DATE DUE

DE 6'99			

DEMCO 38-296

An Historical Geography of Recreation and Tourism in the Western World 1540–1940

An Historical Geography of Recreation and Tourism in the Western World 1540–1940

John Towner

University of Northumbria at Newcastle

JOHN WILEY & SONS

Chichester • New York • Brisbane • Toronto • Singapore

England
7
779777
iries): cs-books@wiley.co.uk
co.uk
com

Other Wiley Editorial Offices

John Wiley & Sons, Inc., 605 Third Avenue,
New York, NY 10158-0012, USA

Jacaranda Wiley Ltd, 33 Park Road, Milton,
Queensland 4064, Australia

John Wiley & Sons (Canada) Ltd, 22 Worcester Road,
Rexdale, Ontario M9W 1L1, Canada

John Wiley & Sons (Asia) Pte Ltd, 2 Clementi Loop #02-01,
Jin Xing Distripark, Singapore 129809

Library of Congress Cataloging-in-Publication Data

Towner, J.
    An historical geography of recreation and tourism in the western world 1540–1940 / John Towner.
        p.   cm.
    Includes bibliographical references (p.   –   ) and index.
    ISBN 0-471-94990-6 (hardcover : alk. paper)
    1. Tourist trade—History. 2. Recreation—History. I. Title.
G155.A1T6283   1996
338.4'791—dc20   96-15922
                                                  CIP

British Library Cataloguing in Publication Data

A catalogue record for this book is available from the British Library

ISBN 0-471-94990-6

Typeset in 10/12pt Palatino from author's disks by Mayhew Typesetting, Rhayader, Powys
Printed and bound in Great Britain by Biddles Ltd, Guildford and King's Lynn

This book is printed on acid-free paper responsibly manufactured from sustainable forestation, for which at least two trees are planted for each one used for paper production.

Contents

Preface

My interest in recreation and tourism in the past stretches back over twenty years to a Master's course at York University, Canada, where George Tatham and Roy Wolfe encouraged me to study tourism and changing attitudes to landscape. This developed into a doctorate on the Grand Tour at Birmingham University, supervised by Tony Travis. I owe a debt of thanks to them for helping provide a basis for the present work.

The wish to write a book which synthesises a whole range of material about past worlds of pleasure stems from a concern that much of the burgeoning field of recreation and tourism studies has lacked a strong historical perspective. At best the past appears as a short introduction to contemporary concerns and the considerable amount of work by historians of leisure is rarely referred to. I therefore wanted to make some contribution to changing this situation, and it is in this spirit that I hope the book will be judged. Inevitably, a work of this kind owes a considerable amount to many authors and I am pleased to acknowledge this. Particular influences that can be detected in the text include the work of James Ackerman on the history of villas and that of Peter Borsay on leisure and English towns, Ronald Neale and Phyllis Hembry on Bath and other spas and John Walton's efforts on seaside resorts. The overall framework for research which is developed in chapter 1 grew from general concepts outlined by Douglas Pearce. I have used their efforts freely but hope I have not distorted their views (or anyone else's) in serving my own purposes. All the faults are mine.

During the course of writing the book, Higher Education in Britain has undergone some interesting changes. My own academic base has moved swiftly from being a Department at a Polytechnic to a Department at a University, to a Division at a University. Fortunately, my colleagues within this changing world have remained, at heart, the same people and I must thank them for their support in this venture as I disappeared at intervals to work elsewhere. They have provided an environment within which the writing of books is still regarded as a proper endeavour for academics.

I must also thank Margaret Boardman and Alison Smith for their efforts in deciphering my handwriting and producing a final copy of the manuscript. Thanks also to Laurence Pallister for sharing the task of compiling the index and to Gary Haley for producing the maps and diagrams.

Finally, a great debt of thanks must go to my parents for introducing me to a lifetime of pleasure in history and travel which, in many ways, lies at the centre of this book. And, of course, to Liz who for too long has endured the tedium which comes from living with someone trying to put pen to paper, even if it is supposed to be about leisure and pleasure.

Introduction

In the middle of the eighteenth century, an Englishman visiting Edinburgh noted how the affluent citizens of that city:

> find great pleasure in walking, to which the soil and country is peculiarly adapted, being dry, pleasant, and abounding in prospects, and romantic scenes. It is likewise customary for them to drive in their carriages to the sands at Leith and Musselburgh, and parade backwards and forwards, after the manner of Scarborough, and other public places of sea bathing resort.
>
> (Topham 1775:18)

During the same century, a local friar in southern Italy showed that he was keenly aware of the benefits that visitors could bring to an area. Pointing to Vesuvius, he exclaimed to an Englishwoman on her Grand Tour:

> Yes, that's our mountain, which throws up money for us, by calling foreigners to see the extraordinary effect of so surprising a phenomenon.
>
> (Piozzi 1789:305)

Moving forward to the early twentieth century, we find a working-class woman in Glasgow recalling her month-long holidays on the Isle of Bute:

> Mother used to take this wee house at Ro'say [Rothesay)]. There was Willie, myself, Rachel, James, Robert and Emma; the young ones went wi' her, but father and them that were workin' or goin wi' milk or papers dinae get down till the weekends.
>
> (Blair 1985:150)

In the same period, holidays on a Cornish farm were remembered from a rather different perspective:

> We started taking visitors at Greenlake in about 1917, and from then onwards. We took them in from Easter to October. Mother did the cooking

and we girls did the cleaning, as well as our dairy and calf-work. The
labourer's wife used to come in and do the washing.

(Bouquet 1985:65)

As well as being a source of pleasure for some people and work for
others, leisure could also be a matter of controversy. In towns and cities,
the unequal access to recreational space between rich and poor was one
cause of bitterness. Thus, in 1884 a letter to the *Worcester Sunday Tele-
gram* in Massachusetts pointed out that:

> Our wealthy citizens live in elegant homes on all the hills of Worcester, they
> have unrestricted fresh air and perfect sewage, their streets are cleaned and
> lighted, the sidewalks are everywhere, and Elm Park, that little dream of
> beauty, is conveniently near. The toilers live on the lowlands, their homes are
> close together, the hills restrict the fresh air, huge chimneys pour out volumes
> of smoke, the marshy places give out offensiveness and poison the air, the
> canal remains uncovered, the streets are different, the little ones are many.
> While the families of the rich can go to the mountains or to the sea during the
> hot months of summer the families of the workers must remain at home.

(quoted in Rosenzweig 1979:37–38)

These quotations serve to illustrate something of the variety of experiences of recreation and tourism in the past which form the subject of
this book. Comments from the eighteenth century range from a day's
pleasure for the affluent in Edinburgh to a recognition by a local population of the benefits that wealthy visitors could bring to a locality. In the
early twentieth century, a seaside holiday away from Glasgow for a poor
family can be contrasted with the hard work (largely undertaken by
females) involved in catering for visitors in rural Cornwall. And across
the Atlantic, in nineteenth-century urban America, the enduring problems stemming from the uneven opportunities for leisure and recreation
were ones which could be found equally in the towns and cities of
Britain and Europe. This diversity of circumstances for different people,
at different times and in different places, is an important theme which
will be developed in the following chapters. At the heart of the book, lies
a concern with the effects of recreation and tourism on people, places
and activities in the past and how they varied across space and time.
Under the heading of people come not only those at play, whether the
rich, middling or poorer groups in society, but those who supported
them, directly or indirectly, through their labours. The term places refers
both to the areas where people went in their leisure time and to the areas
where they lived and worked and where their tastes in pleasure were
formed. Finally, activities encompass not only the pursuits of those at
play but the tasks performed by the workers whose actions sustained the
pleasures of those visitors.

Despite an enormous expansion of research into leisure, recreation and tourism in the last 30 years by both social scientists and social historians, attempts to explore this field through the context of historical geography are comparatively rare. In this book I have tried to synthesise a wide range of material from history, geography and tourism studies to produce a different perspective on this aspect of the past. The claim that this is one of the first books to do this is not a boast but a preliminary defence of its shortcomings. No attempt is made to be fully comprehensive, covering all aspects of the subject over the lengthy period provided. Instead, I have selected a number of episodes in history which can be used to explore certain themes. Thus, I have tried to cover the activities of a wide cross-section of society, from the rich to the poor; to balance the prestigious events, like the Grand Tour, with the more general, routine, pleasures of people. These pleasures are considered in different settings; urban and rural, industrial city or resort. The geographies of those at leisure are, where possible, balanced by a study of the geographies of those who provided for them.

Near the beginning of a book of this kind there is an expectation that terms will be defined. Here, however, I skirt lightly around such an obligation. Social scientists have made many attempts to conceptualise leisure, recreation and tourism and their interrelationships, with varying degrees of success (Fedler 1987; Jafari 1981) and it must be admitted that a desire to define, classify and compartmentalise in this area can be a veritable millstone around the neck of anyone interested in the subject. Historians, by contrast, seem to have largely avoided the problem by using the all-embracing term leisure and thus side-stepping the definitional debates that prevail elsewhere. Some space, however, needs to be devoted to how the words leisure, recreation and tourism are used throughout this book.

Leisure, as Patmore (1983:5) observes, "is more readily experienced than defined" and he suggests that there are three distinct ways in which it can be viewed: as time, as activity and as an attitude of mind. Leisure related to time implies the area of life left over when work and other basic functions have been completed. Not all non-work time is free time, however, and some basic functions (for instance eating, drinking, shopping) can also be regarded as important leisure activities. The second approach to leisure sees it as time when particular activities can take place. These can be varied and range from relaxation and social intercourse to activities simply undertaken for pleasure, such as walking or visiting historic sites. The state of mind approach to leisure, however, argues that what is leisure depends on the individual's perception of what gives them pleasure. Thus, leisure is free from particular times or activities or places and to understand a person's leisure we must enter their mentality and let them define leisure for themselves. This last perspective comes closest to an appreciation of what leisure means and how leisure research should be undertaken (Mowl and Towner 1995). It is, however, very difficult to adopt in an historical context for obvious reasons. This has led the historian Cunningham (1990) to suggest that regarding leisure as time, time left over after work and other obligations, is the most obvious, if ambiguous, approach to the history of leisure and it is this view that is adopted here as a practical working definition. I am not, however, attempting an historical geography of the whole field of leisure itself, but rather leisure provides the context within which more specific forms of leisure—recreation and tourism—take place.

Recreation refers to specific activities that take place within leisure time; activities that are undertaken freely and for pleasure. Thus almost any activity can be recreation if it satisfies certain needs on the part of the individual. A precise definition is elusive but here I am concerned largely with non-work activities which mainly (though not always) take place away from home. A definition of tourism would seem to be rather easier to provide. Statistical convenience and tourist industry self-justification can lead to almost any form of travel being included under the heading of tourism. The view of Pearce (1989:1) that tourism is the "relationships and phenomena arising out of the journeys and temporary stays of people travelling primarily for leisure or recreational purposes", perhaps comes closest to the spirit of the phenomenon discussed here. Also the demand for accommodation implied in this idea of tourism is a useful distinction from day visit recreation. Nevertheless, it is worth remembering Hughes's (1991) argument that definitions of tourism have arisen from economic imperatives; the need to measure the significance of travel whether for business or pleasure or any other reason as long as it involves a temporary stay away from home (usually at least one night). This "industry"-based definition does not really help us understand what it means to be a tourist which, like leisure, should involve a particular state of mind. But, again for practical reasons in an historical context, tourism in this book generally refers to leisure and recreation when staying away from home.

In the process of selection of material for inclusion in the following chapters, a number of activities receive relatively little space. These include the more formal nature of organised sports and important entertainments such as the theatre and the public house. This does not imply a lesser significance but simply a necessary way of coping with a vast range of material. At a later date a fuller "historical geography of leisure" will have to be written. What follows is a first step.

1

An historical geography approach to recreation and tourism

What should constitute an historical geography approach to recreation and tourism? In this chapter I outline a simple framework as a means of synthesising the work that has been achieved by historians, geographers and tourism studies researchers and show how this can contribute to a distinctive historical geography perspective on the subject. Extensive reviews of research have appeared elsewhere (for instance: Bailey 1989; Mitchell and Murphy 1991; Towner 1988, 1994; Towner and Wall 1991; Wall 1989) and do not need to be re-examined here. Rather, a number of arguments raised in these reviews are incorporated into the framework to help map the broad boundaries within which an historical geography can be built. The subsequent chapters in the book try, where possible, to incorporate the ideas outlined here to present a particular approach to recreation and tourism.

The basis for the framework is the elementary one of supply and demand within which any recreation and tourism system can be seen to operate. As supply and demand are usually, in this context, spatially separated, movement is involved between the two areas. Two approaches can be distinguished within this basic concept. One stresses the spatial patterns that arise from the locational attributes of supply and demand, while the other is more concerned with the particular role of place. The former approach has long provided an organisational concept for recreation and tourism studies (Clawson and Knetsch 1966; Gunn 1979; Leiper 1979; Pearce 1989). Leiper (1979) and Pearce (1989) for instance, outline a recreation and tourism system consisting of three main geographical components: the visitor-generating area forming the centre of demand, the visitor destination area forming the centre of supply and the two linked by the third component of transport and communication. This interconnected system is dynamic, open to change and continuity and can be seen to operate at any spatial scale and is influenced by the wider external context of social, cultural, economic, political, physical and technological environments.

In addition to this traditional spatial analysis approach to recreation and tourism, there has been more recently in geography a renewal of interest in a humanistic concern with the role of place (Johnston 1991). Here, the emphasis is on "the study of the diversity of human signifi- cance accorded to places beyond any functions they may play in the search for spatial patterns" (Hughes 1992:31). The two approaches are not mutually exclusive and this book incorporates both perspectives. Thus, the critical role of place in shaping leisure cultures needs to be addressed in the visitor-generating areas. Similarly, the role of dis- tinctive places as leisure destinations and the human values accorded to such places require examination. And, in this way, the journey itself becomes not only a matter of distance, time and cost, but a critical experience for those at leisure. A focus on the role of place rather than simply movement also encourages a geographical examination of leisure environments around the home, where, after all, much leisure has always occurred. These general ideas will now be considered in more detail within the broad framework of generating area, destination area and transport and communication.

The visitor-generating area

Both Nash (1977) and Pearce (1989) have stressed the need to examine processes in both generating and destination areas when studying any form of tourism. The development of Blackpool, Coney Island, Bath or Cannes, the activities of the Grand Tourists or the search for mountain scenery, require an understanding of conditions in the generating areas as much as of the actions which take place when the visitor has arrived at the destination. This balanced approach has not always been present. Detailed accounts of the behaviour of visitors in resorts and elsewhere can be curiously divorced from the home conditions which shaped their attitudes and helped propel them to their destinations. Thus, Black's (1992) account of the Grand Tour in the eighteenth century gives little detail on the conditions in British society which encouraged such visits abroad; the story begins when the English Channel has been crossed. The same applies to numerous studies of seaside resorts which pay small attention to the particular places from which the visitors came. Ideally, the socio-economic, cultural, political and technological context in visitor-generating areas needs to be incorporated into research on recreation and tourism history and some of the most convincing work in the field achieves this goal. Walton's (1981, 1983) studies of the growth of seaside holidays in Lancashire and elsewhere in England and Wales juxtapose conditions in the towns and cities where people lived with developments that took place at the coast. The result is a richer account of the complex process of supply and demand.

Within the visitor-generating areas there are a number of basic themes which can be considered. Primarily, these relate to the participants in the recreation and tourism system and the conditions under which they lived and worked. These include the usual factors of age, gender, socio-economic group, and amount of leisure time available. But there is also the need to explore the "leisure culture" within which tastes were formulated. This is more easily done for the wealthy and famous in society who tend to dominate the historical record (Towner 1995). Other groups, such as the poor and women, are more elusive and rarely appear in such detail. Andrew Davies's (1992) work on leisure, gender and poverty in Salford and Manchester, however, highlights something of these lost worlds.

Particular recreation and tourism activities need to be related to the overall lifeworlds, lifecycles and leisure lifestyles of people (Glyptis 1981). There is a tendency to isolate trips from the rest of people's lives rather than relate them to a broader pattern (Towner 1994). For instance, how did travel abroad for the wealthy fit in detail into the wider aspects of country house visiting, journeys to spas and seaside resorts or explorations of Britain? For the poor, the works' outing or a trip to the coast needs to be placed within their overall work and leisure worlds. Furthermore, these events need to be seen as occurring at particular times in the individual's lifecycle, from childhood to old age. How did the forms of recreation and tourism change throughout their lives? We know little about children's experiences or about the elderly in this historical leisure context (Thompson 1981; Walvin 1983). There is a fundamental problem here, of course, in the lack of adequate source material. Long-term diaries and other evidence are scarce for the wealthy; virtually unknown for others in society. We should at least, however, acknowledge our ignorance about large sections of the population before embarking on theories of leisure, recreation and tourism in the past.

The significance of the places where people lived needs careful consideration. Historians have discussed the adequacy of placing recreation and tourism practices within simply rural or urban environments (Cunningham 1980, 1990; Malcolmson 1973; Rule 1986), arguing the extent to which customs varied between country and town. Beyond this general division of place, a number of studies have revealed important local and regional variations in leisure culture both in Britain (Crump 1986; Cunningham 1990; Davies 1992; King 1987; Walton 1981; Walton and Walvin 1983) and elsewhere (Abrams 1992). Visitor-generating areas cannot, therefore, simply be considered as uniform regions, categorised solely on the basis of socio-economic group. Leisure varied not just with social strata but from place to place and so the concept of a "sense of place" suggests that understanding where people come *from* is as important in recreation and tourism as where people *go*. In nineteenth-century Britain, some working-class cultures clung to older leisure practices, such as local wakes, rather than visits to the seaside (Walton 1981) and Arnold Bennett in *The Old Wives' Tale* (1908:11) wrote of the Staffordshire pottery towns, as late as the 1860s, not yet developing the habit "of going away to the seaside every year". These local and regional variations also occurred within the middle classes. Soane (1993) attributes the lack of tourism development of Germany's north coasts, in part, to the localised nature of German bourgeois culture. The same theme can also be detected in the essentially domesticated *Biedermeier* culture of Vienna's middle class from the 1830s where extensive travel was not part of their leisure culture (Barea 1966). Similar variations could also be found amongst Europe's upper classes. The Italian elite visited spas and other resorts but rarely travelled abroad; a pattern that could also be found amongst the wealthy in Spain (Barke and Towner 1995; Villari 1905).

Generating-area cultures are significant when studying the activities of visitors at their destinations. In the Lancashire mill towns of the later nineteenth century, whole streets would go to the coast together, where on arrival at the resort, they would re-establish their links and regulate codes of behaviour in this new setting. The transfer of localised communities to destinations can also be seen with the merchant classes of Lübeck when visiting the resort of Travemünde on the Baltic coast, portrayed in Thomas Mann's novel *Buddenbrooks* (1902). The social networks and activities in the city were transposed to the seaside. Another novel, Somerset Maugham's *Liza of Lambeth* (1897), vividly evokes the departure of a whole working-class street on a day excursion to Chingford and illustrates how activities at the destination were conditioned by circumstances back home.

The development of informal and formal aspects of the tourism "industry" also needs to be placed in the context of visitor-generating as well as destination areas. Information networks such as clubs, societies, newspapers, journals and advertising (Dent 1975; McInnes 1988), the organisation of transport systems (Towner 1984b), investment in the creation of facilities and developments in the marketing of places (Walton 1983; Ward 1994) all influenced the pattern of different recreation and tourism systems. Did the balance of influence in this sphere lie in the generating or destination areas? Can this pattern of influence be attributed to uneven economic development between areas of supply and demand and the uneven growth of consumer societies and the growing commercialisation of leisure (Glennie 1990; Plumb 1973)? The notion of core–periphery relationships in the political economy of tourism (Britton 1982; Pearce 1989) is clearly relevant here; relating the growth of tourism to the balance of "power" between generating and destination regions. Thus, Fifer (1988) shows that the expansion of tourism in western USA in the late nineteenth century was controlled from the core metropolitan regions of the eastern seaboard and even western Europe, with companies based in those areas both stimulating and then satisfying particular forms of demand and supply. A similar core–periphery relationship, this time between northern and southern Britain, has been argued for the creation of deer forests in the Scottish Highlands in the last century, where the demands and power of a metropolitan-based leisure elite held sway over the interests of the peripheral groups (Orr 1982). On the other hand, there were occasions when the balance of control lay with the destination regions. Some seaside resorts in Britain, for instance, took an active role in both stimulating and controlling forms of tourism (Roberts 1982; Walton 1983) and investment in development schemes often came from locally based groups. Destination areas were not always simply passive recipients of demand generated elsewhere, and we shall now turn to a consideration of them.

The visitor destination area

Similar ideas to those discussed above relate to the destination areas. The extent to which socio-economic, cultural, political and technological conditions varied between areas of supply and demand is basic to understanding the ways in which destination areas developed and the varying impacts of recreation and tourism upon them. These include visitor and host society relationships, the range and pattern of leisure activities taking place and the forms of employment and services created. In general terms, however, it would be true to say that we know less about host societies in the past than about certain types of visitors. Wealthy and educated visitors expressed their views and recorded their activities in diaries and journals; host societies, generally in subordinate roles, have tended to remain hidden from history.

Destination areas, like generating areas, were centres of consumption (Borsay 1989; Fisher 1948; Glennie 1990). The presence of recreation and tourism brought demands for food, fuel and other services which might be supplied locally, regionally or sometimes nationally (Fawcett 1990; Haug 1982; Hembry 1990; Neale 1981). The need to support people at leisure created labour demands which may have had to be satisfied by inward migration from the local area or beyond (Neale 1981; Patmore 1963). These patterns of labour migration created by the holiday industry remain little researched in an historical context, yet a concern with people in the destination area involves not just those at play but those who provided for them, either directly or indirectly. The age, gender and socio-economic background of leisure workers, as well as where they lived, have been studied by Neale (1981) for Bath, Haug (1982) for Nice, Walton (1978) for Blackpool, Gilbert (1954) for Brighton, and Bouquet (1985) for rural Devon, but these are rare attempts to provide a fuller social geography of resorts and regions.

Issues of power and the control of resources and development can be explored in the same context as for the generating areas. The idea of core–periphery relationships is useful for examining the balance between locally based elites and outside developers in resort growth and there has been an interesting debate on this in the historical literature (Cannadine 1980; Walton 1983). Within the resort region, differences in power between different local groups were often critical for shaping the way a town grew. Thus the process of development reflected the interplay between patterns of landownership, public and private agencies and entrepreneurial activity (Neale 1981; Walton and Walvin 1983). Very often, a similar morphology and land use in resorts could conceal a variety of different processes.

The specific places used for recreation and tourism are of evident importance. A whole range of questions can be raised: Where were they located? What activities took place there? Which groups of people used them? Did visitors and local populations mix or were some places socially exclusive? Who owned and controlled these places? From these questions stem basic land use and morphological considerations: Were distinct leisure landscapes created? How did they relate to other land uses? The walks and public gardens of urban centres, the promenades, piers, boarding houses and hotels of seaside resorts, the moves to protect valued landscapes, are all testimony to the role of pleasure in helping to create environments away from home. Conversely, visitor experience in the destination areas could help shape environments back in the generation areas. The spread of villas along the banks of the River Thames in the eighteenth century (Ackerman 1990) or the design of a country house and garden, often reflected tastes nurtured by foreign travel (Burke 1968; Manwaring 1925; Wittkower 1974). Idealised Italian classical landscapes were transplanted into the English rural scene so that the landed estates of the aristocracy and gentry both reflected and stimulated the Grand Tour of Europe.

The values with which landscapes, both rural and urban, were imbued by visitors have a strong tradition of research (for instance:

Andrews 1989; Hussey 1927; Huth 1957; Lowenthal and Prince 1965; Nicolson 1959; Nash 1967). Studies of landscape aesthetics can help in charting the rise and fall of certain destinations over time, how existing places were re-evaluated and how new areas were opened up (Squire 1988; Towner 1985). Shifts in sensibilities were important aspects of change in recreation and tourism patterns, especially as tastes moved from a preference for humanised "garden" landscapes to a preference for wilder scenes.

So far, the implication has been that destination areas are necessarily spatially separate from generating areas. But, as argued at the beginning of this chapter, a renewed interest in the role of place means that attention must also focus on leisure settings in and around the home. The country estate for some, or the terraced house and street for others, were where much leisure time was spent. The geographies created in these settings deserve as much attention as the patterns created by travel elsewhere.

Transport and communications

Although the geography of leisure cultures does not need to imply travel, transport technology and transport networks are clearly basic factors in many patterns of recreation and certainly of tourism. They form the basic linkage between spatially separate generating and destination areas. Beyond this function, the part played by transport in any form of development has long given rise to debate (Hart 1983), with opinions varying between those who see transport as a vital element in the process, to those who stress transport's permissive role within a more complex environment, where social and organisational transformation were as significant as technology.

Some aspects of this debate have penetrated recreation and tourism history, where the specific nature of the relationships between railways and resort growth has been questioned (Simmons 1986; Walton 1979, 1980). Tourism studies research, however, has tended to adopt a less critical stance on "technological determinism". Two recent studies of the evolution of tourism, for instance, were still largely organised around changes in transport technology, arguing that this factor fundamentally determined tourism's history (Burkart and Medlik 1990; Sears 1989). Sears (p. 3), writing of the impact of turnpike roads, steamboats and railways in the USA, claimed that: "this revolution in transport made tourism possible". But, although critical for linking specific areas of supply and demand, the impact of change in transport technology on travel does require careful evaluation. To say that certain modes of transport created certain patterns of tourism is not the same as claiming their role as essential for tourism to exist. In many places, changes in transport had the effect of reinforcing existing patterns (Walton 1980). In other cases, changes in travel patterns were more closely related to changing cultural tastes than transport innovations (Towner 1985).

The role of transport in the recreation and tourism system can be considered not only in terms of linkage between generating and destination areas but as an integral part of the leisure experience (Clawson and Knetsch 1966). Thrift (1990) and Schivelbusch (1977) have written of the way in which railways altered perceptions of time and space and the relationships between traveller and landscape. But a similar effect was also claimed by William Cobbett for turnpike roads at an earlier date (Brandon 1979), and the close attention paid to scenery in seventeenth- and eighteenth-century diaries makes clear that a journey was not merely the distance between two places (Towner 1984b). In addition to these themes, movement is, of course, a recreation activity in its own right, whether this be the fashionable urban promenading of the eighteenth and nineteenth centuries (Borsay 1986; Lawrence 1988) or the growth of hill walking in the early twentieth century (Blunden and Curry 1990; Shoard 1987). Furthermore, particular forms of transport, such as cycling and rowing, have had fashionable periods which, for a time, created significant leisure patterns (Lowerson 1993).

Other forms of communication played a vital role in recreation and tourism systems through the flows of information and ideas. The culture of the English leisure classes, for example, with visits to fashionable seasons in London, watering places, provincial towns and travel in Britain and Europe, was bound together through a network of social acquaintances, clubs, societies, libraries, newspapers and journals. These systems of communication all had a geographical expression at national, regional and local scales (Dent 1974).

A dynamic system

The broadly outlined recreation and tourism system discussed so far is dynamic, subject to both change and continuity. Indeed, for Barraclough (1979), history's emphasis on time provides "the depth which comes from studying society not as a static but as a dynamic constellation of forces manifesting itself in continuous and constant change". Thus history considers the transformation of people, places, institutions and ideas through time, from one state into another.

Within this context, historians have examined the transformation of leisure and the working classes in Britain in the late eighteenth and early nineteenth centuries (Bailey 1989; Malcolmson 1973; Rule 1986). From seeing leisure and recreation closely integrated with the world of work, historians have debated the extent to which leisure was broken down, or transformed, under the pressures of urbanisation and industrialisation (Cunningham 1990). Leisure and recreation emerged in new forms in the later nineteenth century, forms which included working-class tourism (Walton 1981; Walton and Walvin 1983). Historians have also debated the underlying processes of change in the leisure system (Bailey 1989). Leisure, recreation and tourism were not just consequences of industrial change, technological change and class structures. Nor were activities simply initiated by one social class following another. Hardy (1990), Cunningham (1980) and Thompson (1963) argue that working-class culture had its own momentum and was not just waiting to emulate the habits of the higher orders in society. Similarly, Thompson (1988) has shown that the middle classes were not merely following in the steps of the upper classes in their leisure during the nineteenth century. Leisure evolved in a much more intricate manner which did not adhere to simple class stereotypes. The idea of one social class following in the steps of another is just too crude. For instance, Corbin (1994) provides evidence of local populations enjoying the sea long before wealthy visitors arrived to "discover" the seaside and Walton (1983:10) notes "the survival of sea bathing traditions which had hitherto gone un-recorded" in resort development along the Lancashire coast. Bailey's (1989:112) view of the evolution of leisure as "a process that has been erratic, complex and contentious" is a useful corrective to crude notions of change in the recreation and tourism system driven by transport technology or the mechanistic process of successive class intrusion.

Consideration of the pace of change in the system is also part of an historical geography approach to recreation and tourism. Some systems showed remarkable long-term endurance, for instance the attraction of southern Europe for north Europeans, which has now been a feature of travel for almost 500 years. On the other hand, the practice of visiting spas has endured for far longer on the continent than it has in Britain, while the bicycling craze of the 1890s in Britain, Europe and America experienced rapid rise and fall (Rubinstein 1977; Tobin 1974). Distin-guishing between the more profound influences on change and con-tinuity and the more superficial manifestations of fashion is an important objective for research. In addition, the consideration of dynamics in the system requires the study of failures as well as successes. Thus the evolution of England's spa resorts was, in reality, a complex picture of births, deaths and survivors (Hembry 1990) and many spas did not follow a clear lifecycle trajectory (Butler 1980). A tendency to focus on the success stories in the system presents an image of inexorable expansion, whereas at any one time there was always considerable doubt as to the success of many ventures. Finally, there is a need to consider the ways in which different recreation and tourism systems interacted with each other. Were the same or different resources utilised, both in terms of attractions (and how they were perceived) and infrastructure such as accommodation and transport? This aspect of tourism development has recently been considered by Barke and Towner (1995) in a study of Spain. While there was always a degree of overlap between the domestic leisure and tourism systems of the Spanish people and foreign visitors, what was visited and admired by outsiders was often different from the preferences of the local population. Thus at a particular time an area may have layers of different domestic systems and different foreign systems, sometimes coinciding, sometimes operating in different worlds.

Ideology and the system

A critical ideological awareness is required when examining recreation and tourism. Social historians of leisure have a tradition in this field (Bailey 1989; Clarke and Critcher 1985) and historical geographers are also aware of its implications (Dodgshon 1990). Tourism research, however, has rather lagged behind. There has been an uncritical acceptance of the very nature of tourism itself, with a functional, industry-conceived and -defined perspective prevailing (Hughes 1991, 1992). On a world scale this has resulted in ideas of leisure, recreation and tourism being dominated by western societies (Towner 1994, 1995). Little is known of societies elsewhere in the past and there are implications here for understanding historical and geographical processes. Thus, if we conceive of tourism as that practised and developed first of all in the west, then the history of tourism can be seen as spreading outwards from a western core to gradually reach other peoples elsewhere in the world. Furthermore, an industry-dominated view of tourism tends to stress the key role of businesses and organisations, such as Thomas Cook, in this process. Less western-centred perspectives may well provide a rather different picture of events.

Within the western world itself, ideology looms large in concepts of change. Unstated value judgements lead to the idea that a spa resort "declined" when the upper classes forsook it for more exclusive destinations, even though the actual number of visitors might have increased. Too often, the significance of an activity has been linked to social class; hence the overlooking of popular sea-bathing in accounts of coastal development referred to earlier. The "golden age" of recreation and tourism is still evoked in popular writing (Burstall 1981; Gregory 1991;

Wechsberg 1979) but ideas of a decline in standards have also pervaded the academic literature (Boorstin 1962; Fussell 1980). Fussell (1980) for example, distinguishes between "explorers", "travellers" and "tourists" in both historical and contemporary contexts. He assigns exploration to the Renaissance era, travel to the "bourgeois age" and tourism to our "proletarian moment". Thus explorers have sought the "undiscovered", travellers have followed the routes already described by western intellectual thought but tourists have only followed these paths after a mass publicity campaign (see also Horne 1991). Occasionally, a different ideological standpoint has intruded into these views of the past, such as Neale's (1981) Marxist perspective on Bath, but the ideology debate remains largely within the discipline of history and has yet to influence tourism studies' perspective on the past.

A greater awareness of gender is also needed. Women have generally remained hidden from history, either as tourists (Mains 1966; Meyer 1978; Pemble 1988) or as workers (Bouquet 1985; Neale 1981) or as simply having any leisure of their own (Davies 1992). The rapid expansion of research in this area in recent years, however, may well start to correct what is still a major gap in our knowledge of recreation and tourism in previous eras. The relative significance of particular forms of activity also requires careful evaluation. Significance has tended to be equated with easily quantifiable aspects of recreation and tourism, such as length of holiday, or amount of money expended. But the significance of events in people's own lives can easily be overlooked. A short holiday once a year may have been more important for, say, a Lancashire millhand and his family than was a lengthy winter season in Cannes for a member of the leisured elite. It is easy to give more prominence to the prestigious events than to the usual rhythms of people in pursuit of pleasure. Thus the Grand Tour takes precedence over the regular migration of Venetian merchants to their nearby villas or the annual cycle of informal hospitality among the English gentry, while the life of the leisure classes at spas and seaside resorts overshadows the self-help creation of holiday homes by the poor in the countryside and at the coast in the early twentieth century (Hardy and Ward 1984).

The framework which has been outlined in this chapter provides a wide context for the historical geography of recreation and tourism. What follows in the succeeding chapters is an attempt to address many of the themes which have been raised here. Treatment is uneven, however, as neither the evidence nor space will permit a comprehensive approach to all topics. Nevertheless, it is hoped that this book will serve as a pointer towards the rich field of possibilities that lie within an historical geography approach to people's pleasures.

2

The affluent in town and country

Throughout history, both countryside and town have provided settings for leisure as well as work, for both the rich and the poor in society. In this chapter, the recreation activities of the affluent in pre-industrial worlds are considered and they are placed in a broad cultural context derived from Peter Burke's (1978) study of popular culture in Europe. Leisure activities are considered first in terms of movement from town to countryside, then in the countryside itself and finally within the urban environment. These divisions are not, of course, ideal. The world of leisure showed continuity and change across the transition from pre-industrial to industrial-based societies and leisure lifestyles did not neatly divide into either rural or urban arenas (Cunningham 1980). Nevertheless, there is a certain general coherence in conceiving of leisure and recreation within these contexts and as a basis for discussion.

A cultural context

In tracing the history of popular culture in Europe (the culture of the mass of the population), Peter Burke (1978:271) observes: "In 1500 popular culture was everyone's culture; a second culture for the educated, and the only culture for everyone else." By 1800, however, Burke claims that the nobility, gentry, merchant and professional classes: "had abandoned popular culture to the lower classes, from whom they were now separated, as never before, by profound differences in world view." If Burke's thesis is accepted as being generally correct, then there are clear implications for the world of leisure, recreation and tourism. A leisure culture that became split between a social elite and the rest of the population would be reflected in a growth of different tastes and activities from a time when many of them would have been shared. These disparities would thus stem not only from the more obvious variations attributed to economic status but from deep-seated cultural differences. Furthermore, we could expect a cultural split between elite and popular culture to be reflected in the use of different leisure places.

The reasons for "abandoning" popular culture varied with different social groups but for the nobility and gentry they were bound up with the spread of humanist Renaissance ideas. In the fifteenth and sixteenth centuries there was a rediscovery of classical learning with a taste for fine arts. Polished social skills were adopted by the nobility as indicators of high rank, and this replaced the emphasis on military skill. The ancient classics became central to European intellectual and cultural life and texts such as Castiglione's *The Courtier* (1528) identified the ruling classes with education and the arts. An ideal of the well-educated Christian prince and nobleman was strongly influenced by the views of ancient classical writers such as Plato (Caspari 1954), reinforcing the sense of identity with a past era.

The withdrawal of the upper classes from popular culture took place at different times in different parts of Europe. Gradually, however, a common elite culture united different parts of the continent. This culture developed more rapidly than popular culture, driven as it was by a succession of new ideas and thought: the Renaissance, the Scientific Revolution, the Enlightenment and the Romantic eras. By the eighteenth century, the social elite of Europe were closely linked together by a shared cultural outlook in which they had more in common with each other than they had with the mass of their own citizens (Hampson 1968).

In Italy, the process of withdrawal was well under way by the sixteenth century where there was evidence "for an increasing separation between the amusements of the poor and those of the rich" (Burke 1978:275). England began the process during the sixteenth century where the monarchy increasingly relied on a well-educated ruling class rather than a nobility based on military prowess. Thomas Elyot's *The Governor* (1531) reflected Castiglione in stressing the ideal of an intellectual aristocracy. London and provincial centres became more frequented by the landed classes who shared common intellectual values and who became increasingly detached from their local communities. In France, separation began somewhat later but during the seventeenth and eighteenth centuries the nobility, who had previously taken part in local pleasures, retreated to Paris and other centres of fashion and ideas. Elsewhere in Europe, especially in the north and east, the process of cultural withdrawal was more associated with the eighteenth century.

These divisions were never completely clear cut and interaction between elite and popular culture continued in various ways. But the notion that tastes and practices gradually trickled down the social order is too crude and mechanistic. Some aspects of popular culture in fact permeated upwards (Cunningham 1980), while, in the romantic era of the later eighteenth and nineteenth centuries, some aspects of popular culture were rediscovered by the elite. But Burke's ideas do form a useful context for leisure, recreation and tourism history. Did different leisure activities stem partly from the different "world views" of diverging cultures? Did different leisure places in countryside and town develop where previously there had been social and cultural intermixing in the same places? Cultural withdrawal might be expressed spatially with parts of towns and rural areas becoming increasingly reserved and controlled by social elites. This elite leisure culture would take place in private or restricted public places; on an estate in the countryside or in socially exclusive areas of towns. The upper classes would mix together at local, regional, national and even international levels rather than play with locals in local settings. On the other hand, popular culture, the culture of the masses, would be expressed largely in public settings: church, tavern, marketplace, piazza, village street, commons and greens, and would take place most conspicuously at public holidays such as fairs, festivals and carnivals (see chapter 3).

From town to country

The regular movement of the affluent from town to country for enjoyment and relaxation was expressed either as short-term excursions into the surrounding rural area or as a longer term retreat of several days, weeks, or months. The development of the country villa epitomises the latter practice and much of the following discussion will focus on its evolution in parts of Europe. The villa is also a good example of that continuity in leisure practice which can be traced through different societies in different times and places. Its fortunes can be charted from the times of ancient Rome, through the Renaissance of fifteenth- and sixteenth-century Italy, to other parts of Europe in the seventeenth and eighteenth centuries, and eventually to America (Ackerman 1990).

In searching for the underlying causes of this periodic urban withdrawal to the country, historians have stressed a variety of factors. Braudel (1979:28) argued that "changes in the countryside were a reflection and a consequence of the wealth of the town" and that, from the fifteenth and sixteenth centuries, the investment of urban capital in the countryside resulted in "a social take-over" by the towns. Thus, the country villa was simply another luxury to be purchased by surplus urban capital. Ackerman (1990), however, adds a cultural dimension to the process. For him, the villa fulfilled a deep-seated desire to escape from the pressures of the town. Certainly, contemporary writings about villa life evoked an idealised picture of the country as the antithesis of urban values. Whatever the reasons, villas became a feature of the leisure landscape of European urban peripheries and spreading out from Italy they came to be found by the eighteenth century around cities in Spain, the Low Countries, France, and Britain.

In Renaissance Italy, the widespread practice of withdrawal to a country residence acquired the name of "villeggiatura". The re-emergence of prosperous town life in Florence in the fourteenth and fifteenth centuries was associated with the formation of a capitalist economy and city-state with a mercantile and financial aristocracy. The balance of power shifted from rural landowners to city dwellers. Urban investors, such as the Medici, amassed large rural estates to form new, post-feudal, systems of landholding and, although farm incomes from these estates were always important, the pleasurable aspects of rural villa life quickly became appreciated. During the fifteenth and sixteenth centuries, the hills just to the north of Florence became "villa country". The Medicis had villas at Trebbio and Cafaggiolo in the mountainous Mugello valley and later at Careggi and Fiesole.

Contemporary writings of the owners and visitors to these villas were full of Renaissance humanist attitudes derived from classical Rome. They echoed the distinction Horace made between "negotiis" (business affairs and other preoccupations) and "otium", the serenity that came from an ideal country life (Ackerman 1990). Alberti (1404–1472), portrayed the villa as a refuge to:

> flee those uproars, those tumults, that tempest of the world, of the piazza, of the palace. You can hide yourself in the villa in order not to see the rascalities, the villainies, and quantity of wicked men which constantly pass before your eyes in the city.

> (quoted in Coffin 1979:11)

By the mid-sixteenth century, villeggiatura had become a feature of life for the well-to-do in many parts of Italy. Around Rome, however, villas developed under rather different circumstances from Florence and other mercantile centres. Here, the major initiator of rural retreats was the church: the Pope, Cardinals and other members of the ecclesiastical elite. In terms of leisure activities, however, the distinction was not so great. Two zones of villas were created, one in the distant hills and country-side, the other a suburban zone near the old city walls.

For centuries, the Papacy had a summer itinerary (May to October) moving through the hill towns that surrounded the Roman Campagna. Viterbo, Tivoli and the Sabine and Alban hills were favourite retreats from the summer heat and disease of Rome (Figure 2.1). These temporary

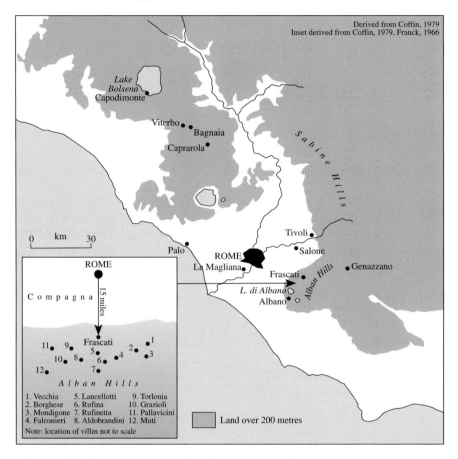

Figure 2.1   Important centres for *villeggiatura* from Rome in the sixteenth century

visitors generally used existing medieval monasteries and palaces for their accommodation rather than constructing new villas and, until the early sixteenth century, there had been a preference for Viterbo and other centres north of Rome. In time, however, partly inspired by the patronage of Pope Paul III (1534–1549), Frascati in the Alban hills to the south became the fashionable centre for villeggiatura (Figure 2.2).

Frascati had a number of important advantages for wealthy Romans, in terms both of general location and immediate site and situation. It lay a convenient 15 miles south of the city across the flat Campagna. The villas could be located on a north-facing slope, all with views back to Rome (Figure 2.1). This slope was attractively wooded, by then a rarity in this part of Italy, and there was access to water supplies (Franck 1966). The villas were carefully located to maximise their position,

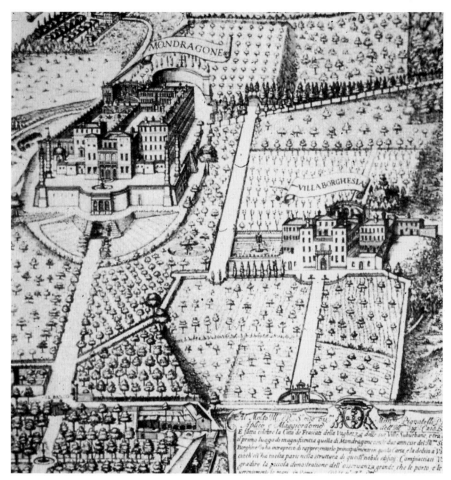

Figure 2.2 Villas on the Alban Hills near Rome as shown in "Frascati" by Greuter (c.1610). This section of the panorama shows the villas of Mondragone and Borghese (the Trustees, the British Museum)

looking back to the city from where their owner's wealth and power derived. Within about 50 years, the slopes at Frascati became covered with villas, many of them grandiose constructions such as Mondragone, Tusculana and Rufina (Coffin 1979). An element of continuity in leisure lifestyle and place existed here, for those villas were near Tusculum, a favourite place for villeggiatura with the ancient Roman elite.

In addition to centres like Frascati, Rome had an outer pleasure zone based on the flat lands around the River Tiber between the city and the coast and further afield. This was hunting land and, from mid-September to October, the Pope, Cardinals and their followers sought for game. Large hunting lodges were constructed at Palo, La Magliana, Bagnaia, Caprarola and Tivoli. Hunting as a suitable ecclesiastical recreation enjoyed only short-term popularity, however. It spread from northern Italy in the early sixteenth century but was in decline around Rome within a hundred years. Fashionable society turned to the theatre and opera in this area as more suitable pastimes for a cultured elite. A less charitable interpretation is that most of the wildlife had been killed off by overenthusiastic dedication to the pleasures of the field (Coffin 1979).

Rome also developed an inner zone of villas around the edge of the city during the Renaissance. Depopulation during the Middle Ages had left large areas empty to the south and east of the city and the land became converted to small farms and vineyards. Gradually, these *vigne* acquired a leisure function. Contemporaries noted how, unlike the Florentines, the Roman elite despised commerce but held agriculture in high esteem and so these small leisure farms became very popular. The Quirinal and Pincian hills were developed during the sixteenth century into suburban villa areas with fine views over the city. When Joseph Spence visited Rome in 1732 he observed:

> 'Tis common for the first noblemen to have a palace in the heart of the town, and a house and gardens (which they call their country-seat) within the walls, but in the less inhabited parts of the city. . . . This mixture of city, country and gardens . . . gives several views of an uncommon sort, and more beautiful than are to be met with in most other cities.
>
> (Spence 1975:114)

But pleasure can never be separated from other aspects of life and the creation of leisure settings around Rome was linked to wider socio-economic and environmental consequences. The process of villa acquisition was based on wealthy Roman families purchasing adjoining *vigne* until they could build suitable country residences in extensive grounds. Gradually, the richest families, such as the Farnese, Borghese and Rufini, bought up the larger holdings until only a handful of families owned vast estates. As the small *vigne* disappeared, the agricultural population left for the towns and the land use on the large estates changed from grain to cattle grazing. General neglect, associated with absentee landlords, led to the spread of pestilence and lawlessness in the Campagna; a legacy that lasted until the early twentieth century (Coffin 1979).

A final example of Italian Renaissance villa development can also be used to point to these wider socio-economic and environmental circumstances. The area of the Veneto, stretching from Verona eastwards to Venice and south from the Dolomite Alps to the rivers Po and Adige, saw extensive villa growth from the sixteenth century onwards. During the fifteenth and early sixteenth centuries Venice, a pre-eminently maritime trading power, gradually gained mainland territory in the Veneto. At the same time, the city-state was facing increased competition in overseas trade from the Turks and Atlantic powers. Thus land became more significant for the Venetian commercial elite than the sea and there was a major shift in the political, economic and cultural environment of the republic (Braudel 1979; Woolf 1968). Venetian capital was invested in the land and there was considerable reclamation of marginal land by draining marshes. Farms developed along improved and new waterways where produce could be easily moved to markets and small peasant holdings were quickly and easily acquired by wealthy Venetian merchants.

Leisure and pleasure soon became grafted onto this economic endeavour. In the early sixteenth century, a retreat from Venice had meant the islands of Giudecca and Murano near the city (Cosgrove 1993) but, during that century, villa retreats combined with "gentleman farming" spread outwards to the lower reaches of the River Brenta and along other river and canal banks (Figure 2.3). The growing demand for elegant villas provided work for a series of influential architects, notably Palladio (1508–1580). He designed a number of villas in the eastern Veneto close to Venice, Vicenza and Padua. His classical designs were to inspire imitation when the villa lifestyle was adopted elsewhere in Europe, including the Dutch canals and rivers and along the banks of the Thames above London (see below).

Some insight into the mentality of villa owners in the Veneto can be gained from the numerous essays and letters that have survived. A leisure culture developed which, like the Florentines, extolled the virtues of the country at the expense of the town. The essays and letters were written by "new men", an urban bourgeoisie who purchased rather than inherited their estates and who felt that rural life epitomised a gentleman. The recreational activities mentioned by the essays ranged from social conversation, games, music, dancing, reading and study to outdoor pursuits such as hunting and fishing. Fashionable Venice was deserted in the autumn for country holidays (Braudel 1979) but many villas were visited throughout the year. Interestingly, the urban-based villa owners did not appear to mix with their old-established landed aristocratic neighbours (Ackerman 1990); a social and cultural divide which can be traced in similar processes elsewhere through time.

The delights of villa retreats shine through the surviving letters and essays. Alvise Cornaro, who gained his wealth through land reclamation projects, wrote in the 1550s of the holidays to his villa at Este near Padua:

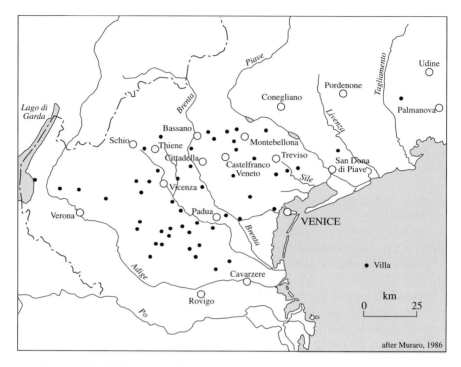

Figure 2.3   Villas of the Veneto in the sixteenth and seventeenth centuries

> I go in April and May, and again in September and October, for several days to enjoy my hill in the Euganean mountains, and in the most beautiful part I have my fountains and gardens, and above all my comfortable and beautiful rooms. Here I can still have enough breath to do a little hunting, such that is suitable to my age, but very pleasurable.
>
> (quoted in Muraro 1986:158)

Evidently, villeggiatura was something to be indulged in throughout the lifecycle. In old age, Cornaro was still travelling to his villa "to revisit my friends" and continually finding pleasure "in the voyage going and coming". By the eighteenth century, the villas of the Veneto had become such a feature of affluent life that the playwright Carlo Goldoni wrote his comedy *La Smarnie per la Villegiatura* (The Craze for Villa Holidays) in 1761 in which he satirised what he saw as a superficial life based on frivolity and show (Muraro 1986).

As Renaissance ideals and urban wealth spread north of the Alps, so did the practice of temporary visits to the countryside for pleasure, although it was always modified by local and regional circumstances. One grand-scale variation on the theme was produced in the Loire

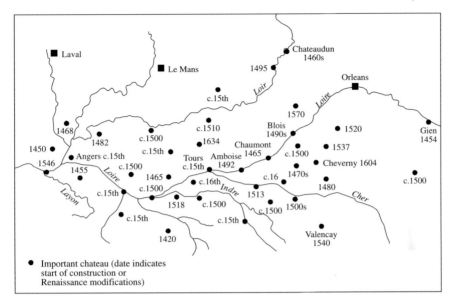

Figure 2.4   The chateaux of the Loire region in the sixteenth century

valley in France in the later fifteenth and sixteenth centuries. Here, a whole region of hunting forests and rivers became a leisure setting for a nationally based elite. The chateaux and estates created there were built either by the monarchy and court attendants or by a new breed of wealthy merchants (Figure 2.4).

The French court was peripatetic. From Paris, it would move down to the Loire region to mix business with pleasure (Knecht 1982). The Renaissance idea of court entertainment and festival was adopted by the French kings Charles VIII (1483–1498), Louis XII (1498–1515) and Francis I (1515–1547), who had all travelled to Italy (Strong 1973). At their courts in centres like Amboise and Blois, medieval chateaux gained Italian Renaissance details and here the cult of beauty, poetry, music and architecture was pursued. As with the Popes in Rome, the more strenuous recreational activities of the *chasse* created royal hunting lodges in the forests, most notably Francis I's fantasy at Chambord. As well as the royal chateaux, there were numerous examples constructed for the rising class of wealthy merchants who were benefiting from the expanding silk trade, banking and administration. Azay-le-Rideau, Chenonceau, Clos-Lucé, Langeais, Valençay, Villandry and Villesavin were built by this new national elite. Along the Loire and other rivers in the region, the "Garden of France" in the sixteenth century saw a burst of building activity which created a leisure setting for the wealthy, a vast stage set for conspicuous consumption and a daily rhythm of life consisting of games, dancing, banquets, tournaments and hunting (Cloulas 1983).

These activities, of course, were for a national elite for whom the Loire was a playground away from Paris. Within the same region, however, a more localised pattern of urban-rural retreat (as found in Italy) may have operated. The father of Rabelais, for example, was a wealthy sixteenth-century lawyer based in Chinon. Withdrawal from the town in his case involved a 5-mile journey to a small farmhouse, La Devinière, at Seuilly. It seems quite likely that beneath the spectacular life of the very rich, the bourgeoisie of the Loire towns were regularly moving out into the surrounding countryside for their leisure. Their lives, however, are only occasionally glimpsed in the historical record and it is easy to overlook this more commonplace experience.

Retreats from the town into the country for bourgeois members of society can nevertheless be seen much clearer further north in Europe, in the seventeenth-century Dutch republic. The combined processes of growing urban wealth and the adoption of Renaissance ideals about country life seem to have operated once again and Schama (1987) identifies a "Dutch leisure ethic" based on rural pleasures emerging by the 1660s. Despite their reputation for frugality, the Dutch burghers were as keen on conspicuous consumption as anyone. An example of villa development was Leiderdorp on the outskirts of Leiden. The original function of the village, to serve the city with dairy and horti-cultural produce, had by 1660 been transformed into a rural retreat for the cloth manufacturers and other elites of Leiden. The villas among the water meadows and copses mirrored, in both form and function, the creations of the Veneto; an escape from the strains of commerce and the chance to become a landowner (Figure 2.5). Similar movements occurred elsewhere in Holland, beginning in the 1630s and accelerating through the 1650s. The rich of Harlem retreated to the dunes and the courtiers at the Hague headed for the surrounding countryside while between Amsterdam and Utrecht elegant villas stretched along the banks of the river Vecht, vying with each other as demonstrations of wealth and taste (Schama 1987).

Vienna also saw country houses developing on the city edge. There were about 400 summer palaces and villas in the suburban belt of the city by the early eighteenth century, forming "a brilliant necklace of summer residences" (Lehne and Johnson 1985:50). Many of them featured elabor-ate geometrically planned parks and gardens (Barea 1966). Similarly, around Marseille, numerous small country houses called *bastides* devel-oped in the eighteenth century, especially for the growing merchant class of the city. In 1808, Millin observed the weekly leisure rhythm: "you go

Figure 2.5 Ludolf de Jonghe's "Farewell before a Country House" (late 1660s) effectively captures an informal aspect of seventeenth-century Dutch leisure culture. (Schama (1987) *The Embarrassment of Riches*, with permission of Fontana Press)

there on Saturday evening, . . . you spend Sunday there with the friends you invite, and you return on Monday morning" (Corbin 1994:253).

In England, temporary retreat to the countryside was accompanied by complaints of the health hazards of towns (Thomas 1983). Again, however, the dominant impulse seems to have been the adoption of Renaissance ideals of country living and growth of urban wealth. It has been estimated that by the early seventeenth century half the aldermen in Gloucester had country houses nearby and merchants in Bristol, Hull and other centres followed a similar pattern. Sometimes, only short-term moves were involved. Pepys' diary records how he and his wife considered buying a country villa but decided to purchase a coach so that they could travel to different places each weekend. Eventually, however, they rented a villa with another couple at Parson's Green, beyond the city edge (Thomas 1983). By the eighteenth century, villas by the Thames near London were common (Brandon 1979). Lord Burlington's Palladian-style residence at Chiswick (1727–1729, and built after his Italian Grand Tour) was simply one of the grander examples of developments at Fulham, Chelsea, Richmond and Twickenham. Small weekend villas were built at Turnham Green and Kentish Town for London tradesmen and their families who would leave the city on Saturday and return on Monday, refreshed for another week of toil and stress.

Edinburgh generated a ring of pleasure villas as early as the mid-sixteenth century (Gifford, McWilliam and Walker 1984). Nobles, politicians, lawyers and merchants purchased relatively small plots of land for weekend relaxation at places such as Brunstane, Caroline Park, Bruntsfield, Liberton, Prestonfield and Cammo. When the Scottish elite visited London in the eighteenth century, they transferred this country villa habit to the capital and Petersham became a Scottish villa enclave. The eighteenth century also saw a growing number of affluent merchants in Glasgow seeking country estates not far from the city. The then wooded rural retreat of the River Kelvin, to the west of the city, became a favourite location (Dicks 1985).

Movement from town to country, in the case of the villa, implies a fairly formalised activity. Land was purchased, house and garden constructed and the same site visited by owners and friends. But rural retreats from the pre-industrial town were also of a much more informal, short-term nature, often a day or half-day outing. This created a different form of leisure hinterland, and one that was visited by a wider cross-section of society. When towns were small in extent, the outskirts were easily accessible and so the "city edge" was an important recreational resource (Kostof 1992). John Stow, in his *Survey of London* (1598), remarked:

> On May Day in the morning, every man, except impediment, could walk into the sweet meadows and green woods, there to rejoice their spirits with the beauty and savour of sweet flowers, and with the harmony of birds, praising God in their kind.

> (quoted in Patmore 1983:31)

Country walks and rambles were popular recreational activities in seventeenth-century England and, by the eighteenth century, London had a pleasure periphery around Chelsea, Hampstead and other villages with numerous inns, beer shops and lodging houses responding to the needs of city excursionists (Thomas 1983). Other cities had similar pleasure peripheries. Newcastle's steeply wooded Pandon Dene on the eastern edge of the town was "a sylvan retreat for strolling lovers" (France and Towner 1992). Edinburgh had its informal leisure zone as well as its villas. Stockbridge, now an inner suburb, was in the eighteenth century a place of resort for the general population with wooded walks along the Water of Leith (Wood 1951). In fact, the edge of the city was an important recreation resource throughout Europe. Beyond the Linienwald, which marked the outer limits of Vienna, the wine-growing villages set up wine gardens where the urban population would come to sample the new wine or *heurige* (Barea 1966). It was to the wine gardens at Grinzing and elsewhere that Schubert and his friends would journey both to drink and to enjoy the countryside beyond the city. Local urban culture was an important factor in recreational activities. The middle-class *Biedermeier* culture, which flourished in the first half of the nineteenth century in Vienna, emphasised the pleasures of "cosy" home-based lifestyles, the importance of privacy and restricted social circles. Many affluent Viennese were thus content with local excursions to the Vienna woods rather than extensive journeys further afield (Lehne and Johnson 1985).

In the country

Moving further from the edge of the town, through the "urbanised countryside" and into the rural heartlands, a further set of distinct leisure settings could be found. Nonetheless, even here, a functional relationship with the town existed. The rural-based affluent classes had lifestyles that embraced urban and rural spheres and their leisure combined elements of both.

Humans are gregarious animals and it is not surprising that a major theme of life in the countryside involved the social round of visiting each other. The modern tourism term "visiting friends and relatives" covers a practice so ubiquitous and yet so difficult to record. Yet it is these routine activities which have always been important. Malcolmson (1973:16) observed for the recreations of the poor that, "the closer we approach the most commonplace experiences . . . the more meagre our information becomes". The same is almost as true for the wealthy.

One surviving source of information, however, has been used to reconstruct the visiting and informal circles of acquaintance for a land-owning gentry family in early sixteenth-century Norfolk (Heal 1990). The detailed account books of Sir Thomas Le Strange of Hunstanton record instances of hospitality by his household and the origins of the visitors can be mapped (Figure 2.6). The pattern reveals a localised network based largely within the county and comprising either Sir Thomas's kin or fellow members of the gentry. Visits were generally for a few days to celebrate births, christenings, festivals or hunting expeditions. Sir Thomas, in turn, spent much time returning these visits as part of the annual rhythm of his life. Pure conviviality and a sense of social obligation to friends and kin seem to have been more important than displays of power and wealth (Heal 1990). This natural human response should not be overshadowed by the more spectacular examples of conspicuous consumption and expenditure. Country visiting in Scotland in the early eighteenth century, for instance, was as much about "friendly intercourse" as display (Graham 1909).

Pleasure settings in the country developed in different places as

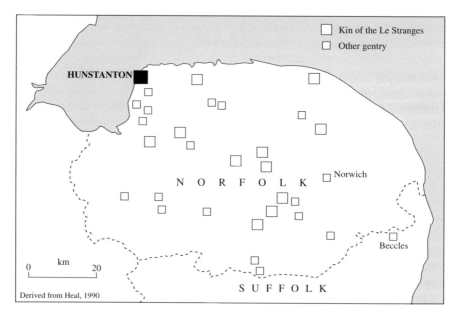

Figure 2.6   The origins of visitors to the Le Strange household, Hunstanton, Norfolk, 1520–1538 (Oxford University Press)

circumstances allowed. More peaceful times, a rise in affluence and the reception of new fashions and ideas in lifestyle clearly varied in time and space across Europe and the design of country property, both house, garden and estate, as appropriate settings for pleasure, reflected these variations.

Leisure-related developments could be on a small scale. As early as 1604, Sir David Lindsay of Edzell Castle, north of Dundee, began to lay out an extensive "pleasure garden" adjacent to his refurbished fortified tower house. Stable political conditions enabled him to indulge in tastes acquired in Europe as a young man. Renaissance ideals were reflected in carvings of planetary deities, representations of the liberal arts and cardinal virtues, placed around the garden. A summer house and bath house were also constructed for the family's pleasure (Douglas-Simpson 1930–1931). That a remote corner of north-east Scotland should see these developments in the early seventeenth century was a sign of the wide-spread urge to modify country residences for enjoyment as soon as conditions permitted.

This process of modification had started rather earlier in England and the sixteenth century saw the transition of wealthy residences from castles to houses. Small medieval gardens moved beyond the confines of defensive walls to form elaborate pathways of knot-gardens, labyrinths and mazes. The large Elizabethan house became a social and cultural centre (Girouard 1978) and classical motifs and styles from Renaissance Italy became architectural features (Allen 1937; Wittkower 1974). A growing taste for gardening as recreation extended around the house (Thomas 1983). Country estates became significant places for leisure and pleasure and it is probable that this process was nowhere more highly developed than in England. Spring (1978) estimates that the English spent more time on their estates than other European elites and so were more inclined to lavish attention on them. Indeed, Ackerman (1990:135) goes further, believing that rural society and economy from Elizabethan times onwards gave country houses and their settings in England "a cultural importance greater than in any other place and time".

The changes in rural society and economy that gave rise to the English landed estate and its role as a centre for leisure and recreation were complex. They require some discussion, however, if leisure is not to be divorced from other aspects of life. The period c.1540 to c.1640 was one of high social mobility with people moving in and out of the ranks of the landed classes (Stone 1966). Church and crown lands were sold by the Tudor monarchy to raise money and between 1534 and 1660 up to 20–30 per cent of the country went on to the private market. New families entered the realms of the landed classes and quickly wished to establish their status. Country house building and demonstrations of fashion and taste were all part of this process and the leisured virtuoso, indulging in collecting, painting and antiquities, became a fashionable ideal (Houghton 1942). Further shifts in landownership came in the late seventeenth and eighteenth centuries with large landowners augmenting their estates at the expense of small farmers (Yelling 1990). By the later eighteenth century, the gentry owned around 50 per cent of England and the aristocracy around 20–25 per cent (Mingay 1976) and landownership units in England became far larger than elsewhere in Europe.

Crucial for an understanding of leisure and recreation is the fact that these landowners were *rentiers*, with their income derived from tenant farmers who worked their estates. Additional income accrued from urban property, mineral rights and investments. Furthermore, the legal strict settlement system helped prevent estates being fragmented between generations (Scott 1982). Thus the landed estate provided ample time and money for leisure as well as an extensive and enduring stage upon which to engage in the pursuit of pleasure.

Landed property was the foundation of English society (Mingay 1963). The leisured country gentleman was the ideal to which society aimed and where house and estate asserted both the power and the taste of the owner. The key term for what owners did with their property was "improvement" (Daniels and Seymour 1990). This involved not just agricultural improvements but extended to refashioning gardens and landscape parks and ensuring that their houses accorded with the latest styles. As land became concentrated into fewer hands, so farmland became converted into a "landscape of display" (Williamson and Bellamy 1987). Country houses and their grounds became more and more divorced from their local communities as landowners saw themselves as part of a national social and cultural elite. This increasing withdrawal from local popular culture, identified by Burke (1978), came to be seen in the creation of landscaped parks from which locals were excluded by the extension of land rights. At times, whole villages were removed if they spoilt tastefully designed "prospects". In Hampshire, over half the landscaped parks contained the relics of former villages (Williamson and Bellamy 1987).

The changing design of houses, gardens and parks has been extensively researched (for instance: Allen 1937; Girouard 1978; Hipple 1957; Hussey 1927; Jacques 1983; Malins 1966; Manwaring 1925; Ogden and Ogden 1955; Prince 1967). The sixteenth and seventeenth centuries saw a preference for formal styles of gardens and grounds derived from the French and Dutch. By the early eighteenth century a more informal style became fashionable, often attempting to imitate idealised classical Italian landscapes depicted in the paintings of Claude and Poussin. William Kent and "Capability" Brown supplied estate owners with sweeping acres of grass and trees in "naturalised" but essentially tamed landscapes. Wilder aspects of nature crept in during the later eighteenth century with the advent of picturesque and romantic tastes. Many of the ideas for landscape design were inspired through the landed classes travelling abroad so that tourism abroad became linked to leisure settings at home (see chapter 5).

Although the aesthetics of house, garden and estate might change, their purposes remained the same. On the one hand they demonstrated the power, wealth and taste of the owner. But, on the other hand, as Habakkuk (1965) and Brewer (1976) have stressed, landowners acquired land not simply to develop it, but also to *enjoy* it. The interests that historians have in finance and power can distort our picture of the world of the landed classes so that, "quite unrealistically, homo economicus has triumphed over homo ludens" (Cannadine 1978:461).

The activities of "homo ludens" on the landed estates were many and varied. House and garden were the setting for entertaining friends and relations, dancing, drinking, card playing, music, reading, promenading, bowls, fencing, and so on. On the estate, fishing and the all important hunting and shooting could be indulged in. Game laws were used to enforce rights and exclude local people (see next chapter) while the consolidation of land holdings made hunting easier. The pursuit of happiness and the pursuit of the animal kingdom were both raised to a high art.

The English country house and estate were not only centres of pleasure for owners and friends; they increasingly attracted tourists travelling in circuits around the country or on short visits from the towns (Ousby 1990). Antiquarians such as Leland, Camden and Aubrey, or the adventurous traveller such as Celia Fiennes, visited estates in the sixteenth and seventeenth centuries but, by the eighteenth century, visitors were increasingly from the urban middle classes. Norfolk, Derbyshire and the west of England were favourite regions due to their high concentrations of country seats. Guidebooks were produced, such as Thomas Martyn's (1768) *English Connoisseur* which directed visitors to the "Palaces and Seats of the Nobility". Some of the larger, much visited houses introduced ticketing systems and guides (Tinniswood 1989). Generally, however, the system was very informal with housekeepers showing visitors around. This form of tourism featured in Jane Austen's (1813) *Pride and Prejudice* when Elizabeth Bennet visited Mr Darcy's estate in Derbyshire and was shown round by the housekeeper. Elizabeth travels there with her aunt and uncle; a London merchant family and part of that urban bourgeoisie who were increasingly exploring their own country.

The enjoyment of a lifestyle associated with extensive landed estates was also found during the eighteenth century in the American colonies of the south. Unlike the New England colonies with their smaller landholdings and somewhat Puritanical overtones in attitudes to pleasure, the large estates and plantations of the south developed a landed gentry way of life (Kraus 1971). Many of the landowners had close connections with England and a similar pattern of leisure can be detected: visiting family and friends, dancing, music, hunting, fishing and horse racing; in short, "the life of the fox-hunting squire" (Dulles 1965). The only real difference with England seems to have been a slightly more open society for leisurely pursuits (Cross 1990a).

If we move back from the rural heartlands of the large landed estates to the "urbanised countryside" around the towns, it is possible to see how a range of processes were at work in creating leisure landscapes in particular regional settings. In south-east England, the pattern of development of landscapes designed essentially for leisure and recreation followed a form of spatial diffusion dominated by London. Brandon (1979) argues that this spread of designed landscapes depended on the complex interplay between changing landscape tastes, a source area for new ideas and fashions, changing accessibility to London and other urban centres, and the availability of land of appropriate quality at a suitable price.

In the early eighteenth century, landscape preference in the south-east was for the "garden-like" quality of the Weald with its lush meadows, hedges and trees. As a romantic and picturesque taste emerged in mid-century, preference was transferred to the higher and wilder scenery of the High Weald, especially on the Surrey–Sussex border. Here was also found a romantic medieval atmosphere of old manor houses and ruined abbeys. By the 1830s even the lowland heaths of the region were admired for their desolate atmosphere.

The first area in the region to adopt landscape parks was the Thames Valley just west of London. This was near to the source of the latest fashions in design with figures like Burlington, Pope, Walpole, Switzer, Kent and Langley developing new styles. From the Thames Valley, parks then spread to areas of accepted beauty elsewhere that also had access to London, Tunbridge Wells or the coastal resorts. Thus the Vale of Mickleham and the North Downs were early centres, a process quickened by the arrival of turnpike roads in the 1750s. Next came the central Weald, combining fine hilly prospects with cheap wooded land, easily converted to varied park scenery. The western High Weald followed, a development delayed until the late eighteenth century by a combination of bleak scenery, difficult soils and few good roads.

Within these different areas, the particular places chosen for "improvement" were closely related to good roads and in fact estate owners would often bear the cost of road improvements to their land. This process led to a significant contrast between the "improved" landscapes along or near good roads and islands of unchanged traditional working landscapes. In one lived a nouveau metropolitan riche, in the other farmers and labourers. William Cobbett, travelling in the area in the 1820s, noted this distinction:

> Those that travel on turnpike roads know nothing of England—from Hascombe to Thursley almost the whole way is across fields or commons, or along narrow lanes. Here we see people without any disguise or affectation. Against a *great road* things are made for *show*.
>
> (quoted in Brandon 1979:174)

From country to town

Before considering leisure and recreation settings in urban centres *per se*, emphasis must be given to the movement of the largely rural-based affluent classes to the town in search of diversions. As mentioned earlier, the lifestyle of the English landed classes, in particular, embraced both rural and urban settings and their leisure reflected this duality (Hughes

1952; Namier 1961). Towns, in this context, refers to those centres with multiple functions. Migration to specialist resort centres is considered in chapters 4 and 7.

The rural tide that flowed to urban settings and back again, took place within fairly clear temporal and spatial parameters (Borsay 1989). Operating within the calendar year were two social cycles. The first was a lengthy urban winter season, and the second consisted of a short-term series of summer events. These two cycles functioned at different spatial scales. At the national scale, a winter season developed in London from the sixteenth and seventeenth centuries onwards. During the eighteenth century London was joined by a number of provincial centres such as York and Norwich which developed similar winter seasons (Cunningham 1990). At the local scale, country towns such as Shrewsbury, Salisbury and Warwick developed smaller winter seasons. The summer cycle depended upon the various fairs, assizes and race meetings that were found in both provincial and local centres. The emergence of these urban seasons can be closely related to the growth of a consumer society which became increasingly broadly based throughout the country (Corfield 1982; Glennie 1990). Towns were centres of consumption and, for leisure, conspicuous consumption. New urban markets for specialist entertainment and services were created as leisure became increasingly commercialised (Plumb 1973).

Pre-eminent for the winter season was London (Cunningham 1990) and from Elizabethan times, the capital had developed rapidly as a centre of conspicuous consumption (Fisher 1948; Stone 1965). A distinct social season grew in the early seventeenth century so that "from October to June, London always contained a substantial population of rural landowners" (Fisher 1948:43). Clubs, coffee houses, theatres, shops, balls and assemblies drew upon a national catchment area. Between late spring and early autumn, however, the tide turned and leisured society left for their country seats, leaving the capital "dull, dusty and abandoned" (Borsay 1989:141). One reason for this was simply climatic. In winter, outdoor recreations were more restricted and travel in the countryside difficult. Indoor entertainment and company were more readily available in an urban setting. During the summer, on the other hand, London and other major centres became dusty, dirty and unhealthy.

During the summer months many local and provincial centres provided short-term attractions for the country elite. Annual fairs were important; that at Bury St Edmunds drew "all the neighbouring nobility and gentry" (Borsay 1989:143). Even more significant were the assizes. They became part of the summer social calendar of the provincial gentry, happily combining an assertion of the power of the law with the other pleasures and privileges associated with their rank.

Thus, during the year, there was a regular seasonal flow of the landed classes in England from their country seats to national and provincial urban centres. If to these flows are added the customary local scale patronage of towns for amusement (Borsay 1989; McInnes 1988), we can see a constant interaction between country and town often based on a search for pleasure.

Urban leisure pursuits

Although the medieval town had spaces for leisure and recreation (Borsay 1986; Kostof 1992), these were generally informal and incidental to other uses. The Renaissance period onwards, however, saw the incorporation of leisure needs into the design of urban open space. In his *De Re Aedificatoria*, Alberti (1404–1472) the Italian Renaissance architect and planner wrote:

> A city is not built wholly for the sake of shelter, but ought to be so contrived, that besides more civil conveniences there may be handsome spaces left for squares, courses for chariots, gardens, places to take the air in, and the like, both for amusement and recreation.
>
> (quoted in Gutkind 1969:116)

During the next two or three hundred years, the Renaissance and Baroque eras saw profound changes in urban functions and form. The leisure and recreation needs of the wealthy were an integral part of these changes, not only creating distinct leisure functions for many towns and cities but also influencing the design and layout of significant spaces in urban areas. The rich and powerful in Europe were attempting to put some of Alberti's ideals into practice.

The period c.1500 to c.1800 saw major political, economic and social changes. In the political sphere, there was the growth of the nation-state and the increased centralisation of government. Capital cities accumulated functions related to their role as power and decision-making centres and they became major arenas for consumption, fashion and display (Smith 1967). Economically, there was a substantial widening of markets associated with urban growth. A proliferation of new forms of employment in luxury goods and services spread throughout the urban hierarchy so that the commercialisation of leisure meant that regional and local centres, as well as capital cities, became locations of fashionable consumption (Corfield 1982). The social changes associated with this period included an elite culture that increasingly delighted in ostentation, parade and display. The Renaissance and Baroque city became, for them, the "city-as-theatre" (Claval 1984), which required appropriate settings for the pursuit of pleasure: fashionable town houses, gardens, parades, promenades, theatres and assembly rooms.

The development of these appropriate settings was facilitated by the increase of central and municipal power over planning and building in towns. Old centres could be remodelled and new ones created according to the Italian models of order and regularity. This process was also associated with an increased specialisation of land use within urban areas including the growth of distinct residential areas for the wealthy in pleasant environments near to specialised centres of entertainment and shops (Smith 1967).

One of the principal features of the urban landscape that was associated with leisure and recreation was the design of open space. Although general open space within towns had long been used for recreation (Kostof 1992), the Renaissance and Baroque periods saw its deliberate incorporation into urban design. Wilkinson (1988) has identified three major components of Renaissance urban planning which influenced open space provision: the primary straight street, gridiron-based district street patterns and enclosed squares. The primary straight street was mainly developed to help movement between different parts of the town, especially for the wealthy in their carriages. These principal streets frequently became major urban symbols with promenades and vistas incorporated and were places where the fashionable could parade and acknowledge each other. Versailles, the Champs Elysées in Paris and Unter den Linden in Berlin were but three of the many examples of this design. New residential districts for the wealthy were often laid out on a uniform gridiron pattern, sometimes incorporating squares and circuses (Gutkind 1969). The development of Edinburgh's New Town from 1767 (Youngson 1966) and the fashionable westward expansion of Glasgow reflected these ideas (Williamson, Riches and Higgs 1990).

Within these overall components of urban design, a series of distinctive open spaces adapted for leisure use can be isolated. They include wall and waterside promenades, garden allées, malls and cours, avenues, squares, boulevards and parks (Kostof 1992; Lawrence 1988). Their design and use developed at different times, but they were mainly derived from Renaissance originals in Italy (Gutkind 1964, 1967, 1969, 1970, 1971).

The defensive walls of towns and cities quickly became an important recreational resource. These were either the old medieval stone walls or the seventeenth-century style ramparts and earthworks. Many became planted with trees and were used by the citizens for walking. This practice was found throughout western Europe and, by the end of the sixteenth century, cities like Lucca and Antwerp were combining their extensive defence systems with use for pleasure. Elsewhere, defences were abandoned and entirely converted to leisure use. France was the first country to abandon defences on a large scale; Louis XIV ordered the destruction of the city walls of Paris in 1670. The moats were filled in and the walls on the north side of the city were razed. These sites were transformed into broad, raised promenades with rows of trees and were open to carriages and pedestrians (Lawrence 1988). Over time, they developed into a series of connected promenades and were an important recreational zone at the edge of the city. By the later eighteenth century, the western promenades of Paris (by then called Boulevards) attracted a whole range of leisure services including shops, cafés and theatres.

The conversion of defences to recreational use was followed elsewhere in Europe according to assessments of defence need and capability. Berlin (1734), Hannover (1763), Graz (1784), Brussels (1810) and Bremen (1802) all converted their walls into promenades (Gutkind 1964). In Vienna, the reforming Joseph II turned the "Glacis", the open strip beyond the fortifications, into a recreation area and employed the army in planting mature trees to achieve an instant visual effect (Lehne and Johnson 1985). It was not just the large cities that acquired this form of recreation space. Small towns in France like Avallon in the mid-seventeenth century and Cluny in the 1780s converted their former walls and moats into tree-lined walks for their citizens.

Riversides, canals and quays provided further settings for leisure use. In the Low Countries, tree-lined canals, notably in Amsterdam, were important areas for fashionable strolling. In Paris, leisurely carriage driving was catered for by the construction of the "Cours de la Reine" along the banks of the Seine in 1616. When Martin Lister visited the city in 1698 he estimated that the Cours could accommodate up to 600 or 700 carriages, the "great Rendezvous of People of the best Fashion" (Lough 1984:114).

Other urban open spaces that had recreational potential were the squares, piazzas or *places* that spread from Renaissance Italy. They were often informal areas for townspeople to gather in but, in exclusive residential districts, they could be closed off by gates. More directly linked to recreation was the development of parks. This was often a piecemeal process and, as Kostof (1992) points out, the idea of the public park "belonging to the public as of right" was more closely associated with the industrial city era (see chapter 8). Before then, we find open spaces, developed on royal or aristocratic estates, gradually being opened up to the public or the construction of pleasure gardens designed specifically for public enjoyment. Thus, in London, the royal parks became more accessible: Hyde Park in 1635, St James's Park in the early 1700s, Kensington Gardens in the 1790s. Pleasure gardens with a wider range of entertainments included Vauxhall (1661) and Ranelagh (1742).

Ranelagh was fairly short-lived, closing in 1802, but Vauxhall continued until 1859 (Chadwick 1966; Rasmussen 1934). Even when they were open to the public, however, parks were generally regarded as being socially exclusive. Joseph II made himself unpopular with the social elite in Vienna when he opened up the Prater to all people (1766) and widened access to the Augarten park (1775). One aristocrat complained to him that there "is no place left where we can solely enjoy society worthy of our standing" (Lehne and Johnson 1985:66).

The spread of the Renaissance ideas for open space planning was not uniform. Spain rather lagged behind these developments (Gutkind 1967). Some ideas were incorporated, such as improved plaza mayores (Valladolid 1560s, Madrid 1617–1619, Salamanca 1729–1733) or tree-lined avenues like the Salon del Prado in Madrid but there was generally very little coordinated town planning until the early nineteenth century. Barcelona did not demolish its walls until the 1860s and the tree-lined walk, or "Alameda" was more a feature of nineteenth-century development. Gutkind (1967:290) writes of the "Spanishness of Spanish cities", where traditional urban structures were retained for much longer and where gardens and parks were less of an integral part of the urban scene.

Many incidental places were, of course, in use in urban areas for leisure and recreation by all social classes. The pictures of Hendrick Avercamp (1585–1634) are a reminder of how quickly a frozen body of water would be converted into a skating arena during the winter by townspeople in Holland of all classes and ages (Figure 2.7).

Across the Atlantic in North America, there were, as in Europe, few early signs of deliberate provision of urban public open space. The towns of the eastern seaboard made do with "commons" and "greens" which served a multiple use with animal grazing, markets, fairs and general recreation. The first signs of setting aside land specifically for recreation seem to have been in Boston where the common was designated in 1634 and protected from development in the 1640s (Kraus 1971). Savannah, founded in 1731, provides an example of a much more conscious plan to provide for recreation, however. The urban scheme of James Oglethorpe included 10 acres of public gardens by the river and 24 small squares and open spaces. In essence, Oglethorpe's ideas harked back to Renaissance city planning concepts (Wilkinson 1988).

New York saw little in the way of open space provision in its early stages, with narrow streets, houses placed close together and only two small open spaces at the "Bowling Green" and "The Fields". The fashionable elite had to make do with promenading around Hanover Square or using the banks of the East River for picnics (Dulles 1965). It was not until 1785 that an appeal was made for more provision for

Figure 2.7   "Winter Landscape with Iceskaters" by Hendrick Avercamp (Rijksmuseum, Amsterdam)

public recreation in the city. A letter to the mayor pointed out that: "there is not in this great city, nor in its environs, any one proper spot, where its numerous inhabitants can enjoy, with convenience, the exercise that is necessary for health and amusement" (quoted in Olmsted and Kimball 1971:18). The letter noted how provision of this kind was made in the great cities of Europe and suggested that the "Battery" and "The Fields" be developed for pleasure. Progress was slow, however. Apart from the pleasure gardens of Vauxhall, Niblo's and Contoit's, New York had little in the way of recreation space. The competition for creating the great resource of Central Park did not commence until 1857.

This section on the affluent and the town concludes with a study of how leisure and recreation affected an English provincial town. Large cities and specialised leisure centres, such as spas and seaside resorts, clearly had a particular concern with catering for the leisured elite. But it was a measure of the pervasive influence of a leisure culture in a society when provincial towns began to seriously address their needs.

Peter Borsay (1989) has claimed that the English provincial town experienced a cultural renaissance from the mid-seventeenth to the mid-eighteenth century. This renaissance was widespread and was largely fuelled by the leisure demands of an expanding social elite. Rising standards of living led to increased demands for luxury goods and

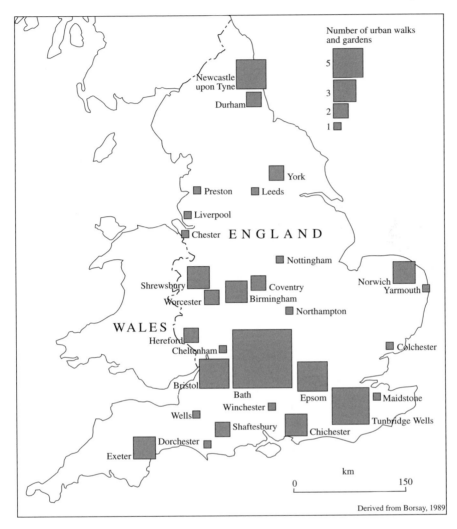

Figure 2.8   The development of urban walks and gardens in provincial England by 1770

services at a time when there was a growing cultural polarisation between polite society and traditional culture (cf. Burke 1978). Borsay traces this cultural renaissance through the urban landscape: houses with classical façades, brick and stone replacing timber, planned streets and public buildings; through the growth of the arts: bookshops, newspapers, music, dancing, society seasons, and through the provision of specific settings for fashionable display: assembly rooms, walks, gardens and promenades (Figure 2.8).

Table 2.1 Occupational analysis of freemen in Shrewsbury, 1650–1675—1750–1775

	Percentage of total tradesmen		
Occupational category	1650–75	1700–25	1750–75
Labouring	0.0	0.8	0.3
Leather trades	19.0	18.1	9.9
Rural occupations	2.0	1.5	1.4
Leisured classes	6.1	7.0	18.4
Textiles	13.8	9.5	5.7
Clothing	5.7	5.5	4.5
Victualling	15.0	20.2	17.0
Building trades	4.5	5.9	5.1
Metal trades	4.9	4.8	4.5
River trades	1.2	3.0	3.1
Household goods	0.8	1.7	2.8
Distribution	2.8	0.3	0.9
Merchants	15.8	8.0	7.9
Luxury trades	4.5	8.6	8.8
Services and professions	4.1	4.3	8.5
Miscellaneous	0.0	0.7	1.1
Leisure sector (services and professions, luxury trades and leisured classes)	14.7	19.9	35.7

Source: from McInnes (1988).

How far did this leisure culture spread through the English urban hierarchy? McInnes (1988) disputes Borsay's thesis that leisure spread everywhere in the seventeenth and eighteenth centuries and points to provincial towns where it was of little consequence such as Uttoxeter or Maldon, or even where it declined, such as Nantwich losing gentry patronage to Chester. McInnes suggests that there was a specific group of provincial towns where the pursuit of pleasure became dominant and that these should perhaps be grouped with resorts as distinctive "leisure towns".

Although this argument remains to be resolved, McInnes's (1988) study of Shrewsbury between 1660 and 1760 provides a useful example of the ways in which a leisure culture operated in the particular setting of the provincial town. He traces the impact of leisure and recreation through four main themes: occupational structure, leisure facilities, amenities and buildings.

The changing occupational structure of Shrewsbury indicates the growing influence of a leisured society on the town (Table 2.1). Registers of the town's freemen show a marked decline in leather and textile employment between the mid-seventeenth and mid-eighteenth centuries.

As these traditional occupations declined, so the leisure sector expanded; services and professions more than doubled and there was a growth in luxury trades. By 1731, there were 5 tobacconists in the town, 3 perfumers, 26 barbers, 4 watchmakers, a dancing master and 3 bookshops. Overall, McInnes estimates that the "leisure sector" of freemen rose from 14.7 to 35.7 per cent of total tradesmen.

New leisure facilities came to Shrewsbury. By the early eighteenth century, gatherings for dancing, tea drinking and card games were well established on a weekly basis using an inn and later an assembly room. The quarter sessions, assizes, hunts and race meetings became important events in the social leisure calendar of the town and demands for fashionable outdoor recreation were met by the provision of public walks around the old abbey as well as promenades and carriage drives by the River Severn. The old town walls were converted into a series of walks with picturesque views across the surrounding countryside. Bowling greens, a tennis court, a racecourse, and a new theatre all emphasised that, by the 1760s, Shrewsbury was an essentially "leisure town".

General urban amenities reflected the presence of an affluent leisure class in Shrewsbury. Conscious of their economic importance, the corporation was anxious to respond to gentry demands. Extensive street paving was initiated as well as street cleaning. From the 1720s, the corporation provided street lighting and improved the water supply. The general urban environment was also being changed by building alterations. Traditional timber-framing and thatch were abandoned in favour of brick and tile, especially in the western part of the town. The owners of these new-style houses were either the gentry or traders who prospered from the world of luxury and leisure.

The transformation of this provincial market town into a leisure town can be related to a number of factors, both general and specific. General factors included the nationwide growth in affluence which permeated down the social ladder, with wage rates generally rising between 1660 and 1760. Also operating at the national level was a changing cultural outlook. Renaissance values of education, taste and refinement had spread to provincial centres, giving rise to a polite urban culture. A general commercial revolution in England was also taking place with the demand for luxury goods being met by increased trade in tea, coffee, sugar, tobacco, fruits and other delights of an affluent lifestyle.

But the transformation of Shrewsbury also depended on certain specific local factors. Its geographical location with the excellent route-ways of the River Severn and its tributaries enabled the town to tap a variety of goods cheaply. Luxury items were brought up the Severn, at lower prices than elsewhere, and this abundance of goods at relatively low prices was recognised by contemporaries as a distinct advantage. Shrewsbury was also the county town and thus the centre for the social occasions which accompanied the quarter sessions and assizes. Finally, Shrewsbury was blessed with a corporation and traders who were particularly responsive to leisure-class demands. The corporation was always keen to provide and improve facilities. It created the town's walks and promenades and the first racecourse was on their land. The tradesmen showed particular entrepreneurial skill in identifying new markets and ensuring that the affluent were supplied with all their needs. As McInnes observes, "it was their vigour and their skill that made Shrewsbury successful as a leisure town" (p. 83).

Shrewsbury illustrates how the affluent in a town could transform that town into a distinct leisure setting. Elsewhere in Europe the Renaissance period onwards saw urban environments modified to accommodate a leisure culture. Beyond the town, the leisure activities of the wealthy spread through the villas of the urban periphery and were a major element in the country estates of the landed classes. Between each of these settings there was a constant migration of the well-to-do in the pursuit of their pleasure.

3

Popular recreations in country and town

The previous chapter was chiefly concerned with the leisure and recreation of the wealthier members of pre-industrial societies. As the nature of the historical record is clearly biased towards the affluent minority, leisure for the great mass of the population is less well known. In addition, as social historians have gradually turned their attention to popular culture and leisure, they have concentrated more on transformations under the pressures of urbanisation and industrialisation (Cunningham 1980; Malcolmson 1973) than on the long-term leisure practices that endured for centuries in pre-industrial worlds (Thomas 1964). This chapter will consider what some of those long-term practices were and where they took place, both in the countryside and in the town. But, as well as continuity, there were also changes in popular recreations before major industrial and urban processes were under way. A gradual "loss of space and time" (Rule 1986) for the leisure and recreation of the labouring classes was already occurring in pre-industrial worlds and a number of these pressures will be examined here before the major impacts of industrial structures are considered in chapter 8.

In the country

Just as the wealthy had their routines of leisure, so a pattern of activity can be observed for the poor. Popular recreation in the countryside throughout much of Europe was rooted in the daily and seasonal rhythms of agricultural life, whether arable or pastoral, and took place in the settings of home, street, village green or surrounding fields and woods. Throughout the year, a distinction can be made between ordinary, everyday leisure and the major annual holiday events, and between activities that were centred around home and immediate locality and those which caused people to move from, say, their village or hamlet to the nearby town or even further afield. Thus the servants of Parson Woodforde in Norfolk could be found engaging in recreations at Whitsun in their local village of Weston but travelling (about 8 miles) for a holiday to the St Faith's Fair near Norwich once a year (Woodforde 1978). On a grander scale, the carnival of Holy Week in Barcelona was able to draw people not just from adjacent villages but from distant provinces also (Burke 1978).

The fundamental basis for the daily and seasonal activities of life was, for many people, the tightly knit rural village community; "the primary locus of identity for most Europeans before the nineteenth century" (Shubert 1990:190). There was the common experience of daily activities reinforced by a shared oral culture. Social relations and contacts were mainly family, neighbours and work; a generally localised world with limited horizons. One should not generalise too much, however, about a uniform way of life and there were important variations throughout Europe. Burke (1978) highlights contrasts in popular culture between lowland zones and poorer, more socially conservative upland zones. Differences occurred between farmers and more mobile herdsmen. Shepherds in central Europe, for instance, developed their own set of festivities with St Bartholomew's on the 24th August marking the transition between summer and winter quarters. Even within a small region like the Beauvaisis in France, there were considerable differences in lifestyle between the rich yeoman or *laboureur* and the poor general worker or *journalier* (Burke 1978). Furthermore, different environments offered different possibilities for leisure activities. Communities near the coast for instance had a long tradition of enjoying the pleasures of sea and beach, long before the elite discovered the benefits of sea-bathing (see Corbin 1994 and chapter 7).

Within these rural worlds, there had been a tradition of mixing between the various social classes for a long time. The French nobility were still taking part "in the business and pleasure of the local community" during the seventeenth century and the local gentry in England joined in village activities right into the eighteenth century (Burke 1978; Malcolmson 1973). The poor and the wealthy had some recreational tastes in common and country houses were, for a time, social centres for local people. Over time, this social mixing declined and the landed classes withdrew, both socially and culturally, from their local communities. It was then that conflict over the use of recreational space became more pronounced and some of the consequences of this will be considered below.

Everyday leisure for the poor occurred mainly in small, informal

Table 3.1 The annual distribution of parish wakes in Northamptonshire in the early eighteenth century

Period of time	Number of parish wakes
January–March	0
April and early May	1
Around Whit and Trinity Sundays	4
Late June–early July	38
Second half of July	20
Early August	1
Around 15th August	14
Late August, first half of September	22
Second half of September	–
Around Michaelmas	31
October	18
Around All Saints' Day	33
Rest of November and December	23

Source: from Malcolmson (1973).

gatherings often mixing pleasure with work. Play in the streets, an evening walk in the surrounding fields, combining a trip to market with socialising, the coming together of relatives and friends during the lifecycle of birth, marriage and death; these were informal gatherings in informal settings. They were also, of course, the dominant, if rarely recorded, experiences of leisure and recreation. Outside this ordinary routine, there was an important holiday calendar of festivals and other celebrations. These were closely linked to the seasonal rhythms of agricultural life and often took place in lulls between labour-demanding tasks, such as sowing or harvesting, or during the winter months. The annual parish feast or wake was one such holiday. Although based in a village and primarily a local event, the parish feast was also a time for friends and relatives from elsewhere to reassemble and so its sig-nificance could extend further afield (Malcolmson 1973). Many of these feasts showed a marked temporal pattern. John Bridges' survey of eighteenth-century Northamptonshire wakes revealed a concentration of events in late spring–early summer and late summer–early autumn (Table 3.1). These wakes often lasted for up to a week and involved a whole range of rustic pleasures such as dancing, wrestling, cudgels, racing, bull-baiting, cock-fighting and music.

Fairs were another important event in the holiday calendar. Most fairs were primarily concerned with commercial functions but it is clear that many incorporated pleasure also. They were generally based in towns and not only served an urban populace but drew in substantial numbers of the surrounding rural inhabitants. Braudel (1979) notes fairs in

Europe occurring at all levels in the settlement hierarchy with hinterlands that varied accordingly. With a seasonal pattern similar to parish wakes, there were, nonetheless, important regional variations in custom. Fairs in East Anglia, for instance, were more explicitly geared to pleasure and this was partly a reflection of a lack of local parish-based festivities in this region (Malcolmson 1973).

Winter was a season for holidays. In England, a time of celebration and festivity was general from Christmas to Twelfth Day. Much of this took place at the local parish scale, centred on family, friends and village neighbours. The difficulties of travel reinforced this tendency. Other winter breaks included Plough Monday and Shrove Tuesday. The Easter period then followed with a whole week of diversions and the start of the fair season. May Day came next with its traditions of flower gathering and dancing, and the later Whitsun holiday could entail up to a week of activities in the villages as well as visits to fairs further afield.

These forms of popular recreation and their seasonal rhythms were to be found throughout Europe. In Germany, parish fairs and carnivals were regulated by seasonal work and religious days. Church festivals took place between Lent and Whitsun and these were augmented by regional and local celebrations of saints' days, church consecrations and pilgrimages. As Abrams (1992:34) points out, these German festivals were "innately local in character". Catholic villages would hold local *Kirchweih* festivals commemorating the founding of a place of worship while all villages had *Brunnenfeiern*, to bless the local water supply, and celebrate harvest festivals. As in England, the most significant occasion was the parish fair or *kirmes*. This was generally held in the autumn, after the harvest, and could last for several days. Thus, the *kirmes* was:

> probably the most important event in the religious, social and recreational lives of lower-class rural inhabitants. It was used to date occasions in the family and community and it functioned as a safety valve too, siphoning off tensions and uniting the community.
>
> (Abrams 1992:35)

The amount of recreational time may have been quite considerable. In some districts of western Germany, more than 100 days a year were officially marked as *Festtage*, with each village timing its festival so as not to coincide with a neighbour.

In Spain, a whole range of church festivals combined religion with pleasure. Following carnivals at Lent, there was Easter week, Corpus Christi in early summer, All Saints' Day and the Christmas period. In addition, there were the local saints' day *feria*; an occasion for celebration that could last for several days. Carnivals were especially important in southern Europe, with a season from January until Lent, which, as with the carnival in Barcelona, could draw people from far afield (Barke and Towner 1995).

This picture of long-term popular custom and recreation began to change, however, at different times and in different places throughout Europe. The transformation of these worlds can be seen most clearly through the processes of industrialisation and rapid urban growth. Irregular habits and a seasonal rhythm of life did not conveniently fit into the new modes of work discipline. But it would be wrong to link all change to these processes. Popular recreation was also under attack in the pre-industrial world, either because of its alleged corrupting influence on the mass of people or because popular recreation could invade space reserved for others. In England, although the moral attack gained pace in the later eighteenth century, puritans of the Elizabethan age and seventeenth century had been hostile to many popular recreations and these attitudes were transported across the Atlantic to the New England colonies. Here, a whole range of restrictions were placed on activities so that, on Sunday, even "unnecessary and unseasonable walking in the streets and fields" became prohibited (Kraus 1971:161).

A major cause for control, however, arose from competition for space. This could occur at a very localised scale. The constant use of churchyards for village games was always, for instance, a cause for complaint in England (Malcolmson 1973). Throughout the countryside in general, however, there was a major undermining of popular recreation, with the social elite appropriating space for its own exclusive pleasures. This was a process that had a long history, as the creation of Royal Forests and medieval game laws testify, but the seventeenth century saw national game laws enacted which restricted hunting to the wealthy while increasingly punitive measures were taken to limit access to land. The most notorious of these measures were the Black Acts of 1723 (Thompson 1975) which introduced the death penalty for poaching. Significantly, the main areas of conflict which gave rise to these Acts were around Windsor and Richmond; areas that were becoming fashionable retreats for the leisure classes of London.

The gradual creation of an essentially "private" rural landscape for the affluent was related to the distancing of the landed classes, in their social and cultural activities, from the local communities. This process created a "solid barrier between the culture of gentility and the culture of the people" (Malcolmson 1973:165). The spread of the landscape park and the creation of the exclusive country house and estate, referred to in chapter 2, was part of this movement. Also at work was the increased enclosure of farmland. With enclosure, more and more of the landscape became subject to absolute rights of ownership. In England, enclosure was under way in the sixteenth and seventeenth centuries and the

Parliamentary enclosure of the eighteenth and nineteenth centuries completed a process that was a major force for restricting access to the countryside and its resources for pleasure (Williamson and Bellamy 1987). Woods became excluded areas and even a simple country walk became difficult. "In the old days you could walk all through the parish and all round it by the baulks and headlands", recalled Tom Lynes of Tysoe in Northamptonshire (Shoard 1987:68), and Robert Slaney observed in 1824 that: "Owing to the inclosure of open lands and commons, the poor have no place in which they may amuse themselves in summer evenings when the labour of the day is over, or when a holiday occurs" (quoted in Shoard 1987:69). Enclosure and the creation of large landed estates, on the other hand, facilitated the growth of recreation and sport for the affluent. Fox hunting and pheasant shooting were made easier if fewer ownership boundaries were involved. As recreation opportunities in the countryside expanded for one group, so they receded for another.

There is some argument over how resilient popular recreations were to the undermining effects not only of loss of space but also of the fundamental social upheaval associated with rapid urbanisation and industrialisation. Malcolmson (1973) sees these latter processes as a potent force for change, particularly with the new demands for labour discipline. In 1772, for instance, Josiah Wedgwood, an early industrial entrepreneur, complained of how his workmen "keep wake after wake in summer when it is their own good will and pleasure" (quoted in Malcolmson 1973:99). In Cornwall, however, the owners of the tin mining industry were having more success. While, in the early eighteenth century, an observer could claim that the miners:

> between their numerous holidays, holiday eves, feasts, account days (once a month), Yeu Widdens or one way or another they invent to loiter away their time, they do no work one half of their month for the owners and employers

by the early nineteenth century it was noted that:

> The occupations in the mining countries fill up the time of those engaged in them too effectively to allow leisure for prolonged revels or frequent festivities.

> (quoted in Rule 1986:217–218)

Some popular recreations, however, survived these forces for change. In Germany, the rapidly growing urban industrial areas around Bochum and Düsseldorf absorbed the traditional rural *kirmes* so that, even in 1860, there were 28 *kirmes* days celebrated within Düsseldorf's city boundaries (Abrams 1992). The notion of popular recreations collapsing under the weight of urban industrial growth can be too simplistic. Cunningham (1980) cites a range of activities and customs that managed to survive in new environments, such as fairs, cock-fighting and bull-baiting, and he suggests that the whole process of the transformation of popular leisure and recreation from pre-industrial rural worlds to industrial urban worlds was far more complex than is often portrayed. These arguments are pursued further in chapter 8.

In the town

Open space for popular recreation in towns can be traced back to medieval times (Borsay 1986). Public spaces such as taverns, market-places, streets and the town edge were always used by citizens for pleasure. Areas would often be taken over for particular purposes such as the street for football (Delves 1981). On Saturday evenings in early eighteenth-century Glasgow, the north and south banks of the River Clyde were occupied by men and boys engaged in stone-throwing contests to gain possession of a mid-channel island (Daiches 1977).

These periodic invasions of public space for popular pleasure were a major cause of social conflict within urban areas for, as in the country-side, the wealthy gradually became more exclusive and wished to create their own leisure preserves, rather than sharing recreational space with other social groups. This trend could be observed in the provincial northern city of Newcastle-upon-Tyne. Before the eighteenth century, the Sandhill area by the river was one of the main recreational centres of the city as well the marketplace and administrative centre. Grouped around this space were the large houses of the merchant classes. Yet the Sandhill was also where Midsummer and St Peter's eves were celebrated as well as other festivities and entertainments. Here also "the good people of the town come on summer evenings to disport themselves" (Charleton 1885:324). Over time, however, this communal area for recreation was lost to commercial developments while the wealthier inhabitants of Newcastle retired to the more exclusive spaces of the Forth, with its tree-lined promenade, the Spring Gardens to the west of the city walls, and the open Town Moor to the north of the built-up area. The poor of Newcastle were left with incidental spaces in the crowded lower town or marginal spaces on the edge. One such space was the Ballast Hills area to the east of the city. Here, ballast from ships was deposited, limekilns and glass-houses located, and open space for walking was shared with a cemetery (Middlebrook 1950). In fact cemeteries, by providing some form of open land, often served towns as spaces of temporary leisure for the living as well as permanent rest for the dead (Kostof 1992).

Throughout the seventeenth and eighteenth centuries, popular recreation in English provincial towns was being squeezed. Just as enclosure restricted access in the countryside, so more parts of the town became "private" preserves for polite society. Admission charges, gates and attendants were some of the methods used to help regulate admission to leisure space (Borsay 1986). These exclusions could, of course, lead to conflict. In eighteenth-century Southampton, wealthy pleasure seekers could find themselves "exposed at night to insult or attack by the rougher elements of the poor, resentful of the amusements of the well to do and fashionable visitors" (Rule 1986:211).

The edge of the town was another space for popular recreation that could be under pressure even in pre-industrial urban environments. These areas had to serve a variety of functions such as agriculture, drill grounds and cemeteries. Public need for recreation could clash with these other interests and, as Kostof (1992:166) observes, "The areas closest to the edge of town . . . were the most bitterly contested". This contest could be clearly seen in the struggles for the use of Moorfields on the northern edge of London. The area had long been a place for recreation and, although poorly drained, it was used for archery and general recreation and, in winter, its frozen surface served as a popular area for skating. Time and again, however, the leaseholders of the area fenced off the land with hedges and ditches to keep people away. Although these were destroyed by mass invasions, Moorfields came under threat in the sixteenth century from the growth of suburban summer-houses and gardens. Eventually, an Act of Parliament (1592) declared that commons and wastes within 3 miles of London should not be enclosed but left, among other reasons, for "walkinge for recreacion comforte and healthe of her Maj. People" (quoted in Rasmussen 1934:82). During the early seventeenth century, part of Moorfields was bequeathed to the city and laid out as a large pleasure ground which attracted the social elite for their promenading. Nevertheless, parts of the area seem to have survived as traditional spaces for popular recreation (Rasmussen 1934).

In the pre-industrial town popular recreation generally took place in areas that served multiple functions and the right to use these areas was often a matter for contest with more powerful interests. The formal provision of space for popular recreational needs was largely absent and it was not until the growth of the industrial city that local authorities and wealthy philanthropists addressed these needs as a matter of urgency (see chapter 8).

4

Specialised leisure places:
the spa resorts

The long history of using mineral water springs for health and pleasure can seem, at first sight, to be relatively straightforward. Depending at first on the patronage of a wealthy elite and then later on, the middle classes, spa resorts moved through cycles of growth and decline. The main variation is that these cycles occurred at different times in different areas. Yet, other than possessing the simple fact of being resource-based attractions (the spring waters), the processes underlying the development of spas are, in reality, extremely complex with variations at national, regional and local scales. Furthermore, a rather simplistic view of spa history can be related to a tendency to focus on the story of successful spas, whereas the full picture must include the equally significant reasons behind those which failed to develop.

Given this complexity, a comprehensive review of the history and geography of spas will not be attempted here. Instead, the chapter highlights a number of aspects which contributed to their development before moving on to a detailed case study of one particular spa, Bath. This forms the core of the chapter and draws together themes referred to in general elsewhere. Bath is considered particularly as a centre of consumption (though not the medical variety) and the geographical patterns which resulted from this aspect of resort life.

The use of spas in the western world dates back certainly to Greek and Roman times (Casson 1974). Numerous *aquae* were scattered throughout the Roman Empire and often formed the basis for the re-emergence of spas in later times. Thus, forms of continuity can be traced from Aquae Sulis (Bath), Aquae Calidae (Vichy), Aquae Sextiae (Aix-en-Provence) and Aquae Mattiacae (Wiesbaden), through different periods of time. Spas in Italy were especially popular with the hot springs around the Bay of Naples (such as Baiae and Puteoli) combining spa and seaside resort functions. These Roman spas were used by people from a wide range of social classes and were rarely exclusive in their social tone.

While some spas declined during certain political and cultural periods, in central Europe their use continued under varying circumstances. In Hungary (Vida 1992), spa use existed under the Romans, through to the middle ages and under Turkish rule (1541–1687). From at least the fourteenth century, there is evidence of social as well as health facilities at Hungarian centres and these were used by a range of social classes. The Turkish baths at Stubnya, for instance, had facilities for the nobility, gentry, peasants, gypsies and women. Following the end of Turkish occupation, Hungary's spas experienced a boom in use and a strong "spa culture" has continued right through to the present day. Further west, the spa tradition also continued to flourish and could compete with other leisure attractions such as seaside resorts. Figure 4.1 shows the numerous flourishing spas in Europe before the First World War.

Themes in the development of spas

Despite the complexity of spa development, it is possible to isolate a number of themes which can be related to the processes and patterns of their evolution. Pearce (1989) has listed a range of factors which underlie many forms of tourism development and these include elements of supply and demand, agents involved in development and the wider context of development within which tourism has to operate. These factors can provide a context for the growth of spas.

In terms of supply, a range of attractions have always been needed in addition to the spa waters themselves. Simply being a spring site was never sufficient and most successful spas served pleasure as well as health needs. The provision of accommodation, utilities such as energy and water supplies as well as transport both for visitors and supplies, were all basic ingredients which development required. To these can be added particular site and local factors. The actual number and position of springs could help determine the morphology of the resort. Harrogate developed two distinct settlements based on separate springs (Figure 4.2) and the spa town did not begin to coalesce until after the arrival of the railway in the 1860s (Patmore 1963). At Cheltenham, seven spas developed at scattered sites and no clear resort centre emerged—resulting in an open and spacious town layout. In addition to the particular spring sites, future development was more likely to occur if combined with sheltered conditions and an equable climate (McIntyre 1981; Patmore 1968). Morphology and the supply of goods, services and

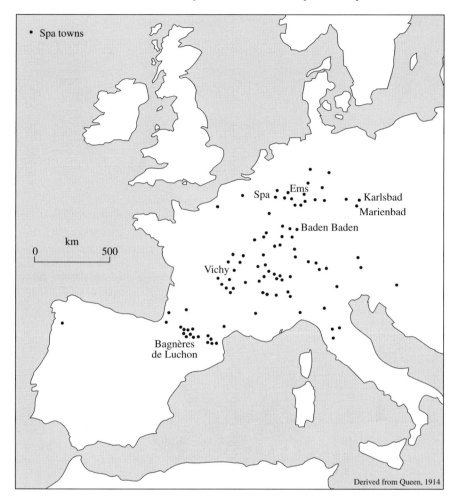

Figure 4.1   Important spas in Western Europe, c.1914

accommodation were also influenced if a spa grew at an already existing settlement. At Bath, the spring site occurred in the centre of the old town and much of the resort expansion took place outside the existing zone. Similarly, Leamington's growth was in the form of a new town of parades and squares laid out on the north side of the River Leam away from the old cramped town centre (Beckinsale and Beckinsale 1980). These new areas were generally for visitor accommodation while many goods and services for the resort tended to remain within the old settlement (Hembry 1990). But an existing settlement which could supply the needs of visitors would not guarantee success. Bishopton

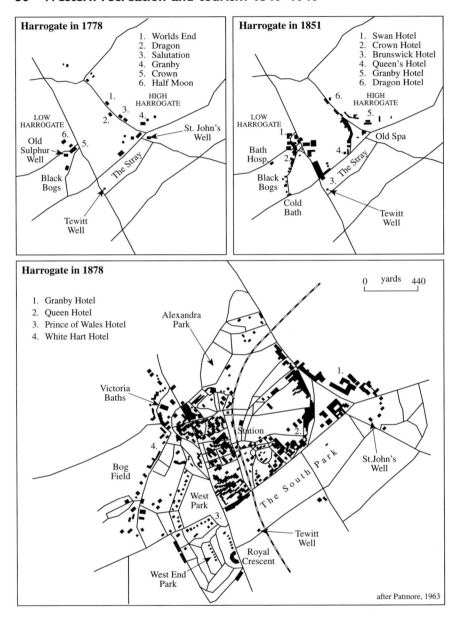

Figure 4.2 The changing morphology of Harrogate, 1778–1878

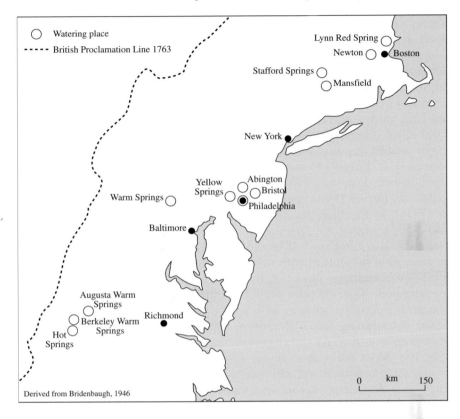

○   Watering place

----   British Proclamation Line 1763

Lynn Red Spring ○

Newton ○ ● Boston

Stafford Springs ○

○ Mansfield

New York ●

Yellow Springs ○   Abington ○ ○ Bristol

Warm Springs ○   ◉ Philadelphia

Baltimore ●

Augusta Warm ○ Springs

○ Berkeley Warm Richmond ● Springs

Hot ○ Springs

0   km   150

Derived from Bridenbaugh, 1946

Figure 4.3   Watering places of colonial America

Spa, near Stratford-upon-Avon, developed in the 1740s utilising the town's services and excellent transport connections but significant investment was lacking until the 1830s, by which time custom had moved elsewhere. Spa resorts could also be created as entirely new settlements, often the case in the frontier conditions of North America (Wightman and Wall 1985; Wall 1982b). But, of all these various components of supply, the provision of accommodation frequently emerges as being crucial for successful spa development. The lack of suitable accommodation inhibited the growth of Cheltenham (Hart 1981) and underlay the demise of many rural spa enterprises (Hembry 1990).

Relative location to population centres and accessibility were also important in influencing spa development. Major urban centres could support a number of surrounding satellite watering places. In colonial America, Philadelphia had its spas at Bristol, Yellow Springs and Abington (Bridenbaugh 1946) (see Figure 4.3). The spa of Baden was a convenient 16 miles from Vienna (Baedeker 1900) and Bad Soden a short distance from Frankfurt am Main (Turgenev 1871). London had a whole clutch of spas at varying distances from its centre. Yet this demand–supply relationship was subtle. For instance, wealth of population was more important than numbers and the catchment area need not be exclusively urban. Thus, the spas of the southern states in the USA and a number of English spas could draw on a hinterland of rural elites (Hembry 1990; Lawrence 1983; Patmore 1968). Proximity to major centres like London influenced not only the number but the social tone of spas. Epsom, 15 miles from London, became a weekend, middle-class resort; Tunbridge Wells, at a further distance, remained more exclusive. Daniel Defoe neatly summarised this access–class relationship in 1724: "As the Nobility and Gentry go to Tunbridge, the Merchants and Rich Citizens to Epsome; so the Common People go chiefly to Dullwich and Stretham" (Defoe 1724:166). Bath, balancing the need to be accessible to London with sufficient distance, was able to maintain its social exclusiveness. And yet, the significance of time–distance can be overstressed. For affluent visitors with plenty of leisure time and planning a lengthy sojourn at a spa, travel time was unlikely to be a major determining factor (McIntyre 1981). The whole role of transport improvements for spa development was complex. Improvements were selective. Most early spas relied on roads and improvements usually brought more people and ultimately widened the social class at resorts. They also tended to favour expansion at the larger centres and thus hastened the decline of less accessible smaller spas (McIntyre 1981). The arrival of the railways was insignificant for the fortunes of some spas (for instance Bath) but was fundamental for the expansion of others. Buxton, Harrogate and Llandrindod Wells were essentially Victorian spas based on the railway system (Patmore 1968; Simmons 1986). In addition, transport innovations tend to be related to their effects on visitor numbers, but transport was equally vital for the supply of goods and services and, here again, improvements were selective. Local advances in water transport reduced the costs of building materials for the construction of Bath but much of the spa's voracious appetite for food, fuel and other necessities and luxuries was maintained over largely unimproved roads (Neale 1981).

Location in respect to other spas could be important for the spatial patterns of emerging spas. In Britain, the successful development of one spa in a region often tempted entrepreneurs to develop spas in the vicinity to catch overflow trade. A crop of minor spas developed in this way in north-west Wiltshire in the late seventeenth century, hoping to tap custom from nearby Bath. Seend (1667), Box (1670), Holt (1688) and Chippenham (1694) briefly flourished in this way but ultimately lacked sufficient investment in attractions and accommodation to take advantage of their relative location.

The demand factors for spas must be placed within regional, national and, on occasions, international socio-economic and cultural conditions. The growing patronage of spas can certainly be related to rising affluence and an emerging elite "leisure culture". The patronage of royalty and nobility was a driving force for a number of successful spas (McIntyre 1981; Patmore 1968) but other conditions also had to be present. Clearly, demand cannot be seen as comprising a homogeneous group. The spas of the northern states of the USA relied on a largely urban-based middle-class clientele in sharp contrast to the rural plantation aristocracy who patronised the southern spas (Lawrence 1983). In Hungary, and other parts of central Europe, visitors came from a wider social class than in Britain (Vida 1992), and spas such as Radium Hot springs in British Columbia were never patronised by fashionable society but catered for the outdoor activities of middle-class visitors (Wightman and Wall 1985). The catchment areas of spas could also vary enormously, from local and regional use to national and international. Bad Ischl served the Austrian court, Bad Homburg appealed to the British upper classes, the Russians were important visitors at Baden Baden, the German court patronised Wiesbaden. The reasons for particular patterns of demand are intricate and no complete picture has yet emerged which would enable generalisations to be made with great confidence.

The coincidence of supply and demand was never sufficient for the expansion of a spa. Successful growth depended heavily on the actions of agents of development, whether private entrepreneurs, public authorities or a combination of both. In Britain, many spas owed their initial growth to the actions of local landowners who were willing to speculate on the expanding leisure industry. Out of 48 minor provincial spas developed in England between 1660 and 1815, 24 were initiated by the gentry and 7 by the aristocracy. Conversely a lack of entrepreneurial spirit could inhibit growth. Spring waters were known at Leamington Spa in the sixteenth century but no exploitation came until 1784 when a local landowner was eventually tempted to invest in baths and accommodation (Patmore 1968). Elsewhere, municipal enterprise was at work. Thirsk in Yorkshire was promoted by the corporation in the 1720s and nineteenth-century Harrogate also relied heavily on public sector initiatives. In Canada, the national government, through the agency of the Federal Parks Department, was largely responsible for developing Radium Hot Springs in the 1920s (Wightman and Wall 1985). Very often, however, growth came through a mixture of both private and public schemes as the Bath case study will demonstrate.

As well as being significant for the development of particular spas, landownership was instrumental in shaping the layout of the resort through patterns of land holdings. Cheltenham's growth in the eighteenth century was constrained by its surrounding open fields with rights of common pasture. These proved very difficult to convert to individual holdings, which could then be developed, until the 1801 Enclosure Act enabled entrepreneurs like Joseph Pitt to move in and construct lodging houses and other facilities to the north of the High Street (Hart 1981). As will be seen, the timing and location of Bath's physical expansion was closely related to the micro-scale patterns of private and public land holdings.

The ways in which the various agents of development, whether local, national, public or private, were prepared to invest in spas, depended on a much wider context of development which embraced social, economic, cultural and political systems. Thus the expansion of spas in Britain in the later seventeenth century has to be related to a general rise in national wealth, the spread of a capitalist free market economy, political stability and a general cultural renaissance in the urban environment centred on an affluent leisure lifestyle (Borsay 1989; Corfield 1982; McInnes 1988; McIntyre 1981 and see also chapter 2). In fact, McInnes (1988) argues that spas should really be seen as a specialised version of a growing number of general urban leisure places rather than as a separate category of towns.

In colonial and post-colonial America, cultural variations between north and south, variations in the stages of economic growth and the geographical spread of settlements created different types of spas (Figure 4.4). Lawrence (1983) suggests that spas emerged later in colonial America than their counterparts in Britain and western Europe partly because of a lingering puritan ethic which resisted the idea of pleasure resorts. However, from the mid-eighteenth century (Figure 4.3) a group of urban spas developed around Philadelphia which contrasted with the more rural spas of New England serving Boston. Further south, primitive frontier spas emerged in Virginia which were on the edge of the outward spread of settlement. These southern spas always maintained their rural ambience, unlike the more developed spas to the north.

North–south variations could also be seen in Britain. The expansion of a capitalist free market economy was important to the overall growth of spas but there was a general lack of investment in northern spas during much of the eighteenth century (Hembry 1990). Major growth had to await industrialisation in the nineteenth century, which provided not only more capital but also a wealthier reservoir of visitors. Harrogate and Buxton's major growth eras were thus from the mid-nineteenth century, considerably later than growth in southern Britain. Initial lack

Figure 4.4 "Congress Spring", Saratoga, New York State, built in the 1830s and rebuilt in the 1870s. Promenades for carriages and walking, gardens and classical buildings reflect similar leisure settings in Europe (Wechsberg (1979) *The Lost World of the Great Spas*, with permission of Orion Publishing)

of investment also affected the social life in northern spas. Entertainment was focused on the inns and boarding houses during the eighteenth century because there were far fewer private lodgings and places of public assembly.

A different context for spa development could be found in central Europe. In western Europe and North America there was a generally clear relationship between new capital wealth and the subsequent creation of spas and seaside resorts for an affluent market. In central Europe, by contrast, the ruling families of the many small states retained much greater control of economic development with a more subordinate, less politically assertive, middle class (Soane 1993). Urban life was more communal with more socially integrated residential areas than were found, say, in England. Local leisure resources satisfied many of the needs of the urban middle classes with little demand for specialised leisure resorts. Political and social structures were more closely bound in Germany than in western Europe, and a middle-class concept of service to the state militated against the more carefree lifestyle of resort life elsewhere. Wiesbaden, for instance, provided a peaceful and healthy environment rather than the cosmopolitan life found at spas further west. Strong state influence was exercised over development so that Wiesbaden

Table 4.1   Periods of spa formation in England, 1558–1815

1558–1659	16	1750–1799	39
1660–1699	39	1800–1815	18
1700–1749	34	undated	27
			173

Source: Hembry (1990)

became as much a symbol of Imperial German achievements as a leisure resort (Soane 1993).

Attempts have been made to conceptualise the development of resorts in evolutionary models. Thus Butler's (1980) hypothetical resort cycle envisages stages of exploration, involvement, development, consolidation, stagnation and rejuvenation or decline. Thurot's (1973) tourist areas pass through a process of class succession with discovery by the rich, followed by the middle classes and subsequent invasion by mass tourists. While aspects of these generalisations can be found in the historical growth of spas, there are numerous difficulties involved in trying to "fit" the models to reality. The absence of historical data (for instance reliable visitor figures) means that measuring growth and/or decline becomes a major problem except in very recent times. This leads on to the length of historical perspective needed to adequately encapsulate cycles. Even in its period of rapid growth in the eighteenth century, Bath followed a number of cycles of growth and stagnation. It then moved into a phase, lasting over 100 years, when its tourist function was fading. In the later twentieth century, however, the city re-emerged as a major "heritage" resort. Therefore fixing the points of growth and decline is quite arbitrary and may be geared more to the availability of statistical sources. Furthermore, terms like "success" and "decline" are often purely value judgements. Popular literature on spas abounds with "lost worlds" and "golden ages" (Gregory 1991; Wechsberg 1979), terms which usually represent nostalgia for when the upper classes held sway, rather than a judgement on economic success or the ability of a spa to attract wider social groups.

The process of spa evolution also suffers from a focus on the history of enduring spas rather than including those that failed. A complete picture of evolution requires both. The growth of spas in England was really the story of many creations and many failures. Most rural spas were short-lived and, although between 1558 and 1815 about 173 spas were created (Table 4.1), the picture at any one time was a shifting pattern of births and deaths.

Thus while Figure 4.5 indicates the changing, and cumulative, pattern of spa formation, it should be remembered that it does not show spas

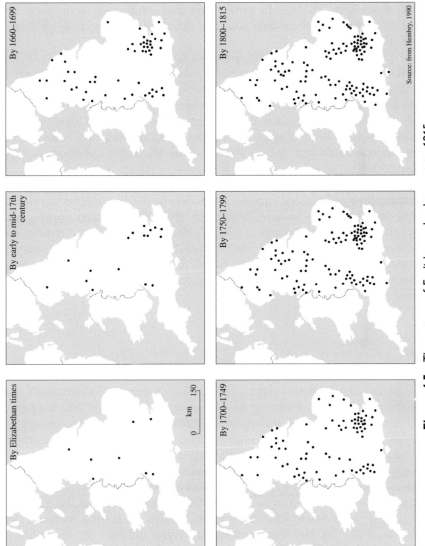

Figure 4.5 The pattern of English spa development to 1815

Source: from Hembry, 1990

that ceased to exist. Information on the creation of spas is easier to obtain than on the period when they ended their operations. Nevertheless, the pattern does show the importance of London for stimulating spas in its vicinity and the effect of Bath on spa formation in the south-west. Elsewhere, the north, north-west and Midlands were important later regions with the eastern counties developing in the final phases of expansion.

By 1841 Granville listed 70 spas in operation in England. Alongside the Baths, Buxtons and Cheltenhams were the short-lived spas such as Wellingborough, mentioned at the end of the seventeenth century but gone by 1711, or Seend in Wiltshire where the antiquarian John Aubrey had unfulfilled dreams of a bowling green and house of entertainment (Tylden-Wright 1991). Similarly in Canada, Cathartick spa near Ottawa grew in the 1860s but had faded away by the early twentieth century (Wall 1982b).

Finally, as geographers and historians increasingly study patterns of consumption as well as production (Glennie 1990) there is a need to study the emerging leisure resorts in this context. The conspicuous display of wealth and fashion created demands for labour, goods and services and these patterns have often been neglected in studies of resorts. In the case study of Bath which follows, the geographical consequences of its role as a centre of consumption are explored as a major theme.

Bath: a case study

This section explores the ways in which a particular spa town, Bath, was transformed from a declining West Country wool town into a specialised leisure resort and the most significant place (after London) for conspicuous consumption in eighteenth-century Britain. The geographical consequences of this transformation, within and beyond the city, are examined, both in terms of the economic, social, cultural and political patterns created and the distinctive townscape that was produced.

Bath has been chosen to provide a detailed case study of the historical geography of a resort because of the wealth of source material and analysis that the city has generated. What follows is, therefore, a synthesis of the detailed research by historians such as Neale (1981), Hembry (1990), and McIntyre (1981), to illustrate aspects of the geography of specialised leisure places. Particular emphasis is placed on viewing Bath as a major centre of consumption; the consumption of goods, services and culture by a leisured elite and the effect this had on trading patterns, labour demands and the geography of Bath. The significance of this theme was recognised long ago by the city itself. In 1839 *The Bath Visitant* observed: "The trade of Bath, will, as at present, be regulated for the future simply by its own consumption" (quoted in Wroughton 1972:7).

Bath can trace its origins as a health resort back to the Romans and its waters continued to be visited throughout the middle ages for medical reasons. By the early seventeenth century, however, the fortunes of the town were rather doubtful. The woollen cloth industry, not the spa, formed the economic linchpin and this was in serious decline. In 1622, the mayor lamented: "We are a verie little poore Citie, our Clothmen much decayed" (quoted in Haddon 1973:60). Yet by the end of that century Bath had successfully changed its role from an essentially manufacturing centre into a health and leisure resort and continued to exploit this role throughout the eighteenth century to become one of the largest and wealthiest cities in Britain. Bath's population in the 1660s was under 2000, by the 1760s it was 13 000 and by 1801 about 33 000. This growth rate was comparable to the rise of the new industrial towns and, in size, Bath came to rank with Newcastle and Portsmouth and well ahead of Bradford, Halifax and Hull (Thompson 1990). To understand how this transformation was achieved requires consideration of factors operating within national, regional and local contexts. The following section examines changes which fostered development at the national level before more detailed aspects of leisure and consumption within Bath are considered.

A context for development

At the national scale, two major spheres of change can be seen as critical for Bath's development. The first concerns the political economy of Britain, with the growth of state institutions and the expansion of a free market economy. The second concerns the spread of a particular leisure culture within the country, with its emphasis on conspicuous consumption, and focused primarily in urban settings (Borsay 1982; Corfield 1982; and see also chapter 2).

Dodgshon (1990) has written of the post-feudal emergence in Britain, from about 1500 onwards, of a set of ideological values and institutional forms which embraced capitalism and its operation through free market systems. A circuit of capital began to integrate different sectors of the economy and different regions of the country and the state aided this process by creating institutions such as the Stock

Exchange (1690s) and by clarifying rights to property and their transfer. Access to capital was further enhanced by the gradual political integration of the country helping to form a "national economic space" (Dodgshon 1990). Non-local capital began to spread into particular projects in the regions; a process that was a vital precondition for Bath's spectacular expansion.

The general rise of capitalism and free markets was closely linked to growing urbanisation, with investment in buildings and services. Opportunities for speculative urban development through site improvement increased and it is notable that the capital value of house building in Bath in the eighteenth century was equal to that invested in fixed capital in the cotton industry. Bath, as Neale (1981) points out, was as much a monument to the credit-raising ingenuity of the eighteenth century and the sophistication of its property law, as simply being a centre of leisure.

As well as changes in the political economy of Britain, the rising wealth of the later seventeenth and eighteenth centuries stimulated a demand for luxury goods and services and catering for the affluent leisured classes became a significant economic activity. Towns and cities became "arenas of public consumption" (Glennie 1990), where wealth was displayed and social status acquired and maintained through a lifestyle of leisure and luxury. London and many provincial towns became centres for conspicuous consumption and spa towns evolved as the most specialised aspect of this process. Leisure was increasingly commercialised (McKendrick, Brewer and Plumb 1982; Plumb 1973) as part of a wider consumer society which permeated much of the urban hierarchy (Corfield 1982).

Linked to these national changes, Bath's rise as a pre-eminent fashionable centre after London depended on regional and local circumstances. There was, of course, its geographical location, accessible to the capital but far enough away to maintain social exclusivity. But the ability to respond to the requirements of the leisured classes was conditioned by the attitudes and actions of local individuals and institutions, the opportunities created by particular patterns of landownership within and around the city, as well as the ability to supply goods and services. Where, when and how Bath's development took place depended on how these more localised factors operated and how they were linked, via investors and speculators, to the national circuit of capital. Bath's success was enhanced by an especially enterprising commercial sector which closely tied the city to an international circuit of fashion and culture (Fawcett 1990). After all, Bath was no mere thriving provincial centre but rivalled London and emulated Paris in the hierarchy of style.

Leisure and consumption in Bath

The presence of a wealthy leisured elite in Bath resulted in a whole range of patterns of consumption of goods and services, distinctive social and political geographies and a celebrated townscape and image. Attention will focus first of all on the visitors and supplying their needs before considering broader social, political, townscape and image aspects of the resort.

The visitors

The patrons of Bath constituted a wealthy set of consumers with special-ised demands for accommodation and services and for a set of arenas for the display of their leisure and prosperity. These demands were not, of course, constant. Visitors descended on the city during the season and the nature of those visitors and their demands changed over time. New responses were constantly needed if the city was to successfully cater for the shifts in taste and fashion and social class of its clients.

Much of the early consumer demand came from London and the south of England (Corfield 1982). As well as attracting the sick and infirm, Bath was popular as a marriage market and social centre. In the sixteenth century, most visitors were from the court and came for cures during the summer months, but gradually a national hinterland which drew on the ranks of the aristocracy, gentry, clergy and professions emerged. Along with these visitors, Bath attracted a migrant population of the poor who came to beg from such a concentration of the nation's wealth. The numbers of visitors are hard to estimate but calculations suggest perhaps about 8000 a year in the early eighteenth century, about 12 000 by mid-century and about 40 000 by 1800 (McIntyre 1981; Neale 1981). About £10 000 a week was spent in the city (Hembry 1990). As critical as numbers, was the time spent in Bath and here an important element was the transition from a short summer visitor season (early July to mid-August) into a prolonged season from late February to early June and from late September to mid-December. Bath's mild climate and cheap coal supplies enabled this change to take place and the long visitor season was essential for attracting investment in the tourist industry (Hembry 1990).

The process and pattern of development

Although much of Bath's eighteenth-century townscape gives the appearance of planned and orderly expansion, it was essentially the result of a multitude of speculative developments by individuals and groups in both the private and public sectors, responding to local opportunities and national economic cycles. The location, sequence and financing of growth took place on areas of land unhindered by lifehold tenancies, with good access to the new attractions of the city and with landowners willing to embark on speculative development (Neale 1981). Physical site conditions were also important. Generally, the buildings for visitors were located on higher land above flood water level on the drier marl and limestones. The buildings for the workers were on the flooded alluvial flats of clay or on the less stable slopes (Weight 1972).

Bath did not develop at a uniform rate over time. The resort grew in a number of building booms: 1704–1707, 1726–1732, 1753–1758 and 1785–1792 (see Figure 4.6). These boom periods corresponded with national upswings, reflecting the city's dependence on national rather than local or regional demand factors (Dodgshon 1990; Neale 1981). Between these booms there were periods of stagnation, for instance in the 1740s, when the resort's success seemed in doubt. Growth was thus not a smooth and orderly progression as models of resort cycles can sometimes suggest (Butler 1980).

The development process within and around Bath can be broadly summarised as follows. Inspired by the demand for housing for visitors and the possibility of rent income, landowners leased plots of land to speculative developers for 99 years. Developers then hired an architect and subleased the land to smaller speculators, often building tradesmen, who undertook to construct houses on the plot within two years. The house and lease of the plot were then sold to a buyer. Thus the builder profited from the sale as did the original developer who received rent from the house buyer. Considerable profits could be made by the developer between the original rent paid to the landowner and the rent from individual houses (Woodward 1992). Buoyant demand for accommodation was essential for capital and land to move into real estate developments but the strengthening of property laws after the 1688 Revolution aided the process as titles to property were certain and leases and subleases became secure in law and could therefore be used as mortgage security. Projects like the Circus and Royal Crescent depended on this legal system and, in fact, much of the investment in Bath in the eighteenth century was raised on mortgages secured by leases of land (Neale 1976).

The pattern of landownership in Bath determined the particular directions in which the city expanded. Until the early eighteenth century,

Figure 4.6   (*opposite*) **A** The spatial development of lodging houses in Bath, c.1700–c.1800 and the physical growth of the city. **B** Bath lodging houses at the end of the seventeenth century (numbers signify number of lodgings)

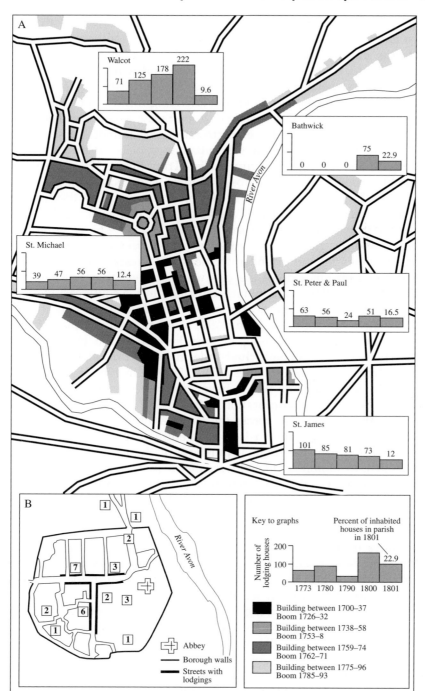

the city was still mainly confined within its medieval walls. Both in the town and immediately to its northern, eastern and southern boundaries, land was only available in small parcels with lifehold leases. Larger blocks of land, controlled by one landowner and with fixed leases, were initially only available to the western side of Bath. Here lay Bath corporation's own common land, the low-lying meadows of Kingsmead and the 85-acre Barton Farm estate of Robert Gay, a barber surgeon from London who had been busy extinguishing local farmers' leases on his land. Although early developments in Bath took place on individual sites within or just outside the city walls—Trim Street 1707, Harrison's Assembly Rooms 1708, Chandos Buildings 1726, Kingsmead 1727—it was Gay's large block of land at Barton Farm that saw the first real expansion to the city with John Wood's building of Queen Square (1728–1734) just to the north-west of the old town (Figure 4.6). New building then spread upwards on this north-west side from Queen Square to the Circus (1754–1758) and extended to the Royal Crescent by 1774.

Expansion on this side of the city was not inevitable, however, and the blank, undeveloped area which remained in the south-east corner of Bath must be related to particular landownership patterns and attitudes to speculative development. John Wood also had elaborate plans for this side of the city (1730), the open area known as the Ham. But the landowners, the Pierrepoints, had little interest in developing the site. Wood's North and South Parades (1740–1743) were intended as one part of a much larger scheme which never got under way and later ideas were blocked by the corporation (Mowl 1990). Pulteney's Bathwick estate also lay to the east, across the River Avon, but here the delay in development was due not to lack of interest in speculation but to the time taken between the original purchase of the land in 1726 and the time taken to eliminate lifehold tenancies (not achieved until 1768). Pulteney Bridge (1769–1774) then linked Bathwick to the city but full-scale growth had to await a new building boom from 1785 to 1793. As with the schemes of Wood and his backer the Duke of Chandos, Pulteney was able to tap into the national circuit of capital for his speculative development (Neale 1981).

Most of these major developments were largely private ventures. Improvements within the city did not come until later in the eighteenth century. Part of the reason for this was, again, landownership. Bath's corporation was the governing body and major landowner within the city, controlling key elements such as the baths, city walls and market-place. In the late seventeenth and early eighteenth centuries, the corporation was composed mainly of craftsmen and traders who often owned lodgings and inns in the city and who tended to oppose developments beyond the boundaries which would conflict with their interests. During the eighteenth century, however, the governing body became dominated by substantial merchants, bankers and the professions—all interested in estate development (McIntyre 1981). Thus the corporation increasingly granted building leases on its land. In 1753, the Town Acre to the north of the city was let to David Milsom whose new street, Milsom Street, rapidly developed from lodging houses to a fashionable shopping arena. Later, the corporation undertook redevelopment schemes such as a new Guildhall (1770s), new streets (the colonnaded Bath Street) and a new Pump Room to try to compete with the successful private ventures away to the west, north and east of the city. Ironically, this burst of civic action came just as Bath was losing its fashionable air (McIntyre 1981).

Transport and communications

The willingness of either private or public concerns to engage in large-scale speculative developments at Bath depended on a large flow of visitors. Britain, in the eighteenth century, was an increasingly mobile society (Thrift 1990) with improvements in transport and communications and Bath benefited from developments that linked it to its main visitor-generating areas: London and the south-east and other major population centres. Furthermore, transport improvements were significant for the physical construction of the city. But these changes should not be seen simply in a deterministic way. As pointed out in the introduction to this chapter, wealthy long-stay visitors were not likely to be influenced by small reductions in travel time and much of the city's increasing demand for goods had to be met by roads largely unaffected by the improvements which occurred between major centres.

Before about 1680, the time taken to travel between London and Bath (107 miles) was around 60 hours. This helped the city to maintain an air of exclusivity but was a barrier to increased numbers. Early road improvements were confined to the area around Bath but the route to London was turnpiked by 1743 (Hembry 1990). In 1750, travel times had fallen to 36 hours, by 1763 to 24 hours and by 1800, the journey took only 10 hours (McIntyre 1981). Furthermore, the frequency of services increased significantly during the eighteenth century (see Table 4.2).

Bath was also increasingly well connected with other potential visitor-generating areas. Services to Oxford rose from one coach per week in 1755 to twelve by 1790, there were five coaches a week to Gloucester by 1780, ten to Birmingham by 1790 and there were good links to Portsmouth, Southampton and Holyhead.

Some local road improvements were significant for visitors. Short excursions out from the city were popular in the eighteenth century for

Table 4.2 Frequency of London–Bath coach and wagon services, 1684–1800

1684	1	1763	37
1740	17 summer	1765	27
	15 winter	1768	39
1744	17 summer	1770	46
	15 winter	1772	46
1749	17 summer	1773	42 summer
	15 winter		44 winter
1752	20 summer	1776	45
	18 winter	1777	46
1755	18 summer	1781	90
	15 winter	1783	90
1757	23 summer	1785	89
	21 winter	1788	101
1760	24	1794	154
		1800	147

Source: McIntyre (1981).

people "taking the air" by carriage. In 1706 the road to Lansdown Hill was improved and those taking a day's recreational trip did not have to pay a toll (Hembry 1990). Within the city, improved street paving and lighting together with an extensive system of chairmen eased movement around the resort. From 1739, the chairmen system was regulated with fixed tariffs and the number employed rose from around 40 in 1714 to 120 in 1743 and 340 by 1799 (McIntyre 1981).

While all these systems of transport were for the direct benefit of visitors and were essentially based on the major roads, poorer local and regional road networks had to suffice for the movement of fuel, foodstuffs and other goods. The physical construction of the city did, however, require significant improvements and these were made to rivers and canals. The River Avon, to the nearby port of Bristol, was unnavigable, blocked by weirs and mills since the thirteenth century. Building materials had to rely on inadequate wagons and packhorses and this undoubtedly delayed the expansion of the city (Hembry 1990; Neale 1981). Between 1724 and 1727, however, the Avon was made navigable, a scheme backed by local quarry owner Ralph Allen and Bristol timber merchant John Hobbs. Timber from the Baltic could now be imported via Bristol on barges (English oak being reserved for the navy). By the early 1730s, Allen had a two-mile wagonway constructed from his quarries on Combe Down south of Bath to reach the Avon and the cost of stone was much reduced (Figure 4.7). The opportunity created for expansion underpinned by these innovations was one of the reasons for attracting the architect and builder John Wood to the city.

But transport innovations do not always have an inevitable effect on

Figure 4.7 "Ralph Allen's Drive" by Anthony Walker (1750). Opened in 1730 this also became a tourist attraction in its own right. Allen's mansion Prior Park fills the background (Victoria Art Gallery, Bath)

growth. A much later transport development, the railways, had little decisive effect on the resort function of Bath. During the nineteenth century, Bath's population did not grow and, in fact, the city was the only town of about 50 000 population which saw no expansion (Simmons 1986). Although linked to London by rail in 1841, Bath was already changing its function from resort to residential and retirement centre. This clientele were people who, in Simmons' (1986:240) words: "did not move about much". Yet at the time, the railway was seen by some as a method for stimulating a new era in Bath's spa function. Granville, writing in 1841, thought that the Great Western Railway, having brought the city within three hours of London, would encourage patrons of continental spas to rediscover their own "Spa of Spas" and so "judge for themselves of its superiority and importance" (Granville 1841:443). Transport innovations were not enough, however, to stimulate a new wave of tourism to a city already adapting to new functions.

Accommodation

The first requirement of visitors to Bath was accommodation and it was in the construction of lodgings and apartments that the physical growth of the city was most evident. The types of accommodation provided, however, underwent change between the seventeenth and nineteenth centuries; from inns and lodgings in the earlier period to rented apartments in the eighteenth century. The location of these different types also changed with time. Generally, the inns were found within the old town, whereas the large expansion of rented lodgings took place in the new developments further out in the Georgian streets, terraces, squares and crescents that came to symbolise Bath's townscape. The nineteenth-century hotels reversed this outward trend, however, tending to be located either on the edge of the old urban core or, eventually, back in the heart of the city.

Figure 4.6 summarises the essential features of the accommodation sector in Bath between 1700 and 1800. The inset shows the main centre for lodging houses at the end of the seventeenth century, clustered around the baths and Abbey or along the north–south Stall Street or east–west Westgate Street. Gilmore's (1692) map of the city shows 22 inns and 28 lodgings all within the borough walls and in the old vernacular architectural style. Many inn and lodging house keepers had dual employment, being also grocers, linen drapers, brewers or doctors, as well as local gentry or members of the corporation (Hembry 1990; McIntyre 1981). Inns were generally for short-term stay, lodgings for lengthier visits.

From about the 1720s, these facilities had to compete increasingly with the new and fashionable lodgings and apartments being constructed beyond the city walls. Figure 4.6 shows how most expansion took place in the parish of Walcot, which included much of the north-western new town, and the parish of Bathwick to the east. Numbers of lodgings in the old town remained stagnant or fell. Mindful of good relations with visitors, accommodation prices were regulated from an early date. A weekly maximum of 10 shillings for a furnished room and 5 shillings for a servant's garret was reduced by half in the off-season. During the eighteenth century, lodgings ranged from the fashionable Queen Square, Gay Street, Circus and Royal Crescent in the upper town to the declining areas of the lower town such as Westgate Street. Pulteney's Bathwick development to the east (1790s) marked a transition in housing provision, however, as many of the streets were as much for permanent residence as for temporary visits. During the course of the nineteenth century, most of the lodgings throughout the Georgian town became permanent residences.

Hotels never formed an important element in Bath's accommodation sector until the later nineteenth century. An early exception to this was the York House Hotel (1765–1769) built at the northern edge of the old town on the coaching road to London and Bristol. It was the first purpose-built hotel in a spa town (Hembry 1990). A later addition was the Sydney Hotel (1796) at the far end of Great Pulteney Street on the Bathwick estate. But it was not until the later nineteenth century that large hotels, catering for affluent but short-stay visitors, came to dominate the shrinking provision of accommodation and replace long-stay lodgings. These hotels were often built back in the centre of the city. Thus, the Grand Pump Room Hotel (1869) was erected on the site of the old White Hart Inn next to the pump room and the Empire Hotel (1899) was located near to the Abbey. Central location was, perhaps, more important for a new generation of short-stay visitors who wanted convenience for sight-seeing rather than leisurely detachment from the bustle of the urban core.

Employment

Visitors to Bath created a whole range of demands for people and materials. Maintaining this society at an appropriate level of leisure and luxury resulted in patterns of inward labour migration and social resi-dential areas within the city. Even as late as 1841, the census suggested that some 87 per cent of the city's workers were, in some way, providing for the affluent visitors (Wroughton 1972).

In the 1680s, about 2000 people were employed in providing the needs of visitors and these lived within the city walls (Neale 1981). In fact, until the 1760s most employment was in the hands of local citizens with some migration from the neighbouring counties of Somerset, Wiltshire and Gloucestershire. Skilled trades, such as clothing, building, baking and shoemaking, were controlled by the city through its apprenticeship schemes but this local monopoly was beginning to break down by the mid-eighteenth century with increased demands for labour in building and services. Unskilled labour was pulled in from surrounding rural areas, especially women looking for jobs as domestic servants (Neale 1981). The need for particular skills would draw in people from further afield. For instance, John Wood initially brought in skilled masons from Yorkshire and joiners, plasterers and carpenters from London for his more demanding standards of building (Hudson 1971).

The range of jobs that supported the leisured elite was considerable, ranging from high-status doctors and surgeons who might be drawn from London, to music and drawing masters, coachmakers, carpenters, tailors, shoemakers, periwig makers, barbers, bakers, as well as the vast range of unskilled and semi-skilled jobs. It is difficult to estimate the occupations in Bath before the end of the eighteenth century, but trade directories permit some generalisations as Table 4.3 indicates.

Table 4.3 Occupations in Bath listed in the *Universal British Directory of Trade and Commerce* (1790)

	Number	%
Victualling	252	28.8
Professional	168	19.2
Clothing and shoemaking	154	17.6
Services, Entertainment, Transport	88	10.6
Building	66	7.7
Other retailers	54	6.2

Source: after McIntyre (1981)

The nineteenth-century census provides firmer ground for employment estimates. The 1841 census reveals the following picture which, although changed from that of the eighteenth century, still shows an essentially resort town. Out of a working population of over 16 000, some 33 per cent were engaged in domestic service, 11 per cent were in clothing trades, 11 per cent in small crafts such as shoemaking and cabinet making, 9 per cent in retailing and distribution, 7 per cent in building and construction, 6 per cent in professional services, 4 per cent in entertainment and hospitality and 4 per cent were sweeps, washers and messengers (Wroughton 1972).

A vital component of Bath's employment structure was the number of women who worked. In fact, as the city moved from a pleasure resort to a place of residence, the number of jobs for women remained buoyant. This was partly because a majority of Bath's affluent citizens in the nineteenth century were women—spinsters or widows, who employed young, single females as companions and servants. Many women worked as domestic servants or in skilled trades such as seamstresses, tailors, milliners or shoemakers. Women in domestic service comprised over 14 per cent of the total city population in 1851, a quarter of all females (Neale 1981).

The seasonal nature of employment always created problems for Bath's workers. Domestic servants were particularly vulnerable, faced with poverty in the off-season and possibly living on money provided by subscription. During the nineteenth century, conditions improved somewhat when the more residential character of the city provided year-round jobs (Hembry 1990).

Bath's workers lived in particular parts of the city. Avon Street and Mill Street in the south were in the low-lying flooded parts of town and were inhabited by the unskilled and unemployed. The parish of St James, in the south-east corner of the city, was the home of artisans and tradesmen: tailors, shoemakers and carpenters. Virtually no domestic servants lived here. The parish of SS Peter and Paul, further north, was the home of the small shopkeeper, while St Michael to the north-east attracted the larger shopkeepers (McIntyre 1981). Domestic servants lived in the same areas as their employers, in the parishes of Walcot and Bathwick, and they were often accommodated in the upper or lower parts of the large houses. Work was often carried out at or near home and the city had a number of small partly industrialised villages around its edge. Leisure and industrial activity are rarely compatible land uses, especially where a leisured elite is concerned, and Bath was largely kept free of necessary industrial activity which located on its outskirts. The expanding city and its consumption demands encouraged small-scale activities and Lyncombe and Widcombe, south of the river and outside the city boundary, were wool cloth centres inhabited by workers who were not freemen of the city. Tiverton and Batheaston had glass, soap-making and brewing for the city as well as clothmaking. By the 1820s and 1830s, however, "industrialisation" was encroaching on the city itself, inevitably locating in the lower town near the river. Thus glass and soapmaking moved into St James with warehouses, workshops and yards beginning to line the river bank (Neale 1981). These developments were, of course, well away from the main visitor areas of Bath.

A study of leisure activities should not be confined solely to that of the transient visitors to resorts. Bath's working population also had some leisure and used certain parts of the city in what little free time they had. In the lower town, the alehouse was an obvious outlet, while the river was used for bathing and its banks played upon by small children. Institutions such as Methodism and Baptists also provided an outlet for non-work time. In the upper part of town, where the domestic servants lived in the same houses as their employers, the more "respectable" were often permitted to share the entertainments of their masters and mistresses, such as the assembly rooms and theatres, until restrictions were introduced in the later eighteenth century. During short holidays, some workers returned to the villages, family and friends from where they had migrated (Neale 1981). A similar pattern is revealed by the 1841 *Royal Commission on the Employment of Children*. Apprentices worked a 12–15-hour day but in the summer off-season could spend between two weeks and a month away, often returning home to family and friends (Wroughton 1972).

While domestic servants occupied the same districts of Bath as their employers, there was clearly a strict spatial as well as economic and social division between visitors and workers in the city (see social geography section below). This could lead to conflicts. Bath was reputed to have one of the worst mobs in England and there were strikes by tailors in 1763 as well as by staymakers and shoemakers and general disorder in 1780, 1800–1801, and in 1812 (see political geography section below). The lower town area around Avon Street was not an area where visitors would generally venture.

The consumption of food

Like any settlement, Bath was a consumer of food and the supply of food for Bath had to meet a number of needs. Basic and luxury items were needed for the visitors and cheap supplies of essential produce were needed for the working population. Provisioning the city was long seen as an important role for the corporation; adequate victualling and control of prices were vital for both civil peace and the attraction of visitors. The city markets were carefully regulated for standards and prices, location and times of operation. Corporation interests extended beyond the city. In 1778 a scheme to preserve fish stocks on the River Severn was opposed because: "the usual supply of fish would be much lessened to the great and manifest injury of the inhabitants of this city and the nobility and gentry who resort thereunto" (McIntyre 1981:238).

Visitors usually praised Bath's markets which were seen as well regulated and well stocked. The *Bath Guide* of 1800 recorded:

> The principal markets are kept on Wednesdays and Saturdays, and plentifully supplied with every kind of provisions, generally at moderate prices, fresh butter . . . is brought from the country every morning, and the butchers . . . supply the inhabitants with the best of meat every day of the week.
>
> (quoted in Lane 1988:55–56)

As noted above, the largest group of retailers (about 30 per cent) were concerned with victualling. In 1799 there were 85 grocers and tea dealers, 37 bakers, 33 butchers and 16 fruiterers, as well as 10 brewers, 10 wine merchants and three brandy merchants (Hembry 1990).

Fresh food provision was largely based on the twice-weekly markets in the city centre. As demand grew, so did market specialisation. By 1754, there was a separate fish market, in 1761 a garden or green market, in 1768 a poultry market and in 1774 a butter market (Hembry 1990). These basic food supplies came from a wide area. Immediately around Bath, the Town Commons to the north-west of the city underwent land use changes in the early eighteenth century with a shift from arable farming to dairy in order to supply the increased demands from visitors for fresh milk, butter and cheese. The undeveloped Ham area in the south-east corner of the city was an area of market gardens and rented smallholdings, famous for its cauliflowers (Mowl 1990). Also near the city, and to the north, the upland plateau of Lansdown supplied much-admired mutton. Meat, milk and butter also came in from north Wiltshire, grain from markets in Warminster and Devizes, as well as fish from the Severn. But Bath also made demands on areas further afield. Garden produce arrived from the Vale of Evesham in the Midlands and cheap Welsh butter came in winter up the River Avon from Carmarthenshire on large bulk barges. Luxury food items for the visitor were also needed as Bath sought to rival the variety of London. Game such as woodcock and snipe went to specialist poulterers and butchers and there were many high-class pastrycooks. Some outlets achieved considerable fame; for instance Gifford and Hemmings for poultry, Hancock the fishmonger and Charles Gill the pastrycook (Fawcett 1990).

Away from this world of plenty and luxury, a smooth supply of basic food for the working population was needed for the efficient functioning of the resort. In times of shortage, the corporation would intervene to buy and supply cheap foodstuffs, especially bread. In 1779, the Provisions Committee in the city used subscription money to buy subsidised food and coal to alleviate hardship and social tension. Earlier, the poor harvest of 1766 had caused disturbances in the city and there were riots in 1800 and 1812 when bread prices rose after poor harvests. In 1800, when wheat prices increased by 50 per cent in two weeks, the corporation sought supplies from neighbouring rural areas. Fundamentally, Bath was a low-wage economy with the majority of its workers living a very marginal existence. In times of shortage, attacks on market supplies, poaching and robbery from gardens increased significantly (Neale 1981).

Water supplies

Apart from taking the spa water, there was, of course, a rising demand in Bath for general water supplies for visitors and locals alike. In medieval times, water was conveyed to the city from springs immediately to the north and south at Walcot and Beechen Cliff. Supplies were never adequate, however, for the increase in demand, with ownership of springs divided between the corporation and private landowners. Even so, sufficient supplies for the visiting population were generally maintained (McIntyre 1981).

During the eighteenth century, various schemes were undertaken to secure supplies. In 1765, a reservoir was constructed at Beechen Cliff and in 1791 improvements were made to waterworks at Beacon Hill. By 1799, the corporation had a new reservoir at High Common and the rights to three springs in Bathwick. Nevertheless, real improvements did not come until long after Bath had ceased to be a major resort. The schemes of the 1870s and 1880s were more related to Victorian public health concerns than visitor demands (Haddon 1973).

Fuel

The provision of relatively cheap coal supplies for Bath was a significant factor in the resort's successful development. Providing warm lodgings in winter at reasonable prices enabled the city to move away from the short summer season of the seventeenth century to the more profitable lengthy winter season of the eighteenth century. On his visit to the city in the winter of 1780, Edmund Rack observed contentedly: "cold winds but we are happy in being so near the coal mines" (quoted in Hembry 1990:143).

Most of Bath's coal supplies came from two areas: the Kingswood coalfield around Brislington, south-east of Bristol, and the Somerset coalfield centred on Radstock and Midsomer Norton, 10 miles south-west of Bath (Flinn 1984). Some Welsh coal was also brought up the River Avon. The Somerset coalfield expanded from the 1750s to meet Bath's demands, a development initiated at a local level by landowners and coal masters and largely drawing on local capital (Bulley 1953). The demand for coal was such that it overcame the problem of poor transport systems using packhorses over difficult roads and steep gradients and the landsale of the Somerset field was, in fact, wider than the usual 10–12-mile limit (Flinn 1984). Bath's coal was considerably cheaper than London's, and this became a particular attraction for the winter spa resort (Hembry 1990).

Roads dominated the movement of coal to Bath and canals had very little impact on this aspect of consumption. Competition from cheap Welsh coal brought up the Avon led to a proposed Somerset coal canal but the eventual opening of the Kennet and Avon Canal to Bath in 1810 had little effect on coal prices in the city. Thus although the movement of visitors to Bath may have been partly related to improvements in transport (see above), the lack of innovation for critical fuel supplies is a useful caution against relating too many aspects of resort development to technical innovations.

Construction materials

One of the many attractions for visitors to Bath was its fine architectural style and attractive building stone. The proximity of the city to good stone was thus a further asset that it was able to draw upon. For the speculative builders who constructed the city, building materials were the greatest cost, far more than labour costs (Woodward 1992) and, until the 1720s, most limestone and timber were obtained from the immediate local area. But costs remained high and supplies inadequate and, as noted above, this was a check on the growth of the city.

The building boom of 1726–1732 and the expansion of the city was stimulated by the Avon Navigation and Allen's Wagonway to the nearby quarries on Combe Down referred to earlier, reducing the price of timber and stone. Other construction materials brought in via the Avon were Cornish and Welsh slate (which gradually replaced local stone tiles), lead, and iron bars used for railings and other details which came not only from the Forest of Dean but also from Sweden and Russia (Woodward 1992).

Lighting, cleansing and protection

The successful functioning of a leisure resort like Bath required a whole system of street cleansing, lighting and protection for its wealthy clientele. As so much of the leisure culture of the affluent in the eighteenth century involved public display in streets, squares and promenades as well as in assembly rooms and theatres, an attractive and relatively safe urban arena had to be maintained and enhanced. Clearly, most attention was paid to those areas in and around the "tourist areas" of the city and, by and large, this was seen as a civic function.

By-laws were introduced as early as 1646 to compel householders to clean in front of their properties, and in 1707 a local Bath Act included provision for lighting and cleansing in response to "the complaints of the Company that resort to the City" (McIntyre 1981). A night watch system was later established. Good lighting was especially significant for a leisure resort as the visitors had to be encouraged to use the evening entertainments as much as possible, and important for Bath with its winter season. In common with many urban places in eighteenth-century England, Bath obtained a whole series of Improvement Acts— 1708, 1720, 1739, 1757, 1766—designed to give powers to improve the urban environment (Borsay 1989; McIntyre 1981). The 1766 Act unified the maintenance of the city through a body of commissioners who had the duty of looking after the streets and public places of Bath.

Law and order was an important part of visitor experience. Eighteenth- and early nineteenth-century Bath was usually regarded as having a good protection system. The real trouble spots, the slums of Avon Street and Milk Street and parts of the villages of Widcombe and

Lyncombe, were well off the tourist map although occasional disorders did intrude into the centre of the city. Most official crime was committed by the poor among themselves rather than assaults on visitors and property (Neale 1981).

The importance of lighting, cleansing and protection for visitor estimation of the city is clear in Johanna Schopenhauer's views in the early years of the nineteenth century:

> It is true that its very hilly position provides much inconvenience, but the splendid paving, the great cleanliness of the streets and, at night, the fine lighting combine to ease greatly these discomforts, while the police guard everything in an exemplary fashion which adds to the security and peace of mind of visitors.
>
> (quoted in Michaelis-Jena and Merson 1988:122)

The consumption of luxury goods

One of the most important aspects of eighteenth-century Bath, which set it apart from other urban areas in Britain other than London, was its consumption of luxury goods. Conspicuous expenditure was a necessary part of the lifestyle of the leisured classes and the forms of consumption created particular patterns of trade as well as a changing geography of outlet within the city itself.

A recurrent theme in visitors' accounts to Bath was the enthusiasm for its shops and the variety of luxury goods on display. As Fawcett (1990) observes, Bath's pre-eminence lay in its "supreme fashion-consciousness" and its shops ranked second only to London's West End. Bath rapidly acquired the latest styles from Paris and London and, in the urban hierarchy of fashion, it was second only to the capital.

The commercial core of Bath underwent change with the city's expansion. Until the early eighteenth century, most traders were ranged along the old medieval north–south route through the centre of the town. But as small fashionable areas developed to the east of the centre, with the Gravel Walks (1690s) and Harrison's Assembly Rooms (1708) near the river, so fashionable shops gravitated towards this zone. Shops, coffee houses and public rooms came to line the Walks and cluster around the Abbey churchyard. This area remained the luxury retailing centre of Bath until the 1760s when high-class shops spread into the newly constructed Milsom Street to the north and the Pulteney Bridge area to the north-east. A final luxury area was created in the 1790s with the corporation's inner city renewal scheme creating the colonnaded Bath Street (1791–1794). Shops for Bath's working population were separate from these fashionable zones and lay in the western and southern parts of the city around Kingsmead and Avon Street (Fawcett 1990).

Luxury retailing activity fluctuated widely between the high and low seasons. In the summer off-period, traders would journey up to London to inspect the latest fashions and visit their suppliers in the Midlands and north. This reverse migration, out of the city, was essential for maintaining Bath's close links with current trends. Within the city, the high level of free market activity helped to break down the local control over trade and crafts. The city simply could not maintain its grip over commerce and, by the 1750s, retailing in Bath was a "free-for-all" with outsiders able to establish themselves easily within the city, either permanently or for the season (Fawcett 1990).

The range of shops was enormous. Luxury food outlets, wine shops, music, books, perfumes, china, glassware, furniture, haberdashers, drapers, milliners, florists, goldsmiths, watchmakers and toyshops selling gifts and curiosities all flourished in this centre of consumption and a wide hinterland was drawn upon for supplies. Nearby Bristol and the West Country, South Wales, the Midlands, Ireland, Yorkshire, Lancashire, Scotland and London and the Home Counties all provided Bath with its luxury goods. Tea kettles and lacquered metalware came from Pontypool, stockings from Nottingham, lace from Devonshire, shawls from Norwich, Wedgwood pottery from Staffordshire and toys and gifts from Birmingham and Sheffield (Fawcett 1990).

Numerous bookshops and circulating libraries were another feature of a leisured society. By 1770, Bath had six libraries, by 1790 this had risen to nine and each one served as an important social and information centre. This helped bind society together in what was an essentially transitory place and linked Bath to the wider world through books and national and local newspapers (Hembry 1990; Thrift 1990). Eighteenth-century Bath functioned as an important national centre for social and cultural communication.

Coming to Bath to shop was one of the chief pleasures of the city. In *Northanger Abbey* (1818:1067), Jane Austen's Catherine Morland cannot have been untypical of the new visitor in spending the first three or four days "learning what was mostly worn, and buying clothes of the latest fashion" and it is notable that the three streets which reoccur in Jane Austen's Bath episodes are Bond Street, Milsom Street and Bath Street.

Places of entertainment

Spa waters were evidently one of the principal attractions of Bath, unique in Britain for their heat and volume. Real or imagined illness was often one of the chief excuses for a visit to spas and Bath was no exception, especially when this could be combined with the more general pleasures of eating, drinking, conversation, gambling and vice. In sixteenth-century Bath, five baths were available and were placed under civic control in 1552. Even at this early stage, Bath was able to provide a range of entertainments not found outside London: a company of players, two tennis courts and two bowling greens, though real growth had to wait until the end of the seventeenth century. It is perhaps indicative of the true role in resort life of the baths themselves that very little change occurred to them throughout the eighteenth century and they remained hemmed in by houses and inns (McIntyre 1981).

Together with shopping, entertainment was a major reason for visiting Bath. Both the public (corporation) and private sectors were involved in supplying places for entertainment within and around the city. During the eighteenth century, the geographical focus of entertainment gradually shifted from the east side of the Abbey in the lower town to the expanding upper town. Bath was not unique of course in the growing provision of leisurely entertainments. Theatres, music, assemblies, walks and gardens, were a feature of many provincial towns throughout the country (Borsay 1989). However, Bath was not simply another provincial centre but was at the pinnacle of the urban leisure hierarchy. Consequently it was often amongst the first to provide particular forms of entertainment and these were generally of national significance. So, in the world of theatres, Bath was one of three places outside London (with Norwich and York) to have a town theatre by the 1720s. It was an early centre for public concerts with bands at the baths in 1668 and concerts by the early eighteenth century. Walks and gardens emerged by the 1680s, assembly rooms by 1708 (Borsay 1989).

Assembly rooms, walks and gardens formed part of the all important urban "arenas of display". Harrison's Rooms (1708) were located near the Abbey and were joined by Lindsey's in 1730. From the late 1760s, however, the upper Assembly Rooms were built nearer to the fashionable new town and the focus of social life migrated uphill to the north. The corporation tried to counter this drift by renovating the old town and building the Guildhall in the 1760s, a new Hot Bath (1773–1777), new Private Baths (1788–1789) and a new Pump Room (1790) (McIntyre 1981).

Bath quickly acquired the most impressive urban walks and gardens. In the 1680s, walks lay outside the city walls to the west but major developments came in the east with the Gravel Walks and Harrison's Commercial Gardens. These were followed in the same part of the city by the Terrace Walk (1728), Orange Grove (1734) and Grand and South

Parades (1743) and formed the "principal place of public resort in the city" (Borsay 1989:168). Together with the Spring Gardens (1742) across the river and the nearby luxury shops, this part of Bath "constituted the most sophisticated complex of leisure facilities to be found in the provinces" (Borsay 1989:168). Elsewhere, the streets and squares of the upper town formed other arenas of display where the Circus, Royal Crescent and the adjoining districts were important for leisurely promenading and conversation.

Space for entertainments gradually extended further outwards. In 1795, Sydney Gardens opened at the eastern end of Great Pulteney Street with groves, vistas and walks, emulating London's Vauxhall Gardens. On gala nights, the area attracted crowds of 3000–4000 people (Hembry 1990). Social access was controlled by the use of subscription fees. The 1800 *Bath Guide* recorded:

> During the summer are publick nights, with musick, fireworks and superb illuminations. Surrounding the Garden is a Ride for the accommodation of Ladies and Gentlemen on horseback, supported by a subscription of 2s 6d for one month, 5s for three months, or 15s per year, non-subscribers pay 6d each time. It commends beautiful and romantic views, and has the advantage of being free from dust in summer and dirt in winter.

> (quoted in Lane 1988)

Informal leisure space extended beyond Bath during the eighteenth century as the fashion for rural walks and picturesque scenery grew—sentiments captured in Jane Austen's *Northanger Abbey*. The fields below the Royal Crescent and the village of Weston lay to the west, Beechen Cliff immediately to the south and the country beyond Sydney Gardens to the east. Further afield, it became fashionable to take an "airing" by carriage on Landsdown to the north and Claverton Down and Kingsdown to the east of the city. Thus a whole system of walks and drives evolved creating a leisure periphery around the city linking both urban and rural pleasures for visitors (Lane 1988).

The forms of entertainment provided and the spaces utilised, reflected the culture of the leisured classes and these changed as culture changed. Entertainment and mixing with society was, for much of the eighteenth century, a matter of public display. The pump room, assembly room, theatre and promenade were part of a public show regulated by masters of ceremony such as Beau Nash. During the late eighteenth and early nineteenth centuries, however, private entertainment became increasingly fashionable with the house providing a focus for leisure rather than public space. Fanny Burney, in 1780, noted these changes: fashionable visitors began to keep to a round of private parties and concerts and withdrew from the assembly rooms now patronised by the "nouveau riche". By 1800, Bath society was fragmenting with a number of cliques using their own private spaces rather than public gatherings (Hill 1989). In *Northanger Abbey* Catherine Morland and Mrs Allen lament the lack of genteel company in the Pump Room and retreat outwards and upwards to the Royal Crescent to "breathe the fresh air of better company" (Hill 1989).

In the nineteenth century, suburban villa and private garden replaced the public street, square and crescent as Victorian family life centred on the house. The rise of this domesticated leisure space is reflected in Bath's early Floral and Horticultural Society founded in 1834. Even public open space was of a different type. Victoria Park, opened in 1830, to the west of the city, was very different in tone to Sydney Gardens. Victoria Park was a middle-class, family arena, instructive and moral (Haddon 1973). Social access was still restricted, of course, with wardens employed to eject any undesirable intruders (Weight 1972).

Although Bath ceased to be the innovator in entertainments it had been in the eighteenth century, concerts, theatres and balls continued to be successful right through the 1830s (Neale 1981). The population of over 33 000 in 1801, grew by 16 per cent between 1801 and 1811 and by 21 per cent between 1811 and 1821; growth rates similar to the country in general (Neale 1981). Bath and its entertainments were adapting to a different social class and culture. Decline is too often linked to the departure of the rich and fashionable. After all, if Bath's new patrons were "poorer and less influential, they were more numerous" (Salter 1972). A more fragmented and domestic society may have been less ostentatious than its predecessor, but transition seems a more appropriate description of change than decline.

Social and political geographies

The growth of Bath as a leisure resort created distinctive geographies. These included social and political patterns as well as a distinctive townscape and sense of place.

Social geography

Neale (1981) emphasises that Bath's space was never really planned but was socially organised. The spatial arrangements of visitors, prosperous residents and workers became increasingly clear during the eighteenth century, with a fashionable leisured society in certain parts of the city supported by a population largely concentrated and confined in areas of the lower town.

Yet this clear spatial separation did not happen immediately and, in the early eighteenth century, distinct areas for different social classes were not evident. Initial developments were scattered on sites within the old town rather than in the creation of separate specialised areas. Subsequent development, however, spreading outside the town, began to create clearer social areas. The 1766 rate books for instance, reveal zones of low-quality housing around the old north gate of the city and in the low-lying areas to the south (McIntyre 1981) as well as in areas that were close to busy trading streets and where food, fuel and other supplies were brought into the city. These tended to become areas for the poor. Thus, the growing flow of wagons in Avon Street accelerated its decline from medium-quality housing when built in 1726–1732, to a notorious slum later in the century. The Saw Close inside the old west gate was the area where coal wagons delivered their supplies, a noisy and dirty area to be avoided by polite society.

At the end of the eighteenth century, the social geography of Bath was clearly defined. The low-lying south-western areas including Milk Street, Avon Street and Kingsmead Street, were the working-class heartland of the city. Other labouring areas, also on low-lying ground, included the Dolemeads across the river to the south-east and the Holloway area south of the river. Poor housing also stretched along the busy traffic routes of the London road in Walcot Street to the north-east, while Hedgemead and Snow Hill in the same area were built on land found to be unsafe for higher class housing. Increasingly separate from these working-class areas were the fashionable districts for visitors and wealthy residents, laid out uphill to the north and north-west and east across the river. This geography of social contours is captured in Jane Austen's *Persuasion* (1818:134) when Anne Elliot descends from fashionable Camden Place (c.1788) to Westgate Buildings in the lower part of town to visit a friend. She is subsequently admonished by her father:

> Everything that revolts other people, low company, paltry rooms, foul air, disgusting association, are inviting to you . . . Westgate Buildings must have been rather surprised by the appearance of a carriage drawn up near its pavement.

Separation of leisured class from serving class was not simply by areas of the city. The huge class of domestic servants occupied the same houses as their employers but were segregated within the building, living in the attic rooms and working in the basements (Woodward

1992). Thus Walcot, the principal area for visitors, also had the highest numbers of domestic servants living in it (Wroughton 1972).

Political geography

The maintenance of a well-ordered city with a favourable image for visitors has long been a necessity for towns and cities engaged in tourism (Gold and Ward 1994). The process of places being "fashioned in the image of tourism" (Hughes 1992:33) thus carries clear political implications. Presenting a desirable external face and regulating the internal structures of a town to satisfy visitors, shapes particular forms of political organisation. Bath had to develop external relations with Britain's ruling groups who formed much of its clientele and thus had to carefully select appropriate political positions. Internally, the spa had to cope with the presence of a very prosperous sector of society directly supported by a large number of some of the poorest members of society.

In the early seventeenth century, Bath, like other spas, was closely linked to national politics as a centre of dissent and political intrigue (Hembry 1990). Later, however, Bath's fortunes were favourably connected to the court and the spa became known as the "loyal city" to the Stuart monarch. A rapid change was needed, however, after the 1688 Revolution. Loyalties had to be switched and new ideologies adopted. Under the Hanoverians, Bath was initially suspected of being a Stuart and Tory centre of dissent but the city carefully returned both a Whig and a Tory MP. As the second social centre of the country, Bath needed to adopt a judicious brand of parliamentary politics.

Within the city, the need to satisfy both visitors and other social groups affected the politics of the town. The corporation was the main instrument of local government, chosen from the freemen of the city, and many of their actions were conditioned by the need to balance their own business interests in the town with external schemes for development. Thus, there was a constant tension between developers like John Wood and a corporation wishing to maintain control of expansion on their own terms. As shown earlier, many of the actions of the corporation in the eighteenth century were concerned with improving the city for the visitors while maintaining food supplies and law and order amongst the working populations (Poole 1990).

This working population was excluded from all political life during the eighteenth century. The electoral franchise extended to 0.1 per cent of the city's population (Poole 1990). As Bath's fortunes depended on the social elite being supported by this subordinate servant class, it might reasonably be assumed that this would give rise to an especially deferential society; one where political consciousness would not be greatly developed. And yet Bath did not neatly fit this picture (Neale 1981). Its leisure industry workers did develop forms of political consciousness, aggravated perhaps by the fact that the "physical and social manifestations of arbitrary power of elites were all around them" (Neale 1981:367). There were riots in Bath in 1731, 1738, the 1740s, 1765,1780 and 1799 resulting from food shortages as well as strikes by tailors, shoemakers and staymakers. Workers also organised themselves in self-help and self-protection societies and joined dissenting movements such as Quakerism and Methodism. By the early nineteenth century, Bath had become one of the main radical political centres in Britain and part of the national map of Chartism (Gregory 1990), where its mixture of tradesmen and artisans was part of an aspiring political community. Their heartland was in the parish of St James, voting for the Radical candidate in the 1841 election and sharply contrasting with the Tory vote in the wealthier areas of the city (Neale 1981). Wroughton (1972:3) describes this contrasting political geography of the early nineteenth century: "[Bath] was a city of memories—a city of the retired and the genteel. It was also a city of hopes—a city of the Chartist and the Radical. It was a city vigorous and alive in thought". During the disturbances of 1812 the corporation was afraid of the effect on the tourist trade and so it is perhaps not so surprising that one field in which Bath *was* an innovator in the nineteenth century was in the introduction of a police force (1830).

Townscape and sense of place

Townscape

It has been stressed elsewhere that a number of the features found in Bath in the eighteenth century were not unique to the city but could also be found in the more general urban renaissance of the late seventeenth century onwards. But Bath was often an early innovator and the scale of its developments was generally far larger than found elsewhere.

This same argument applies especially to the townscape that was created for the wealthy leisured class. Architectural features and spatial arrangements in the city could be found elsewhere in provincial centres but Bath was fundamentally *not* another provincial centre. As Borsay (1990:232) critically observes: "Whereas most towns identified closely with a particular region or locality, Bath was first and foremost a cosmopolitan centre, catering for the medical, recreational and aesthetic needs of the nation's elite." And thus its townscape reflected this exalted position. Both in terms of innovation and scale, it was to become the architectural showpiece of eighteenth-century England, even, at times, being ahead of London (Mowl 1990).

Certain features of Bath's townscape can be associated with general trends within Britain from the later seventeenth century onwards. First, was the abandonment of essentially vernacular styles in building in favour of national and international forms. Local designs were forsaken in favour of Renaissance town planning ideals, transforming a decaying but fairly typical West Country wool town into a Renaissance-style city. Second, were the actual building forms adopted: terraces, squares, crescents, and streets; the stages upon which people could parade and observe status. Together with other "arenas of display", the assembly rooms, walks, gardens and promenades, this was a townscape which reflected social and cultural aspirations (Borsay 1982). In common with other expanding urban areas, Bath developed this townscape in new residential areas adjacent to the existing town, with change more limited within the old centre. Also similar to developments elsewhere was the fact that commercial activity tended to remain confined to the existing town with little spread into new residential areas (Hembry 1990).

Bath's townscape and organisation of space also reflected class relations and ideological views. Thus not only were the leisure spaces of visitors separate from the workers' areas but the design of the new town reinforced this sense of exclusion (Figure 4.8). John Wood's views on squares in Bath illustrate this point:

> But yet I preferred an inclosed Square to an open one, to make this as usefull as possible: For the intention of a Square in a City is for People to assemble together; and the Spot whereon they meet, ought to be separated from the Ground common to Men and Beasts and even to Mankind in General, if Decency and good order are to be observed in such Places of Assembly; of which I think, there can be no doubt.
>
> (quoted in Neale 1981:171)

Bath's townscape was never formally planned but developed during the eighteenth century in an informal manner. However, physical coherence of common architectural style, building material, sensitivity to topography and an underlying conjunction of common social and cultural purpose present a picture of unity. Thus Queen Square, the Circus and the Royal Crescent were assembled by Wood and his son over a 50-year period but they link together in one grand scheme. When Bath's leisured group changed during the nineteenth century into a more permanent, residential, middle-class society, so the streets, squares and crescents of outward display were succeeded in the newer suburbs by villas and enclosed gardens; a townscape which reflected different cultural forms.

Figure 4.8 "Queen Square" by Thomas Malton (1784). John Wood's Queen Square (1724–1739) in a townscape for leisure. Houses for visitors enclose an open space providing a setting for assembly and promenading; sweeping the gravel walks provided local employment (Victoria Art Gallery, Bath)

A sense of place

Recent movements in human geography have witnessed the rise of place-centred studies and a concern with "the diversity of human significance accorded to places beyond any functions they may play in the search for spatial patterns" (Hughes 1992:31). Therefore we can consider the ways in which the resort of Bath, as an archetypal leisure setting, has been expressed in a variety of social and cultural forms which have highlighted and reinforced a particular sense of place.

Herbert (1991) has shown how an insight into the role of particular places in society can be explored through imaginative literature and this is the cultural form which will be explored here. The visual arts and music would be other very obvious fields to consider but the links between Bath and imaginative literature are especially appropriate. The city played a critical role in the development of the eighteenth-century novel and these novels, in turn, give an insight into the role of Bath as a place in eighteenth-century society (Hill 1989).

At one level a straightforward visitors' map of Bath can be constructed (Herbert 1991). Jane Austen's novels reveal the confined use of space in the city with the fashionable centres of Milsom Street, Royal Crescent, Camden Place, Lansdown Crescent and the Assembly Rooms dominating the map. Beyond this analysis, the relationships within a tight social circle and the ways in which people related to particular spaces in the city can be portrayed. We see the more genteel repelled from the nouveau riche at the Pump Room, the social gulf between visitors in the upper town and the lower town, while the almost complete lack of reference to the serving classes and the poor is, itself, revealing in a city where such people counted for so little.

These ideas can be taken further by considering the role of Bath in the eighteenth-century novel and how the place functioned in literary culture. Virtually every person of letters in the eighteenth century visited Bath and the city became the subject of novels, plays, letters, diaries and poems. Consequently Bath came to epitomise the illusions, values and conflicts of that century. The rise of the eighteenth-century novel was associated with the philosophical concept of realism; the central role of individual experience. Realistic depictions of characters and places in fictional literature reflected this concern and Bath was especially useful in novels because it was such a familiar backdrop against which actions could take place. Furthermore Bath came to represent the good and bad aspects of contemporary society. Smollett's *Humphry Clinker* (1771) uses the enthusiastic Lydia to indicate the pomp and show of the city with its shops, concerts, gossip and news. The splenetic Bramble, however, points out the chaos, ugliness, dirt and danger of the streets and the poor workmanship which often lay behind the veneer of polished townscape in the showcase that was Bath.

The changing social use of public places can also be traced through the novels. In the early eighteenth century, the upper classes seem to have kept separate from other visitors (Fielding's *Tom Jones* 1749) but an increasingly regulated society drew them into its mixed company at the assemblies, balls and concerts. By the end of the century, the upper classes again withdrew to private functions. Thus the Pump Room became the hub of social activity by the mid-eighteenth century; a dominant image in novels of the period such as Charlotte Lennox's *Female Quixote* (1752). By 1771, Smollett's *Humphry Clinker* reveals the increased presence of the middle classes encroaching on the preserves of the elite and by the time of Jane Austen's *Persuasion* (1818), the Pump Room is avoided by polite society. Whereas the baths in the resort receive scant attention in novels, perhaps reflecting their lack of a central function in social and cultural life, shopping received increasing refer-ences. Early novels make little of this leisure activity but later ones show Milsom Street as significant a place as the Pump Room (Hill 1989) in the leisure world of the visitor.

Other aspects of Bath as a place are suggested through contemporary novels. As a centre of inward migration, whether as leisured visitor or as worker, Bath was a place of strangers. Visitors could adopt higher status to gain access to society, the rascal could pretend respectability, the ill-used could hope for a new start. Thus the character of the pretender looms large in novels set in the city. Bath was depicted as a place of pretence where a particularly vulnerable group who were drawn to the city were the young women who came for romance, culture, manners and entertainment.

A further insight into contemporary culture and the significance of Bath is revealed by the part played by the city in the structure of novels. The journey was an important structural principle in writing in general (Fussell 1965) and Bath was an obvious device, given that its very existence depended on travel. It was a believable place for events, a national meeting point for literate society. It was also an essentially transitory place, a place of frivolity and shallowness from which the characters in novels move on for more worthy activities such as work or settling down. Ultimately, however, Bath ceased to feature prominently in novels just as it was ceasing to play a central role in the world of leisure. Literature forsook the city, anticipating the gradual withdrawal of fashionable visitors. Bath's world of convention and display did not fit the new romantic subjects of nineteenth-century writing: nature, the common man and freedom of spirit. Bath was not a place where these new interests could be set, as a place of retirement for the genteel it ceased to be a place of action. When Dickens sent Mr Pickwick and his friends to Bath (1837), the city and its customs had become a subject for mockery with the fawning master of ceremonies welcoming Mr Tupman, Mr Winkle and Mr Snodgrass into the company of Lord Mutanhed and Lady Snuphanuph.

Nineteenth-century change

Although the novel emphasised the "decline" of Bath in the nineteenth century, not just in terms of visitor numbers but as a central and vital part of the social and cultural life of the leisured classes in Britain, it is misleading to finish an account of the city at this point. Bath's population did stagnate and its wealthy visitors left but it was generally successful in transforming itself into an upper-middle-class residential and retirement centre. The history of resorts does not end when the social elite move on and we should not subscribe to the view of one Bath citizen that "Bath has had no history since Queen Victoria came to the throne" (Ball 1977:5).

For some people, the changing nature of Bath brought benefits. The working population found more secure employment in serving the needs of an affluent permanent population rather than seasonal visitors (Hembry 1990), and Neale (1981) considers that, overall, the conditions of the labouring population improved during the nineteenth century. The forms of employment changed, with more opportunities for young single women to act as servants and companions to the high proportion of wealthy female residents (see above).

Bath also benefited from general improvements in the urban environment. Gas lighting came in 1819, and a number of hospitals were built: the Eye Hospital (1811), the United Hospital (1826), and the Ear, Nose and Throat Hospital (1837) (Haddon 1973). The economy began to diversify into light engineering and printing and the city developed into a major middle-class educational centre with boarding schools for boys and girls (Ball 1977). There was even a temporary revival of interest in spas in the later nineteenth century with the practices flourishing at continental spas being introduced into Britain. The Grand Pump Room Hotel was built in 1869, the original Roman baths were discovered in 1880 and drew visitors, and the King's and Queen's Baths were re-designed by the corporation in 1881. The immense Empire Hotel opened in the 1890s and the Bath Pageant of 1909 was an example of urban boosterism designed to raise the profile of the city.

Furthermore, decline was not seen as inevitable at the time. Granville's (1841) survey of the spas in England was optimistic for the future of Bath. He observed that ten times more visitors came to the city than in its fashionable heyday but that the city was too big and bustling to be exclusive any more. He suggested improvements to the spa facilities to rival continental spas and felt that the season should move to the more benign summer period. Nevertheless, there is no doubt that the city's population and economy did stagnate during the nineteenth century and that it never recovered its position as a major visitor centre.

Paradoxically, however, Bath's very stagnation during the nineteenth century bequeathed a largely unchanged Georgian townscape to the twentieth century and this laid the foundation for the next stage of the "resort cycle". In the later twentieth century, Bath has experienced a new tourist boom based on the appeal of "heritage" and has developed into a major national and international tourist centre. Perhaps inevitably, that "heritage" appeal is based on the eighteenth-century visitor areas of the city. Redevelopment in the 1960s destroyed much of workers' Bath (Fergusson 1973). But then today's tourists are probably as uninterested in these areas of the city as were its visitors 200 years ago.

This chapter has drawn attention to the extensive fields of research that are possible when piecing together the historical geography of spa resorts. It has emphasised the complexity of the picture rather than attempting to simplify it because it is based on the belief that historical

research suggests that the generalisations often found in tourism literature when looking at the past cannot be sustained without major
qualifications (Towner 1994). There is a considerable amount of research
still to be done before a full picture of the role of spas in social, cultural,
economic and political life can be presented.

There are other themes which require more understanding. First, spas
should not be seen as isolated from each other in terms of patronage. In
many cases there was a "circuit of spas" rather than visits to individual
centres. The rural spas in England were often linked in this way
(Hembry 1990) and Bath and Hotwells in Bristol had visitors moving
back and forth between them. Spas also need to be related to other
leisure places and other forms of leisure. Thus the spa seasons in Britain
were often connected to the winter seasons in London with a migration
from home to the capital and on to a spa. Harrogate's season in the early
nineteenth century was placed between the race weeks at York and
Doncaster (Patmore 1963). The leisure world of north-country gentry
placed spas among hunting, racing, sea-bathing, visits to provincial
towns and journeys to London and abroad (Hughes 1952; Neave 1991).
Similarly, the spa of Baden near Vienna was one of a variety of destinations for the local leisure class (Barea 1966). As centres for ideas and
communication, spas were part of the process of stimulating travel
abroad (see chapter 5) and so part of a much broader leisure system.
Establishing these links will eventually enable us to see the spa resort,
not as an isolated development, but in a much more comprehensive
lifestyle context (Towner 1994).

5

Venturing abroad: the European Grand Tour

The Grand Tour, that circuit of western Europe undertaken by the wealthy in society for culture, education, health and pleasure, is one of the most celebrated episodes in the history of tourism. It was a major feature of travel abroad from the sixteenth to the first part of the nineteenth century (Towner 1985) and, although it has been argued earlier that an emphasis on prestigious events can distort our view of tourism history, there is no doubt that the practice of visiting the major cultural centres in France, Germany and, above all, Italy, assumed an important role in the lives of the affluent in Britain and elsewhere in Europe. Grand Touring developed in the sixteenth and seventeenth centuries, reached its zenith in the eighteenth century, and survived in modified form into the nineteenth century. Indeed, its legacy can be traced right through to today with cultural tours to Paris, Florence, Venice, Rome, Vienna and other embodiments of European culture, neatly packaged by the modern tourist industry.

The Grand Tour is thus a good example of continuity in tourism history. In fact, it can be seen as a re-emergent form of cultural tourism which had existed in the ancient world. Wealthy Romans, for example, travelled to Greece in search of the culture to which they ultimately aspired and which reaffirmed and validated their own beliefs and practices (Casson 1974; Lowenthal 1985). So although Pimlott (1947:65) was correct in claiming the Grand Tour as the ancestor of "the continental holiday in its various modern forms", it in turn was derived from practices that were a feature of tourism over a thousand years earlier.

The Grand Tour and the tourists

How should the Grand Tour be interpreted? Should it be defined by the social class of the tourist or by where the tourist went? If the Grand Tour is viewed as essentially aristocratic in nature, then wherever the aristocracy travelled would constitute their tour and areas such as Portugal, Spain, Greece, the Near East, Russia and Scandinavia would have to be included (Black 1992). On the other hand, the Grand Tour can be seen as a distinct tourist circuit of western Europe which, over time, attracted a range of social classes and nationalities and which persisted in its essential outline through numerous changing circumstances. This latter perspective is adopted here in order to explore change and continuity within a particular tourist circuit.

There have been many accounts of the Grand Tour. These have usually concentrated on the journey itself, drawing upon the vivid accounts of tourist activities which emerge from the numerous letters, journals and diaries left by the travellers (Black 1992; Hibbert 1969; Mead 1914; Trease 1967). Rather than repeating this picture, emphasis will be given here to themes which contribute to an historical geography of the tour. A number of the processes which created a "travel culture" in the tourist-generating regions will be considered at some length before examining the actual travel patterns in the destination regions. In this way, an attempt will be made to provide a perspective on what might be termed the "Grand Tour system". A fully balanced view of this system is not, unfortunately, possible. Other nationalities apart from the British under-took Grand Tours, such as the French, Germans and Russians (Schudt 1959) but, although many travel accounts exist from these sources, it is less easy to discover the broader context within which the tours took place. Therefore this chapter focuses on the British experience. Further-more, amid all the information we can obtain from tourists' records and guidebooks, one particular group of people remain largely silent. The attitudes and behaviour of the tourists can be explored, but what of the host societies within which the Grand Tour operated? What were the reactions of people in France, Italy, or Germany to these visitors, whether they were directly concerned with providing tourist services or simply detached observers? As yet, we have few records from this equally important side of the Grand Tour system and we can only indirectly infer the likely social and economic impacts.

Bias in the historical record also applies to who were the Grand Tourists. Estimates as to their social composition and numbers have to rely on informed guesswork. The diaries and journals which have survived in manuscript or published form are the main source of information but they present a one-sided picture. The wealthy and literate who had time (or a tutor) to keep travel accounts are over-represented at the expense of the dilatory tourist. Also, the records of the wealthiest and most famous are more likely to have survived over time. Contemporary references in periodicals focus on the activities of the rich and powerful and thus the stereotype of the Grand Tourist as a young aristocrat accompanied by a tutor is probably an oversimplification and there was always a greater variety of travellers to Europe (Dent 1975; Towner 1984b). Nevertheless, a preponderance of the landed classes on the Grand Tour from the mid-sixteenth century to the later eighteenth century seems likely after which the middle classes formed the majority (Towner 1985). This later rise of middle-class travel also saw a significant increase in family travel and women travellers (Meyer 1978).

The number of Grand Tourists is a matter of guesswork. No statistical records were kept and contemporary estimates fluctuated widely. A possible figure of 15 000–20 000 British tourists abroad per annum in the mid-eighteenth century has been suggested; about 0.2–0.7 per cent of the total population (Towner 1985). Certainly the number and wealth of the potential groups from which tourists would be drawn increased over time. The landed classes grew from c.126 000 to c.239 000 between 1688 and 1803 and their incomes rose two and three fold. At the same time, the middle classes expanded from c.368 000 to c.410 000 and incomes for some of them rose dramatically also (Mathias 1957–58; Mingay 1976). The landed and middle classes in Britain in the eighteenth century formed between 7 and 9 per cent of the population and they formed the dominant groups from which Grand Tourists were drawn.

The development of a travel culture in Britain

Travellers from Britain had journeyed through Europe long before the Grand Tour developed. Pilgrims and merchants had visited many of the places which were later to become part of the tourists' itinerary and their needs helped establish a well-understood system of routes and centres of accommodation (Parks 1954). But there was a crucial change in the sixteenth century with travel for religious conviction evolving into travel for secular curiosity. This was not simply due to the split away from Rome of the English church in the 1530s, but stemmed from the development of a "travel culture" in Britain which derived much of its inspiration from the Renaissance movement in Europe. This section will explore the processes by which this "travel culture" was developed in Britain and then go on to consider the pattern of particular geographical settings through which this culture was transmitted to the landed and middle classes throughout the country.

The underlying causes of the Grand Tour are to be found in the changing cultural relations between different parts of Europe which evolved from the sixteenth century onwards. Until the later eighteenth century, the culture to which the social elite in Britain aspired was geographically located outside the country—in Italy and later also in France. Therefore, to use Cohen's (1979) terminology, the "centre" to which Britain's social elite adhered lay elsewhere and this spatial separation underlined the need to develop travel as part of their culture. Furthermore, the desire to travel was reinforced by many of the ideals of the Renaissance itself. The intellectual movement of humanism revering classical antiquity became central to European cultural life (Caspari 1954) and Italy was not only the source of classical inspiration but the centre of its reinterpretation through the Renaissance. Developments in philosophy and scientific thought also encouraged the desirability of travel. The new astronomy challenged the medieval scholastic view of a static universe. Outward-looking thought and the urge to explore and understand encouraged a new spirit in movement (Graburn 1978). Certainly, some contemporaries made a clear link between travel and the expansion of the human mind. Justus Lipsius wrote in 1578: "Humble and plebeian souls stay at home, bound to their own piece of earth, that soul is nearer the divine which rejoices in movement, as do the heavens themselves" (quoted in Parks 1951:264). The importance of gathering factual evidence and the use of reason, argued by seventeenth-century philosophers such as Bacon and Descartes, encouraged tourists in their travels through Europe (Frantz 1934). To the lure of classical antiquity and the achievements of the Renaissance, was added the appeal of being part of a scientific quest for knowledge. By the eighteenth century, the social elite of Europe were further united by the philosophy of the Enlightenment; a common system of thought and attitudes based on human reason. A Europe-wide social and intellectual "club" made travel congenial for the upper classes when similar views and ties of kinship and patronage gave easy access to society (Hampson 1968).

As a common European elite culture was forming, so the wealthy were withdrawing from locally based popular culture (Burke 1978; and see chapter 2). Thus the Grand Tour can also be seen as part of a social and cultural process of withdrawal that occurred not only at the local scale of country house and estate or the regional and national scale of fashionable seasons, but was extended to foreign travel. This socio-cultural and geographical split was never clear-cut, of course. Within the English landed classes there were always differences between "court" and "country" and a distinction between "the insular fox-hunting squire and the travelled and cultivated nobleman" was an enduring image (Stone 1965:330).

The British upper classes were susceptible to the influence of Renaissance thought. They became exposed to the changing cultural climate abroad and the Grand Tour developed into a significant medium for transmitting ideas from Europe to Britain. This evolving "travel culture" can be considered through a number of related themes including education and career, cultural pursuits and health.

British elite education was largely directed by the spread of Renaissance practices from the sixteenth century onwards and a close association developed between the needs of education and travel. A knowledge of the classics, art and architecture, and the development of social skills, all emphasised the idea of travel *as* education (Parks 1951). Italy and France exerted a strong pull on the educated Englishman (Lee 1910; Stone 1965) and by the eighteenth century, travel abroad was widely accepted as essential for a gentlemanly education (Brauer 1959). Travel abroad was also required to enhance a government career in Britain in the sixteenth and seventeenth centuries. The Tudor monarchy selected people of intellectual rather than military merit and the ambitious wealthy needed to acquire diplomatic and linguistic skills abroad (Stone 1965).

Gradually, however, the distinct motives of education and career travel became absorbed into a much broader cultural field with the growing ethos of the leisured gentleman. Certain aspects of these cultural interests can be clearly related to travel, such as the classics and classical antiquities, art and architecture, landscape tastes and the popularity of travel literature. To see the places associated with the great writers and deeds of classical antiquity was always an important motive for travel to Italy and was a natural extension of an education which stressed the central role of the classics. Similarly, art and architectural interests were dominated by Italian classical and Renaissance ideals, and a growing interest in the fine arts in Britain in the seventeenth century was associated with the rise of the virtuoso; the wealthy amateur who united an interest in science with the collection of antiquities, paintings and sculpture (Houghton 1942). These collections came primarily from abroad, especially Italy (Haskell 1959).

Tastes in landscape reflected travel abroad. Gardens and parks were inspired by scenes on the continent, changing from the formal Dutch and French styles of the seventeenth century to the Italian landscape ideal of the eighteenth century (Allen 1937; Malins 1966; Manwaring 1925; Ogden and Ogden 1955). The rise of a picturesque and romantic taste for landscape, although possibly a distinctly British cultural creation, has also been attributed to travel in Europe as well as to the

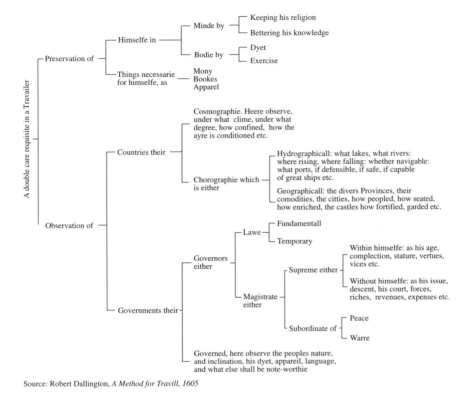

Source: Robert Dallington, *A Method for Travill*, 1605

Figure 5.1 An early seventeenth-century theory of travel

influence of Renaissance scientific thought (Hussey 1927; Manwaring 1925; Nicolson 1959).

The development of a travel culture in Britain was reinforced by the immense popularity of travel literature (Batten 1978; Wright 1935). English books on foreign countries began to appear in the sixteenth century. William Thomas's *The History of Italy* (1549) was the first English book on that country and, along with a whole series of later publications, began to develop a theory of travel. Figure 5.1 indicates that proposed by Robert Dallington in the early seventeenth century and it reflects the wide range of subjects that early travellers were expected to study and record. Between 1660 and 1730, seven large collections of voyages and travel were published and by then, "books of travel provided the principal secular reading of a growing readership" (de Beer 1975:1). Travel literature formed a major part of literary culture in the eighteenth century (Curley 1976; Kaufman 1960) and periodicals such as the *Spectator, Tatler, Critical Review* and *Gentleman's Magazine* were full of advice and comments on travel, especially travel abroad (Golden 1977; Towner 1984b). Many writers such as Swift, Defoe, Addison, Fielding, Smollett, Boswell, Johnson and Sterne employed the travel format in their works (Fussell 1965) and these publications helped spread the culture of travel to the literate middle classes.

A further theme that was bound up with an urge to travel abroad was the perceived benefits to health. The warmer climes of southern France and Italy were always important attractions for the wealthy of Britain and the spas and seaside resorts of Britain had to compete with the benefits of spending the winter in the milder climates of southern Europe. Distinct centres, such as Montpellier, developed in the seventeenth century for treating consumption and were often linked to a more general Grand Tour (Towner 1984b). Later on, places like Nice and Cannes fulfilled similar roles, either as health centres in their own right or serving as a winter pause for more extensive travel (see chapter 7). The idea of travel for health was part of a more general leisured-class concern for its mental and physical welfare which linked spas, seaside resorts and "healthier climates" with other cultural forms of touring.

It was suggested earlier that the centres for culture for Britain's social elite lay outside the country. In fact, the need to travel abroad was so strong that it possibly led to the neglect of travel *within* Britain itself until the later eighteenth century. Apart from the fashionable season and visits to spas and seaside resorts, contemporary accounts suggest that exploration of Britain was disregarded. The *Gentleman's Magazine* (1748) urged the upper classes "to be better acquainted with the beauties and rarities of their own Britain" and Thomas Hurtley (1786) complained that: "An universal rage for Foreign Travel has long occasioned an unaccountable neglect of the Beauties and Wonders of our own Country." More recently, Norman Nicolson (1955:76) explained the neglect of the English Lake District until the late eighteenth century in largely cultural terms: "It was not so much a matter of distance as of history—the [Lake District] did not belong to the civilisation from which the eighteenth century drew its culture." Placing the growing travel culture exclusively within terms of journeying abroad is, however, probably an exaggeration. Moir (1964), Dent (1975), Ousby (1990) and Andrews (1989) provide evidence of travel in Britain during the time of the Grand Tour and the historical record is likely to be distorted by the fact that travel abroad conveyed more prestige and attracted more attention.

We can trace the various elements that constituted the British travel culture by analysing the range of interests that the tourists revealed in their European tour journals and how these interests varied over time. Figure 5.2 attempts to summarise the main interests shown by a sample

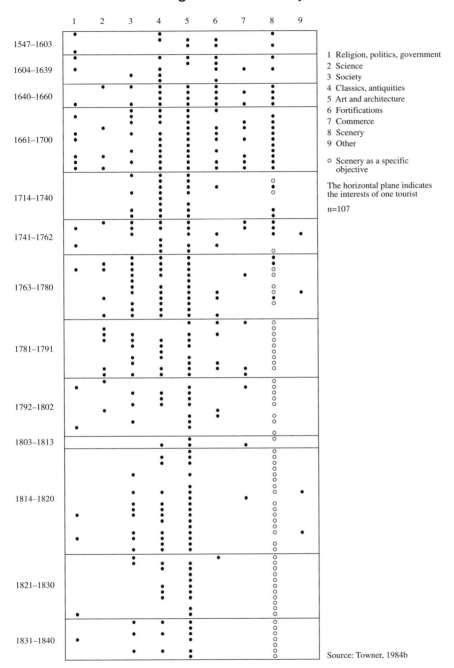

Figure 5.2   The changing range of interests of Grand Tourists in Europe

of Grand Tourists' accounts. Certain themes always dominated the tour: the classics and antiquities, fashionable society and art and architecture. Scenery was always commented upon but, from the mid-eighteenth century onwards, the quest for picturesque and romantic landscapes became a major goal for tourists. Other interests declined over time. Thus, travel abroad to examine politics, government and religion, the recording of fortifications and commerce, or an interest in scientific phenomena became less significant. It is also noticeable how the range of interests of individual tourists declined so that, by the early nineteenth century, the discovery of scenery, viewing works of art and architecture and admiring classical antiquities became the main concerns recorded in travel journals. (However, the material contained in the tourists' journals needs to be treated with great caution. Plagiarism and sheer invention were common and much of the real experience of travel was omitted; see Batten 1978; Towner 1984a.)

The development of a culture for travel abroad took place within specific settings in Britain which both encouraged and reflected the world of the Grand Tour. There was, therefore, a geographical pattern to the process by which continental tourism was formulated. Certain places were of great significance and a generating region cannot simply be considered as a uniform area. Important geographical settings included the landed estate, London, certain urban provincial centres and resorts, schools and universities. It was a major characteristic of British landed-class culture that there was considerable movement between these settings (Namier 1961); from country house and estate to the London season, from public school to university and from provincial town to leisure resort. The movement of the middle classes may have been more circumscribed, but during the eighteenth century they were increasingly part of this circuit of cultural centres and open to the influence of travel literature.

The landed estate must be seen as one of the principal places within Britain for cultivating an interest in the Grand Tour. Some of the characteristics of these estates as leisure settings have been discussed in chapter 2 and their economic role in providing income and time for leisurely travel is clear. But the landed estate also served other functions. The country house became an important centre for the informal education of the landed classes and where ideas were transmitted between social circles (Dent 1974; 1975). Much use was made of the extensive libraries with their travel books and illustrations and tourists' diaries and journals were circulated among friends and relatives (Nichols 1812–1815; Nichols and Nichols 1817–1858; Towner 1984b).It was in these country settings that tastes in art and architecture could be demonstrated and enjoyed. Palladian villas and their variants spread across rural England in the eighteenth century and as their exteriors reflected Italian tastes, so their interiors were adapted to accommodate the books, pictures and ornaments acquired on a Grand Tour (Girouard 1978). Cabinet rooms were constructed at houses like Felbrigg in Norfolk and Corsham Court in Wiltshire to house this cultural baggage.

The gardens and parks of the estate were ideal places for putting into practice the latest fashions. Here, the Grand Tourist could recreate images of a real or imagined Italy (Malins 1966; Manwaring 1925; Williamson and Bellamy 1987). Landowners like Hoare at Stourhead and Lyttleton at Hagley attempted to capture idealised Italian scenes; one view at Stourhead, for instance, closely resembles Claude's *Coast View of Delos with Aeneas* complete with classical temple. A reciprocal role with the Grand Tour is clear; settings were created in house and garden that both reflected and stimulated the desire for continental travel (Wittkower 1974).

London was another important place for developing a travel culture. Chapter 2 has indicated how the landed classes descended on the capital for the winter season of balls, assemblies, concerts and dinners and the fashionable season must be seen as a potent element in taste formation. It was in London, too, that a large number of fashionable clubs were found (Timbs 1898). Some, such as the Dilettanti Society (founded 1732), were especially for Grand Tourists (Cust 1898; Mougel 1978). As Horace Walpole acidly observed, it was: "a club for which the nominal qualification is having been in Italy and the real one, being drunk" (Gay 1967:84).

The rise of the provincial leisure town (see chapter 2; Borsay 1989; McInnes 1988) formed regional centres contributing to the development of a travel culture (Dent 1974). Attendance at an assembly or ball, a visit to the provincial bookseller or circulating library, or joining local clubs and societies was part of a cultural network encouraging travel. To these provincial centres should be added the spas and seaside resorts which from the seventeenth century onwards became part of the fashionable circuit after the London season. With their own rounds of balls and assemblies, these resorts were where continental travel, either planned or experienced, would be a distinct asset.

A small number of public schools, such as Westminster and Eton, together with Oxford and Cambridge universities, were the centres of formal education for the landed classes and, although their educational role declined in the eighteenth century (Dent 1975; Stone 1975), it was here that important social contacts were made. In the eighteenth century, a number of "smart" colleges at Oxford and Cambridge developed clubs and societies similar to those in London (Stone 1975). For some middle-class students, public school and university gave them the entrée into society which ultimately led to their undertaking a Grand Tour, either as tutors or as friends of the wealthy (Towner 1984b).

These travel culture places were also linked to the wider development of the growing commercialisation of leisure in Britain (chapter 4). The circulation of information in the form of newspapers, journals and books, the growth in the consumption of luxury goods and the increased importance of fashion were all part of an economic structure that was responding to and encouraging leisure and travel (Black 1992; Glennie 1990; Plumb 1973).

A useful way of synthesising these different cultural processes and the settings within which they took place is to link them to particular lifestyles and lifecycles. Thus for a member of the landed classes, the Grand Tour was part of a leisurely lifestyle based on the country estate, certain forms of education, the London and provincial season, visits to fashionable resorts and, perhaps, travel within Britain. Unfortunately, few studies have been made of the role of leisure and tourism in this wider context of lifestyle and lifecycle. The lack of good primary data covering a lengthy time-span for individuals is one problem. Also, the tendency to view episodes like the Grand Tour in isolation from other activities has contributed to this lack of a wider context. Black (1992) has recently suggested that, for most travellers, the Grand Tour preceded travel within Britain and that, after the tour, few travelled abroad again. More research is needed before this view can be substantiated, however, and placing the Grand Tour within the wider context of the lifestyle and lifecycle of individuals has yet to be fully considered.

The patterns of travel in Europe

The scene now moves to the tour in Europe itself. Journeys around western Europe from the sixteenth to the early nineteenth century reveal a wide range of patterns some of which remained virtually unchanged for 300 years, while others fluctuated according to the tourists' tastes or conditions within the destination regions themselves. Three main themes are considered in this section: the spatial patterns of the tour, the temporal patterns which emerged and some of the characteristics of the embryonic tourist "industry" which supported the various activities of the visitors.

Spatial patterns

Figure 5.3 shows the principal routes and places described in Thomas Nugent's (1756) Grand Tour guidebook. This comprehensive guidebook

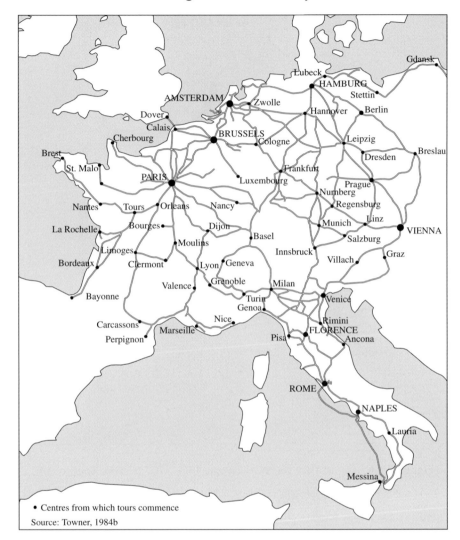

• Centres from which tours commence

Source: Towner, 1984b

Figure 5.3   Nugent's Grand Tour routes in 1756

gives an idea of the maximum extent of eighteenth-century Grand Tour destinations. In four volumes Nugent covered France, Italy, Germany and the Netherlands and for each country a variety of itineraries radiated outwards from the main centres of Paris, Amsterdam, Brussels, Hamburg, Vienna, Venice, Florence, Rome and Naples. The tourist was to select those routes which suited his overall plan best and the network was largely based on the post road system (see below) of Europe as it then existed. Although Nugent provided information on Spain and

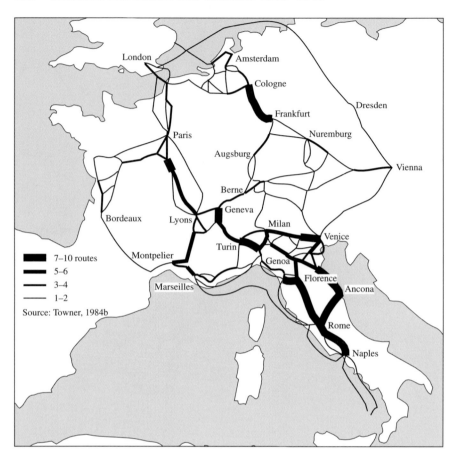

Figure 5.4A   Grand Tour routes in Europe, 1661–1700 (Elsevier Science Ltd)

Portugal, Sweden, Russia, Poland and Denmark these did not constitute major destinations for the Grand Tour. Furthermore, the general lack of outstanding foci in Germany can be contrasted with a very clear idea of what to visit in Italy. The actual routes undertaken by tourists are shown in Figure 5.4 based on a sample of tours in the late seventeenth century and the early nineteenth century. These show that there was little departure at the European scale from Nugent's outline and that the overall pattern of tours did not vary considerably over time. There was always a concentration of travel to Paris, through France and on to Turin, Florence, Rome, Naples and Venice. Away from these centres, the pattern of routes was always more diffuse. Important changes did occur, however, at more regional scales. The rise of Switzerland as a major

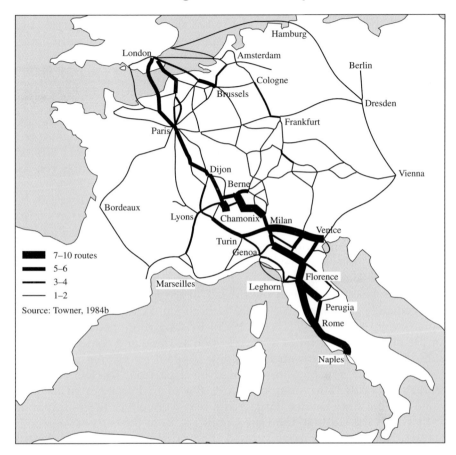

Figure 5.4B Grand Tour routes in Europe, 1814–1820 (Elsevier Science Ltd)

touring centre and the shift of Italian routes from the Adriatic coast to Umbria were significant alterations in Grand Tour practices. On the other hand, some local-scale itineraries remained little altered. The short circuit of classical antiquities based around Naples or the excursions from Rome to Tivoli and Frascati remained very much the same throughout the whole tour period.

Although these basic spatial patterns formed the framework of the tour, the evaluation of places by the tourists changed over time. Early seventeenth-century tourists saw Rome, the plain of Lombardy and the Alps in a very different light to their early nineteenth-century counterparts. In fact, it is possible to broadly distinguish between an essentially "classical" tour of Europe from the later sixteenth century to the mid-eighteenth century where attitudes were dominated by classical and Renaissance tenets, and a "romantic" tour influenced by the sensibilities of the Romantic Movement with a quest for sublime and picturesque scenery and a new enthusiasm for the medieval world (Towner 1985).

Thus a dynamic element always existed in the patterns and processes of the tour. From the sixteenth to the early nineteenth century, new attractions and interests were either being physically created in the art, architecture and urban designs of Europe or were being produced through perceptual re-evaluation as changes in tourist taste and fashion occurred. Certain places rose or fell in popularity as existing centres were reassessed or new centres discovered and admired.

The main influences on the spatial patterns of the Grand Tour can be examined in terms of culture, wars and disease and transport systems.

Transport systems will be examined first as their network was clearly basic to the particular routes that travellers could follow. Nevertheless, it should be emphasised that transport infrastructure rarely determined the choice of locations visited on the Grand Tour. Underlying cultural factors (see below) governed the overall structure of the tour and transport generally facilitated movement rather than dictated what cities and regions were to be seen (Towner 1985). Existing route networks created for the needs of other types of travel, such as trade and commerce, were utilised and new improvements readily adopted by visiting tourists.

A number of transport forms could be used from the late sixteenth century onwards. For water transport, the main European rivers provided a *coche d'eau* service, large boats that were either horse-drawn or drifted with the current. The Low Countries, from the early seventeenth century, developed a sophisticated horse-drawn canal boat system known as *trekvaarts* (see below). On land, again from about the sixteenth century, much of western Europe was covered by the post system, where stages provided a relay of fresh horses (Rowlands 1576). A much slower, but cheaper, service of stagecoaches evolved in the seventeenth century with extensive coverage across Europe. In addition, France and Italy, from the sixteenth century onwards, created the *veturino* (Italy) or *voiturin* (France) form of travel. Here, a contract was made with an agent to travel between specific places with no change of horses. It was fairly slow but had the advantage of not confining the traveller to post routes (Towner 1985). A number of the wealthier Grand Tourists bought or hired their own carriages and then used the *veturino* or post system (Towner 1984b). Inevitably most tourists used a variety of transport modes on their travels (Baillie 1911; Nugent 1756; Moryson 1617) and used both land and water systems. The use of the latter did have a general effect on the *overall* direction of a Grand Tour through Europe as travel was quicker down river. Thus, an anti-clockwise movement

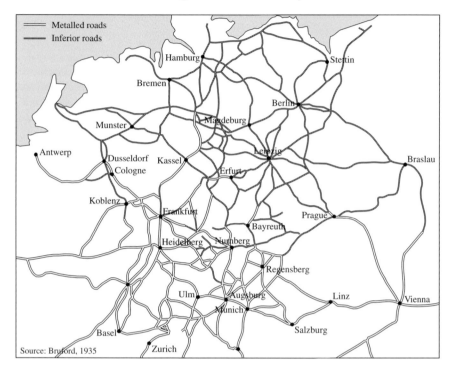

Figure 5.5   Road conditions in Germany at the end of the eighteenth century (Bruford (1935) *Germany in the Eighteenth Century. The Social Background of the Literary Revival.* Cambridge University Press)

around the continent, journeying down the River Rhône in France and returning down the River Rhine through Germany to the Low Countries and the Channel was preferred.

Overall, there were few really significant improvements in journey times during the Grand Tour era and the tempo of a continental Grand Tour did not change radically (Derry and Williams 1960). The upper limit of a horse's speed and stamina was always the final control on journey times (Thrupp 1877).Therefore the journey from Rome to Naples took five days in the mid-sixteenth century and remained the same to the early nineteenth century when road improvements reduced the time by one day. Florence to Rome took from between four and six days for the whole tour period (Towner 1984b). Also, travel conditions varied enormously. Figure 5.5 shows how even by the end of the eighteenth century there was a clear distinction between the fairly good roads of southern Germany and the still often unmetalled roads to the north. Seasons and local weather conditions could play havoc with journey

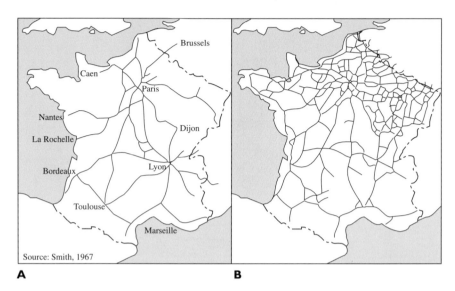

Source: Smith, 1967

A   B

Figure 5.6 A French post roads, 1632. **B** Major roads in France by the end of the eighteenth century (Smith (1967) *An Historical Geography of Western Europe Before 1800*, Addison Wesley Longman)

times. Fynes Moryson (1617) took three days in the 1590s to travel from Dresden to Prague but Mrs Piozzi (1789) took five days in 1784.

Improvements in travel were made in certain regions. France, especially, saw a great advance in the main road system from the later sixteenth century onwards with centralised government control and specific administrative bodies (Forbes 1957; Singer et al 1957). Figure 5.6 shows how extensive these improvements were and French roads were frequently praised by the tourists. Even so, as Braudel (1979) shows, the journey times on the "privileged routes" (e.g. Paris–Lyon) remained much the same over time. The reduction in time spent on a Grand Tour was due to shorter stays in individual centres rather than speedier journeys (Towner 1984b).

A notable transport network was the *trekvaart* system in the Low Countries (Figure 5.7). This was a highly organised system where long narrow boats (*trek schuiten*) worked to a regular and strictly enforced timetable on the canals. They linked with overland coach services and sailing vessels (De Vries 1978) and provided a cheap, efficient all year round transport system which was much praised by the tourists and featured in the guidebooks (Nugent 1756).

As scenic tourism increased in popularity in the later eighteenth century, so some transport systems were used extensively for this

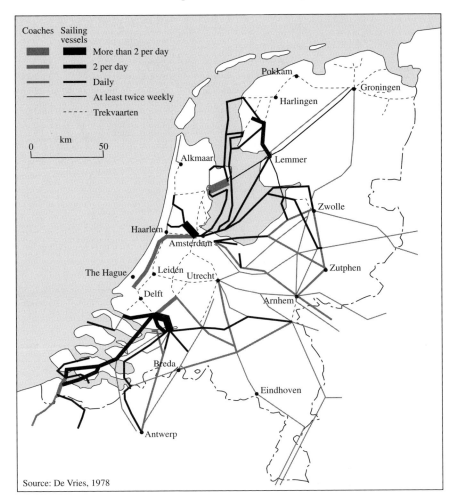

Source: De Vries, 1978

Figure 5.7   The Dutch coach and sailing vessel services in the mid-eighteenth century

purpose. The journeys on the Swiss lakes and on the Rhine were as much for viewing scenery as for travelling from one destination to another and the introduction of steam-powered boats running to time-tables accelerated this process. Steamers were on the Rhine by 1819 and appeared on the Swiss lakes in the 1820s.

Changes in transport technology are sometimes seen as decisive in different phases of tourism's history (Burkart and Medlik 1990). For the Grand Tour, a number of writers have seen the coming of the railways as the dominant factor which marked its demise. Thus, Lambert

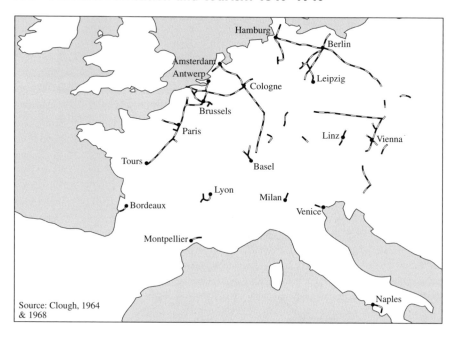

Figure 5.8 The railway network in France, Belgium, Germany and Italy by 1846 (Clough (1964) *Economic History of Modern Italy*, Columbia University Press)

(1935:12) declared: "It was speed that killed the Grand Tour, as it was slowness, that is time for leisurely travel, that made it what it was." Yet the time spent on a Grand Tour, and the social composition of the tourists, changed long before the railways could have had any major influence. Figure 5.8 shows the overall European railway network by 1846 and its fragmented nature is clear. In France, travel to Paris was possible by railway but otherwise there was little of real value to Grand Tourists. Brussels and Cologne were linked by 1846, valuable for visiting the Rhine, and in Germany the borders of Switzerland could be reached fairly quickly. Italy, however, had very little other than the local services based on Venice, Milan and Naples. Even by 1865, Rome could not be reached by rail directly from the north (Clough 1964). Thus railways had a limited regional influence on the later Grand Tour and they were certainly used where possible. But their effect was probably more symbolic than decisive and the transition of the Grand Tour into a few months travel to Europe was well established long before an integrated railway network existed.

One final method of transport should be mentioned. Travel on foot was an exceptional way of visiting centres and few affluent tourists would consider it an acceptable way of behaving. But romanticism changed attitudes considerably and by the 1820s and 1830s walking tours of Switzerland had become grafted onto the usual Grand Tour. These were low-altitude expeditions during the summer months accompanied by guides and quickly attracted a wealthy clientele. In 1820, Mariana Starke noted that walking was now: "a mode so commonly adopted that the foot passenger is as well received, even at the best inns, as if he came in a splendid equipage" (Starke 1820:76). A more fundamental influence than transport systems on the pattern of the Grand Tour was the prevailing cultural attitudes of the tourists. Cultural aspirations determined the parameters within which a particular pattern of tour was organised, and this cultural effect can be analysed through education and society, the quest for classical antiquities, art and architecture and the wider appeal of landscape tastes.

The contribution of education and society to the spatial patterns of the Grand Tour passed through two stages; from a quest for a formal acquisition of practical training and social skills at specific educational centres to a broader and more informal social and cultural education that was best attained at the main courts and social and artistic centres in Europe. Formal education for the early Grand Tourists could be pursued at centres such as Padua, with its famous university, Venice or Florence, or Montpellier; all providing language, scientific and diplomatic skills (Sells 1964). Generally, however, this career motive declined and the more social skills of a gentleman—riding, dancing, fencing, good conversation, a knowledge of fine arts—came to dominate. Consequently centres like Paris and the academies of the Loire valley such as Tours and Saumur, became important foci in the seventeenth century (Lough 1984; Stoye 1952). The Loire academies, however, enjoyed a relatively short-term influence on the patterns of the Grand Tour and were losing their hold by the later 1600s (Towner 1984b). Possibly these small centres lacked a sufficiently wide range of attractions to maintain a hold on pleasure-seeking visitors. Paris and the court at Versailles, on the other hand, could combine training with a wider range of experiences and remained major centres for the tour. John Clenche observed of Paris in the 1670s that: "The principal Traffick of this city, is, their Language, Dancing, Fencing, and Riding Masters . . . with which they supply all Europe" (Clenche 1676:3). Other educational centres included Turin. Joseph Spence took his pupil, Lord Lincoln, there in the 1730s "to ride, fence and dance" while elsewhere, virtuoso tastes in the fine arts could be developed at the various academies such as in Florence and Rome (Skinner 1966; Spence 1975).

During the eighteenth century, travel itself and mixing with fashionable society replaced more intensive educational practices. At the various courts and artistic centres of Europe the Grand Tourists could mix not only with other nationalities but with friends and acquaintances from home. This process intensified the appeal of established centres like Paris, Rome, Florence and Naples but it also helped to create new destinations at the emerging court societies of the German states. When James Boswell was on tour in Germany he moved from one court to another—Brunswick, Berlin, Dresden, Kassel, Hannau, Mannheim, Karlsruhe—and used letters of introduction from one centre to gain entrée to the next (Pottle 1952–1955). In Vienna, John Moore found that tourists "may mix, on an easy footing, with people of rank" (Moore 1781,2:313). Attending assemblies and balls, mixing with the rich and famous, were powerful influences on the Grand Tour in the eighteenth century.

Nevertheless, mixing with fashionable society did not always control tourist behaviour and choice of destination. As the "romantic" tour began to replace the "classical" tour, so a number of tourists began to shun this mannered world. Fashion encouraged a new interest in viewing local inhabitants and culture (Burke 1978). In 1819, Maria Graham ventured away from Rome to see the "peasants of the hills" east of Rome. The dances and costumes of these "quiet, simple people" dominated her enthusiastic and sympathetic account (Graham 1820) and the *Monthly Review* 1821:173, commended her:

> modestly retiring from the beaten track to illustrate a feature of the country on which modern travellers have unaccountably been silent—the state of the present inhabitants of the near neighbourhood of Rome.

In the same vein Mariana Starke wrote of the peasants in Tuscany and Lady Morgan observed local customs at Novi (Starke 1820; Morgan 1821). No doubt much of this was fashionable sentimentality but it did reflect a changing attitude to what constituted "society" in destination regions. The process was further accelerated by the growing numbers of middle-class travellers on the Grand Tour who lacked the social contacts of the landed classes to gain admission to polite society, even if they had wished to.

The location of classical antiquities was always a major determinant of Grand Tour spatial patterns, from the earliest tours right into the nineteenth century. This classical heritage was largely that of the Roman era. Greece was little known until the later eighteenth century; partly because it was firmly under Turkish control (Jenkyns 1980; Spencer 1954). The principal classical remains were in Italy: Rome and its environs, Tivoli, Albano and Frascati, the Appian Way from Rome to Naples, the Phlegrean Fields west of Naples, the amphitheatre at Verona and the bridges and arches at Narni, Fano and Ancona. From the mid-eighteenth century, the discoveries at Herculaneum (1738) and Pompeii (1748) added new classical destinations to the Naples area as did the discovery of the Greek temples at Paestum. The other major centre for antiquities was in France, concentrated in the southern part of the Rhône valley at Vienne, Orange, Arles, Nîmes and the Pont du Gard.

The attraction of visiting classical sites rarely lost its grip on the Grand Tourists. Not only did they help fix a basic tour pattern, but distinct circuits of sites at a local scale were established that were to endure for centuries. One of the clearest of these was the tour of the classical remains west of Naples. A visit to Lake Agnano, the Grotte del Cane, Pozzuoli, Baia and Lake Avernus was part of the late sixteenth-century tour; Misson's guidebook provided a detailed map and description of the area in the early 1700s (Misson 1714) and the same itinerary was being followed in the 1820s (Towner 1984b).

Over time, however, these antiquities were seen in different ways. Until the mid-eighteenth century, the "classical" tourists visited them with a mixture of wonder and pleasure at seeing reminders of a civilisation that lay at the centre of their own world. The remains were studied with great care, inscriptions noted down, dimensions recorded in minute detail. Joseph Addison's tour of the early 1700s was typical of the sentiments expressed. As he followed the Appian Way he enthused:

> The greatest Pleasure I took in my journey from Rome to Naples was in seeing the Fields, Towns, and Rivers, that have been described by so many Classic Authors, and have been the Scenes of so many great Actions.

> (Addison 1761:115)

From about the 1760s, the tourists' journals reveal a changing attitude towards the classical past and its remains, especially amongst the influential taste setters such as poets and novelists. So although the locational pull exerted remained as strong, the attractions underwent a re-evaluation. Remains became appreciated for their evocation of a vanished civilisation and their romantic and picturesque qualities. They were often visited in the evening to heighten the melancholic effect. Samuel Rogers visited the Roman bridge at Narni and "by the grey light of evening contemplated the vast and splendid ruin" (Rogers 1956:206). As always, literary effect was mixed with genuine sentiment.

As well as visiting classical antiquities, the Grand Tourists were keen to visit the principal works of art and architecture in Europe. For much of the Grand Tour era this meant the creations of the Renaissance and subsequent Mannerist and Baroque styles. Until the mid-eighteenth century, British tastes in this field were derived from abroad; Italy and France were the innovators. Native British styles traced from the medieval Gothic period were of little interest to the fashionable elite. It was only with the onset of romanticism that Britain took a lead in formulating fashion and taste and later tourists travelled to Europe with an interest in the medieval legacy of the continent and explored a new set of attractions.

It is important to emphasise that visits to centres of art and architecture were often visits to relatively new developments as well as past creations. In this sense, the physical supply of cultural attractions was expanding, whether in Italy, France or, later, Germany. For the early tourists many of the great Renaissance works in Italy were comparatively recent. St Peter's in Rome was largely a late sixteenth-century creation and quickly became one of the prime objects of a Grand Tour. The activities of Popes such as Sixtus V (1585–1590) and Urban VIII (1623–1644) were transforming the eternal city into a Baroque spectacle, while the newly completed villas at Frascati (chapter 2) and the papal residence at Castel Gandolfo rapidly attracted the attention of travellers (Towner 1984b). In much the same way, the late sixteenth-century villas of Palladio in and around Vicenza soon became part of the tour itinerary between Venice and Verona. The increased attraction of Bologna in the early eighteenth century was partly due to a fashionable enthusiasm for the seventeenth-century painting school of the Carraccis.

That visits to centres of art and architecture were often visits to recent or contemporary developments can be clearly seen in France and Germany. The rise in power and influence of France in the seventeenth century created new objects of interest for tourists outside Italy. Paris and Versailles became major cultural centres with art collections and monumental Baroque styles of architecture. The Louvre Palace was developed from 1624, the Luxembourg Palace in 1625 and, and all, Versailles from 1661. All quickly attracted admiration from visitors.

The gradual shift in wealth and power away from Italy to north of the Alps during the seventeenth and eighteenth centuries had an important influence on the Grand Tour in Germany. As individual German states rose in economic prosperity, so their capital cities were remodelled along Renaissance and Baroque lines. Major art collections were established and so a number of cities began to attract the attention of the Grand Tourists. Early visitors to the region had found little of cultural interest and, in any case, many places had been devastated in the Thirty Years' War (1618–1648). Yet by the 1670s, Edward Brown on his travels noted that recently:

> Buildings have been better modelled and ordered, Fortifications and Outworks more regularly contrived; Convents and Publick Houses more neatly and commodiously built.
>
> (Brown 1677:148)

The construction of the Schönbrunn Palace in Vienna (1695), the Royal Palace in Berlin (1698), the Zwinger at Dresden (1711) and the Nymphenburg Palace in Munich (1714) all contributed to the growing appeal of German cities. Dresden was especially admired for its Baroque architecture and, in the 1770s, acquired a major picture collection. When Düsseldorf similarly gained an art collection (in 1767) the city soon became incorporated in tour itineraries (Towner 1984b).

For early tourists from Britain, the major buildings they encountered on the continent were only to be gazed at in awe and wonder; they far exceeded anything to be seen at home. Thus, Francis Mortoft in the 1650s encountering his first major Italian city:

> Genoa, is a very large and stately Citty, having without doubt as faire and gallant Houses and Pallaces as any Citty in Christendome. When wee first entered into the suburbs, some 3 miles before wee came to the gates of the Towne, wee saw all the way fild with very stately and fine Pallaces, which indeed would make a man wonder how man should be able to contrive such rare and superb buildings.
>
> (Mortoft 1925:40)

Even the Gothic styles of cathedrals like Milan and Siena were acclaimed, such was their splendour. By the 1680s, however, Burnet commented on Milan cathedral that it "had nothing to commend it of Architecture, it being built in the rude Gothick manner" (Burnet 1686:105). But this dislike of the Gothic was relatively short-lived for, within a century, the romantics eulogised the style. In the 1780s, Mrs Piozzi acclaimed Milan's cathedral as "first in all Europe of the Gothic race; whose solemn sadness and gloomy dignity make it a most magnificent cathedral" (Piozzi 1789:55).

Throughout the whole Grand Tour period, travellers showed a considerable interest in the scenery around them. Both urban and rural landscapes were carefully assessed according to prevailing tastes and fashions. From the second half of the eighteenth century landscape, especially that deemed "romantic" or "picturesque", became a primary goal for many tourists, resulting in new regions being discovered and existing regions being re-evaluated (and see also chapter 6).

In an age of busy observation, the early tourists had an extensive list of features to record when visiting towns and cities. They were concerned with the overall plan of the city, the building materials employed, the layout of the streets, the system of fortifications and the general site and situation. The outline shape of the urban area was often recorded; a relatively easy feature to note in an age when the city edge was clearly defined by town walls and systems of fortifications (Figure 5.9). This was always the first task for Fynes Moryson when arriving at

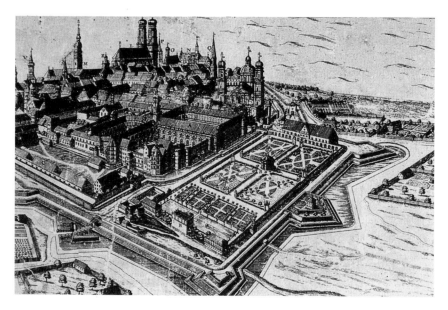

Figure 5.9 "Munich", detail of an engraving after M. Wenig (1701). By the nineteenth century many of the defensive walls were converted into urban leisure promenades (Fiorello H. La Guardia Archives)

a town; Bologna and Florence were essentially circular in shape, Padua was triangular and Verona resembled the outline of a lute (Moryson 1617).

Within the city, a regular or irregular plan was critically assessed. Those cities which were redeveloping or expanding according to Renaissance schemes of broad, straight streets and uniform building styles were generally admired but medieval towns with narrow crooked streets were disliked by seventeenth-century visitors. Mannheim, rebuilt after the Thirty Years War on a regular gridiron pattern, was greatly esteemed as was Turin with its uniform Baroque styles. Further south, Naples was for Burnet (1686:200): "one of the Noblest Cities of Europe . . . the streets are large and broad, the pavement is great and Noble, . . . and it is full of Palaces and great Buildings." Building materials were a significant element in the assessment of a town. The neat brick construction of towns in the Low Countries was praised, in contrast to the old method of timber and plaster. Moryson found Châlons "low and base, being of Timber and Clay" (Moryson 1617,1:401) and Nugent dismissed Ulm as "mean and irregular" (Nugent 1756,2:436). The most admired material was stone and, in this respect, Italian towns had a distinct advantage. Elsewhere, construction varied more widely. In

Germany, for instance, the traveller would encounter the brick of Lübeck and Lüneburg and the stone of Dresden and these would be favourably contrasted with the timber and plaster of Prague and Frankfurt (Towner 1984b). Variations within cities were carefully observed such as the elegant modern sections of Lyon contrasting with its old, wooden and crooked areas. As the Romantic era introduced new sensibilities, however, this aspect of townscape underwent a reappraisal. Narrow winding streets and crooked timber-framing lent a picturesque tone to the scene. Visiting Frankfurt in the 1820s Dorothy Wordsworth preferred the old gabled parts of the town to the "dull regularity" of the newer developments (Wordsworth 1941).

The general site and situation of a town was always recorded. James Howell, in his *Instructions for Forreine Travel* (1642:21), advised the following scheme:

> At his first coming to any Citie he should repaire to the chief Church (if not Idolatrous) to offer up his sacrifice of thanks that hee is safely arrived thither, and then some have used to get on the top of the highest steeple, where one may view with advantage, all the Country circumjacent, and the site of the city, with the advencies and approaches about it, and so take a landskip of it.

In the early tours, cities were often seen as contrasting favourably with surrounding rural areas and were signs of human progress (Tuan 1971). This urban–rural contrast was particularly clear in parts of Germany where cities and their garden-like peripheries of agriculture rose, like oases, from barren wastes. Thus, Nürnberg was praised by tourists because the industry of its citizens had made it rich in contrast to the untamed nature around it (Moryson 1617; Brown 1677). The later romantics, however, saw things in a different light. They looked out from the city assessing its attractiveness in terms of the surrounding scenery. Whereas Francis Mortoft had focused on the internal attributes of Genoa in his appraisal of the city, Thomas Martyn and Mariana Starke were later to praise its magnificent setting rather than its palaces and houses (Martyn 1791; Starke 1800). Similarly, John Owen saw the beauty of Florence as lying in the vistas of surrounding country glimpsed at the end of its streets (Owen 1796).

The Romantic era also brought to the tour a fashionable anti-urban sentiment. The neat and orderly towns of Flanders and the Low Countries began to lose their appeal. While Nugent (1756) found Antwerp "so beautiful and uniform", the arch-romantic William Beckford complained of being "pent in by Flemish spires and buildings, no hills, no verdue, no aromatic breezes" (Beckford 1928:15). A dislike of towns and cities was a minority taste but it was a reflection of a shift in balance of admiration from town to countryside.

The ways in which the landscapes through which the tourists travelled were to be viewed and assessed always received careful attention. Misson's (1714,1:590) Grand Tour guide provided a detailed assessment of scenery and road conditions in Italy and his classification of landscapes provides not only some insight into the close observation of rural scenery that a tourist might make but also the unsentimental way in which it might be viewed:

*	Denotes a Country and a Road indifferently fine and good
**	A Road better than the Former
***	An extraordinarily fine Road, and fertile Country
X	Bad Road in bad Country
†	Difficult Road in a Country either bad or good
‡	Road extraordinarily bad
–	Plain or even Country
^	Mountain
H	Eminences or little Hills
R	River
P	Bridge and River
L	Lake
F	Forests

Figure 5.10 is a summary of Misson's assessment of the routes in Italy. It shows clearly how the flat northern parts of Italy combined good roads with fine scenery as did small areas around Florence, Rome and Naples. Mountainous central Italy suffered by contrast with its poor roads and what was then considered unattractive scenery.

The *Gentleman's Magazine* provided a more simplified method for recording the landscape (Figure 5.11). It suggests that even by the later eighteenth century, an essentially compartmentalised view of scenery prevailed, not searching for the total effect but assessing a view by its constituent parts.

Between the sixteenth and the earlier part of the eighteenth centuries, scenery was closely observed but rarely formed the main object of a journey. Rural landscapes were generally evaluated in terms of their productiveness and a sharp distinction was drawn between fruitful and humanised scenes and barren and mountainous landscapes. Regions such as the plains of Lombardy in northern Italy, the Low Countries, the Rhône valley, the Foligno area of central Italy and the Campania around Naples were especially admired (Towner 1984b). Evelyn (1955,2:324), in the mid-seventeenth century, considered Campania "the most fertile spot that ever the sun shone upon" while for Nugent (1756,3:145), Milan stood "in one of the most fruitful and pleasantest plains in Europe".

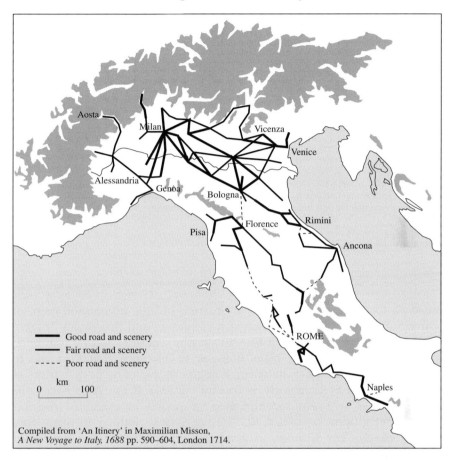

Compiled from 'An Itinerary' in Maximilian Misson,
A New Voyage to Italy, 1688 pp. 590–604, London 1714.

Figure 5.10   The nature of the roads and scenery in Italy (1688)

Grosley's (1769) trip from Venice to Padua was through an "earthly paradise". After travelling amongst hills and mountains, travellers frequently lavished praise when arriving in fertile areas. Lombardy was a welcome relief from the Alps and the area around Foligno a delight after the Apennines. Of the latter, the Earl of Perth enthused: "It lookt like a bason of flowers and greens, for the hills seemed to surround it, one's fancy cannot exceed the beauty of this delightful valley, and no spot of ground can be more rich" (Perth 1968:74).

Barren and mountainous landscapes were just as strongly despised. The rocky Riviera coast, the barren "desert" Mountains of Radicofani between Siena and Viterbo, and the sandy north German plain were always criticised. Edward Brown (1677:146) travelling towards Hamburg

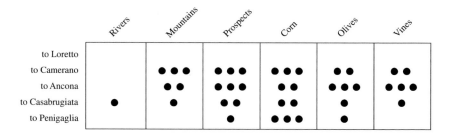

	Rivers	Mountains	Prospects	Corn	Olives	Vines
to Loretto						
to Camerano		● ● ●	● ● ●	● ● ●	● ●	● ●
to Ancona		● ●	● ● ●	● ●	● ● ●	● ● ●
to Casabrugiata	●	●	● ●	● ●	●	●
to Penigaglia			●	● ● ●	●	

"Set down the names of all the parts or places where you are to change horses, and opposite to them make columns for what remarks you choose to make; then, by dotting with a pencil as the objects present themselves, you form an exact description of the face of the country; for example, from Loretto to Ancona, in the above table, appears to be a mountainous country, beautiful in prospects, and abounding in corn, olives, and wines."

from a letter "On Foreign Travel", the *Gentleman's Magazine*, June 1783 p.501

Figure 5.11   Recording the landscape, c.1780

noted "a Country for the most part barren, of little accommodation, or scarce anything remarkable". Between Hannover and Brunswick Nugent (1756,2:235) observed only "a few villages in a desert" and he reminded tourists in Italy crossing from Bologna to Florence that "we are to observe that the country between Bologna to Florence is as barren as that on the side of Lombardy is fruitful" (3:324). If the Alps had to be crossed it was an event accomplished as quickly as possible. Misson's (1714,1:158) guidebook observed: "I have almost nothing to relate concerning Savoy. The Country is generally mountainous, and we found hardly anything remarkable in that Part of it thr' which we pass'd."

Landscape was evaluated in terms of human progress and travellers such as Addison (1761) and Burnet (1686) viewed many scenes in terms of the governments and ideology they reflected. Burnet contrasted the prosperity of Protestant Switzerland having few productive landscapes with the poverty of Catholic France and Italy and similar observations were made about the deprivation in the Papal possessions around Rome contrasting with the prosperity of the more progressive rulers of Tuscany.

By the 1730s and 1740s, however, the beginnings of an appreciation for wilder scenery become apparent in the tourists' accounts. This gradual change in taste has been attributed by some authors to the Grand Tour itself, forcing travellers into intimate contact with wild nature (Hussey 1927), or improvement in travel conditions (Manwaring 1925). More convincingly, Nicolson (1959) links a new love of mountains to the scientific revolution of the seventeenth century, which, by revealing a vastly expanded universe, began to encourage a feeling of awe when contemplating the greater objects of the earth itself (see chapter 6).

As early as the 1680s some travellers noted with pleasure mountainous scenery as a backdrop to a view; Burnet (1686) at Chambéry referred to an "entertaining prospect" and Addison in the early 1700s commented: "[Geneva] has its view bounded on all sides by several Ranges of Mountains, which are however at so great a Distance, that they leave open a wonderful Variety of beautiful Prospects" (Addison 1761:258). Nevertheless, it was not until the later eighteenth century, under the full influence of the Romantic movement, that the spatial patterns of tours began to change and reflect the quest for dramatic scenery. Clear examples of this trend can be found in Switzerland and in central Italy. In Switzerland, Grand Tours of the 1770s and 1780s show the development of "scenic tourism" with Geneva as the centre for a circular tour to Chamonix and the south shore of Lake Geneva. Tours based on Lauterbrunnen, Grindelwald, Thun and Interlaken evolved as well as a circuit of lakes Lucerne, Zürich, Walensee and Konstanz (Towner 1984b). A tour of Switzerland as a subcircuit of the Grand Tour was firmly established by the later eighteenth century and wild areas like the Jura also began to be explored. This new taste for mountain scenery created a reversal of earlier tastes, for while seventeenth-century travellers lavished praise on Lombardy after crossing the Alps, romantic tourists enthused about the approaching mountains, having crossed a plain where there was "little to please my eye, but the eye of an agriculturalist" (Matthews 1822,2:45).

While purely barren landscapes in Italy, such as around Radicofani, continued to be despised, many other regions rose in estimation. Unlike Nugent, 40 years before, Adam Walker (1790) considered the journey between Florence and Bologna "romantic and beautiful". The quest for romantic scenery also opened up new areas in Italy. Until the later eighteenth century, the preferred route between northern Italy and Rome lay along the Adriatic coast to Ancona before crossing the Apennines (Figure 5.4). Then, quite quickly, tourists switched to the route through Umbria visiting Perugia and Arezzo. These medieval towns and rolling hills became more desirable than the flat coastal plain and, although there is evidence of some road improvements acting as an incentive (Herbert 1939), changing landscape tastes seem to have been of greater significance in causing a new route pattern to emerge.

The River Rhine provides an example of an established Grand Tour route that underwent re-evaluation. For early tourists the Rhine was simply a convenient routeway northwards through Germany to the Low Countries. But the romantic tourists saw the journey in a very different light, enthusing over the "abrupt romantic views" (Walker 1790). In order to reach the area as quickly as possible from the Channel, travellers began to avoid the Low Countries and headed further south directly to Brussels and Cologne. The Low Countries also suffered because their productive landscapes, evidence of the successful conquest of nature (Howell 1642), were now seen as dull and uniform (Frye 1908; Bernard 1815).

A final element in the landscape that tourists were influenced by comprised the "natural curiosities" such as waterfalls and volcanoes. As with so many other aspects of landscape, they too underwent a process of re-evaluation. For early tourists these curiosities were sites of great scientific interest, to be examined closely, to be measured, and for their origins to be debated. Fynes Moryson (1617:24) explored the Falls of the Rhine at Schaffhausen, "passing with huge noyse and ending all in fome". John Evelyn (1955:355) closely inspected Vesuvius, "one of the most stupendious curiosities in Nature", and Misson (1714) spent time trying to estimate the height of the waterfalls at Terni. But forms of scientific assessment were of no interest to romantic tourists. It was the *effect* on the senses of dramatic scenes which counted. For Mrs Piozzi (1789:419), Terni produced "a thousand senses of sublimity".

Although a variety of cultural interests determined the main patterns of the Grand Tours and transport systems directed the particular routes selected, a number of other factors can be seen to have had an influence on where tourists went at particular times. Significant amongst these were the effects of wars and diseases.

The European wars from the mid-sixteenth century to the end of the Napoleonic wars in 1815 had varying effects on tour patterns. Some conflicts, such as the War of Spanish Succession (1701–1713), Austrian Succession (1740–1748), Seven Years' War (1756–1763) and French wars (1792–1815) tended to close down widespread continental travel but, very often, tourist routes were diverted to other regions rather than travel prevented altogether. The French civil wars (1562–1595), for instance, deflected tours to Italy via Germany while the Thirty Years' War (1618–1648) virtually closed Germany to tourists and they travelled to Italy via France instead (Towner 1984b). Problems were also created at a more localised level. England was at war with Spain from 1588 to 1604 and, as Spain had possessions in Italy at Milan and Naples, this caused problems for tourists. Fynes Moryson (1617) had to pass quickly through Milan for fear of discovery by the Spanish. A complicating factor for early tourists was fear of the Inquisition and Venice provided a valuable safe haven for Protestant travellers with its policy of religious toleration (Sells 1964). The impact of the Inquisition, however, rapidly declined as a problem for visitors during the seventeenth century.

Tourists were generally aware of the likely onset of war and the regions likely to be affected. In 1740, as the War of Austrian Succession was about to break out, Thomas Gray (1909,1:75) wrote from Italy: "You see we are now coming northward again, though in no great haste; the Venetian and Milanese territories, and either Germany or the south of France (according to the turn the war may take)." Generally, tourists were given time to leave areas where war was declared and, until Napoleon (who imprisoned visitors in the early 1800s), allowed three months for departure. The relative calm with which travellers selected their routes was reflected in their willingness to pass close to the theatre of war itself. Mrs Radcliffe, the romantic novelist, skirted the French border along the Rhine in 1793–94 and her travel account was full of the excitement of nearby fighting (Radcliffe 1795).

If war did close down much of Europe for the tourists then they sought out new destinations. During the Seven Years' War Lord Breadalbane wrote from Taymouth in Scotland: "It has been the fashion to travel into the highlands, many have been here this summer, I suppose because they can't go abroad" (Holloway and Errington 1978:63).

When the French revolutionary wars had a similar effect, tourists explored the Mediterranean area, protected by the Royal Navy, and visited Sicily which had been occupied by the British in 1800. Travel always resumed very rapidly after peace treaties were signed and war was regarded as a matter for governments and armies. There seems to have been little residual hostility between populations.

Grand Tour itineraries were also temporarily influenced by outbreaks of disease, particularly the plague. John Reresby reached Lyon in 1656 intending to visit much of Italy. He learnt, however, of severe plagues in Rome, Genoa and Naples (Cipolla 1981) and so confined his visit to Padua and Venice before retreating northwards to Germany as the plague spread from Rome (Reresby 1904). On his return journey he was forced to skirt Wesel and Dordrecht because of localised plague outbreaks in the two cities. Edward Wright's tour coincided with the last major European outbreak of plague, in southern France from 1720 to 1722. He travelled back to England from Italy via Germany instead.

Malaria had a longer term but more localised effect on travel. Rome and other cities in southern Italy were particularly hazardous during the summer months and this influenced the seasonal migration of both affluent locals and visitors to the surrounding hills or into northern Italy. Outbreaks of fever occurred right into the nineteenth century and Thomas Barlow (1836) needed a cholera certificate before entering the Papal States in 1835.

Other localised hazards included attack by bandits. Two particularly difficult areas were the sea voyage between Marseille and Genoa, with the dangers of Barbary corsairs, and the land route between Rome and Naples. Although the coastal pirates were largely removed during the eighteenth century, bandits between Rome and Naples were a recurring problem. After a quiet period between the late seventeenth century and the late eighteenth century, the dangers increased again and were especially difficult near Rome in the 1820s (Towner 1984b). Even so, these hazards rarely diverted tourists, they were an inconvenience rather than a deterrent, and the road between Rome and Naples was always one of the busiest of the Grand Tour routes. Most visitors would have endorsed John Raymond's (1648:113) view that:

> The voyage from Rome to Naples, though it bee the most dangerous passage in Italy, because the wayes are so throng'd with Bandites, yet in the upshot it proves no lesse requisite to mindes inquisitive in the Roman Antiquities, no lesse delightfull to men that would see the Wonders of Nature, than any other in Europe.

Temporal patterns

As well as its distinctive spatial patterns, the Grand Tour over its 300-year period showed distinctive temporal patterns. These can be traced in such features as the start of a tour, the seasons for travelling and staying in particular places, the length of stay in those places, the daily routine of travel and the total length of a continental tour.

From the later sixteenth century, right up to the 1820s, there were two very clear seasons for starting on a Grand Tour. These were April and May and late August–September. Very few tours started in either summer or winter (Towner 1985). The reasons for these two pronounced peaks are not entirely clear, though they can be related to factors such as climate, the London fashionable season and certain popular festivals in places such as Rome and Venice (Figure 5.12). Richard Lassels' (1686) guidebook suggested leaving for Europe in the autumn after a summer's tour of England and the *Edinburgh Review* in 1806 pointed to the influence of university terms and the London season:

> At the close of every term, our universities send forth their raw productions to be exported in abundance to the continent; and no sooner is the season for fashionable gayety concluded in London, then the roads are covered with "tourists" and "travellers".

> (*Edinburgh Review* 1806:35)

Figure 5.12   (*opposite*) "A Regatta on the Grand Canal, Venice" by Canaletto in the eighteenth century. Spectacular events such as this attracted affluent visitors from across Europe (Bowes Museum, Co. Durham)

If a Grand Tour commenced in spring after the London or provincial season, it would also be the first opportunity to travel after the poor winter road conditions. An autumn departure meant that the Alps were crossed before the winter snows and the tourists could avoid summer travel in southern Europe. Many tourists aimed to be in Rome for Christmas and Easter and Venice for Ascensiontide to witness the many celebrations and festivities in the two cities. Patterns for returning to England were never as clear, although May and October were the most common times.

When examining the seasons for travel within Europe and the seasons and length of stay in particular places, a distinction can be drawn between transit centres visited en route, and the main destination centres which formed the principal goals of the Grand Tour. At a continental scale, seasonal patterns in northern Europe can be related to the departure times from England and the crossing of the Alps in autumn. In Europe north of the Alps, travel occurred throughout the year despite the problems of German roads in winter. Many tourists simply struggled (and grumbled) through the poor conditions (Towner 1984b). In Italy, however, there was a much clearer seasonal pattern to travel. Most tourists moved around the country during the winter months, especially further south around Rome and Naples, and they tried to ensure they were in the northern regions by the onset of summer. The growth of excursions in Switzerland in the later eighteenth century also showed a distinct seasonal pattern. Most tours took place during the summer months from July to September and were sometimes extended to a tour of the north Italian lakes.

A seasonal pattern for staying in particular places was very marked. This could be seen in transit centres such as Lyon, Geneva and Turin. Most tourists were in Lyon in September or October before crossing the Alps. Gailhard (1678:140) described the city as "the great gathering Rendezvous of all those who intend for Italy". A similar seasonal pattern could be found in Turin where tourists gathered in October after crossing the Mt Cenis pass. Geneva had a similar trans-Alpine season but, by the 1820s, had also developed into a summer base for tours of Switzerland (Towner 1984b).

The main Grand Tour destination centres were Paris, Venice, Florence, Rome and Naples. Paris had two seasonal visitor peaks: April and September. As the city was generally the first centre visited on a tour, these two peaks reflected the departure date from Britain. Venice had a pronounced visitor season between May and June during the spectacular Ascensiontide festival. Because of its northern location, however, the seasonal fluctuations at Venice were not so marked as for cities further south. Rome and Naples had very clear seasonal patterns. Rome was busy during March and April for the Easter festivities and again in December and January for Christmas. The very clear reasons for being in the city at these times were combined with very clear reasons for not being there during the hot and unhealthy summer months. In Naples, climatic reasons seemed to dominate the visitor season. Tourists clustered there between December and March but the city was rarely visited in the summer months. Florence, on the other hand, had a rather complex seasonal pattern. There were peaks of visitors in August and November and fewest in May and June, but overall the fluctuations were not pronounced. The city was possibly seen as not too hot in summer for those retreating from the south but being attractively warm for winter visitors (Towner 1984b). Some centres, such as Rome and Naples, also had local migration patterns. During the summer months both visitors and affluent local residents might move to the cooler hills to the east of Rome or to the coast at Sorrento south of Naples.

North of the Alps, seasonal patterns for staying in the major destination centres in Germany and Austria were less clear. Vienna seems to have been visited more frequently during the winter months but otherwise, as with travel in general, visitor seasons do not seem to have developed as clearly as in other parts of Europe.

An important part of Grand Tour temporal patterns was the overall length of stay in particular places. Certain centres dominated the time spent abroad. Rome, Florence, Naples, Venice and Paris were pre-eminent in this respect with stays of three or four months or often longer. Apart from these centres, the fortunes of others fluctuated. Saumur and Tours in the Loire valley were very significant in the seventeenth century with their educational academies but they later faded from the picture. In the early eighteenth century, Turin's court and academy attracted some tourists to stay for long periods but it gradually lost its appeal and simply became a short-stay transit centre (Eustace 1815; Spence 1975; Sharp 1767). At the same time, other places became more significant. Some of the new and fashionable German courts like Vienna, Dresden and Berlin attracted lengthy visits in the mid-eighteenth century while Switzerland as a whole changed from being a region through which to pass quickly to a region where two or three months in the summer would be spent.

The daily routine of travel for the tourists is worth noting because it emphasises the point made earlier that the tempo of a Grand Tour did not vary greatly over its 300-year period. This was an era of slow but not necessarily leisurely travel. On their journeys, most tourists rose early and arrived late at their destinations. In averaging 26 miles a day between London and Turin in 1754, the Earl of Cork and Orrery claimed, "you cannot call us dilatory travellers" (Boyle 1774:44); yet this pace was not dissimilar to times taken by Anglo-Saxon pilgrims (Parks 1954). Lady Miller, in France in the eighteenth century, left every morning at 5 a.m., and Mrs Piozzi travelled all day and night across Germany. As late as 1823, David Wilson (1825:95) recorded:

> We generally rise in the morning at five and start at seven, and so a stage of 4 or 5 hours, sixteen or eighteen miles; dine at twelve, or half past, staying 3 hours; and then take our second stage of four or five hours, till seven or eight; then we drink tea or sup, as we like, and retire to our rooms at nine.

Faster journey times were simply achieved by non-stop travel. In 1835, Thomas Barlow arrived in Padua at 6 a.m., left immediately for Ferrara, arriving there at 4 p.m., departed immediately for Bologna and arrived there at 10 p.m. (Barlow 1836). He did not appear to have seen very much of Italy.

Finally, the total length of time spent on a Grand Tour showed a distinct trend over time. There was an almost continuous decline in the length of Grand Tours so that three years or more in the seventeenth century reduced to two years or more in the eighteenth century and fell to sometimes only four or six months by the 1820s. Individual tours, of course, fluctuated around this average considerably; middle-class tours were generally shorter than aristocratic tours. Faster forms of transport had little to do with this decline in time. The reductions were achieved by spending less time in the various centres in Europe, particularly the transit centres. Destinations like Rome, Florence and Naples tended to retain lengthy periods of stay while much of the rest of the tour became composed of one or two night stops (Towner 1984b).

The contemporary tourist industry

The amount of information available from tourists' journals and letters as well as from guidebooks, enables something of the nature of the tourist "industry" that supported the Grand Tourists to be pieced together. The tourist industry can be considered as the firms, organisations and facilities which served the specific needs of tourists as well as incidental enterprises where tourists formed just one component of total clientele (Leiper 1979). Throughout most of the Grand Tour era, the tourist industry can be considered as being of this incidental type. With the exception of one or two transport services and forms of accommodation it was not until the 1820s and 1830s that clear signs of larger scale tourist services can be discovered. Until then, the Grand Tourists used the accommodation, transport and information services available to all travellers in Europe.

In the area of accommodation provision, the early tourists were evidently a small proportion of travellers and so they used services created for other purposes. Early guidebooks, in fact, saw themselves as serving a range of demands. Rowlands' (1576) guide claimed to serve "Gentlemen, Marchants, Factors or any other persons disposed to travaile" and Wadsworth's (1641) was "Usefull for all Gentlemen, who delight in seeing forraign Countries; and instructing Merchants where to meet with their conveniences for trade".

Over time, despite the usual tourists' complaints about accommodation, a number of centres and individual inns emerged which had a good reputation. Misson's (1714) guide recommended Nürnberg, The Hague and Frankfurt as well as the "Star" at Padua and the "3 Kings" in Milan. Furthermore, some cities developed their own distinct areas for accommodation. In Paris, in the seventeenth century, the Faubourg St Germain catered not only for the French nobility but also for wealthy visitors (Jeffreys 1742). In Rome, the area around the Piazza di Spagna developed early on into a centre for tourists and other visitors to the city. By the early nineteenth century, Florence emerged as a notable place for its good standard of accommodation. A Scotsman, Collins, provided lodgings in the early part of the eighteenth century (Baillie 1911) but later on Vaninis and Schneiderff's had an international reputation and Mariana Starke (1820) considered that Florence had the best hotels in Italy. At Secheron near Geneva, Jacques Dejean responded directly to the tourist trade and had built up a considerable name by the later eighteenth century. His "L'Hotel d'Angleterre" provided a courier and carriage service throughout Europe. He catered especially for the British, some of whom found it "à l'Anglaise to a defect" (Lemaistre 1806). In Calais, another enterprising hotel owner, Dessein, bought and resold carriages to travellers for their European tour. Between 1766 and 1776 he was reported to have made a fortune of £50 000 (Lambert 1950).

Tourists' comments about accommodation generally improved over time, particularly in the larger centres; but rural inns encountered en route seemed to have remained very poor. Some areas responded quickly to specific tourist demand. Apart from Dejean at Geneva, hotels and inns in Basle, Berne and Lausanne were highly praised and Switzerland established a reputation for good accommodation during the later eighteenth and early nineteenth centuries. Chamonix, until 1770, provided only a lodging with a local curé but two inns came in the 1780s; the "Ville de Londres" and the "Hotel d'Angleterre" and another was added in 1815 (Towner 1984b). German accommodation, having been disparaged in earlier periods, had improved greatly by the 1820s;

Augsburg, Cologne, Dresden, Hamburg, Nürnberg and Frankfurt were particularly praised by travellers (Towner 1984b).

When tourists planned to stay in a city for any time, however, they usually moved into rented accommodation. This was a practice fully developed during the sixteenth century. Fynes Moryson (1617,2:332) observed that: "all the Cities of Italy have many houses wherein strangers may hire Chambers called Camere locanti" and in Rome the Piazza di Spagna area was the main centre for renting accommodation. At one stage in the eighteenth century much of this business was in the hands of an Englishman called Taylor and Tobias Smollett (1979:250) observed that: "Strangers that come to Rome seldom put up at public inns, but go directly to lodging houses, of which there is great plenty in this area."

In these rooms and apartments tourists would arrange for all the usual services to be provided by a household of servants (Baillie 1911). As the wealth of the continental aristocracy declined in the early nineteenth century, a number of their palaces became converted into ready furnished lodgings for visitors (Starke 1820). The economic decline of Venice, in particular, ensured a steady supply of this form of accommodation in the city (Ritchie 1832).

Most of the transport services outlined earlier served a variety of travellers. The post, stagecoaches, *trekvaart* and *veturino* services were all part of the general transport system and the Grand Tourists simply provided extra custom. But the 100 porters at Lanslebourg who carried travellers over the Mt Cenis pass could expect a profitable time when a party of Grand Tourists arrived. Joseph Spence's party required four porters for Lord Middlesex, six porters for the Duke of Kingston, eight porters for Kingston's governor and four porters for Spence himself (Spence 1975). But this trade disappeared when the pass was converted to carriage use between 1803 and 1810, creating local unemployment problems (Brockedon 1828–29).

New services geared entirely to tourists were created elsewhere in the Alps, however. At Martigny, 30 guides with 70 mules awaited tourists to take them into the mountains (Cobbett 1830), while Lausanne had a brisk trade in supplying carriages for Swiss tours in the summer and Italian tours in the winter (Wilson 1825). The popular ascent of Vesuvius had long provided employment for guides who would pull visitors by ropes to the top of the mountain. Elsewhere, transport in the form of mules would take tourists to the waterfalls at Terni or into the hills around Tivoli. Many of those developments came in the later eighteenth and early nineteenth centuries and they indicate an informal local response to visitor demands.

The early nineteenth century also saw the growth of more widespread transport services geared entirely to the needs of tourists. These were long-distance inclusive packages for tours to Switzerland. Sometime before 1820, a Mr Emery, operating from the "White Bear" in Piccadilly and Cockspur Street, Charing Cross, undertook to transport passengers to Switzerland in sixteen days, including two in Paris. The fare included lodgings, food and all transport (Ebel 1820). Together with innovators like Dejean and Dessein, Emery was clearly a precursor of developments later to be refined by Thomas Cook.

The Grand Tourists used an extensive range of informally organised services for information and advice and for transferring money around Europe. Diplomats and bankers were important sources of information to travellers who would generally call upon them as soon as they arrived in a centre. The British diplomatic service was thus part of a network of "ports of call" around Europe. In the sixteenth century, England had representatives in France, Venice, Vienna and the Low Countries. Sir Henry Wotton, the ambassador in Venice in 1604–1610 and 1616–1623, provided an "open house" for visitors from Britain (Sells 1964). It was not until the late seventeenth century onwards that a more extensive system of ambassadors, envoys, residents and consuls spread throughout the continent (Lachs 1965; Horn 1961) but they quickly became a significant part of the Grand Tour. Horace Mann, envoy to the Florentine court from 1738 to 1786, was much visited by tourists. Lady Grisell Baillie (1911:395) advised her grandson, "if Mr Mann is still Resident here he will conduct and take care of you in everything". At the Palazzo Manetti, Mann held weekly receptions for visitors as well as providing a coffee house atmosphere where friends could meet and letters be forwarded (Moloney 1968). Sir William Hamilton, British minister in Naples from 1764 to 1800, performed a similar service for British tourists further south, though it is possible that his wife, Emma, was the main attraction for some visitors.

Bankers throughout Europe also provided a range of services to the Grand Tourists. They could help with finding lodgings (Pottle 1952–55), forwarding baggage, and general advice and information. One banker in Geneva provided weekly assemblies for English visitors (Mayne 1909). By the 1820s, large banking firms such as Herries were providing lists of their agents abroad who would be able to proffer advice and assistance to the tourist (Reichard 1829) but the main role of the banks was, of course, to transfer money for visitors in Europe. Two systems were in use from the sixteenth century: bills of exchange and letters of credit. With both systems, money deposited in London with a merchant provided bills which could be exchanged for cash with the merchant's contacts abroad. The system seems to have worked very well with few complaints from tourists.

The important task of viewing the cultural attractions of an area, especially antiquities and works of art and architecture, required guides and the concentration of wealthy visitors at certain centres stimulated the growth of employment in this activity. According to Misson (1714), Venice was the only city in Italy which did not have guides. Rome, especially, was full of *cicerones* who as Evelyn (1955,2:214) noted in 1644, "get their living only by leading strangers about to see the Citty". Before the mid-eighteenth century most guides to the antiquities in Rome were Italian but, after that, a leading role was taken by expatriate Scots (Skinner 1966). As well as existing in established tourist places, it is notable how the opening up of new tourist areas quickly attracted local guides. Chamonix by the 1820s had 40 guides in the area, all under the control of a magistrate, and they apparently could earn very large wages (Wilson 1825).

Information could also be gained from the extensive provision of maps and guidebooks. The mapping of European countries developed in the sixteenth and seventeenth centuries and detailed maps of regions and provinces followed (Harvey 1980). Maps of direct use to travellers indicating post routes and other roads came with Tavernier's map of the post roads of France in 1632, later to be up-dated by the Jaillots' in 1716 (Fordham 1925). Otherwise post routes, itineraries and roadbooks appeared in the form of extensive lists. Guides to individual towns appeared before 1600 for cities such as Venice, Verona, Milan and Florence. Pompilio Totti's (1638) *Ritralto di Roma moderna* was intended for pilgrims but could be used by secular visitors also (Barwick 1904; de Beer 1952). By 1700 most Italian towns had guidebooks and by 1800 town guides were common throughout Europe.

Specialist guidebooks developed for the Grand Tourists themselves began to appear. Thomas Nugent's *Grand Tour* (1749 onwards) was the most comprehensive and others included Misson's guide (1714) and Lassels (1686). Published tourists' accounts were also used as guides such as those of Burnet (1686) and Addison (1705). During the early nineteenth century these guidebooks became less descriptive and more practical. Mariana Starke's (1820) work reflected this trend but the real developments came in the 1830s with the efforts of Murray and Baedeker.

While there is very little direct evidence of the impact of the Grand Tour on host societies, there are some indications that the effects may have been quite noticeable at a local level. For instance, there are many references in the tourists' accounts of prices rising in particular visitor centres. Montpellier, an important health resort, was considered to be prosperous due to the tourist trade. James Fall (1931:61) in the 1680s noted that "the town draws a great profite by them" and Smollett (1979) in the 1760s felt it was the most expensive town in southern France. Lemaistre (1806,2:81) in Naples in 1803 wrote: "The great concourse of English families has rendered all the conveniences of life extremely dear; and since I have been here, Naples has been more expensive than either London or Paris."

Prices also seem to have fluctuated with the tourist season. The cost of lodgings in Rome could fall by a half once the Easter season had finished (Matthews 1822) and prices in Pisa were always lower in the summer "off-season" (Pennington 1825). Furthermore, areas that declined in popularity became cheaper. As the Loire region became less important, so prices fell. By the time Thomas Pennington was in Tours and Blois in 1818 he found prices much lower than in England (Pennington 1825). Many of these variations were extremely localised. Verona, less popular than Florence, was cheaper to stay in by the early nineteenth century. But by the 1830s it does seem that tourism was beginning to have not just localised economic impacts but wider regional effects. Murray (1838:xix) claimed that tourism was a vital part of the Swiss economy, "of the same importance . . . that some additional branch of industry or commerce would be", and he pointed out that Swiss innkeepers were often very wealthy and rose to positions of political importance in their areas.

The souvenir trade also brought employment and wealth. There was always an extensive and important art trade, especially in Italy (Ford 1974; Haskell 1959; Sutton 1982), as well as local mementoes (Towner 1984b). Nugent (1756,3:389) recorded that in Capua: "The country-people dig a large quantity of medals in this neighbourhood, the most valuable they sell to virtuosos in the neighbouring cities, and the refuse they offer to travellers." Shops in Portici and Naples sold specimens of lava (Martyn 1791) while souvenir craftsmen in Rome did a brisk trade during the winter season (Morgan 1821). Forsyth (1813:239) in Rome in 1802 referred to "an inferior class of artists who work chiefly for the traveller".

The lack of information from the "supply-side" of the Grand Tour system means that these estimates of the nature of a tourist "industry" and its likely local and regional impacts must come from visitor accounts. Opinion varied from journal to journal and, until more research is done on the provider groups, any consideration of the likely impacts of a numerically small, but financially strong, group of visitors on local and regional economies must remain largely speculative.

This chapter has highlighted a number of aspects of the Grand Tour of Europe. It was the first episode in international tourism for which there exists an extensive body of primary information, although much of this information tells only part of the story. Emphasis has been given to processes within Britain that created a strong travel culture; a culture that was reinforced by the tourists after they returned from their travels. This context is as important for understanding the Grand Tour as the activities of the travellers during the tour itself.

As the social elites of Europe moved out to the peripheral areas of Spain, Portugal, Greece and the Near East, or created exclusive enclaves within Europe, the tradition of Grand Touring of Europe's cultural centres was taken over by the Americans who, in essence, followed the established tour circuit (Baker 1964; Dulles 1964; Strout 1963). By the mid-nineteenth century, a Grand Tour was but one of many forms of travel for pleasure in Europe and yet the appeal of a cultural circuit of the continent has persisted in modified form right to the present day. Indeed the term "Grand Tour" is still used by marketeers in the travel industry to evoke an image of refined and cultivated travel.

6

The search for wilder places

the 4 Sunday we attended morning prayers and the preaching; at 4 o'clock
we left for Penreathe [Penrith] whose situation can be regarded as beautiful
and agreeable, if one considers it moreover in relation to the frightening
wastes, the stony places, and the highlands which are in all the remaining
part of this country.

(De Blainville 1703:28)

we got in in the evening, travelling in a post-chaise from Penrith, in the
midst of a gorgeous sunshine, which transmuted all the mountains into
colours, purple, etc, etc. . . . Such an impression I never received from
objects of sight before, nor do I suppose I can ever again.

(Lamb 1802; in Simmons 1969:165)

A period of 100 years intervened between these radically different sentiments for the same area of the English Lake District. They were noted in
private diaries and letters rather than being addressed to a wider public,
yet they reveal a profound change in attitude towards the wilder scenes
of nature. This change was to lead, from the mid-eighteenth century
onwards, to the "discovery" of new regions for tourism and a taste for
particular forms of landscape which have persisted right through to the
present age.

Until the first half of the eighteenth century, the preferred rural landscape was generally a humanised scene of cultivation; evidence of the
successful control of nature. Fertile and productive land was directly
beneficial to people and beauty and fruitfulness thus went hand in hand.
This attitude was not confined to Britain and could be found throughout
Europe. The influential eighteenth-century French naturalist and philo-
sopher, Buffon, enjoyed scenes of well-ordered nature with moors, fens
and forests being won for cultivation (Glacken 1960) and the journals of
travellers both in Britain and abroad largely reflected these opinions as
different scenes were viewed from a carriage window or from astride a

horse (Baridon and Chevignard 1988; see also chapter 5). As the eighteenth century progressed, however, a taste for wilder scenes developed—mountains, gorges, waterfalls, forests—and this was to draw visitors into the peripheral regions of Britain, Europe and later North America. These romantic and picturesque conceptions evolved in Europe, inspired by figures such as Rousseau, whose writing on unspoilt nature and society appeared in *La Nouvelle Héloïse* (1759) and *Emile* (1762). In *The Reveries of a Solitary* (1778) Rousseau declared: "No flat country, however beautiful it may be, ever appeared so to me. I need torrents, rocks, firs, dark woods, mountains, rough tracks to climb up and down, precipices by my side to give me a nice fright" (quoted in Hampson 1968:205). Eventually, areas with these characteristics were to acquire a special status, to be protected and conserved as national parks and reserves; first in the USA and Canada and later in Europe.

This chapter considers the implications of this change of attitude. New patterns of tourism were created with the search for a new set of attractions not previously found on the tourist map. At the same time, a new set of values was accorded to places as they became re-evaluated. The changes in attitude concerned a whole range of landscapes, from the fully humanised to the wild and untouched. Thus although part of the focus here is towards the further end of that spectrum of landscape which Tuan (1971) envisaged extending from the city, to the garden, to the wilderness, it also embraces human artefacts such as ancient ruins, castles and abbeys and the historical associations which become attached to place. Furthermore, a particular interest here is on "eras of discovery" rather than the subsequent eras of established patterns. Therefore I am more concerned with the processes of "opening-up" new locations than the developments which took place once a tourist flow was well established. Discovery eras are often passed over rapidly in studies of tourism where there is a preference for moving on to periods where visitor numbers can be quantified more clearly. Although most of the following discussion is confined to Britain and North America, similar changes were taking place in Europe for which there exists a relevant literature (for instance: Adhémar 1938; Charlton 1984; Green 1990).

A number of issues need to be considered for tourism "eras of discovery". First, the change in taste for wilder landscapes took place at different times in different places. Thus the process cannot be neatly pigeonholed into particular periods. Second, this change took place at different times for different social and cultural groups. Innovators such as artists and writers influenced particular circles and new ideas were not adopted wholesale across society at one time. Another issue concerns the geographical locations where new tastes were formulated. What was happening in the new destinations, such as the Lake District or the Catskills, depended on processes evolving elsewhere. In fact the taste for wild nature is often portrayed as an essentially urban feeling. This, then, leads to a consideration of likely variations in attitude to places between visitors and local inhabitants just as there were variations in attitudes to scenery in the home country compared to that found abroad. Evaluating the relative merits of landscapes at home compared with foreign lands influenced the growth of tourism within Britain in the eighteenth century just as it was later to stimulate tourism within the USA in the nineteenth century.

The first part of this chapter reviews a number of explanations which have been suggested for changing tastes in scenery, before turning to Britain and considering where and when new forms of tourism took place. This is followed by a study of North America, comparing and contrasting the process of re-evaluation with the British experience.

Changing landscape tastes

The search for explanations of a change in landscape tastes must inevitably recognise that a whole range of interrelated factors were in operation and that many of them had a reciprocal role in both stimulating and reflecting a growing enthusiasm for less cultivated scenes. Four broad themes are suggested here:

- Movements in science, philosophy and religion which, from the seventeenth century onwards, influenced attitudes towards the relationship between humans and the natural world.
- The influence of art, literature and travel on developing aesthetic tastes for landscape.
- The role of transport technology in lessening the hazards of travel and improving access to peripheral and isolated areas.
- Social, economic and related environmental changes associated with increasing urbanisation and the spread of cultivated landscapes.

Thomas (1983) has suggested that an important cause of change in human attitudes towards the natural world was the rise, during the seventeenth century, of the study of natural history. Methods of classifying natural phenomena became less anthropocentric and more objective; utility and relationship to man became less central (see, for instance, the work of John Ray 1691). There was also a growing appreciation for the sheer diversity of nature, which did not have to be continually related to human purpose. At the same time, studies of geology were emphasising the great age of the world and the profound changes which had occurred long before the arrival of humans. Scientific enquiry through exploration was also revealing extensive areas of the planet—mountain ranges, forests and deserts—which did not immediately seem to serve mankind. Seventeenth- and early eighteenth-century travellers saw themselves as part of this information-gathering enterprise (see chapter 5) and Adler (1989) has argued that this new emphasis on observation in travel was a precursor of later forms of tourism where the objective collection of information was replaced by objectifying visual senses into the rules of picturesque taste and travel.

Astronomy was also changing human horizons. As the earth was shown not to be the centre of the universe, so the relative insignificance of mankind in an ever expanding cosmos questioned the notion that the world was solely created for the use of human beings. These ideas were intertwined with contemporary debates in theology which were also rethinking the relationship between people and the natural world. The orthodox Christian view was that the earth had degenerated and been deformed since the Creation and that mountains and other "useless" aspects of nature were all products of this change. As late as 1681, Thomas Burnet's *Sacred Theory of the Earth* upheld this belief, considering mountains the "very Rubbish of Noah's Flood". Other theologians, however, increasingly maintained that the earth was not imperfect and that mountains were all part of God's design. Indeed, during the eighteenth century, mountains, especially, were to be accorded a form of spiritual value with the belief that to be among them was to be brought closer to the Creator.

The scientific revelations of the seventeenth century and the decline of religious objections to non-utilitarian nature are considered by Nicolson (1959) to be a fundamental reason for the growth in admiration for mountainous scenery which was to gain momentum during the eighteenth century. She argues that the awe once reserved for God was transferred to the vastness of the universe and hence to the greatest objects on earth: mountains, oceans and deserts. But other factors were also at work in this process and threads of evidence from the closely interrelated worlds of art, literature and travel help to illuminate taste in landscape. They both provide evidence for changing attitudes to the landscape and were, themselves, part of that process of change. In Britain, art and literature not only show how a new taste for wilder nature was evolving but, through the forms in which this process took place, emphasise the growth of more nationalistic schools which were part of a critical phase of national "self-definition" (Andrews 1989). This had implications for the growth of domestic tourism in Britian for, as discussed in chapter 5, the cultural "centre" of the nation began to move from classical and renaissance Italy to Britain itself. Part of this changing cultural emphasis was the discovery of the landscapes of home.

Landscape painting and drawing have long been used as evidence for landscape tastes. Clark (1949) and Rees (1973) consider landscape painting as an expression of the relationship between humans and nature and they trace the change from the symbolic representations of landscape in medieval art to the realistic portrayals in the Flemish and seventeenth-century Dutch landscape schools. Later, the eighteenth-century English landscape tradition popularised landscapes and thus painters, in an aesthetic sense, helped in the "discovery" of new places. The influence of the seventeenth-century Italian school of Claude, Poussin (generally not referring to Nicolas Poussin but to his brother-in-law Gaspard Dughet, who adopted the Poussin name) and Rosa was considerable and Manwaring (1925) and Hussey (1927) linked this development to travel, arguing that continental tastes in landscapes were brought back to Britain through the art collections of the Grand Tourists. Thus, this school of thought has stressed the role of the artist in forming tastes, not simply reflecting them, helping to sharpen perceptions and develop aesthetic awareness (Andrews 1989; Herbert 1988, 1994).

The images that artists captured were not simply confined to a very small clientele either. Picturesque and romantic views could be disseminated amongst a wider middle-class audience through the production of topographical prints (Russell 1979); a process which was itself all part of the eighteenth-century commercialisation of leisure (see chapters 2 and 4). Certainly, in England, landscape painting evidence does suggest a growing appeal of more rugged scenery from the later seventeenth century. Early hints come from works such as Henry Peacham's *The Art of Drawing with the Pen and Limning in Water Colours* (1612), which linked the pleasure of landscape painting with the collection of notable prospects gathered through travel, and Edward Norgate's *Miniatura or the Art of Limning* (1649), which enthused over wild scenery (Ogden and Ogden 1955). At this time, however, Peacham and Norgate were still looking primarily to Italian landscapes for inspiration rather than scenes within their own country. It was not until the later eighteenth century that the mountains of Britain began to appear before the public and the more overtly Italianate vision began to wane. Then a British school of painting represented by figures such as Richard Wilson, Thomas Gainsborough, Paul Sandby, Thomas Smith of Derby, Francis Towne, Thomas Rowlandson, John Cozens and later John Constable and Joseph Turner captured British landscapes, some of which became sights for discerning tourists (Andrews 1989; Bicknell 1957; Grigson 1975). Paul Sandby's watercolours of the Falls of Clyde, for instance, helped to popularise that area when they later appeared in print form (Holloway and Errington

1978; Thomas 1983). Art, travel and the search for picturesque views reached its most explicit form with the work of William Gilpin, whose travels, writings and illustrations from the 1780s attempted to define what constituted a picturesque scene worthy of viewing. In essence, Gilpin's picturesque landscape required variety and ruggedness and the major centres he championed included the Wye Valley, the Lake District, North Wales and parts of the Scottish Highlands (Gilpin 1782, 1786, 1789, 1809). Amongst an educated public, the correct appreciation of a picturesque scene was a matter of significant debate (Hipple 1957), the absurdities of which became neatly satirised by Jane Austen in *Sense and Sensibility* (1811) and *Northanger Abbey* (1818).

Like art, literature has also been closely examined for evidence of landscape tastes (Andrews 1989; Barrell 1972; Malins 1966; Newby 1981; Williams 1973). Poetry, essays and novels have helped to form and also reflect new attitudes to nature. Particular influence has been claimed for James Thomson's poem *The Seasons*, which appeared between 1726 and 1730 (Andrews 1989; Wilton 1980). Joseph Warton observed in 1756:

> The "Seasons" of Thomson have been very instrumental in diffusing a general taste for the beauties of *nature* and *landscape*. It is only within a few years that the picturesque scenes of our own country, our lakes, mountains, cascades, caverns and castles, have been visited and described.
>
> (quoted in Andrews 1989:9)

As with painting, a national school of literature grew in the eighteenth century, favouring native medieval Gothic and Celtic themes, redis-covering Shakespeare and Milton rather than venerating classical models. Together with art, it reinforced the process of cultural self-definition, without which there would have been no desire for the leisurely exploration of one's own country. In this way Wordsworth and the Lake Poets celebrated the beauties of the Lake District and Walter Scott popularised the Scottish Borders and parts of the Highlands through his poetry and prose (Drabble 1979; Holloway and Errington 1978; Newby 1981). Eighteenth-century essays helped form notions of good taste in landscape (Parks 1964) for the upper and middle classes and *The Spectator, The Tatler, Critical Review, The Connoisseur, Gentleman's Magazine* and many other periodicals contained advice on travel and viewing scenery (Towner 1984b). Indeed, it was the *Gentleman's Magazine* in 1748 which drew attention to the lack of exploration of Britain's landscapes:

> If our great ones were, previously to their crossing the sea, to be better acquainted with the beauties and rarities of their own Britain, they would not be so imprudently fond of such as merit less regard.
>
> (*Gentleman's Magazine* 1748,18:561)

To art and literature must also be added the influence of anti-quarianism, which developed in seventeenth-century Britain, and which explored the relics of Britain's past, its own ancient monuments, and so fuelled a growing awareness of the country's cultural and scenic attractions. The work of figures like John Aubrey (1626–1697) and William Stukeley (1687–1765), was part of the discovery of Britain (Piggott 1950). To antiquarianism must be added the growth of regional descriptions of Britain which included Camden's *Britannia* (1586) and Dugdale's *Antiquities of Warwickshire* (1656) (Butlin 1990), and the increased production of maps and road books such as Ogilby's *Britannia* of 1675. Consequently the "travel culture" which evolved in Britain from the seventeenth century, which was formed in the wealthy and educated societies of London and provincial centres, and which initially revolved around the Grand Tour (chapter 5), began to include tours of Britain as well as tours to the continent (Dent 1975).

The production of road books, country maps, descriptions and guide-books helped to build up the general infrastructure of travel (Vaughan 1974) and improvements in transport conditions have formed another broad theme for explaining changes in landscape tastes. The argument is that as a consequence of having safer and easier journeys, travellers were likely to regard mountains and difficult terrain with more pleasure than discomfort. Clearly, improvements in transport and travel infra-structure were important in developing tourism in regions *after* a new taste in wild nature had developed (Jakle 1977). But it is more difficult to see a decisive influence in those critical eras of discovery which are the main concern here. We have already seen that on the Grand Tour, tourist routes were altered in the eighteenth century to explore the Alps and central Italy before any road improvements and, as Moir (1964) points out, poor roads did not prevent the early explorations of Britain. Furthermore, Thomas (1983) argues that improvements in transport do not explain the taste for scenery as such; they can only explain how more people ultimately came to see it. Buzard (1993) makes a related point by linking technology to the type of visitor, with minimal influence on the adventurous traveller but greater effect on the succeed-ing, more cautious, tourist. Separating cause and effect is ultimately bound to be difficult but it does seem that the earlier arguments of Manwaring (1925) and Hussey (1927), who tried to relate changes in landscape taste directly to improvements in transport, were too sim-plistic and that a complex process of interrelationship between cultural change and technological change was at work.

A final, wider theme can be seen as providing a context for many of the ideas examined so far. The social, economic and physical environ-ments within which people lived, worked and played in Britain and

North America were being transformed, especially from the early eighteenth century, through the processes of urbanisation and agricultural improvement. These changes have also been felt to have contributed to alterations in attitudes to nature (Thomas 1983; Williams 1973). Throughout the eighteenth century, towns in Britain were expanding both in number and size, so that urban dwellers were a significantly growing minority. In 1700, less than 20 per cent (1 million) of the population of England and Wales lived in towns of over 2500; by 1800 this had risen to 30 per cent (over 2½ million) (Corfield 1982). At the same time, the growing industrialisation of towns overshadowed the notion of the city as a civilised centre of learning, culture and manners. Instead, the countryside began to embody idealised images of simplicity and purity, so that the love of rural landscapes became a strong urban-bound sentiment (Williams 1973). In North America a similar process, though at a later date, was at work (Huth 1957; Nash 1967).

Change in the countryside itself reinforced these ideas. In 1500, about 45 per cent of agricultural land in England and Wales was enclosed, by 1760 this had risen to at least 75 per cent (Yelling 1990), with the reclaiming of marshes, fens and heaths for arable land. But of course, actual figures are not critical. People *felt* that there were widespread forces changing the world around them. The spread of regular patterns of enclosure led to the idealising of the informal and picturesque scene (Thomas 1983). As people moved from the land, so there was an increased sense of separation of agricultural production from areas of consumption which heightened the division between the practical and the aesthetic assessment of landscape. As Williams (1973:120) observes: "A working country is hardly ever a landscape. The very idea of landscape implies separation and observation." An urban-based intellectual society and a prosperous landed society could afford to indulge in the aesthetic consumption of scenery, supported as they were, ironically, by the profits from agricultural change and expanding trade and commerce. Agricultural improvement also contributed to the notion of wilderness in North America. Veneration of the wilderness was intimately bound up with the westward march of the frontier and the humanised landscape which followed in its wake (Nash 1967).

There seems to be general agreement that the taste for wilder landscapes was developed amongst an elite; the wealthy and educated in society with their attendant circle of artists and writers. In fact, the scientific and aesthetic approaches to nature produced a gulf between educated and popular culture from the seventeenth century onwards. Furthermore, Thomas (1983) and Nash (1967) both make the crucial point that the new taste for the picturesque and romantic had to be *acquired*; it was not intuitive. Aesthetic appreciation required a knowledge of literature, art and history, so that enjoying the "correct" landscape became a form of social distinction. Generally, the new tastes were formulated where most of the visitors originated: London, the fashionable watering places and provincial centres of Britain and the growing towns of the eastern seaboard of North America, together with the country houses and estates which all formed part of the elite's lifestyle (see chapter 5).

Inevitably, contrasting attitudes to landscapes arose between the local populations of the newly discovered tourist regions and the visitors. This was observed at the time. Alison, in 1790, commented that visitors saw features in the landscape in terms of "majesty", "solemnity" and "terror", whereas for the locals they served "only as topographical distinctions, and are beheld with the indifference such qualities naturally produce" (Thomas 1983:264–265). These contrasting views were common in the Lake District of the later eighteenth century (Andrews 1989) and could also be found elsewhere. In Wales, there was a considerable time lag between the appreciation of harsh landscape by English visitors or Welsh landowners and native Welsh culture. Welsh verse, right through the eighteenth century, continued to celebrate landscape in terms of human activity, production and skills, and romantic legends attached to place were often pure inventions by entrepreneurs in the incipient tourist industry. The story surrounding the grave of a dog at Beddgelert in Snowdonia was devised by the local innkeeper. It was not until later in the nineteenth century that the Welsh came to see their mountainous regions as symbolising an essential ingredient of their culture (Morgan 1983).

The discovery of Britain

A general increase in travel for pleasure can be detected from the sixteenth century in Britain, although it did not attract the prestige associated with travel abroad (Moir 1964). Early travellers' accounts reveal, for the most part, a predictable taste in scenery: delight in fertile rural landscapes and praise for trade, production and the energy and enterprise of towns and cities. The oft-quoted views of Celia Fiennes, travelling through Britain from the 1680s (Hillaby 1983), and Daniel Defoe in the 1720s (Defoe 1724–6), probably typify the general educated assessment of Britain's scenic attractions. Places such as the Lake District were passed through with comments on their barrenness except for the occasional signs of industry and fruitful agriculture. There is little hint in journals such as these that, within a relatively short space of time, new patterns of tourism were to be created through a virtual *volte face* of aesthetic judgements.

Certain areas were particularly associated with the "discovery" of Britain's scenery during the eighteenth century: the Wye Valley, North Wales, Derbyshire, the Lake District and parts of Scotland. Three of these regions—the Wye Valley, Lake District and Scotland—will be examined in more detail and the processes involved in their discovery and initial development for tourists discussed.

The Wye Valley on the Welsh borders, especially the deeply incised stretch of the river which runs between Ross-on-Wye and Chepstow, combined a number of elements which appealed to visitors seeking picturesque scenes and romantic historical associations. The steeply wooded banks, the series of changing vistas, ruined castles such as Goodrich and Chepstow, together with Tintern Abbey, coincided exactly with the new landscape taste. William Gilpin, who came to the area in 1770 and published his account of the scenery in 1782 (Gilpin 1782), is often credited with the discovery and promotion of the area. In fact, the Wye Valley was appreciated before Gilpin, in the 1740s, by figures such as John Egerton, Bishop of Durham, and the Revd Davies whose poems in 1742 praised Tintern Abbey (Andrews 1989). By 1770, when Gilpin and the poet Thomas Gray came, there were well-organised boat trips on the river. Knowledge of the Wye accelerated in the 1770s amongst connoisseurs of scenery when Gilpin's account was circulated in manuscript form and his description was followed by others such as Heath (1799) and Fosbroke (1818) together with Wordsworth's celebrated poem on Tintern Abbey in 1798 (Wordsworth 1940–1949). Artists were also an important part of the discovery process: Paul Sandby in the 1770s, Day in the 1780s, Turner in the 1790s and de Loutherbourg in the early 1800s. Prints of many of the scenes appeared, separately or in guidebooks, and by the 1820s tourism was well established in the area.

The discovery of the Wye Valley seems to have been principally by outsiders to the area, whose journals, books and prints were circulated to an educated audience. This initial promotion was followed by a small-scale response to demand by some local inhabitants. Thus local boatmen were ferrying visitors up and down the river from the 1740s, a local Monmouth printer produced a guide to Tintern in 1793 and the landlord of the inn next to the abbey became its unofficial custodian. As early as 1770, a poor local population was begging from visitors to the ruins or offering to show them round as guides (Andrews 1989; Ousby 1990). Significantly, this initial phase of tourism did not rely on any obvious improvement in transport access. Visits were made by river partly because, even as late as 1800, the local roads were so bad.

In northern England, the Lake District was to became one of the major areas to benefit from the new taste for wild and romantic scenery. By the 1790s it was the most popular summer excursion in the country (Moir 1964) and tourism had become a useful additional economic asset for a peripheral area which, since the seventeenth century, had suffered decline. The wool trade and mining industries were moving out from the central dales to the periphery, leaving poverty and depopulation (Nicolson 1955; Winchester 1989). At Wasdale, in the heart of the region, the 18 farm holdings of 1578 had declined to 10 in 1750 and only one remained by 1800 (Winchester 1989). Celia Fiennes in the 1690s (Hillaby 1983) referred to the "sad little hutts" she had encountered in the area. Thus the Lake District's traditional resources were in decline just as its new aesthetic resources of lake and mountain scenery were about to be discovered.

Raising awareness of the scenic assets of Lakeland shows an important difference with the process at work in the Wye Valley for, while much of the promotion of the Wye seems to have come from those outside the area, the cause of the Lake District was espoused by people living immediately around its circumference (Woof 1986). This was a group of landed proprietors such as the Lowthers, Howards and Wyndhams, together with a local intellectual society of gentry, doctors and clergymen. Key promotional figures such as Gilpin, Brown, Dalton and West were all from the general region around the Lakes.

Early evidence of praise for the Lake District appeared in 1748 with the reference in the *Gentleman's Magazine* referred to earlier. In the same year, Gilpin's *Dialogue upon the Gardens . . . at Stow* also celebrated its scenery. Gilpin came from Scaleby near Carlisle and his later work on the picturesque scenery of the Lakes (1786) must be seen as a second phase in the opening up of the area to visitors. Other important evidence for a growing enthusiasm comes in the Revd John Brown's letter of 1753 which was circulated in manuscript form until its publication in 1766 as *a Description of the Lake and Vale of Keswick*. The Revd John Dalton's published poem of 1755 also praised the Lakeland scene (Moir 1964; Woof 1986). Brown came from Penrith and Dalton from near Cockermouth. Thomas West, whose *Guide to the Lakes* (1780) became the standard text for the region (10 editions by 1812), lived at Tytup near Dalton in Furness (Rollinson 1967). The most significant enthusiast for the Lakes, Wordsworth, was born in 1770 at Cockermouth but his writings belong to a later phase of promotion. Other notable early events for tourism development in the Lake District included the visit of the poet Thomas Gray in 1769, but his account was not widely circulated until the second edition of West's guide in 1780.

As with the Wye Valley, artists were also closely involved in projecting the new image of the Lake District, although more of them

Figure 6.1   "View of Derwent Water" by William Bellers (1753?). Such landscape depiction represents an early stage in growing appreciation for more "natural" scenes. However, nature forms a stiff and stagelike backdrop to the main interest—the elegantly dressed ladies and gentlemen in the foreground (Provost and Fellows, King's College, Cambridge)

seem to have been outsiders than the first writers. Early portrayals of the scenery, such as Stephen Penn's (1733), show a place where people lived and worked—fishing, farming and transporting—but by 1752, William Bellers's images in engravings show a growing appreciation of the landscape itself (Woof 1986) (Figure 6.1). The view of Smith of Derby (1761) shows a Derwentwater full of drama and atmosphere. From the 1760s, a whole series of artists produced scenes which helped promote an interest in the Lake District's landscapes: George Barrett in the 1760s, Thomas Herne and George Beaumont in the 1770s, Turner, Girtin and Wright of Derby in the 1790s (Bicknell and Woof 1982; Russell 1979; Woof 1986). Views appeared in prints or in guidebooks such as Gilpin's and West's and were therefore widely circulated.

Writers and artists, locally based or coming from elsewhere, raised the awareness of the Lake District for the leisured classes. But they also critically influenced the particular geography of tourism which developed within the Lake District in its first phase from the 1740s to the 1780s. This geography was essentially observation of landscape from a low altitude, confined to a small number of recommended sites. The values accorded to places were their scenic qualities as measured against prevailing standards of picturesqueness. Most visitors arrived from the south via Lancashire and crossed Morecambe Bay. From here, the tours were based on Coniston for Coniston Lake, Bowness and Ambleside for Lake Windermere, and Keswick for Derwentwater. Most of the excursions were for viewing certain scenes only and visitors remained at or near the lakeside and the indicated vantage points. There was little exploration of the hills themselves and little interest shown in other aspects of Lakeland life. This early pattern and experience became highly formalised; tourists carried Claude glasses (convex mirrors which distorted the view to resemble a picture by Claude) and West's *Guide* providing a series of stations, or viewing points, which were also marked on the ground with access cleared and improved for visitors. Thus there was a station at Coniston, Lake Windermere had five, then on to Rydal's station before a circuit of the eight surrounding Derwentwater (Andrews 1989). It is noticeable how many contemporary accounts of visits to the Lake District refer to West and his stations (e.g. Wilberforce 1779; Gell 1797). Beyond the well-defined routes, however, there was little tourist movement and the remoter dales, such as Wasdale and Haweswater, were rarely visited until the 1820s (Walton and McGloin 1981).

During the later 1780s and 1790s, Lake District tourism moved into a second significant phase, creating a new geography with modified patterns and values of place. A notable development was the first signs of hillwalking as a pastime. Some visitors were no longer content with a passive observation of scenery but wished to experience the landscape and this took them away from the standard itinerary. A pioneer was Joseph Budworth who, from 1792, climbed many of the region's mountains and whose account *A Fortnight's Ramble in the Lakes* appeared in 1810 (Nicolson 1955; Rollinson 1967). A second innovation was the addition of entertainments for the less adventurous tourists, for whom scenery was no longer a sufficient reward. Regattas appeared on Bassenthwaite lake in 1780, followed by a whole series on Derwentwater. This same period was also marked by a third development, the increased presence of second-home villas. These were rural retreats for wealthy outsiders drawn by the scenic beauty of the area. The first villa appeared on Windermere in 1774 and lakeside leisure homes quickly spread here and at Derwentwater. With their landscaped gardens and parkland, they were a notable modification to the Lakeland scene (Taylor 1983; Winchester 1989). The process of urban retreat to a rural arcadia, discussed in chapter 2, had now extended to one of the "wilderness" areas of Britain.

Therefore by the time Wordsworth and his Lake Poet friends, Coleridge, Southey, Lamb and De Quincey, were writing about the region, certain forms of tourism were long established. Wordsworth and his circle really belong to the second phase of development which lasted until the 1840s and was symbolically ended by the coming of the railway to Windermere in 1847. Wordsworth's influence on tourism was not only to increase the popularity of the area but also to present a richer view of landscape for visitors than Gilpin's picturesque theorising. For Wordsworth, all nature was to be celebrated; landscape was to be experienced not just observed. This can be seen in *The Prelude* (1805) (Wordsworth 1940–1949) and later in his guidebook to the district which stressed the underlying structure of the area and the effects of light and season. An appreciation and understanding of the countryside would come through seeing it, "as an organic unity and not as a series of pictorial scenes" (Moir 1964:155). Wordsworth's *Guide to the Lakes* first appeared in 1810 attached to another work on the area but it was subsequently published in its own right in 1822, reaching a fifth edition by 1835. The more practical information added in 1842 suggests that tourism to the Lakes was beginning to enter a new era, not of discovery but of reinforcing knowledge of well-known areas.

The second phase of tourism development had impacts on local society, and the poor economic situation of the area no doubt influenced the response to the needs of visitors. Peter Crosthwaite, the son of a local farmer, established a museum in Keswick in the 1790s and sold prints and guidebooks. Prices of accommodation and goods rose in tourist centres, such as Keswick and Ambleside, during the season; sometimes approaching the costs in London (Andrews 1989; Moir 1964). By the later eighteenth century, visitors were beginning to lament a change in attitude amongst the local people, with children, for instance, gathering around carriages hoping for tips (Nicolson 1955). In 1817, the *Westmorland Advertiser* commented on the former "simplicity and hospitality" of local people being changed by "the great influx of strangers [who] destroyed the original character of the natives" (Walton and McGloin 1981:179). Much of this, of course, was based on a romantic ideal of rural innocence but, nevertheless, it does show that 30 years before the coming of the railway, tourism was seen as a powerful agent of social change.

This study of the Lake District suggests that its process of discovery can be divided into two phases: an initial era from the 1740s to the 1780s based on the influence of artists and writers who helped initiate a low-altitude, formalised tour of observation points for scenery, followed, from the 1790s, by greater exploration of the hills themselves and a romantic veneration of landscape which went beyond mere observation, together with a growing provision of tourist facilities and the growth of second homes. In these two phases the role of transport had some influence but was probably not crucial. Improved access to the Lake

District from elsewhere came later in the eighteenth century. The London to Kendal carrier wagon replaced packhorses in 1758 but a map of the turnpike roads shows the Lakes unattached to the national network in 1750. By 1770, they were linked to the national system from both north and south (Thrift 1990) and by 1800, Penrith, Cockermouth and Kendal were important coaching centres (Rollinson 1967). Roads within the Lake District remained unimproved until the middle of the eighteenth century when, in the 1760s, a turnpike was opened which ran through the area linking Cockermouth, Keswick, Ambleside, Windermere and Kendal. No doubt this improved road eased the movement of visitors but it is difficult to agree with Hindle (1989) who sees a direct link between maintained roads and the "beginnings of tourism". As late as 1801, Dorothy Wordsworth felt it was newsworthy to note in her diary, "Today a chaise passed" (Rollinson 1967:127). A more decisive transport influence has been credited to the coming of the railway to Windermere in 1847 which introduced a new social class and new forms of tourism to parts of the southern Lakes during the 1850s. In the northern part of the district major changes came later. Keswick's morphology remained little changed until the mid-nineteenth century, with tourist accommodation and services largely absorbed within the existing settlement structure or scattered beyond the town. Expansion came after the railway arrrived in 1864, when major boarding house development occurred in a block to the east of the old town and leisure facilities such as Fitz Park enhanced the town's attractions (Figure 6.2) (Marshall and Walton 1981).

This section on the "discovery of Britain" concludes by examining the early phases of scenic tourism in parts of Scotland. It would be a mistake to see the growing taste for wild and romantic scenery applying only to the Highlands region and in the first stages of tourist growth, areas south of the Highland line, near Edinburgh, Lanark and the Borders, were very much involved in this process. In many places, it was a combination of scenery with the associations of history and legend that was to make them popular, unlike the Lake District which relied almost exclusively on its natural beauties.

An important aspect of Scotland's tourism discovery phase involved a national cultural re-evaluation. This transformed it, during the eighteenth century, from being perceived as a peripheral part of Britain, where even Scottish intellectual society looked to cultures elsewhere (Skinner 1966), to an appreciation of Scotland as a culture with a romantic Celtic and medieval past and possessing spectacular natural landscapes. Thus the nation's history and scenery became tourist attractions through a coincidence with prevailing educated tastes. That many of the cultural traditions were invented or strongly modified, such

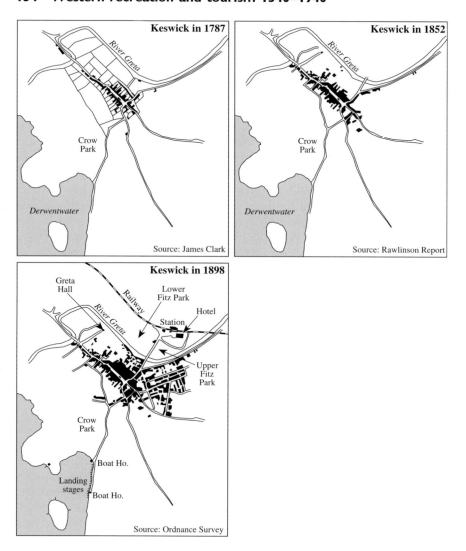

Figure 6.2 The changing morphology of Keswick, 1787–1898

as the myth of the ancient Celtic bard "Ossian" (Trevor Roper 1983), mattered little in the process of raising Scotland's tourist attraction to a high level of interest. Tourism, after all, has never been too concerned with matters of authenticity, and Scotland is still being reinvented by the tourist industry (Hughes 1992).

Early visitors to Scotland focused their attentions on signs of human endeavour in the landscape: towns and cities, trade and improved agricultural land. Most visits were confined to Edinburgh and Glasgow before heading south again, so that by the end of the seventeenth century much of the nation still remained "terra incognita" to the outside world (Hume Brown 1891).

One of the first areas to experience large numbers of visitors was the Esk Valley to the immediate south-east of Edinburgh and within walking distance of the capital. Variety was the key to its appeal with steep wooded banks, rocky scenery at Dryden, Dalkeith Park, the romantic castle and chapel at Roslin and the castle at Hawthornden; a mixture of the visual with historical associations. Hawthornden had a certain early fame as the retreat of the sixteenth-century poet Drummond who was visited there by Ben Jonson, and the area later featured in Allan Ramsay's poem, *The Gentle Shepherd* (1725). John Beugo's poem, *Esk Water* (1797) later praised the valley and Roslin and Hawthornden appeared in Scott's *Rosabelle* in his *The Lay of the Last Minstrel* (1805). But the first visitors to the Esk Valley were the local citizens of Edinburgh, for whom it provided a pleasant summer's day outing, together with the city's group of artists and writers. Thus Roslin Castle was frequently painted and drawn by artists such as Alexander Nasmyth and both Robert Burns and later Turner visited the valley as a matter of course. Through the influence of Edinburgh-based writers and artists, the local recreationists were joined by more distant visitors who included the Esk in their tour of Scotland. The area exactly fitted the rules and theories of picturesque scenery (Holloway and Errington 1978) and travellers including Sarah Murray from London made the customary detour from Edinburgh to the valley, enthusing over "Roslin! Sweet Roslin!" (Murray 1799:27).

The spectacular Falls of the Clyde near Lanark, south-east of Glasgow, was another early site involved in the discovery of Scotland. Here, although it was largely raw, spectacular nature that was the appeal, romantic historical events were soon linked to the area. By the 1790s, the Falls were a well established part of the tourist circuit. Early promotion has been partly attributed to the artist Paul Sandby who was in the area with the English army in the 1740s (Holloway and Errington 1978; Thomas 1983). Sandby's watercolours were later widely circulated in print form and were followed by Gilpin's (1789) observations on the Falls. For Gilpin, part of the landscape's attraction lay in its possible connection with a hideout of the Scottish patriot William Wallace; "these traditional anecdotes, whether true, or fabled, add grandeur to a scene" (Gilpin 1789:73).

The combination of historical association with landscape was a potent force in the rise of the Scottish Border country as a tourist area in the early nineteenth century, especially the area of the Tweed Valley. In pure visual landscape terms, the bare rolling hills lacked enough variety to satisfy observers such as Gilpin in the 1770s or the artist Joseph Farington in the 1790s (Holloway and Errington 1978). But this was Walter Scott's local area and, although it is often dangerous to attribute major changes in perception to one individual, there is no doubt that the writings of Scott fostered a whole new dimension to the Border scenery. *The Minstrelsy of the Scottish Border* (1802–1803), *The Lay of the Last Minstrel* (1805) and *Marmion* (1808) embraced the whole Border region, evoking traditional ballads and romances and legends of the Border struggles. Through the power of historical association, Scott gave the area a new attraction. The ruined abbeys of Jedburgh, Melrose, Dryburgh and Kelso, the medieval castle at Norham and the tragedy of the battle at Flodden Field, exactly suited the romantic sentiments of early nineteenth-century visitors. Through Scott's writings a number of artists were attracted to the Borders and saw them in a new light: James Ward, John Thomson of Duddingston, Patrick Nasmyth and later William Turner. In this way art and literature were effectively combined to add a new value to places which had previously failed to interest tourists.

The gradual discovery of the Highlands region also owed much to Scott's writings although, by the later eighteenth century, a number of visitors were penetrating into remote regions. The naturalist Thomas Pennant (1774) toured the Highlands in 1769, while perhaps the most celebrated journey was that of Johnson and Boswell in 1773 (Johnson 1775; Boswell 1774). In 1792, Sarah Murray, with only a servant, travelled through much of the Highlands and she provided detailed information for visitors in her *Companion and Useful Guide to the Beauties of Scotland* (1799). But it was Scott who added the extra romantic dimension to certain specific places in the Highlands. Murray could delight in the scenery of Loch Katrine in the Trossachs but Scott immortalised it in *The Lady of the Lake* (1810). It was his description which visitors clutched as they were rowed across the water. In the wake of Scott, there came artists such as Horatio McCulloch, in the 1840s and 1850s, who painted scenes of Highland landscapes which mirrored the sentimental expectations of the tourist.

There is insufficient space here, however, to fully explore the complex initial phases of tourism development in the Scottish Highlands (Butler 1985; Lindsay 1979; Youngson 1974). Rather, this section concludes by commenting on the relationship between leading artists and tourists, so frequently stressed in this chapter, as it developed in Scotland during the nineteenth century. Many artists lived or stayed in Edinburgh and journeyed into the distant countryside on painting expeditions, capturing those scenes beloved by visitors. During the later years of the century, however, the artist–tourist relationship began to break down.

Groups of painters such as Guthrie, Hornel, McTaggart, Henry and Walton, collectively known as the "Glasgow Boys", began to react against the grand scenic art of figures like McCulloch, with their stock tourist images of mountain and glen. The new artistic mood was to capture the ordinary, more domestic scenes of everyday life and landscape in small towns and villages, nowhere near the tourist tracks. Thus the "Boys" visited places like Cockburnspath on the Berwickshire coast or Kirkcudbright in Galloway (Billcliffe 1985). In this sense "tourism and serious art had ceased to run together" (Holloway and Errington 1978:164). The majority of tourists were seeking a romantic vision of Scotland, a stereotyped scene of mountain and glen, while artists were increasingly seeking a more matter-of-fact image of the country. Even today, the wider interests of artists such as the "Boys" rarely coincide with the gaze of a later generation of visitors.

Wild nature in North America

The development of an appreciation for wild nature in North America, and its links with the growth of scenic tourism, provides a range of interesting comparisons with the situation in Britain and Europe. At first, attitudes to nature flowed from the Old World, in being at first hostile to the wilderness but then gradually coming to admire it. In the nineteenth century, the wilderness came to be seen as something unique to North America, a defining national cultural symbol, which helped distinguish the New World from the Old. And it was in North America that the earliest moves to legislate to preserve the wilderness originated; an attitude which was slowly transferred back to Europe in a neat reversal of influence.

When William Bradford landed in New England in 1626 he observed nothing "but a hideous and desolate wilderness" about him (Nash 1963:3) and Michael Wigglesworth in 1662 felt that outside the settlements of the coast there existed only:

A waste and howling wilderness,
Where none inhabited,
But hellish fiends and brutish men
That Devils worshipped.
                    (quoted in Huth 1957:6)

The business of subduing the wilderness was an understandable priority for the first European settlers as their very survival depended upon it, but this hostile view remained long after the immediate pioneer conditions were past (Nash 1967). Views of the wild began to change amongst the growing urban intellectual societies of the eastern seaboard; the scientists, artists, and writers who were in close contact with current attitudes in Britain and Europe (Huth 1957). Thus the forces contributing to a rise in appreciation for romantic scenery, outlined at the beginning of this chapter, were transferred wholesale across the Atlantic from one leisured elite to another.

New attitudes to landscape can be discerned in the writings of early travellers in America. William Byrd, on the boundary between Virginia and North Carolina in 1728, enthused over the wild scenery around him as did John Bartram in Pennsylvania in the 1750s. William Bartram expressed "rapture and astonishment" for the wilds of the Carolinas in 1770 and Jeremy Belknap was in the White Mountains in 1792 praising their beauty (Nash 1967). These pioneers helped to spread the romantic ethos and, by the 1840s, the literati of the eastern towns and cities were making excursions into the wilds to collect "impressions". As in Britain, artists were also part of the early discovery phase. Painters were capturing scenes on the Hudson River north of New York City by the 1790s, and were in the Adirondacks by the early nineteenth century. Huth (1957) describes the general pattern of discovery that took place in these areas as follows. First, artists and writers arrived using only local farms and lumbermen's cabins or simply camping for accommodation. These groups then returned to the city with material for their pictures and writings which were subsequently reproduced and published for a wider audience. In the 1840s, "Summer Books" containing travel essays on New England and New York State proved very popular and visits were made to these regions to confirm the sights and descriptions that had been encountered on the page. During the 1820s and 1830s, artists and writers had established more permanent bases in the wild country by constructing summer cottages and these early visitors were charac- terised more by a love of nature and the simple life than by wealth. Artistic colonies sprang up around places such as Lake George and Lake Placid while North Conway in the White Mountains was known as the "American Barbizon". From the 1850s, however, the discovery phase was over in areas like New England with the arrival of wealthy urban dwellers derided by the term "cockneys". The discerning few were driven out and sought refuge on the Canadian borders or further west (Huth 1957).

As in Britain, the taste for wild scenery was a form of social dis- tinction. Nathaniel Hale, in the 1830s, recommended that if parents wished their children to have good taste then: "let them look at, and become familiar with the woods, the wilds, and the mountains" (Nash 1967:60). There were also similar distinctions in attitudes to landscape between visitors and the local population. Early European travellers on the frontier were interested in the scenic qualities around them, whereas the Americans working there had a more utilitarian view. But the practical sentiment towards nature moved west with the frontier; a dynamic process unknown in Europe. The frontier in Michigan was visited by De Toqueville in 1831:

> In Europe people talk a great deal of the wilds of America but the Americans themselves never think about them . . . they may be said not to perceive the mighty forests that surround them till they fall beneath the hatchet.
>
> (quoted in Nash 1967:23)

Until the early nineteenth century then, American attitudes towards the wilds were largely inspired by tastes in Britain and Europe. From about the 1830s, however, a new dimension was added to these sentiments whereby the idea of wilderness was seized upon and glorified as something distinctly North American. Nature was on a scale unknown in Europe and so the wilderness became a national cultural form of identity. What is interesting in this process, however, is the similarity with the development of cultural self-definition which had evolved in eighteenth-century Britain and which underlay the growth of domestic tourism. As Britain's history and scenery were deemed as worthy as that found in Italy, so the wilderness in America was deemed as important as the culture of Europe. Americans were therefore urged to visit their own attractions such as the Hudson River or Niagara Falls. As in Britain, however, there also remained a strong attachment to centres elsewhere amongst the social elite and Americans continued to travel to Britain, France and Italy (Baker 1964; Mulvey 1983) just as many Britons remained attached to the Mediterranean world (Pemble 1988).

There was also a similarity with Britain in the process of tourism development whereby areas which had formerly seemed devoid of romantic historical associations acquired a literature which did much to enhance their appeal. So, just as the Scottish Borders through Walter Scott gained legends and history, parts of the American landscape gained similar attributes. Fenimore Cooper's *The Pioneers* (1823) marked an important early stage in attaching history and legend to place, as did his *The Last of the Mohicans* (1826), which was set in the upper Hudson Valley. Similarly, the work of Washington Irving in "Rip van Winkle" and "The Legend of Sleepy Hollow" (1819–1820) evoked the earlier days of the Dutch pioneers in the Hudson region (Huth 1957; Sears 1989). Irving presented an area which retained its historical past:

it is in such little retired Dutch valleys, found here and there embosomed in the great State of New York, that population, manners, and customs, remain fixed; while the great torrent of migration and improvement, which is making such incessant changes in other parts of this restless country, sweeps by them unobserved.

(Irving 1819–1820:372)

History and legend were also rapidly linked to a process which was happening on a far grander and more dramatic scale than anything in Europe: the westward movement of the frontier. As urbanisation and agricultural settlement pushed back the wilderness, so the frontier quickly absorbed historical place associations. In the Ohio Valley, by the mid-nineteenth century the frontier had only recently shifted further west, leaving behind an agrarian landscape. And yet the romance and legend of frontier life was already a tourist attraction and "many travellers expended as much energy imagining this past as describing the contemporary scene" (Jakle 1977:103).

Although there were many similarities in the processes associated with the development of taste for wilder scenery between Britain and Europe and North America, there were important differences. The moving frontier sweeping across a continent had no parallel in Europe. Also the scenic wonders were on a scale unknown in the Old World. Niagara Falls and the Mississippi River had no equivalents in Europe and visitors struggled to fit them into contemporary aesthetic rules. Previous travel experience was important. Europeans who had seen the Alps found the Alleghenies disappointing, whereas Americans who had not been to Europe were impressed (Jakle 1977). There were also variations in attitudes to the wilderness between Americans and Canadians. Whereas in America, the frontier advanced on a wide front, in Canada only small outposts amongst the wilderness were established. The wild thus remained a formidable barrier rather than a symbol of national identity. Furthermore, Canadians retained closer links with Europe during the nineteenth century and adhered to more European attitudes to nature (Wall 1982a). But perhaps the main difference between European and North American reactions to their wilder country was the rapid move in America towards *preserving* the wilderness. Having adopted European ideas on landscape in the seventeenth and eighteenth centuries, the concept of preserving the wilderness was, essentially, an American innovation. As early as the 1820s and 1830s there were calls for preservation, and Yosemite (1864), in California, became the first area of wild land to be established for recreational use, followed by Yellowstone National Park in 1872 and Niagara Falls Reservation in 1885 (Brockman and Merriam 1973). It is significant that, for the early preserved areas, the main interest was in aesthetic values—the scenery of the landscape, rather than its ecological value (Nelson 1982).

New places for North American tourists

The growing appreciation of wilder landscapes created new patterns of tourism in North America. Figure 6.3 gives an impression of the areas which formed the leisure and tourism system of the eastern USA by the mid-nineteenth century. To the coastal resorts and inland watering places have been added the rural landscapes of the Hudson and Connecticut Rivers and the wilder scenery of the Adirondacks, Catskills, Berkshires and White Mountains together with Niagara Falls and the Ohio Valley. These regions were among the first to be discovered in the earlier part of the century as a result of changing landscape tastes.

The valley of the Hudson River, north of New York City, was one of the earliest of the new places discovered for tourists. A great glacier valley cut through the Catskills, its initial popularity owed much to the fact that it fitted a European-derived model of picturesque scenery. Therefore it was compared to the Rhine Valley in Germany and even to parts of the Scottish Highlands. Indeed, Britons in the Hudson Valley and Americans in the Highlands, wrote very similar descriptive pieces (Mulvey 1983). The standard trip which evolved was up the river to Albany with excursions to the Catskills or further afield to the Adirondacks and the White Mountains. Another early tourist region was the Connecticut River whose scenery appeared in early nineteenth-century dioramas (Sears 1989). An influential publication was Timothy Dwight's *Travels in New England and New York* (1821–1822), which helped to establish many of the attractions of the area. Mount Holyoake, near Northampton, Massachusetts, became a major viewpoint for the valley. Artists and writers were important in the initial discovery and promotion phases of tourism in the two valleys. The English artist, Thomas Cole, painted scenes on the Connecticut in the 1830s and, with friends such as Asher Durand, created the influential Hudson River School of Painters (Cornell 1983) (Figure 6.4).

While many of the New England regions owed their early popularity to a similarity with British and European landscapes, Niagara Falls presented a different situation. The Falls were too vast to fit notions of the picturesque but they were clearly sublime (Figure 6.5). Thomas Moore in 1804 observed: "We must have new combinations of language to describe the Falls of Niagara" (Mulvey 1983:187). An earlier visitor, in 1792, evidently struggled with this problem for, after calculating the dimensions of the Falls, he could only refer to them as "most picturesque" (Clarke

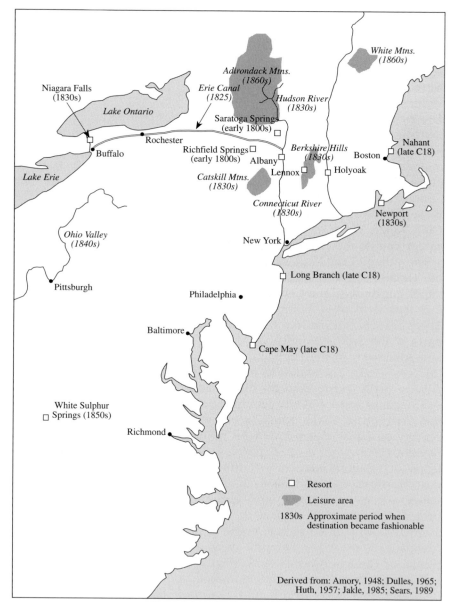

Figure 6.3 The development of selected leisure destinations in the eastern USA by the mid-nineteenth century

Figure 6.4 "View from Mount Holyoke, Northampton, Massachusetts, after a Thunder-storm (The Oxbow)", by Thomas Cole (1836). Such romantic visions encouraged Americans to explore their own country for pleasure (Metropolitan Museum of Art, New York, gift of Mrs Russell Sage, 1908 (08.228))

1974). Later romantics, however, equated seeing the Falls with emotional and quasi-religious experiences. Visits to the area were hampered by British-French and then British-American conflicts until 1814, but after this the exploration phase for Niagara was rapid and short-lived. Getz (1992) estimates that it was over by the 1820s, hastened by the construction of the Erie Canal in 1825 (see Figure 6.6), which brought tourists to nearby Buffalo. By the 1830s, the Niagara area was already commercialised with staged events attracting over 10 000 visitors (Getz 1992; Sears 1989).

Further west, the Ohio Valley was undergoing rapid change and development as the frontier moved through it. From the 1740s, the first English settlers arrived in the Ohio Valley and gradually advanced westwards. Their views of the landscape, as might be expected, were essentially utilitarian. By the early nineteenth century, the first tourists were in the valley, mainly wealthy Europeans and Americans, who came to see what the pioneers had achieved and to record factual information about the regions travelled through (Jakle 1977). This view, however, quickly changed to a more aesthetic appreciation of landscape and an interest in the history and legends of the frontier. Although initial itineraries were fairly *ad hoc*, there seems little doubt that, in this case,

Figure 6.5 "Niagara Falls" by Charles Lyell (c.1845) from his "Travels in North America 1845". Natural scenery on this vast scale was increasingly seen as something distinctively North American, providing images for the tourist unlike anything seen in Europe (Mulvey (1983), *Anglo-American Landscapes*, with permission from Cambridge University Press)

rapid transport innovations quickly influenced the patterns of travel (see Figure 6.6). Before the 1820s, rivers and stagecoaches created a diffuse pattern of movement but the introduction of steamboats on the main rivers concentrated routes and focused attention on major centres such as Cincinnati. During the 1850s, railways had spread across the northern part of the region and visitors were increasingly drawn away from the agrarian states of the south towards the towns and cities further north. In addition, many of the scenic wonders had become "packaged" for tourists. Mammoth Cave, Kentucky, for instance, although nationally known by the early nineteenth century, was little visited until the arrival of the railways in the 1850s when it was firmly placed on the tourist circuit (Sears 1989).

To the north, in Canada's Maritime Provinces, a process of exploration and development was also under way. Here, a distinct time-lag with views prevailing in Europe can be detected. Early nineteenth-century visitors to Nova Scotia valued the landscape in much the same way as seventeenth-century travellers in England. Joshua Marsden, in the early 1800s, found the area, "naked, wild, barren and mountainous" (Moffat 1982:124), and the utilitarian objectives of settlement development

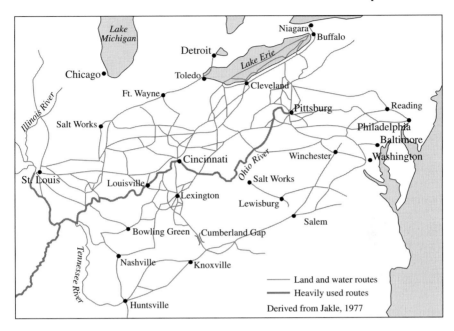

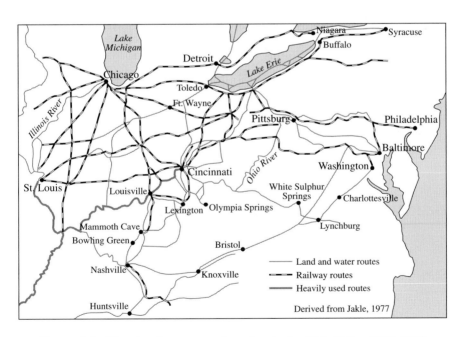

Figure 6.6 The changing pattern of tourism in the Ohio Valley, 1820–1860

prevailed. But although this emphasises that perceptions of wild nature varied with time and place, the transition to more aesthetic evaluations current elsewhere was fairly rapid. This was happening by the 1840s in Nova Scotia as more visitors began to celebrate its rugged scenery. Many of them were naturalists and sportsmen (Sleigh 1853; Hardy 1855) but the healthy climate of the region also appealed to tourists from the eastern seaboard cities of the USA. After this short exploration phase, the development of Nova Scotia's tourism was accelerated by the arrival of steamships from Quebec in the 1840s and 1850s which brought wealthy visitors from America and Britain. Access from other parts of Canada, however, remained difficult until the construction of the Intercolonial Railway in the 1860s (Moffat 1982).

In many parts of North America there was a rapid transition from eras of discovery and exploration to larger scale tourism developments. This happened not only in the eastern regions but also in the West. From being "discovered" in the 1850s, the Yosemite Valley was created a park in 1864. Yellowstone was known by the 1860s and was a National Park by 1872. The stages from exploration, to development, to protective legislation were passed through at a great pace. Contrast this with the experience of wild places in Britain. From discovery in the eighteenth century, to development in the nineteenth century, it took until the early 1950s to create the first National Parks in the Lake District, Peak District and Snowdonia. Scotland has none. The search for wilder places, despite their common cultural origins, has ultimately led to significant differences in the protection accorded to such areas. Although there are clear distinctions in land use and scale between the wild areas of North America and Britain, the New World was far quicker in valuing them as special places of aesthetic and ecological value to society.

7

At the coast: the development of seaside resorts

Few places created for the pursuit of pleasure have received as much attention from scholars as the development of the seaside resort. Geographers and historians have both devoted considerable space to this phenomenon, such that there is a danger that leisure at the coast can sometimes overshadow leisure elsewhere. Nevertheless, there can be little doubt that, from the mid-nineteenth century, the lure of the sea and the consequent creation of seaside resorts have been the most impressive manifestations of the power of leisure to create new landscapes, to shape new patterns of activity, and to generate new social and economic relationships.

Geographers have long had an interest in the seaside resort and E.W. Gilbert's (1939, 1949, 1954) early studies have been succeeded by, amongst others Barrett (1958), Stansfield (1972, 1978), Cosgrove and Jackson (1972) and Pearce (1978, 1987, 1989). A concern with the form and function of resorts has been supplemented by studies of resort evolution in the form of lifecycles and models attempting to link both spatial and temporal aspects of resort regions (Butler 1980; Gormsen 1981). Geographical studies have tended, however, to focus on the resorts themselves, the area of supply, and have paid less attention to the equally important spatial variations in the areas of demand. Some attempt to redress this imbalance is made later in this chapter. For historians, Pimlott's (1947) classic study of English holidays provided a firm basis for research on seaside resorts, which has subsequently been updated by Perkin (1976), Walvin (1978), Walton and Walvin (1983) and especially Walton (1983). Comparisons between developments in Britain and the USA have been provided by Demars (1979), Lewis (1980) and Pearson (1990), while the French historian Corbin (1994) has recently attempted a wide-ranging study of the appeal of the coast in European culture from the eighteenth century onwards. There has also been a host of regional and local case studies of resorts, which include: Cannadine (1980); Farrant (1987); Haug (1982); Jarvis (1993); Liddle (1982); Roberts (1982); Sigsworth (1980); Snow and Wright (1976); and Whyman (1973).

Despite all this research, however, there have been few substantial links forged between historians, geographers and those involved in tourism studies and this has had important implications for an understanding of the development of tourism *per se* (Towner 1988). Tourism researchers have tended to look for broad, general frameworks which summarise historical change in a simplified form rather than revealing its complexity. Gormsen's (1981) model of the "spatio-temporal" development of international tourism can be used to illustrate this point. It attempts to conceptualise the growth of the European seaside from c.1800 onwards and brings together a number of elements such as the spread of resort regions, or peripheries, social class of visitor and the amount of local or outside involvement in resort development. But the model is too simple. For instance, it suggests that most development came initially from outside interests whereas evidence from Britain (Walton 1983), Spain's north coast (Walton and Smith 1995) or Germany (Corbin 1994) points to local groups being the key agents in the early stages of growth. The French Riviera (Haug 1982; Nash 1979; Rudney 1980) may have been developed from outside but this characteristic was far from universal. Similar strictures apply to the model's portrayal of the wealthy as always being the initiators of coastal tourism. This overlooks the prior existence of local popular culture at the seaside (Corbin 1994; Walton 1983) and suggests that one class simply followed the example of others. Yet, as the historian Hugh Cunningham (1990: 312) writes: "We misunderstand the history of the seaside holiday if we think of it as something initiated by the middle class and in due course imitated by the working class." The broad sweep of Gormsen's model is superficially attractive but it conceals the complexity of what was really taking place along Europe's seashores.

In this chapter, the development of seaside resorts is considered through a number of themes which link to the tourism system discussed in chapter 1. Also, a number of the themes discussed here can be related to the processes involved in the development of spa resorts outlined in chapter 4. Although spa and seaside were different leisure places, it is possible, at a general level, to see similar factors operating in their creation. The nature of demand for leisure at the coast is considered in some detail, including both the overall rise in taste for seaside areas and how that demand varied at national, regional and local scales. An outline is then provided of the evolving pattern of supply of resorts in different countries and areas, and this picture is related to local or external agents of development and the role of transportation in these patterns of growth. The more localised factors, those operating within and around the resorts themselves, are then considered, together with aspects of the social geographies that emerged at the coast. A brief discussion then follows on the seaside as a distinctive place; one which combined strong visual images with the capacity to engender strong emotions. These images influenced not only ordinary visitors but also artists and writers and were later to be used by place promoters in the marketing of the seaside resort.

The nature of demand for the seaside

The demand for coastal holidays comprised a whole range of factors. A growing general taste for these locations as places for leisure was allied to health considerations and the changing appeal of seaside resorts *vis-à-vis* the spas. These, in turn, must be related to the role of social class, rising affluence, and the growing popularity of family holidays for which the coast had a particular allure. Such general trends must then be set within specific national, regional and local contexts because the development of demand for seaside resorts was never a geographically uniform process, varying only with social class.

In the previous chapter, the growth of taste for the wilder aspects of nature was considered and it is possible to include the coast and the sea within this type of environment. Thus the changing evaluation of the seaside was part of the romantic taste for sublime effects that increased from the mid-eighteenth century onwards and Corbin (1994) charts a similar range of changing religious attitudes and the influence of artists and writers to that outlined earlier. Coastal scenery, like mountains, was not viewed with any great enthusiasm before the eighteenth century. But during the late seventeenth century, Corbin records the growing appreciation of French poets such as Saint-Amant for cliffs and sea-scapes and the praise of beach scenes by travellers at Scheveningen in Holland. The enthusiasm of Grand Tourists for the Bay of Naples and its classical seaside villas (chapter 5) also forms part of Corbin's argument of the development of seaside taste. Although this evidence is all rather fragmented, there seems little doubt that the changing landscape tastes of the eighteenth century included the coast among the new areas to be explored and admired. The growing aesthetic appreciation of coastal landscapes with their picturesque cliffs, dramatic sea views and ever-changing lights, drew an increasing number of artists and writers to the shore. In Britain, Sandby, Cozens, Constable and Turner were among the most notable of a whole group of artists who contributed to the vast expansion in the number of coastal views that were recorded by the early nineteenth century (Corbin 1994; Grigson 1975). To this aesthetic movement must be added the contribution of science, particularly the amateur interest in geology which encouraged the collection of fossils and shells at the coast.

Grafted onto this growing taste for coastal scenes was the influence of health awareness and a desire to escape from the effects of rapid urbanisation. Health was an important factor in the growth of spa resorts in Europe and North America (chapter 4) and, from the mid-eighteenth century, the claims of the seaside were added to those of spa waters. Increasingly, the medical profession was urging the value of exercise and fresh air, which were easier to obtain at the coast than at inland spas, and this was taken up by a leisure class preoccupied by its own state of health. As early as 1667, Dr Robert Wittie was advising bathing at Scarborough to ease gout (Corbin 1994) and John Floyer's *History of Cold Bathing* (1701–1702), helped to establish a new fashion (Pimlott 1947). By the time Celia Fiennes (Hillaby 1983: 113) visited Scarborough in 1697, the value of the local spa water and the exercise of walking along the beach was clearly recognised: "on this sand by the Sea shore is the Spa Well which people frequent, and all the diversion is the walking on this sand twice a day at the ebb of the tide and till its high tide." Dr Richard Russell's (1752) celebrated *Dissertation on the Use of Sea-Water*, which recommended drinking seawater as a purgative as well as sea-bathing, confirmed what society was already beginning to do. There was a similar situation in France when the Académie de Bordeaux held a debate on the value of seawater as a health cure in 1766 (Corbin 1994). As at the spas, however, the health reason for visiting the coast was soon combined with motives of fashion and pleasure.

The growing wealth in European and American societies in the eighteenth and nineteenth centuries brought an ever-expanding middle class to the spa resorts and this encouraged the social elite to seek out new destinations so that Brighton, for instance, began to rival Bath as the most fashionable place outside London. But this was not a simple process. In Europe, spas retained their fashionable prestige, not only the large ones such as Baden Baden, Karlsbad or Aix-les-Bains, but small centres such as the mountain spas in northern Spain which maintained their regional patronage throughout the nineteenth century (Barke and Towner 1995). Also, within Britain, inland Cheltenham and Leamington were very fashionable in the 1820s and 1830s at the same time as Brighton. Perhaps the seaside resort should be seen as an addition to the leisure places of the elite; a new element to be included in the social round of visits to London, spas, provincial towns and landed estates (chapter 2). Certainly, the forms of behaviour adopted at the spas were initially transferred to a coastal setting, so that Brighton had its season and the cultural trappings of reading rooms, assembly rooms, bookshops, walks and excursions. The coast, however, did become a less rigid and formal social setting and this widened its appeal. It was also more capable of catering for the demands of families and children which became especially important with the middle-class family culture of the Victorian era and a growing recognition of the particular needs of the child (Pimlott 1947; Plumb 1975; Walvin 1978, 1983). The seaside may have been one of the first places that catered especially for children and their leisure.

So far, the rising appeal of the coast has been discussed only in terms of outsiders and has portrayed the coast as a leisure setting largely in terms of the upper classes and artists and writers "discovering" its qualities. At this point, however, it is useful to emphasise the evidence for an older popular culture of beach use which existed independent of the sensibilities of elite culture. Along the coasts of the Baltic, North Sea and Mediterranean there was a tradition of sea-bathing that lay beyond the codified practices of the leisure classes. This custom of "popular sea-bathing" lay within the usual round of collective festivities (Corbin 1994). Thus on the last Sunday in September, villagers in the Basque region would descend to the seashore at Biarritz in an atmosphere "full of shouts, songs, and untroubled, unbridled pleasure" (Bouet 1837, quoted in Corbin 1994: 314). A similar situation could be found at Bordeaux which, again, had a long tradition of popular sea-bathing. On the shores of the Mediterranean it was the peasant classes who bathed for pleasure well before it was adopted by the ruling classes. Travellers to Italy noticed this and, on occasion, imitated the locals. Further north, in Britain, a popular sea-bathing culture existed on the Lancashire coast, not emulating the rich but having "a prior and independent existence" (Walton 1983:11). And later, when working-class visitors from urban areas came to visit the coast, it was generally more a process of transposing their popular urban culture to a new setting than a process of one class imitating another (Cunningham 1990). This long-established popular culture at the seaside did not create the organised development of the coast for pleasure but the tendency to overlook its presence is one of many cases where those who dominate the historical record are assumed to have been the innovators of custom.

The wide range of social classes who used the coast for pleasure was an important distinction from the spas. Part of this wider class involvement in seaside leisure can be related to the general increase in leisure time for the middle and working classes during the nineteenth century, although information on the working day, week and year is very fragmented. General trends in Britain for the working classes and middle classes are first discussed and then national, regional and local variations in demand for the coast by the upper, middle and working classes are considered. For the industrial working classes, the early nineteenth century saw an *increase* in the working day until about the 1830s. Twelve to thirteen hours a day in textile factories, twelve hours in coalmines were common. From 1850 onwards, however, a general decrease in working hours is discernible, so that by the 1870s a nine-hour day was practised, reducing to perhaps eight hours by 1919 (Cunningham 1990). There was also a greater regularity in the working week with a Saturday half-holiday increasingly recognised. But for visits to the seaside it was the change in the working year that was critical and, in this context, it was not the national picture that was important but the regional and local variations in holiday culture that created distinctive patterns of demand for the coast (see discussion below). Official legislation gives a broad idea of increased potential leisure time; the Bank Holiday Acts of 1871 and 1875 provided four days statutory holiday, but before then holidays were common in some areas. As employers also increasingly conceded holidays to their workforces, so local variations became important. Many of these holidays were without pay, however, certainly until after the First World War (Cunningham 1990).

Only scattered information is available for the working hours of the middle classes. Until late in the nineteenth century, it seems that the working hours for the professions and civil service were relatively light: a day from 10 a.m. to 4 p.m. for the civil service, 9 a.m. to 5 p.m. for businessmen. Hours were very long in shops, however. By the 1840s, annual holidays were increasingly common; Bank of England workers were getting six to eighteen days by 1845, and in the 1870s office clerks were taking at least two weeks holiday a year. As might be expected, the working middle classes had more extensive holidays earlier than the working classes, and owners and managers of firms and organisations had even greater freedom.

Demand for the seaside must be considered, however, as it varied internationally, nationally, regionally and locally. At the international level there were differences in the timing of the development of organised sea-bathing cultures. Britain appears to have been an innovator in the 1730s, France followed by the 1780s, Germany in the 1790s and Spain in the 1830s (Walton and Smith 1995). This cannot be entirely attributed to variations in wealth and leisure time; there was also a cultural dimension. Thus, the United States closely followed the British example and had a sea-bathing culture developing by the later eighteenth century, but in northern Germany the localised and work-orientated Prussian culture suppressed the expansion of resorts on any large scale until later in the nineteenth century (Soane 1993).

Within the national picture, the demand for the seaside varied with class and area. If we consider first the upper, or leisure classes in Britain, it is possible to see a level of demand that operated at the national and international scale. Few areas were potentially out of their reach in terms of either time or cost and so they patronised the French and Italian Rivieras for exclusive winter seasons, the resorts of the Normandy coast such as Deauville and Dinard, and enclaves within Britain such as Folkestone and Eastbourne, or the remoter resorts of West Wales and the West Country. Some resorts, such as Allonby in Cumbria, relied on the patronage of the local gentry (Walton 1983). The seaside for the upper classes was always, however, part of a much wider leisured lifestyle which embraced a variety of different places throughout the year rather than being the dominant annual holiday event.

The growing numbers of those who considered themselves middle class constituted a buoyant demand for the seaside in the nineteenth century and their two- or three-week summer holiday visit provided the main stimulant for resort growth in Britain. The constraints of time and money meant that initial demand was generally provincial in nature, so that the coasts nearest the main urban centres, especially London, were the early beneficiaries. Thus London generated middle-class visitors to resorts in Kent, through Sussex and down to Weymouth in the South West, while in the north the middle classes were served by Scarborough, Blackpool and Southport. Bristol merchants were served by Weymouth and Lyme Regis and later Weston-super-Mare and Clevedon. Wealth and demand were not always simply related and there were some regional cultural variations. The prosperous classes of Birmingham, for instance, developed a strongly localised inland urban culture which was not purely a reaction to lack of access to the coast (Walton 1983). During the nineteenth century, middle-class demand became less provincial and, fuelled by increased wealth, time and improved communications, spread out to cover virtually all the seaside resorts of Britain.

Working-class demand for seaside holidays was always the most constrained geographically and local and regional work practices, wage rates and adherence to local leisure practices were always far more varied than for other social groups. These led to significant variations in demand for visits to the coast and Walton (1981) has identified six types of area in England and Wales where these differences could be found:

1   The Lancashire textile towns.
2   The woollen districts of the West Riding of Yorkshire.
3   Areas of well-paid piece work for craftsmen, such as Sheffield and Birmingham.

4   Less prosperous areas of factory and workshop economies, such as the Potteries and Black Country.
5   Areas of mining and heavy industry.
6   Other areas of southern and eastern England.

The Lancashire textile towns formed a centre of demand which stimulated the first specialised working-class seaside resort development in Britain (Walton 1981). Figure 7.1 summarises this holiday system in terms of demand factors and their location, access routes in the form of cheap railway travel, and the location of the resorts. There were a number of reasons for high levels of demand for seaside holidays in this region. First, there were opportunities for sizeable family incomes to be earned in the form of high levels of employment and wage rates, not just for adult males but for females and the young. The cotton industry in the later nineteenth century provided fairly regular and reliable employment. Furthermore, within these areas there was a tradition of self-help with saving and mutual insurance schemes which, in the form of "going-off" clubs, encouraged saving for holidays. In addition to income, the communities of the cotton towns achieved blocks of consecutive holiday time before other working-class industrial societies in Britain. The local fairs and wakes survived the introduction of the factory system and employers came to accept the tradition of regular holidays from the 1840s. These increased in length so that by the late 1880s Oldham and Darwen had achieved a week's summer holiday and were soon followed by Chorley, Nelson, Burnley and Blackburn. A regular working week for the rest of the year helped to discourage surplus income being spent on pleasures nearer to home.

This growing ability to take holidays away was made even more effective by the fact that the textile towns took their holidays at different times. Thus, a steady flow of tourists arrived in the resorts from early July to early September and Blackpool and Morecambe as well as centres further afield such as Douglas, Isle of Man, and Rhyl responded by investing in accommodation and entertainments.

Elsewhere in England, working-class demand for the seaside varied with economy and culture. The woollen district of the West Riding of Yorkshire closely followed Lancashire in forming a seaside holiday habit although lower family incomes and less tradition of coastal visits meant that it lagged about ten years behind. Traditional holidays had survived the factory system and there was also that local tradition of thrift and mutual assistance. The favoured resorts for holidays were Scarborough, Morecambe and Blackpool.

Away from the textile economies of the north, other variants in demand emerged. In the steel industry of Sheffield workers were well

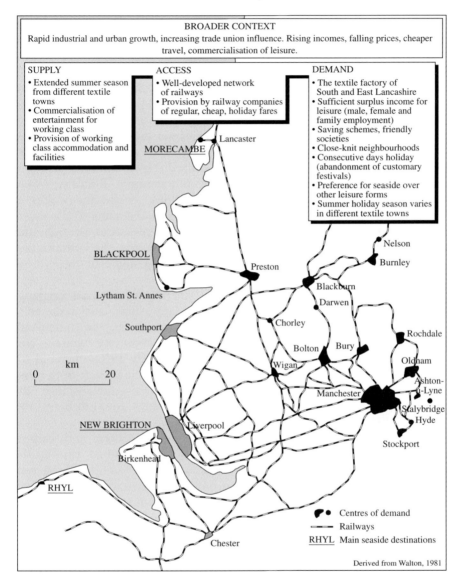

Figure 7.1 showing content:

BROADER CONTEXT
Rapid industrial and urban growth, increasing trade union influence. Rising incomes, falling prices, cheaper travel, commercialisation of leisure.

SUPPLY
• Extended summer season from different textile towns
• Commercialisation of entertainment for working class
• Provision of working class accommodation and facilities

ACCESS
• Well-developed network of railways
• Provision by railway companies of regular, cheap, holiday fares

DEMAND
• The textile factory of South and East Lancashire
• Sufficient surplus income for leisure (male, female and family employment)
• Saving schemes, friendly societies
• Close-knit neighbourhoods
• Consecutive days holiday (abandonment of customary festivals)
• Preference for seaside over other leisure forms
• Summer holiday season varies in different textile towns

Lancaster
MORECAMBE

BLACKPOOL
Lytham St. Annes
Preston
Nelson
Burnley
Blackburn
Darwen
Chorley

Southport
Bolton   Bury
Wigan
Rochdale
Oldham
Ashton-u-Lyne
Manchester
Stalybridge
Hyde
Stockport

km
0   20

NEW BRIGHTON
Liverpool
Birkenhead

RHYL

Chester

• Centres of demand
— Railways
RHYL Main seaside destinations

Derived from Walton, 1981

Figure 7.1   The Lancashire working-class seaside holiday system in the later nineteenth century

paid but their income came in short spells of intensive labour rather than through regular hours. Absenteeism was rife in the summer months and this lack of labour discipline became incorporated into a few days visit to the coast by the 1870s, to resorts such as Bridlington and Yarmouth. Therefore, in this region it was not the survival of old festivals that became translated into holidays away but irregular work practices combined with sufficient income. It was a different picture again in the workshops of Birmingham, for here strict labour discipline retarded the growth of seaside visits until the 1880s when a few extra days became attached to the August Bank Holiday. Close to Birmingham, strong local culture also played a part in influencing demand. In the Black Country and Potteries not only were wages lower but there was a tradition of keeping the old wakes and festivals, scattered throughout the year. These localised leisure patterns persisted right through to the end of the nineteenth century; Burslem Wakes survived until the 1890s as a separate holiday as did the wakes in Walsall. Thus, despite the availability of cheap excursions to the coast, there remained a strong attachment to local pleasures of pub and fairground so that, in Arnold Bennet's (1908:11) words, the Potteries had not yet "understood the vital necessity of going away to the seaside every year".

Areas of mining and heavy industry, such as North-East England, South Yorkshire, South Wales and South Lancashire, also retained a preference for local festivities throughout much of the nineteenth century. These areas also presented fewer chances for women and children to boost the family income. Until the early 1920s, demand for the coast was still largely confined to the day excursion even from those areas which lay close to the sea. In South Wales, for instance, the railways brought day trips from the mining valleys down to Barry and Porthcawl (Howell and Baber 1990).

For the urban working classes throughout southern and eastern England, traditional holidays had been severely curbed during the nineteenth century. Other than excursions at Whitsuntide, there was little drive for amassing consecutive days' holiday except where there was a substantial core of skilled workers such as in Bristol and London. The introduction of the August Bank Holidays in the 1870s was a much needed stimulus to demand for a few days' holiday at the seaside throughout much of the south and east and, in fact, short excursions were still the general rule until the end of the century. Thus the resorts of the Lincolnshire coast were slow to grow partly because their catchment area, the East Midlands, was late in extending holidays beyond a Monday. Outside these urban areas, the rural working classes, everywhere, were amongst the last to adopt any form of seaside culture. Compared to the eighteenth century, agricultural hours became longer and more regular, while low pay, poor accessibility and a stronger attachment to local traditions reinforced a lack of demand from these areas (Cunningham 1990; Walton 1981 and see chapter 8).

As well as important regional variations, there were local differences which influenced demand for the seaside amongst the working classes. Work practices, wage levels and attitudes to leisure varied at the scale of town or individual company. In the railway settlement of Crewe, for instance, employment was dominated by the London and North Western Railway (LNWR) and its patronage and paternalism permeated most aspects of society in the town (Redfern 1983). Rapid population growth (from around 500 in 1841 to over 24 000 by the 1880s) was largely due to the inward migration of skilled workers and the company tried to instil a new sense of community amongst them. High wage rates and an annual week's holiday created before the 1880s were combined with travel concessions to workers and their families. This resulted in a relatively high level of mobility so that, by the turn of the century, Crewe was generating holiday visits not only to Blackpool but to the Isle of Man, Aberystwyth, Barmouth, Bournemouth, Ireland and even the continent. Local variations in demand were created by the involvement of companies and firms in organising excursions to the seaside (Delgado 1977). Cheap travel rates were often provided by many railway companies for their employees from the 1840s onwards, so that Weymouth became known as "Swindon by the Sea" (Williams 1915). Large firms, such as Huntley & Palmers in Reading, could organise major expeditions; five special trains for Margate and Ramsgate, and five for Portsmouth in June 1914, or the Coatbridge Phoenix Iron Works steamer excursions to Rothesay 50 years earlier (Delgado 1977). A multiplicity of other organisations including churches, temperance societies, and charities were also involved in seaside outings, especially for the poor and deprived. The 1890s saw the founding of the Newcastle-upon-Tyne Poor Children's Holiday Association and Rescue Agency which every week sent groups of children to South Shields for the day. The Association aimed "to provide a day's holiday at the seaside for every poor child in Newcastle who had no other means of enjoying one" (Delgado 1977:78). At a more informal level there were simply local groups organising visits such as the village of Slad's annual trip to Weston-super-Mare recalled so vividly by Laurie Lee in *Cider with Rosie* (1959).

The evolving supply of seaside resorts

The evolving patterns of the supply of seaside resorts in response to the demands traced in the previous section are examined here for a selection of regions in Britain, Germany, France, Spain and the United States. Where information allows, these patterns of growth and development are related to notions of core and periphery. Did the balance of initiative and control of growth lie more in the metropolitan core regions or within the resort areas themselves?

The growth of seaside resorts in England and Wales has been presented in considerable detail by Gilbert (1939), Pimlott (1947), and more recently, Walton (1983). The following is therefore a summary of the more important trends. Figure 7.2 presents the picture of resort growth from about 1750 to just before the First World War and it identifies those areas which experienced resort development in different periods. These broad locational patterns are a starting point for analysis for the maps do not indicate the relative size and importance of individual resorts.

A simple but basic geography underlies the overall pattern and significance of the resort system in England and Wales. No large cluster of the population was more than about 70 or 80 miles from the coast and this helped the rising economic wealth and the growth of a seaside culture to find expression in these countries sooner than those where the potential attractions were more distant (Lewis 1980). Beyond this obvious fact, of course, the reasons for the varying patterns were more complex. Resorts did not simply wait for demand to create them but took a major role in shaping their own destinies. Topography and physical environment and accessibility to regions of demand all provided a context within which landowners, entrepreneurs and local governments attempted to capitalise on an expanding holiday market.

Figure 7.2 shows that by about the middle of the eighteenth century, there was a handful of recognisable seaside resorts in England and Wales. Scarborough in the north combined a spa and seaside function and must be reckoned amongst the first of the coastal resorts, but all the others lay to the south with Brighton, Eastbourne, Deal, Portsmouth and Margate together with Exmouth in the south-west. London was the main centre of demand for these places. By the late eighteenth century and the 1801 census, a cluster of very small resorts in south Devon and Dorset had emerged: Exmouth, Sidmouth, Dawlish, Teignmouth, Weymouth and Torquay, serving a regional market of gentry and merchants. But while Exmouth and Sidmouth contained about 2500 and 1200 people respectively, Brighton, by then, had grown to c.7000, Margate c.5000 and Scarborough c.6000. On the Lancashire coast, Southport and Blackpool were still tiny and served only a local hinterland.

The 1851 census revealed that the original pattern of resorts had been extended considerably. A string of resorts lay along the southern coasts from Kent to Devon, but concentrated particularly in Kent and Sussex where 44 per cent of all the seaside resort population was located. The Isle of Wight had emerged as a further centre serving London but beyond here, the less accessible resorts of the West Country had, apart

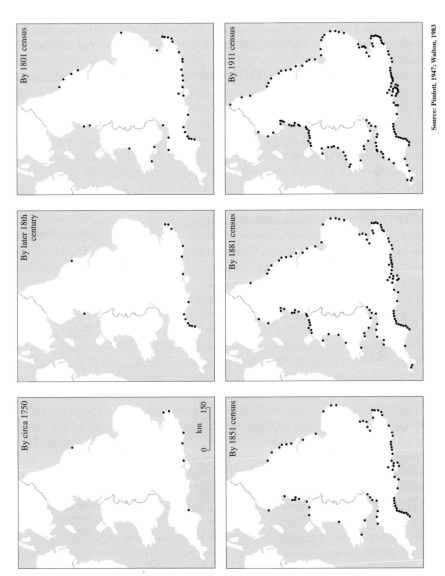

Figure 7.2 The pattern of seaside resort growth in England and Wales, 1750–1911

Source: Pimlott, 1947; Walton, 1983

from Torquay, grown only very slowly. Everywhere else, the pattern reflected local and regional demands. Bristol had its nearby resorts at Weston, Clevedon and Portishead, Aberystwyth and Tenby looked to a Welsh hinterland, Blackpool and Southport were just beginning to grow and, on the east coast, the line of resorts in Lincolnshire and East Anglia was still very small. The resorts of Kent and Sussex continued to dominate the map.

After another 30 years, the 1881 census reflected a period of increased wealth and growing accessibility to the seashore for an ever-widening range of social groups. Resorts became more specialised in the markets served, so that Blackpool and Southend focused on the working-class trade, while others, such as Bournemouth and Torquay, began to concentrate on the genteel middle classes who were retreating from the mass resorts. Within this process, the railways tended to accentuate existing trends rather than create fundamentally new patterns (see discussion in next section). Railways certainly helped the more distant coasts to grow more rapidly, so that although Kent and Sussex continued to dominate, the regional resorts in areas such as Lancashire, North Wales and the Bristol Channel grew considerably. By 1911, buoyant working-class and middle-class demand was coupled to an increasing trend to either commute from, or retire to, the coast. Over 1.6 million people were then living in the seaside resorts: 4.5 per cent of the population of England and Wales. Although major expansion continued to lie in parts of Sussex and Kent, regional resorts also saw large growth whether catering for middle-class or working-class sectors. Colwyn Bay and Llandudno in North Wales and Lytham St Annes in Lancashire looked to the middle classes but Blackpool was especially successful with its working-class visitors and became the fifth largest resort with a hinterland which now extended beyond Lancashire, Manchester, Yorkshire and Liverpool to include the West Midlands. Brighton and Bournemouth were also gaining a national hinterland by the Edwardian age. But the pattern of growth was uneven. The resorts on the Lincolnshire coast were held back by lower demand in the East Midlands and the South Devon resorts had very sluggish rates of growth before 1914. Despite the coming of the railways, they were still relatively inaccessible to large urban populations.

Within these broad patterns, there were always a variety of different types of resorts in any one region. This can be seen in the evolving system along the Sussex coast. Until the early nineteenth century, despite the presence of resorts on the coast, Sussex was still a largely rural-based economy. But from the 1840s, these resorts were responsible for a movement of population from the Weald to the coast, while new demands for dairy and market garden produce helped offset the effects of agricultural depressions felt in many other areas of Britain. Yet although the resorts had a similar regional effect and all looked principally to London for their clientele, they had different origins and fluctuating histories of success (Farrant 1987). There were, essentially, four main groups of resorts. First, were those which developed early, proved successful, and were able to adapt to changing conditions. Brighton and Hastings acquired fashionable autumn and winter seasons as well as summer middle-class visitors and a day excursion market. Success brought considerable private sector investment in facilities and Brighton grew into a regional service centre and residential area and served commuter functions as well as being a tourist resort. Hastings was rather less successful, it had poorer communications and had to compete with neighbouring resorts such as Eastbourne and Bexhill. There was then a group of smaller Georgian resorts such as Bognor Regis, Seaford and Worthing which developed slowly and looked to the middle-class London market. Poor communications and a lack of significant investors checked their growth and they depended on short seasons and cheap family holidays. Bognor stagnated until the 1920s with no railway until 1897, and had an image of being quiet and dull. Seaford evolved into a convalescent and residential area. Both resorts, in a sense, benefited from their lack of development and Worthing ultimately made a great success of its uneventful character by becoming a major retirement centre.

A third group of resorts, represented by Hove and St Leonard's, were essentially fashionable off-shoots of larger resorts: Hove from Brighton, St Leonard's from Hastings. Hove flourished in the later nineteenth century as an up-market resort independent of its bigger neighbour while St Leonard's ultimately merged with Hastings. The final group were the new Victorian resorts where major landowners invested heavily in development. This was the case at Eastbourne and Bexhill. From 1849, Eastbourne was developed by the Duke of Devonshire as a high-class resort, expanding very rapidly in the 1870s and 1880s. At Bexhill Samuel Scrivens and Earl de la Warr imitated Eastbourne's success with a middle-class trade in visitors and, later, attracted respectable independent schools and residential growth. In both resorts, exclusivity was aided by strict zoning policies which helped ensure a separation of resort function from workers' areas.

The variety in the fortunes of these resorts was matched by certain similarities, however. By the early twentieth century, they were all vulnerable to seasonal and trade cycle depressions which was a problem for workers even in wealthy Eastbourne and Bexhill. Also, although the origins of the visitors may have varied, employment in these resorts continued to be drawn largely from the Sussex area so that the coast continued to be seen as an area of economic opportunity.

A core–periphery relationship?

The links between demand and the patterns of resort supply can be considered not just in terms of visitors but in patterns of investment and control. Commentators on tourism development such as Nash (1977), Hills and Lundgren (1977) and Britton (1982) have argued for a core–periphery relationship between metropolitan areas which generate and control both tourists and capital for investment and the recipient resort areas, which are dependent on decisions made in the core regions. Thus resorts can be seen in a geographical, political and economic sense as peripheral areas. This concept of dependency has generally been applied to international relationships between the developed and developing worlds but it can apply equally to intranational levels as the development process is rarely evenly spread at any scale. The balance of dependency will evidently relate to the extent to which economic levels vary between the core and peripheral areas.

These ideas can be usefully related to the history of resort development in Britain. Investment in any resort was a risky venture involving a considerable amount of capital and this had to be met either through the resources of the local resort population or elsewhere. Historians have debated aspects of this issue. Cannadine (1980:413) argues that the aristocracy were critical in resort development with their influence spanning both core and periphery. Thus, they owned land at the coast and their "high status and credit-worthiness gave them access to the London money market". Walton (1983), however, suggests that these aristocrats were only active at a small number of high-class resorts and that most landowners in the resort areas were local gentry who worked with neighbouring tradesmen and professionals in raising capital. Also, few resorts were created on "green-field" sites with grandiose schemes but were piecemeal additions to existing settlements, and so the demands for capital were correspondingly smaller.

Until the 1840s, most of the expanding resorts in England and Wales were initiated by small groups or individuals in the resort areas with little external control. Development was, at first, very cautious, with facilities created by converting or replacing buildings within the existing built-up area. Margate, for instance, grew in the eighteenth century by conversions in the old town rather than by outward expansion. Thus many houses were "now applied to a use for which they were not originally intended" (*New Margate Guide* 1770; quoted in Walton 1983:111). A similar picture obtained in Brighton, with replacements and conversions in the original centre utilising capital drawn from rural east Sussex and Lewes. Local lawyers, solicitors, doctors and gentry together with traders such as brewers, hoteliers and innkeepers were behind much of the speculative development in the first phases of resort growth. If these initiatives were successful then external resources might be drawn in, such as the involvement of London's Covent Garden and Drury Lane in Margate's theatre in 1790 (Walton 1983). It was after 1840 that the larger landowners began to invest large sums in resort development, tapping into the national circuit of capital (Dodgshon 1990) and creating high-class resorts. But even then, this involvement was to decline later in the century. Furthermore, outsiders who tried to speculate in resort development often lacked sufficient resources to make significant impacts on resort growth; for instance the London-based entrepreneurs at Swanage and Seaford or the businessmen from Manchester and the West Midlands at Colwyn Bay, Towyn and Pwllheli.

For much of the nineteenth century, the provision of accommodation and attractions in most resorts in Britain thus depended on local and regional efforts. Weston-super-Mare's baths were financed from Bristol, Southport's Assembly Rooms were financed from Manchester, Liverpool, Bolton and Wigan and much of the momentum for resort entertainments came from tradesmen in and around the resorts. The expansion of piers illustrates this. They evolved from commercial use to fashionable promenade and the 1860s saw a boom in their construction. Yet despite this being an expensive and risky venture, initial investors were generally local shopkeepers, tradesmen, and the professions. As entertainment schemes grew larger, however, so the balance of investment shifted from the resorts to wider regional and national investors. Winter gardens, aquaria, pavilions and grand theatres needed more than local capital. By the 1870s, a broad north–south divide could be seen in investment patterns. London money was increasingly penetrating the southern resorts, so that money for Bournemouth's Winter Gardens and half the share capital for Margate's Aquarium came from London. Further north, the resorts of Lancashire and North Wales looked more to the industrial areas of Lancashire itself and the West Riding for capital rather than their local areas or London. This basic pattern persisted even when resorts became more dependent on outside finance in the 1890s. Many of the investors in these schemes, however, continued to be individual tradesmen, professionals, widows, spinsters, clerks and even skilled workers so that, in time, the customers of the resorts were also some of their financial backers (Walton 1983).

The west coast of Scotland presents an interesting variation on the themes traced so far in England and Wales. One similarity was the initial provision of facilities in the Clyde resorts by largely local effort. The piermaster at Kirn, for instance, built the first tenement block for visitors to the town and he also provided shops and summer houses to let. Other locals simply let out rooms in their own houses (Blair 1985).

But with a large working-class centre of demand lying in the industrial centres of Glasgow and Clydeside, together with week-long holidays from the 1880s (Fraser 1990), it might be thought that an equivalent to Blackpool would have emerged from the resort system of the Clyde coast. One reason blocking the intensive capital development needed for such a resort was the fact that Glaswegian industrialists and merchants and local landowners had appropriated large sections of the coast as holiday retreats for themselves. Thus the one sector of society which could have initiated a Blackpool equivalent wanted as little tourist development as possible (King 1987). The Marquis of Bute, the dominating influence at Rothesay, blocked a number of schemes in the resort which would have led to an overt commercial presence. Given the size and diversity of the region, however, it is difficult to see competition for leisure space as the only barrier and there may have been a more deep-seated cultural objection amongst the Scottish moneyed classes, shaped by work and religion, which would not encourage stimulating hedonistic pleasures especially amongst the "lower" orders (Fraser 1990; Morgan and Trainor 1990).

In terms of a general core–periphery relationship, seaside resort development in Britain showed a changing pattern from local initiative and investment to more regional and, later, national core area involvement. But the picture was always complex. Investment patterns for the northern resorts tended to be more regional, looking to the growing wealth of the industrial towns and cities, while London extended its influence to many of the resorts in the south. Dependence on outside investment increased almost everywhere during the nineteenth century for the large sums of money needed to keep resorts competitive. The significant role played by the resorts themselves and their regions was a reflection, however, of the greater spread of wealth and entrepreneurship in Britain than in some other countries as will be seen later in cases such as the French Riviera.

Patterns of seaside resort development in Germany, France, Spain and the United States

Germany's coastal resorts fall into two distinct geographical areas: those on the North Sea and those on the Baltic coast. Figure 7.3 indicates the overall pattern which had evolved by the early part of this century with large resorts of the North Sea such as Norderney on the East Frisian islands receiving about 40 000 visitors a year, and Westerland on the Island of Sylt in the North Frisians receiving about 25 000 visits. Sassnitz (around 20 000 visitors), Swinemünde (17 000 visitors) and Heringsdorf

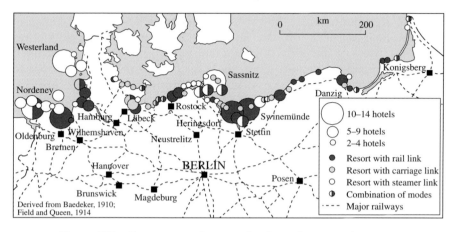

Figure 7.3   German coastal resorts by the early twentieth century

(15 500 visitors) were major resorts in the Baltic zone (Baedeker 1910; Queen 1914). Most of these resorts served the cities of northern Germany but some further east, such as Memel, also attracted affluent Russians.

Resort development in Germany was on a considerably smaller scale than in Britain. For instance, at the end of the nineteenth century, Great Yarmouth could receive up to 800 000 visitors a year, Margate 700 000, Scarborough 450 000 and Blackpool perhaps about 2 million (Walton 1983). But as in Britain, the resort system had evolved to serve a wide variety of markets with high-class and popular resorts often in close proximity. Thus Norderney was the most fashionable of all German resorts with summer and winter seasons and a full range of facilities. Heringsdorf, near Stettin, was the most fashionable and expensive of the Baltic resorts yet Bansin, only two miles away, was far cheaper and the same area also included Sassnitz, Crampas and Swinemünde, which were amongst the most popular of German resorts (Baedeker 1910). As well as serving a wide range of social groups, the variety of modes of transport upon which the resorts depended is striking (Figure 7.3). Many places had rail links to the inland urban centres but some of the larger resorts (for instance on the Frisian Islands) had to be reached by steamer, while the smallest still relied on horse carriage.

As late as the 1770s there was almost no seaside development in Germany (Corbin 1994). In the 1790s, Dr Georg-Christoph Lichtenburg raised the question of why Germany had no sea-bathing resorts although the region possessed many spas. There followed a medical debate on the relative merits of the North Sea and the Baltic with the former possessing greater tidal range, wave power and salinity and the latter possessing calmer and warmer summer waters. The Baltic zone won the argument and the first seaside resort was developed at Doberan in 1794 near Rostock on the lands of the Duchy of Mecklenburg-Schwerin. Most of the early development was sponsored and controlled by the various governments along the coast, unlike the freer response to demand in Britain, but the rapid transition from health to pleasure and fashion was similar. Thus, Doberan could boast a vibrant social life by the 1820s, with a theatre, promenade, pier, music pavilion and library. Other resorts included: Travemünde (1800–1802) the resort of the merchants of Lübeck, Colberg (1802) encouraged by the King of Prussia, Rügenwald (1815), Putbus (1821), Swinemünde (1822–1826), Warnemünde (1805–1821) near Doberan, Apenräde (1813–1815) and Kiel (1822). There were fewer resorts on the North Sea: Norderney (1797) modelled itself on Doberan, and was followed by Cuxhaven (1816) and Wyk (1819), off the coast of Holstein.

The slow development of the German seaside resorts has been partly attributed by Soane (1993) to the more localised and regulated culture of the German middle classes who were less inclined to indulge in the notion of coastal resorts dedicated largely to the principle of pleasure. The hinterland of most resorts remained local and regional so that, by 1900, Swinemünde's main demand was still generally from Berlin and Hamburg. Thomas Mann's *Buddenbrooks* (1902) emphasised the role of Travemünde as the local seasonal leisure resort of the merchant class of Lübeck with few outsiders intruding into the social scene.

It is not feasible here to consider the sequence of resort development along the whole of the coasts of France but, instead, two contrasting areas are selected: the French Riviera from Hyères in the west to Menton on the Italian border, and the coast of Brittany.

The Riviera began as a winter health region for affluent north Europeans, especially the British (Gade 1982; Haug 1982; Nash 1979; Pemble 1988; Rudney 1980; Soane 1993). It was especially fashionable from the 1830s when the winter visitors, or *hivernants*, created an area of "elitist space" for themselves during the season from October to April (Gade 1982). Until the early part of that century the Riviera had been a largely poor region dependent on wine, fruit, olive oil and fishing and cut off from other areas by the Maritime Alps and poor coastal roads.

Hyères was one of the first centres to develop as a resort; it was near Toulon and benefited from easier access down the Rhône valley. But growth along the coast was not simply a matter of distance and accessibility. By the 1830s, Cannes was still a small fishing village while further east, Nice was already growing considerably. Nice's fortunes were shaped by a change in political geography when the city was annexed by France from Savoy in 1860. The subsequent arrival of the French railway system then fuelled expansion so that Nice grew from

16 000 people in 1754 to 48 000 in 1861 and 143 000 by 1910 (Haug 1982). Visitor numbers expanded from about 5000 in 1861 to 150 000 in 1914 (Rudney 1980). Nice, Cannes and other Riviera resorts modelled themselves on high-class spas such as Baden Baden, Vichy and Aix-les-Bains and, until the 1920s, focused almost exclusively on the winter season. From the 1920s, however, the region began to undergo a major shift in the temporal patterns of visitors with the growth of a summer season. The rise of the suntan as a fashionable accessory and the increased numbers of Americans, used to summer seasons in the States, helped to popularise this trend. Juan-les-Pins was one of the first resorts to embrace the summer season, while Nice continued to look to winter patronage. A further change to the Riviera came in 1936 when the French Government introduced paid holidays (*congé payé*) and a wider social class arrived on the Mediterranean shores for their summer holidays. Significantly, however, this did not lead to a wholesale exodus from the Riviera by north Europeans. Foreign tourists and *congés payés* mixed successfully at the old resorts like Nice, Menton and Cannes and at the new resorts like Juan-les-Pins (Rudney 1980).

The process of development on the Riviera can be related to core–periphery relationships. Gade (1982), for instance, places tourism growth in the region within a wider political and socio-cultural context. He argues that the highly centralised French political and social life radiated a series of "deeply rooted cultural premises to its far borders" (Gade 1982:19), and these included elitism and a hedonistic lifestyle. This rapidly gave the Riviera a national rather than a regional hinterland and can be contrasted with prevailing German attitudes discussed earlier. There was also a significant difference with the British experience in that the Riviera was an extremely poor peripheral region which had to look to the metropolitan core for its initial development. From the outset, there was a considerable amount of outside control with many of the hotelkeepers and other major developers coming from elsewhere in France or Europe and with the local population tending to react to initiatives coming from outsiders (Nash 1979; Rudney 1980). For example, the English colony inspired the construction of the Promenade des Anglais at Nice and the Russian colony lobbied for better roads to Villefranche. Local administrations improved the infrastructure of the coastal region but had to look to the central government for funds (Nash 1979). Much of the considerable expansion of Nice from the 1880s, for instance, depended on banks and developers from Lyon, Paris and Britain (Soane 1993) and the large hotels, which replaced villas as the centres of social life, required much larger capital investment than could be supplied locally. Thus Nice, through tourism, became linked to the national economy so that although "the city was geographically further

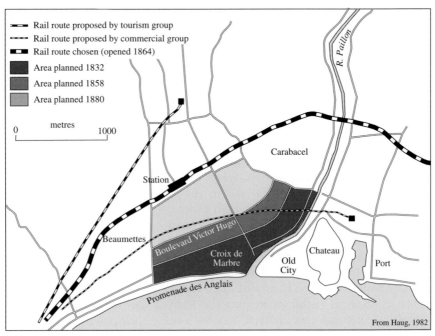

Figure 7.4 Nice: proposed railway routes and planned urban expansion (University Press of Kansas)

from Paris than any other, financially Nice was closer than any other" (Haug 1982:85).

There were, however, local initiatives that countered a simple core–periphery relationship along the Riviera. The Cooperative Banque Populaire de Menton provided cheap credit for local projects and a number of major building supply firms remained in local hands (Soane 1993). It was also businessmen and officials within the area who, after the Napoleonic wars, realised the importance of tourism to the economy and adopted an extremely compliant attitude to the needs of outsiders, whether tourists or investors.

This balance between internal and external interests can be shown in the debate over the location of the railway station in Nice (Figure 7.4). As a new part of the French state, Nice was to be linked by rail to Paris and the Paris–Lyon–Méditerranée Railway (PLM) advanced eastwards along the coast from Marseille and Toulon. Within Nice, however, there was an argument between local interest groups which reflected two contrasting ideas on the city's future. One group argued that the city's future lay in commerce and trade, building on the new political ties and communications and hoping that Nice would rival Marseille as a trading centre. In which case, the new railway station should be located near the port on the east side of the River Paillon. The tourism group saw the future of Nice as fundamentally linked to the needs of outside visitors and consequently the station should be located on the western side of the city but keeping the noise and smoke of trains away from their villa quarters. The final choice, however, was made externally by the French government and the PLM who decided that Nice was essentially a tourist resort. But the station was located closer to the sea than the local lobby suggested, to ensure easier access to the city. It was a victory for tourism but an outside perception of how that would be served.

At the opposite extremity of France, the coast of Brittany developed in a very different way to the Riviera. Here, growth was not directed by an affluent group of *hivernants* but by the process of "discovery" by romantic artists, writers and travellers. French poets celebrated the wild scenes on the Breton coast and, in the 1790s, Jacques Cambry's survey of the region amounted to an "emotional mapping of the sea-shore" (Corbin 1994: 135) which urged Parisians to visit not just the Alps and Italy but Brittany as well. A romantic interest in the Celtic culture of a remote periphery was similar to that which added to the appeal of the Scottish Highlands for British tourists (see chapter 6). In the early nineteenth century, the writings of Chateaubriand and Michelet inspired painters such as Gudin and Isabey (Cariou 1992) and centres such as Pont-Aven were later to attract an artistic colony which included Gaugin.

Thus tourism evolved slowly in Brittany during the nineteenth century, based on its appeal to a discerning few for whom its remote and difficult country were all part of its attraction. Railways gradually penetrated the region from the 1850s so that, by the early years of this century, it was possible to identify a resort system which extended around much of the coast (Figure 7.5). The Joanne guide for 1912 indicated a whole range of resorts, varying from the fashionable to the quiet and simple, from the popular "familial" resort to those just experiencing discovery, and resorts which served both domestic and foreign visitors. Thus there was a complex mix of closely juxtaposed places serving different markets. The overall "tone" of Brittany, however, was for the fairly simple family holiday market rather than the elite space of the Riviera. Figure 7.5 indicates no very clear pattern of resorts related to distance from the entry points to the region, although there was a tendency for the quiet and simple to be found in the far west and for the more fashionable and popular to be at the eastern end of the peninsula.

The Joanne guide identified a northern tract of resorts from St Malo in the east to Brest in the west and a southern tract from St Nazaire to

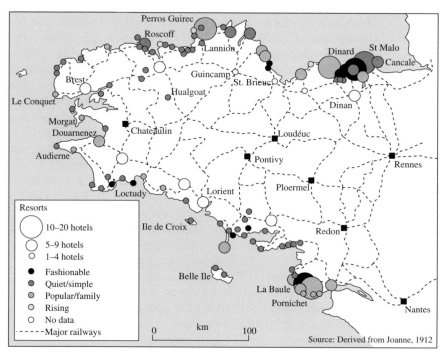

Figure 7.5 The "social tone" of seaside resorts in Brittany in the early twentieth century

Brest. Access to the region was by two main railway routes, from Rennes and Nantes, with branches leading off to the coast. From Britain, steamers ran regularly from Southampton to St Malo and Roscoff and from Plymouth to Brest. At the northern and southern "gateways" to Brittany there were pronounced clusters of resorts. In the north, Cancale, Paramé, St Malo and Dinard were important and could be reached from Paris in about seven hours. The variety in this cluster was considerable. Cancale was described as quiet and simple, while Dinard was the most fashionable resort in Brittany with English and American patronage. Popular St Malo lay close to fashionable Paramé, while on the western side of this cluster there were a number of small, simple, resorts. At the southern gateway, fashionable La Baule was mixed in with popular resorts such as Pornichet. Both La Baule and Dinard had summer seasons with casinos and other extensive entertainment and were the closest Brittany had to the large resort complexes on the Normandy coast. Along the northern coast, moving west, Perros-Guirec was a considerable centre despite its relative inaccessibility, depending on a local train from Lannion. Furthermore, in the far west Morgat, near

Brest, was described as one of Brittany's most popular resorts "increasing by leaps and bounds" (Joanne 1912:158); a trend confirmed by the 1930 Blue Guide (Guides Bleus 1930). A fine beach and local scenery were apparently the reasons for this remote resort's success. Other resorts, such as Pont-Aven, were artists' colonies but a further attraction here may have been that "its women are known for their alluring charm" (Joanne 1912:195). The sheer variety of different types of resorts around the Brittany coast suggests that it was local conditions, such as physical environment, and the presence or absence of local entrepreneurs, which must have been critical in the story of an individual resort's success.

The first seaside resort system in Spain to be developed lay, not along the now famous "costas" to the south, but on the north coast. Expanding from the 1830s, this system served an essentially domestic market of a variety of social groups. The principal resort was always San Sebastian, with a secondary centre at Santander (Walton and Smith 1995).

Spain was slow to create an organised coastal tourism system. Whereas in Britain it had clearly appeared by the mid-eighteenth century, in France by the 1780s, and Germany by the 1790s, it did not reach Spain until the 1830s. Certain factors limited development here. An overall lack of economic growth restricted wider demand for holidays and the coasts lay a considerable distance from Madrid, the one centre that could generate a sufficient wealthy clientele. In general terms, the leisured class of Spain preferred their small inland spa resorts (Barke and Towner 1995) or they could simply cross the French border to fashionable Biarritz. San Sebastian, however, began to attract visits to the Spanish coast in the 1830s and was the first resort to really expand. Rail access from the Madrid–Paris line in 1864 provided a further impetus for the city. Further west, most resorts had to rely on horse-carriage transport from a number of railheads and access to them remained difficult right through to the present century. Nevertheless, by about 1870, 14 resorts had grown along the coast from San Sebastian to Santander, varying in size and social tone. San Sebastian was then receiving about 25 000 visits in the summer season, Santander about 3000, Bilbao's three resorts about 3000 all together, Deva, between San Sebastian and Bilbao, about 2000 and Saturruran about 1800 visits. All the other resorts were extremely small. Even so, there was a growing commercial interest in resorts during the 1860s and 1870s with heavy investment in the two main centres.

A notable feature of these resorts was their interest in catering for a wide range of social groups, with even San Sebastian providing relatively cheap as well as luxury accommodation (Walton and Smith 1995). But distinctive social tones can be identified. San Sebastian aimed for a

European-wide elite market; Santander, combining resort with port functions, aimed for the middle classes of Madrid and Castille province. Bilbao's resorts failed to grow successfully: Las Arenas developed into a high-class suburb, while Algorta became a day trip destination for the city's working classes. Deva became a middle-class resort serving Madrid and Bilboa and Zaranz grew into a fashionable outlier of San Sebastian.

The early phases of coastal resort growth in the United States were, in many ways, similar to the situation in Britain. Colonial spa development has been referred to in chapter 4 and the first seaside resorts were off-shoots of these leisure places. There are references to sea-bathing from the eighteenth century with local and regional patronage of certain resorts: Nahant for Boston, Cape May and Long Branch for Philadelphia. By the early nineteenth century, Newport, Rhode Island, was serving the affluent from the urban north and the southern gentry and, by 1850, had overtaken Nahant as the more exclusive resort (Huth 1957). Figure 6.3 shows a number of these evolving resorts by the mid-century but it is important not to see them in isolation. As in Britain, the leisured classes had annual migration routes to a variety of different environments: summer at Newport, winter at Palm Beach, Florida, spring and autumn at one of the inland spas such as White Sulphur Springs (Amory 1948).

These socially exclusive resorts were pre-eminent in the USA until the 1850s, after which a wider social base came to be served (Lewis 1980). Atlantic City on the New Jersey shore near Cape May lay 60 miles from Philadelphia but developed rapidly after the coming of the railway in the 1860s and Coney Island, 10 miles from Manhattan, was receiving some excursion trade by the 1830s. One proclaimed difference with Europe was a desire for seaside resorts to appear relatively classless; the New York Times in 1868 referred to the sea as "the old Democrat", erasing class distinctions among the bathers (Snow and Wright 1976:972) and Atlantic City aimed to be "a thoroughly democratic place" (Lewis 1980:47). Coney Island liked to view itself as a melting pot for all the classes of New York, mixing together in pleasure. This was perhaps wishful thinking in a new republic which hoped to break with the customs of the Old World. Furthermore, the USA had to confront the issue of race on a larger scale than in Europe. Segregation was apparent in Atlantic City, with blacks having their own pier and a section of the sea front, which effectively transferred the divisions of Philadelphia to a seaside setting. Jews, facing anti-Semitism at the inland spas like Saratoga Springs, found, however, that the coastal resorts such as Long Branch, Cape May and Atlantic City were more tolerant and so they gradually established summer colonies in these places (Lewis 1980).

Atlantic City was essentially created by, and for, Philadelphia. Busi-nessmen in the latter centre were aware during the nineteenth century of the potential demand for a new seaside resort as Cape May, despite difficult access by steamer, was receiving up to 110 000 visitors a year by the 1850s (Stansfield 1978). Much of the initial development of the new resort came, in fact, from a railway company which had a wholly owned land company subsidiary which sold the real estate on the coast. As Atlantic City grew, so Cape May, further by rail from Philadelphia, declined.

Just as Atlantic City was linked to Philadelphia, so Coney Island's future was inextricably bound up with New York and Brooklyn. Lying on the tip of Long Island, Coney was, at first, an excursion for the affluent of Brooklyn but the arrival of horse-drawn trams in the 1850s and the steamer from New York in the 1870s helped change it to a popular urban resort. Nevertheless, the developers in the 1870s created three expensive hotels at Coney Island to tempt back the patronage of the social elite and, for a time, the resort did serve a range of social groups. At the far western end of the island, Norton's Point was a zone notorious for gambling and prostitution. Next to this was the working-class area centred on the amusements and further east Brighton Beach served the respectable middle classes. Manhattan Beach at the eastern end of the island was the most socially exclusive zone. Despite this spatial segregation of visitor types, for short periods there was a degree of social mixing. Middle- and upper-class males would head west to enjoy the pleasures of Norton's Point and gamblers and prostitutes headed east to the back stairways of the major hotels. Meanwhile, the middle-class families would walk to Manhattan Beach to mingle for the evening with the social elite. Eventually, however, Coney Island came to be associated with massive mechanised amusements, such as Luna Park in 1903, which eclipsed all other attractions on the island (Snow and Wright 1976). In this phase, there was much resemblance between Coney Island, Blackpool (which had its own Luna Park) and Atlantic City and they came to represent extreme cases of Wolfe's (1952) "divorce from the geographic environment", where the original natural attrac-tions of a place are largely supplanted by human creations.

The relationship between Britain and America in terms of seaside resort development has produced conflicting opinions. Demars (1979) argues that most of the activities, structures and philosophies that were found on the American seashore were borrowed from Britain. Only bathing machines and zones for single sex bathing failed to cross the Atlantic. Lewis (1980) on the other hand, sees the large-scale mechanised amusements of the later nineteenth century as being an American inno-vation, later adopted by the British, with only the pleasure pier as an

Old World creation. Whatever the true degree of influence, there was clearly a closely related common seaside culture which evolved during the 1800s in Britain and America, whose differences were perhaps more a question of degree than of kind.

Transport and the resorts

The general theme of the relationship between transport development and tourism development has been discussed in chapter 1. Arguments range from those seeing transport as a fundamental factor in the development process to a view which stresses its permissive role within wider social and organisational change (Hart 1983). In this section, the role of transport is considered in more detail in terms of the growth of seaside resorts.

The question is not whether transport was important; at the simplest level it was the vital link between generating and destination areas (Simmons 1986). However, there is a question over the extent to which specific modes of transport were decisive in creating or transforming resorts and determining patterns of movement.

Some of the earliest systems of seaside resorts can be related to water transport or a combination of water and land carriage and, later, water and rail transport. Examples in Britain include the Kent resorts, the Clyde, the Solent, and the Mersey and Tyne. Kent was one of the first regions to develop coastal resorts and Figure 7.6 indicates the principal centres which are related to key modes of transport. A number of places, including Margate, developed considerably during the era of sailing vessels and horse-drawn carriages, others such as Whistable and Folkestone were more clearly related to the later railway age. Before tourism developed in the mid-eighteenth century, the economy of the Margate region was based on arable farming and maritime activities, and Margate harbour exported corn to London using sailing vessels known as hoys. In time, these ships brought passengers out from London to Margate at a very low cost and the growth of resort trade encouraged more luxurious sailing packets to tap into this new market. By the later eighteenth century, the hoys were bringing working-class excursionists from the capital in large numbers and this established pattern was reinforced, from 1815, by the introduction of fast, cheap and regular steamboat services. Water-borne visitors to Margate increased from about 22 000 in 1815 to over 88 000 by 1840; a dramatic increase in the pre-railway era (Whyman 1980).

In the west of Scotland, the resort development referred to earlier on in this chapter was based on a dense network of steamer operations

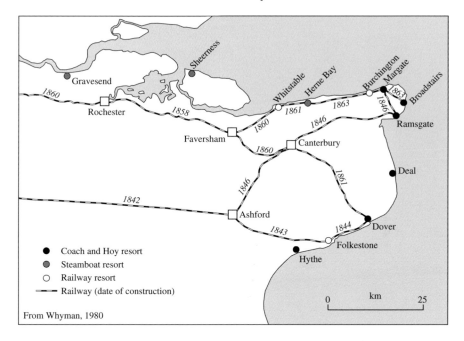

Figure 7.6   Kent seaside resorts and principal modes of transport

from the Clyde which was later intensified by an interlinked rail and steamer system which could move large numbers of people quickly and cheaply (McCrorie 1986; Paterson 1969, 1972). Steamboats first appeared on the Clyde in 1812 and within ten years there were 50 passenger boats with regular services to Campbeltown, Inveraray and Rothesay carrying both day trippers and staying visitors. By 1833, half of Rothesay's 600 houses were providing holiday accommodation (King 1987). Figure 7.7 shows the network of piers that were created to serve this extensive trade and it is clear that, from the 1860s, a trip "doon the watter" had become an established part of the working-class Glaswegian leisure experience with significant centres of accommodation by the turn of the century (Figure 7.8). Railways became integrated into this already established pattern with lines to Greenock in 1841, Helensburgh by 1858 and Wemyss Bay by 1865. This development cut the time of travel down the Clyde itself so that Greenock and Wemyss Bay grew at the expense of the Broomielaw pier in the heart of Glasgow. Nevertheless, it was not until the 1880s that the combined steamer and rail routes won supremacy over the "all the way" water network (Paterson 1972) and it can be argued that the innovation of railways in this instance modified rather than created patterns of movement to the resorts.

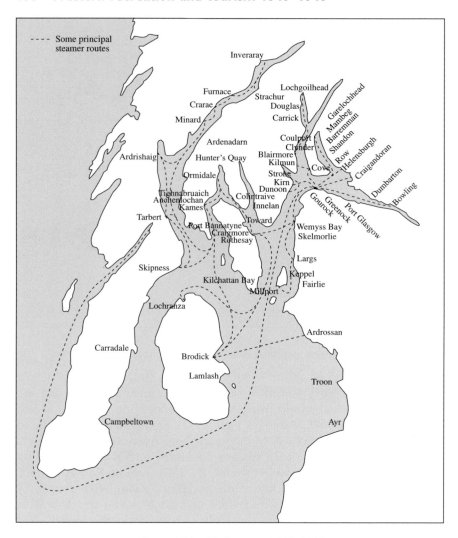

Figure 7.7   Clyde piers, 1864–1888

The large-scale growth of seaside resorts in England and Wales from the mid-1800s onwards has often been attributed to the spread of the railway network. However, although the scale and pattern of development was strongly influenced, other forces were also at work. In general terms, four main links can be discerned between railways and resort growth (Walton 1979). First, railways could give new life to resorts that were stagnating because of inadequate transport capacity. This was happening at Brighton and Margate. Brighton's growth actually slowed

Figure 7.8   "Embarking at the Broomielaw, Glasgow", photograph by George Washington Wilson (1885). Crowds boarding the steamers for the ritual exodus to the Clyde estuary resorts (University of Aberdeen)

in the 1830s so that its 242 per cent population increase of 1801 to 1831 fell to only 15 per cent between 1831 and 1841. Many contemporaries felt that the town was overbuilt with many houses for sale and that it had "outgrown its transport system" (Simmons 1986:236). Another impact of the railways was in giving extra impetus to small resorts that were beginning to grow; a recurring influence throughout the nineteenth century. In this way Blackpool and Southport were stimulated at an early period, while Bournemouth was influenced much later. A third effect of the railways was to help accelerate the changing economies of existing urban centres away from traditional activities such as commercial trade and fishing towards tourism. This happened at Scarborough, Yarmouth and Aberystwyth. Finally, the railways could have a direct influence on creating entirely new resort centres on vacant land. This, most decisive, influence was however extremely rare, with Silloth and Seascale on the Cumbrian coast and Withernsea on the east coast being some of the few clear-cut cases (Walton 1983).

Railway companies were usually more interested in the year-round profit which could be gained from minerals and commerce rather than highly seasonal tourist flows. There were instances where resorts grew from these other forms of trade. The Furness Railway along the Cumbrian coast was developed for iron and coke traffic but small resorts like Grange-over-Sands, Seascale and St Bees were spawned once the railway was established (Marshall 1971; Walton 1979). On the Lincolnshire coast, the growth of railways was geared principally to the agricultural trade and only at Cleethorpes was a stronger rail–resort link in evidence (Pearson 1968). For most of the railway companies, resort traffic was viewed as a useful additional income and Walton (1979) points out that it was the response from *within* the resort areas which proved decisive, relying on the ability of landowners and business entrepreneurs to maximise the opportunities that the railways created.

Silloth and Seascale in Cumbria provide two examples of close railway involvement in seaside resort development. Silloth was initially promoted as a commercial port for Carlisle with a railway link in 1856. Poor trade, however, persuaded the railway company to develop its own resort there and it created all the accommodation, roads, pavements, gardens and other services. For a time there was some success, with 4 hotels and 38 lodging houses by 1860, but when the local railway was absorbed by the larger North British Railway the resort's fortunes waned and the infrastructure was neglected by a company whose main concerns lay elsewhere. Seascale, along the same coast, was the creation of the Furness Railway which had a grandiose scheme for a villa and hotel resort (Figure 7.9). An industrial boom at nearby Barrow and a general increase in tourism in the Lake District provided a climate of optimism for a new resort. By 1900, golf, tennis and croquet facilities existed together with shops and a library. But Seascale never flourished. Barrow suffered depression and the Lancashire resorts proved a stronger attraction for holidaymakers. The town plan simply became a reminder that seaside resort growth was never an inevitable process (Marshall 1971).

Railways, by providing cheap and rapid transport, helped to convey the working classes to those coastal areas which lay within easy reach of the large urban industrial centres. But at the same time, they also helped the middle classes move further afield in a search for exclusivity. In the later nineteenth and early twentieth centuries, this process benefited the more peripheral areas such as Cornwall and East Anglia, which provided safe havens for those who had greater time for travel. But the influence of the railway on the social tone of resorts was rarely clear-cut. Perkin (1976) has pointed out that Scarborough and Skegness were similar distances from the West Riding and yet they developed very different social tones. Blackpool and Southport produced contrasting forms of resort but Southport, more middle class in tone, lay closer to the main centres of demand in Lancashire. In this instance, local land-ownership factors were more decisive and this is discussed in greater detail later in the chapter.

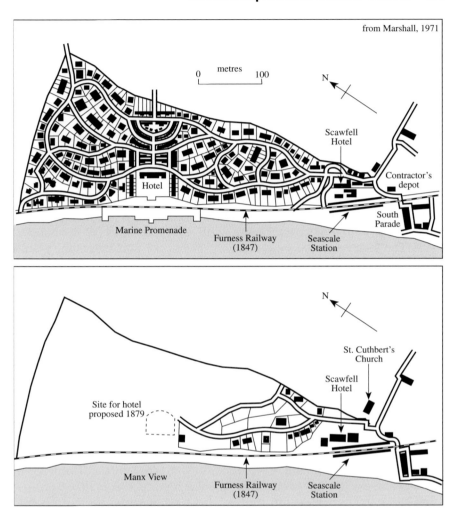

from Marshall, 1971

Figure 7.9   The proposed and actual development of Seascale, 1879–1898

Thus, it is too simplistic to see the links between resorts and transport as a form of technological determinism. To be effective, new technology also requires new organisational and social changes. After all, the railway companies did not, at first, see the possibilities of leisure travel and it required organisational innovators such as Thomas Cook to demonstrate the traffic that could be generated (Brendon 1991). Social attitudes also had to change. Giddens (1991) has argued that travel involves social relations being "disembedded" or lifted out from a local context and that people must have trust and confidence in institutions and processes before willingly departing for new areas. Any transport link was never sufficient, in itself, to create new patterns of tourism and it is perhaps useful to conclude this section by briefly considering how seaside resorts may have evolved without the presence of railways. We can employ a form of counterfactual argument, discussing what could have happened in order to place what did happen in perspective (Norton 1984). The railways created specific patterns and scales of movement to the coast, they moulded the catchment areas, but they did not *create* the seaside resort. The slower and lesser capacity of the road- and water-based systems of transport would have produced different patterns and scales of movement. There would probably have been a closer identity of resorts with their local and regional markets: Liverpool with its outlets at Bootle and Crosby, Edinburgh with Portobello, Sunderland with Roker, or Bristol with Clevedon and Weston-super-Mare. Far fewer resorts, possibly only Blackpool and Brighton, would have had national catchment areas. Centres closest to the large urban industrial regions may have grown even larger, while more distant resorts would have remained considerably smaller. It is possible that the social tone of the resorts would have been more clearly differentiated, with the distant coastlines maintaining a more pronounced fashionable air, just as the resorts nearest the urban centres would have been the preserve of those with less time for pleasure. Regions further from the coast, such as the Midlands, would have continued their greater reliance on inland recreational resources and, in general, the seaside would have played a smaller part in the overall leisure lifestyles of the British population.

While all this is speculation, it does serve as a reminder that there is no simple and inevitable dependent link between transport innovation and recreation and tourism. The seaside resort, albeit in a different form, would have existed just as it did in Roman times (Casson 1974), or as it came to be in the eighteenth century, because of wider socio-economic and cultural processes of which transport was an important but a not determining aspect.

Local factors in resort areas

The nature of demand for seaside holidays and the role of transportation present only part of the picture of resort development. A crucial element was the way in which localised factors, such as the physical environment, local economies, landowners, local government and business entrepreneurs responded to the opportunities provided by a growing market. These not only shaped the ways in which resorts developed, they created the particular geographies of the resorts: their morphology, patterns of land use and the social, economic and cultural relationships between visitors and local populations.

The physical environment was a basic influence on the development of a resort, setting limits to the type and scale of response to demand. Dr Richard Russell's (1752:230) famous dissertation on sea-bathing outlined the conditions for a model seaside resort and it gives an insight into mid-eighteenth-century perceptions of suitable coastal environments:

> [It] should be clean and neat, at some distance from the opening of a river; that the water may be as highly loaded with sea salt, and the other riches of the ocean as possible, and not weakened by the mixing of fresh water, with its waves. In the next place one would choose the shore to be sandy and flat; for the convenience of going into the sea in a bathing chariot. And lastly, that the sea shore should be bounded by lively cliffs, and downs; to add to the cheerfulness of the place, and give the person that has bathed an opportunity of mounting on horseback dry and clean; to pursue such exercises, as may be advised by his physician, after he comes out of the bath.

This statement was often copied in local guidebooks to resorts, with claims that they exactly fitted Russell's ideal (Gilbert 1954). The early assessments of suitable coastal environments were extremely detailed with small variations at the micro-level pointed out. Soil, wind direction and strength, air quality, temperature variations, local birth and death rates, were all employed in a form of scientific analysis of healthy environments. In general, the southern coasts of Britain were held to be superior, especially those of Sussex. They were found to be sheltered from northerly winds, but were exposed to sea breezes and had lengthy hours of sunshine. Some resorts claimed to have bracing air, which encouraged exercise (for instance, Brighton, Eastbourne, Scarborough, Yarmouth), others claimed soothing air, conducive to rest (Bourne-mouth, Falmouth, Torquay). Along with this detailed analysis of health benefits, the aesthetics of coastal environments were championed: picturesque cliffs, extensive sea views, the variety of scenery, and the possibilities of studying and collecting shells, fossils, seaweed and other flora (Corbin 1994).

In general terms, certain aspects of the physical environment were significant for resort development at any large scale. Easy access to a clean, sandy beach was important as was a straight shoreline with gently sloping cliffs. This permitted the spatial spread of visitors along the beach so that different social groups could be accommodated without conflict. Brighton, Blackpool and Great Yarmouth benefited considerably from this aspect. A lack of steep gradients was also an asset, especially for families and the retired, although the secluded fishing port with cliffs was an asset for resorts catering for the discerning middle-class trade (Walton 1983). Beyond these general considerations, topography influenced conditions within the resort itself. Steep slopes and cliffs provided more extensive views and encouraged the growth of social contours. At Eastbourne, the better residences lay on the slope leading to Beachy Head, with the working-class terraces confined to the low marshy land to the east. If the highest points were too exposed to the elements they would, of course, become relegated to the poorest families, as happened in Brighton (Gilbert 1954). Climate always remained an important factor, influencing as it did the ability of a resort to have a winter as well as a summer season. Temperature range, shelter and assessments of bracing or soothing air continued to be referred to from the eighteenth century to the twentieth century. Just as Jane Austen's Mr Woodhouse in *Emma* (1815) worried over the relative merits of Southend and Cromer in these terms, so the *Queen Book of Travel* in 1914 was still carefully assessing resorts in climatic terms including a detailed comparison between Switzerland and the "English Riviera". Thus the more sedative climate of the English resorts was recommended for residents of dry, inland districts and also for the "numerous sufferers from the effects of the overexciting air of the east coasts of England and Scotland" (Queen 1914:198–200). It is difficult today, perhaps, to appreciate the significance of these details for Victorian and Edwardian readers, as the travel brochures of the 1990s present a standardised image of beach and sunshine across the globe.

The nature of local and regional economies—the range of alternative forms of economic activity and the perceived significance of tourism within them—was an important influence on the fortunes of resorts. In some cases, tourism came to dominate the economy, as it did in Nice, elsewhere it was submerged by more profitable alternatives, or tourism could co-exist fairly harmoniously with a variety of different activities. At a small scale, this latter aspect can be seen in the case of Portobello, lying about three miles from the centre of Edinburgh. The resort grew modestly from the mid-eighteenth century with villas along the sea front and it later acquired a pier and promenade (Gifford et al 1984). From the outset, however, Portobello combined leisure with two potteries and a brickworks and successfully maintained its "dual character as a seaside resort and an industrial town" (Keir 1966:87).

On a larger scale, Swansea in South Wales provides an example of a town where the local economy ultimately offered more attractive alternatives to tourism and its resort function declined. The dilemma of opting for tourism or trade and industry dated back to the eighteenth century and was observed by the Revd Evans in 1804: "It is [now] the wish of the inhabitants that Swansea should be viewed in the light of a fashionable resort, rather than as a trading town: and a bathing place rather than a sea-port" (quoted in Stevens 1990:264). In 1762, an area of common land to the east of the town known as the Burrows became enclosed and the town corporation saw an opportunity to create a resort in the area. It leased land for lodging houses, bathing facilities and the building of an assembly room, theatre and fashionable walks. The corporation also promoted its resort in Bristol, Cork and Dublin. By the 1780s, its marketing slogan had the rather optimistic claim of the "Brighton of Wales" and it was receiving a daily mailcoach from Bristol, and regular sailing vessels from that city, as well as from Gloucester and other ports on the Severn estuary. Boat races and trips to the Gower organised by local seamen were all part of the attractions of a rising seaside resort. However, at the same time, industry and commerce were also expanding in the area (Boorman 1990). Heavy industry grew rapidly in the Lower Swansea Valley, especially the copper smelting industry, where copper ore from Cornwall came to Swansea and utilised the local coal supplies. All this demanded better port facilities and the Burrows was the ideal site, notwithstanding its tourist function and affluent clientele. In 1852, the South Dock was constructed and this effectively killed off the seaside resort. More modest leisure facilities moved away from the Burrows towards the western side of Swansea but the town never again saw a major future in the holiday industry and essentially provided a local outlet for the western industrial valleys of the coalfield.

Landownership and the control of land could be decisive for the way in which a resort evolved and this aspect of resort growth will be examined in some detail. A comparison of the fortunes of Blackpool and Southport can provide a clear illustration of its importance (Liddle 1982; Perkin 1976; Walton 1978; Urry 1990). Both resorts had fine beaches but Southport was nearer to large centres of population. Both began through local innkeepers, farmers and fishermen providing sea-bathing facilities for visitors. In Southport, however, the land was unenclosed and the squatters there, who provided the leisure facilities, became tenants of the lords of the manor who decided to lay out spacious and elegant avenues and villas. These major landlords effectively resisted industrial and commercial development so that Southport evolved into an upmarket resort and retirement centre for industrial magnates. Blackpool, by contrast, was a community of small freeholders who controlled only limited areas of land. There was no scope here for a planned high-class development dominated by large landowners. Instead, Blackpool grew as an ill-planned, high-density mass of small properties, boarding houses, small shops and amusement arcades, which offered cheap accommodation and entertainment for an expanding working-class market.

Until the arrival of the railways, many resorts had a uniform market to serve and this made it easier for individual developers, builders and investors to have a clear idea about the type of resort to aim for. After the railways, resorts were able to serve a variety of clientele and they faced more competition from rivals. This could lead to differences of opinion in the local community and the successful resorts were those which could control their growth carefully to suit particular markets. A number of large landowners saw this possibility and so became involved in resort development, for instance the Devonshires at Eastbourne, Radnors at Folkestone, Mostyns at Llandudno and the Scarisbrick and Hesketh families at Southport. An alternative approach was the formation of land companies, combining the resources of groups of businessmen, such as those from Manchester involved in the expansion of Colwyn Bay (Walton 1983). Later in the nineteenth century, this unity of vision could be provided by local governments who became increasingly significant in shaping the future of resorts. The interrelationship between landowners and resort growth can be examined using the example of Bournemouth.

The Enclosure Act of 1802 resulted in most of the land in the Bournemouth area being held by a few individuals. Before 1840, much of this area consisted of a few scattered cottages with one street of villas, the result of a speculative development by a local landowner. Gradually, adjacent landowners followed this example so that, from its beginning, Bournemouth was the creation of its landowners, who controlled its pattern of growth and its social tone. About twelve private estates and six land companies were involved in the process and virtually all the land developed was leasehold. The leasehold system enabled owners to maintain a tight grip on what happened to their land. It was this concentration of landholding with the leasehold system which gave the resort its particular character. These landowners nevertheless restricted themselves to the control of overall growth and left the provision of amenities and promotion to an especially active local authority (Roberts 1982).

Bournemouth grew rapidly from a population in 1851 of under 700 to 80 000 by 1911 and this growth took place in three phases, each the result of distinctive social and economic circumstances. Figure 7.10 (map A) shows the overall sequence of spatial growth during this time. Phase one was from the 1840s to the early 1870s when large detached villas were built around the valley of the Bourne and on the East and West Cliffs. Visitors mainly came for the winter and their servants also lived in the villas. Other workers travelled in from nearby Poole, Christchurch and local villages. Phase two, from the 1870s to the 1890s, saw the

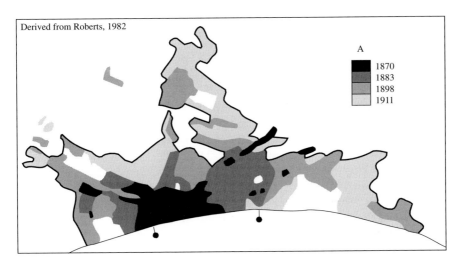

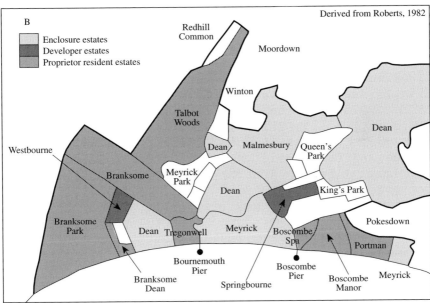

Figure 7.10   The spatial growth and patterns of landholding in Bournemouth in the nineteenth century (Roberts (1982) with permission of Leicester University Press)

arrival of the railway in 1870 which helped create a two-season resort with middle-class summer visitors supplementing an elite winter season. Winter-season villas continued to capture the best locations on the cliffs and at Dean Park, while a summer resort developed at Boscombe to the east. Here, semi-detached houses were quickly converted into lodging houses. This second phase also saw the growth of workers' housing with satellite settlements to the north and north-east of the resort at Winton, Springbourne, Pokesdown and Moordown. These were physically separate from the visitor zone as no working-class housing was permitted on the landed estates. This strict segregation of classes reflected the landowners' desire to maintain Bournemouth's respectable image. The third phase of Bournemouth's development was from the 1890s to 1914. This saw the decline of the winter health season but an increase in the summer visitors and the retired. Better rail links also brought lower-middle-class visitors. From the early 1900s, the large villas at the centre of the resort were converted to hotels and there was an expansion of workers' housing beyond the main estates.

This story of the resort's growth must be related to the land-holding pattern in Bournemouth and Figure 7.10 (map B) shows the different landholding types. Enclosure estates were created by the 1802 Act and three owners controlled 59 per cent of this land, largely in the Meyrick, Malmesbury and Dean estates. The proprietor resident estates belonged to wealthy outsiders, who bought land in the area from the early nineteenth century, and who established secluded villas in substantial private grounds. As the original owners of these properties died, so the land was laid out for development. By the end of the century only the Portman and Talbot estates remained undeveloped. Developer estates were those purchased by land companies with the specific intention of developing them for building.

The first developments took place on the Meyrick, Tregonwell, Branksome and Dean estates with new villas. The Portman estate resisted development until much later, while Malmesbury Park was developed for artisan housing for boarding-house keepers and pensioners in the 1880s. Talbot Woods remained unbuilt until the 1920s. The developer estates at Westbourne and Springbourne were used for artisan terrace housing from the 1850s and 1870s away from the heart of the resort. The pattern of expansion that resulted from the mixture of different forms of estates created an irregular outward spread with many gaps in development. There was certainly no neat progression of concentric lines of growth.

Within this system, leaseholding to builders and 99-year leases for homeowners enabled the estates to maintain control over development and the landowners took a long-term view of "desirable" development rather than the short-term attraction of immediate profit. No commercialisation was permitted along the seafront and no shops or public houses were allowed amongst the villas, which could have happened with a looser freehold system. Although the leasehold system began to break up in the 1920s, its influence on Bournemouth and its exclusive districts long outlived its demise.

Local government had an important role to play in the development of resorts. The case study of Bath (chapter 4) revealed the significance of the corporation in the affairs of the spa in the eighteenth century and, during the following century, local government became increasingly influential throughout the whole urban system. Surprisingly, however, government in the seaside resorts showed a very slow response to the obvious need to maintain a healthy and safe environment for visitors through the provision of water, sewage, paving and lighting of a high standard. Most active involvement in Britain did not come until the later nineteenth century (Walton 1983). The principal ways in which the infrastructure of resorts was improved before then were through an *ad hoc* system of public subscription, the initiative of private companies or the work of the Improvement Commissioners. The 1835 reforms of municipal corporations and the 1848 Public Health Act influenced conditions at the coast but the 1849 cholera epidemic with 124 deaths in Margate, 65 in Hastings and 26 in Southport, together with a succession of critical reports from Board of Health inspectors, revealed what little progress had been made in places whose chief claim to fame was their apparently healthy environments. It might be expected that seaside resorts would have been in the vanguard of health reforms, but poor water quality and drainage were common tales, with sewage on the beach even at resorts like Brighton and Margate.

Major improvements came in the 1870s, 1880s and 1890s, not only in health control but in municipal involvement in the provision of attractions. As a result not only were better sewage and drainage schemes installed in resorts like Bridlington and Brighton but piers, concert halls, winter gardens and eventually promotion, came within the active sphere of corporations. Bournemouth was particularly enterprising in this area, with the corporation investing heavily in parks and gardens, cliff-top walks, winter gardens, piers and an orchestra (Roberts 1982). Local by-laws were also introduced to help control visitor behaviour and a system of sanitary certificates maintained high standards of hygiene. Local government was thus an increasingly vital element for the success of a resort in a competitive world.

A similar situation could also be found abroad. The prosperity of San Sebastian in Spain depended ultimately on the excellent provision of local government (Walton and Smith 1995), which provided strict planning controls, excellent gas and water supplies and a sewage system. Local police controlled public behaviour and a good relationship with the private sector resulted in San Sebastian being the best governed city in Spain. Local government provided a stable environment and a long-term sense of continuity and ideology which encouraged the resort to renew its attractions and image in a controlled response to changing situations. The same picture existed in Nice, where the role of local government was a significant element in the success of the resort (Haug 1982). From the early nineteenth century, local officials came to the verdict that the future of Nice depended on wealthy winter visitors and consequently adopted policies that organised the city around the needs and desires of the *hivernants*.

In 1832, a planning commission was created in Nice to control growth—the *Consiglio d'Ornato*. Its functions were to oversee the alignment and improvement of streets and approve plans for new buildings. This resulted in a new tourist district, the Croix de Marbre, with a gridiron pattern of streets, which was laid out to the west of the old town. Therefore, in the initial phases of growth of the resort, there was strong planning and regulation rather than a pattern dominated by speculators and builders. This level of control was, however, difficult to maintain during the period of rapid growth in the second half of the century and speculative development came to dominate with a rash of villa apartments and hotels. In fact, the degree of planning varied with economic circumstances. In boom periods, entrepreneurs developed areas as they wished within certain guidelines But in periods of stagnation, the city planners would impose stronger controls on the urban fabric. Consequently the map of Nice reflects these economic cycles, with the more regular patterns representing phases of stagnation, the less regular patterns eras of expansion (Haug 1982).

As well as facing the pressures of speculative interests, the city council in Nice had to appease the demands of the winter residents. Here was a group of wealthy people who lived on the edges of the city and who had only limited connections or interests with its overall well-being. Their demands consisted of access to desirable views, a healthy environment and exclusive entertainment. Thus, the *hivernant* suburbs were not functionally linked to Nice and roads were forced to wind around the villas and extensive gardens rather than being in the form of planned streets. Not only did these property rights have to be accommodated within the growth of Nice, but the public health of the city had to be skewed towards the needs of the visitors (Haug 1982). Within the city there was a district gulf between a local population, largely unaware of advances in public health, and a cosmopolitan elite from around Europe who were fully aware of the standards required and whose own health was their major preoccupation. A cholera epidemic in 1865, which resulted in a disastrous tourist season, emphasised how vital these matters were for the city's prosperity. Improved water supplies were a key element in the campaign. Before 1864 Nice depended on local wells and springs or the River Paillon but a new scheme tapped Alpine springs from the nearby mountains. As might be predicted, the best water was channelled to the tourist districts, and the local population continued to use the inadequate local supplies.

Waste disposal also saw uneven provision between the hosts and guests in the city. Improving the situation, as in the case of the location of the railway station, split the local business community. The tourism group argued for large-scale sewage schemes to ensure the continued patronage of wealthy visitors, but the commercial business group opposed public expense on schemes which were geared to a purely seasonal sector of society. They were joined by local farmers who wished to continue using the waste for their fields. A compromise was reached with limited improvements which ensured that the tourist district benefited most and it was not until the 1890s that major improvements for the whole city took place (Haug 1982).

Social geographies of the resorts

The uneven provision of services in Nice between visitors and local inhabitants highlights the varying social geographies that were created by tourism development of resorts. This was evident in spas (chapter 4) as well as at the seaside. The different groups of people at these places included the visitors, who could themselves be from different social backgrounds, and the inhabitants, who could consist of local social elites, business interests, workers and those not directly involved in tourism at all.

Thompson (1988:292) has pointed out that one of the distinctive roles of resorts as places was their function of bringing different social groups together. In Britain, they formed "easily the most widely experienced set of middle-class encounters with the working classes". Thus seaside resorts were a set of arenas where class divisions were especially sharply accentuated, not just between visitors and local workers but between different types of visitors. These divisions often amounted to a process of contesting space within the resort.

There was always, of course, a basic division between visitors and the local working population. In middle-class resorts it was often the case that local elite and affluent visitors would share much the same space.

This happened in Nice (Haug 1982) and in the genteel villa districts of Bournemouth (Roberts 1982). But those who served the tourists were confined to very different parts of the towns. Again, in the case of Bournemouth, we have seen how the workers' districts were carefully segregated from the exclusive visitor spaces but these divisions were also very clear in less planned contexts. In Brighton, Gilbert (1954:175) observed that, "the contrast between Disraeli's two nations was clearly visible"; the zones of the consumers and the producers were evident in sharp relief. The wealth and fashion of Brighton was on display along the sea front with its hotels, shops and large houses, but behind this façade there was a labyrinth of narrow streets and courts, often more overcrowded than northern industrial towns. In the 1840s, the worst part of the resort was around Edward Street in Carlton Hill, a factor highlighted by the 1849 Board of Health Report. But not only were living spaces sharply differentiated, the leisure spaces of visitors and locals were largely separate. Much local working-class leisure for males in Brighton centred around the public houses and cheap theatres and music halls known as "penny gaffs". The distribution of these amenities in the resort reflected, not the visitor map, but the back streets of the local working population (Lowerson and Myerscough 1977).

The growth of tourism in the resorts of southern Europe could introduce new forms of social areas. Nice, for instance, in its pre-tourism era reflected a fairly common pattern of living, with diverse social neighbourhoods of all income groups living in close proximity. The establishment of a tourist colony to the west of the old town, however, began to draw the local social elite away from the old town towards the *hivernants'* quarters. The old town became a neglected ghetto for the poorer workers, often unskilled Italian migrants. Skilled workers moved out also, not to the tourist districts but distributed more widely around the city (Haug 1982).

Those who supplied the needs of visitors cannot be simply grouped together. There was a world of difference between the providers of large hotels and villa accommodation and the landladies and street entertainers who catered for the working classes. Conflict was possible between these different groups of providers, each trying to influence the direction of resort development. In Blackpool, the pro-working-class lobby became increasingly influential on the local council and this helped the resort to grow in a way that served their interests (Walton 1983). The nature of the services provided was reflected in the social structure of the resorts. Elite resorts, like Brighton, had high numbers of female domestic servants while Blackpool was below the national average in this respect. Much of the work required was filled by females but male employment was significant in the resorts in retailing, transport and building operations.

Most of the resorts relied on significant amounts of seasonal labour migration to cater for visitor needs (Walton 1983). In the area of accommodation, it was local men who were generally involved at the early stages of growth with an additional income provided for local tradesmen and their families. Over time, however, the growth of tourism encouraged outsiders to move in and lodging-house keeping was particularly attractive for lower-middle-class women seeking an occupation (Walton 1978).

Resorts catered for an immense diversity of visitors: middle-class families, bachelors, respectable working classes, rowdy excursionists or fashionable society. The problem was that they often wanted access to the same spaces: the beach, the promenade and the sea. This issue was complicated by the vagueness over who owned and controlled the tidal foreshore. Some corporations, as at Scarborough, owned this area but generally responsibility was divided and debatable. In this disputed zone, regulating visitor behaviour and forms of entertainment was always difficult and, where the beach lay within easy access of a railway station, the working-class excursion trade would often colonise the route and the foreshore. They brought their own customs with them and failed to modify them in a new setting. This tended to force the middle-class visitors further along the front to the more peripheral areas of the resort. Satellite resorts could then develop at one remove from the main centre, where the sensibilities of the middle classes could still be preserved. A number of resorts had these middle-class "havens": Westcliff for Southend, Westgate for Margate, Bexhill for Hastings, Sheringham for Cromer and Lytham St Anne's for Blackpool (Jackson 1991). The frequency of class conflict between visitors at Britain's seaside resorts declined, however, in the later 1800s, attributed in part to an increased social tolerance amongst the middle classes together with a growing modification of working-class behaviour in resort settings. Therefore by the 1890s, a more all-embracing common "resort culture" emerged amongst visitors. Where problems continued, they stemmed not from the tightly knit communities of the industrial towns, who often holidayed together and regulated their own behaviour, but from excursions from the more anonymous urban environments of big cities such as London and Liverpool (Walton 1983).

Image and place

The coast has always produced strong visual images and emotional reactions. The natural landscape of sea, sky, cliffs and beach or the resort townscape of promenade, piers, pavilions, entertainment and exotic architecture, provide a distinctive sense of place: a holiday landscape that represents an escape from the ordinary routine of life. As artists and writers increasingly responded to these scenes and as competition arose between resort areas, so the opportunities to both reflect and reinforce this aspect of the "tourist gaze" (Urry 1990) increased.

The seaside in the nineteenth century came to assume the role of a special place in many people's lives, bound up with expectations, hopes and desires. It formed part of their "geography of hope" (Wright 1947), where even a short annual visit to the coast could be something to make the rest of the year endurable. There was a sense of excitement and anticipation on arrival. A Bolton worker in the 1930s recalled a visit to Blackpool:

> We emerged from the station . . . me feeling like a schoolboy again for it was as a schoolboy I had last been to the seaside and my wife's cheeks glowed with the salt air of the incoming tide.
>
> (Cross 1990b:61)

Some of the Revd Francis Kilvert's most ecstatic passages in his diary were when he was at the seaside and experienced "a delicious feeling of freedom": freedom from the constrictions of Victorian life (Kilvert 1977:212). A working-class woman from north London remembered a childhood excursion to the coast "what an adventure that was! My first sight of the sea!" (Delgado 1977:107). Numerous examples of similar reactions testify to the significance of the seaside in people's lives.

Coastal landscapes produced strong reactions from artists. Chapter 6 discusses how artists could play an important part in the "discovery" phase of areas for recreation and tourism by helping to form new aesthetic standards, and their work can be used to gain an insight into contemporary attitudes to the coastal environment. Herbert's (1988, 1994) recent studies of Monet's paintings on the Normandy coast in the 1870s and 1880s, between Dieppe and Deauville, raise some interesting ideas. The pictures provide now familiar images of the coast as it apparently seemed at that time but, in fact, Monet omitted much of the development that had already occurred through the agency of tourism (Figure 7.11). Hotels and visitors are generally excluded from Monet's vision, although some of the views were clearly painted from hotel bedrooms. Etretat had developed since the 1860s, but Monet painted a pre-growth landscape excluding most signs of labour and hard work which merely appear as an occasional decorative backdrop. Other painters, such as Pierre Outin and de Poittevin, depicted the reality of gregarious groups of tourists on the cliffs (Figure 7.12) but Monet's view coincided with the desired image of many bourgeois urban visitors. The

Figure 7.11   "Etretat: the Beach and the Falaise d'Amout" by Claude Monet (1883). Monet carefully omitted signs of tourist development to make his views more appealing (Joseph Winterbotham Collection, Art Institute of Chicago, © ADAGP, Paris and DACS, London 1996)

Figure 7.12   "Bathing at Etretat" by Eugene de Poittevin (1865–1866) shows how by the 1860s Etretat was attracting the middle classes of both sexes. The resort was well known for its mixed bathing culture and informed social life (Musée des Beaux Arts de Caen)

Figure 7.13 "Etretat, the Beach and the Porte d'Amout" (1888), a photograph of the same scene as Monet painted which shows the reality of development in Etretat with a beach full of fishing boats and a resort already beginning to grow (Roger-Viollet, Paris)

coast represented an escape from the everyday urban world—an image that was an illusion which fitted their needs. Although they had used the newly improved roads to reach the resort, stayed in the hotels, patronised the restaurants and were surrounded by the whole social organisation of tourism (Figure 7.13), this is not what they "saw". They sought the solitary views that Monet captured and, when they returned home, they "carried away images of the pre-modern landscape" (Herbert 1994:1).

That pronounced gap between image and reality revealed by Monet's paintings has been a continuing aspect of the relationship between tourism and place (Ashworth and Voogd 1990; Boyle and Hughes 1991; Gold and Ward 1994; Hughes 1992; Kearns and Philo 1993). Place promotion, although very much associated with the marketing of tourism today, has in fact a lengthy history (Ward 1988, 1994) and is part of that enterprise of places being "fashioned in the image of tourism" (Hughes 1992:33). It is perhaps significant that seaside resorts were amongst the earliest parts of the urban system in Britain to experience place promotion. From the late nineteenth century, local authorities tried to secure local powers to advertise themselves. Blackpool succeeded in 1879 but progress was slow until the Health

Resorts and Watering Places Act of 1921. The "boosting" of urban areas was far more common in the ever-changing American urban scene, however, and it is probably no coincidence that seaside resorts were also the most dynamic parts of the UK urban system (Ward 1994).

Railway companies were involved in the place promotion of British seaside resorts as well as local authorities. Their first efforts were confined to posters and handbills and newspaper advertisements for day excursions But by the 1890s, they were promoting the coastal zones (rather than individual resorts) that lay within their operating area. The Great Western Railway (GWR), for instance, began to advertise the Cornish Riviera (Burdett 1970) and the South Eastern and Chatham Railway somewhat bizarrely termed the Kent coast "Caesar's Choice!". Individual resort promotion soon followed, Ilfracombe by 1908 with the GWR, Skegness ("Skegness is so Bracing") by the Great Northern Railway (Richards and MacKenzie 1986). Even the railway companies themselves became part of the image; the GWR termed itself the "Holiday Line", and the London, Brighton and South Coast Railway presented itself as the "Sunshine Line" (Cole and Durack 1990). But the railway posters were the most visible of the companies' efforts and they, in themselves, reveal important aspects of image creation and its role in shaping visitor expectation of place. The earliest posters lacked strong place images, instead they were a confused jumble of small vistas of resorts with uninspired scenes of piers, promenades, bandstands and hotels. By the early twentieth century, a more professional, stronger, image creation was evident (Cole and Durack 1990; Shackleton 1976). There was a particular appeal to families with images of open space, fresh air, children playing—reassuring and comforting scenes of uncomplicated pleasure. There was also the apparently uncomplicated ability of marketeers to associate one place with another; not only did the Cornish Riviera ape the South of France but even the Moray Firth Coast was termed the "Scottish Riviera" by the Great North of Scotland Railway. The landscapes of the resorts were also carefully distorted. A poster of Weston-super-Mare in the 1930s portrayed a resort curiously free from its familiar Severn estuary mud and with a townscape nearer to the Côte d'Azur than Somerset (Palin 1987) (Figure 7.14).

As images of the coast became simpler and stronger (see especially the series of posters by Tom Purvis for the London and North Eastern Railway in the late 1920s), so did the language that was employed reveal a change. The Edwardian terms "breezy" and "bracing" became supplanted, by the 1930s, with "sunshine" and "warmth". The rise of the fashionable suntan in the 1920s and the competition from resorts abroad meant new images had to be sought and the nature of the seaside resort experience redefined. These changing images of the coast repay careful

Figure 7.14 "Weston-super-Mare" by Claude Buckle (1930s?). Manipulating place images has a long tradition in the tourism industry (National Railway Museum, York/ Science and Society Picture Library)

analysis as they are all part of the evolving relationship between the seaside and society which has now been in existence for over 200 years. This relationship shows little sign of weakening; the coast still dominates tourism patterns at national and international scales and the stock image of the travel brochures continues to be the sea, the beach and the resort—the epitome of the holiday experience.

8

Recreation and tourism for all?

How should one characterise the geography of recreation and tourism in the later nineteenth and early twentieth centuries? For most social groups in western Europe and North America, there was more time and income for leisure activities and new patterns of leisure were stimulated by increased socio-economic and physical mobility. For the social elites, new opportunities existed, with exclusivity found either in visits to exotic destinations available on a global scale or within the expensive winter and summer resort enclaves of Europe. The middle classes were also ranging further afield, both within their own countries and in making attenuated versions of the old Grand Tour. Greater wealth, shorter working hours and the gradual provision of holidays with pay permeated down the social ladder so that the working classes were also able to extend their leisure patterns to include visits to destinations ever further away from home.

Leisure activities were also changing. As some traditional entertainments declined, so new ones arose. Spectator sports might replace bull-baiting, cock-fighting or street football in popular culture, while country walking, rowing, skiing and golf became important pastimes for the more affluent. Many of these activities saw increased commercial intervention, whether it was travel firms like Thomas Cook or the Polytechnic Association, entertainments at the seaside or home-based diversions. And, after the First World War, the significance of tourism activity was beginning to attract the attention of national governments who saw a role in planning and the gathering of travel statistics (Jones 1986, 1987; Lickorish and Kershaw 1958; Newton 1995; Norval 1934; Ogilvie 1933; Pimlott 1947). While all these trends can be discerned, it is less clear how far they represented fundamentally new experiences in people's lives or were variations on longer term themes. Having more holiday and travelling further do not necessarily represent a complete break with earlier conditions. Furthermore, there is a danger in overemphasising the occasional new experience at the expense of the daily and weekly routines in leisure which may not have undergone any substantial alteration over time.

The ways in which leisure changed for different social groups in different areas during the nineteenth century have fostered a lively debate amongst social historians (Bailey 1989). This is not the place to consider the debate in detail but a few salient points can be outlined. One theme concerns the degree of continuity and change in leisure practices in the transition from pre-industrial to industrial societies (Bailey 1989; Cunningham 1980, 1990; Walton and Walvin 1983). There is the view that an urban industrial society was less significant in creating new forms of leisure than was once believed. Thus Cunningham (1990:336) doubts that the industrial revolution was "a cataclysmic force" which destroyed a self-contained pre-industrial world of leisure and he argues for transformation rather than destruction. Another theme in the debate concerns the nature of leisure forms, where it has been pointed out that too much attention has been paid to large institutionalised practices rather than to ordinary day to day experience. A similar bias has been detected with leisure settings, where the large industrial town has dominated the picture at the expense of the small town, suburbs and rural areas (Walton and Walvin 1983). There has also been a social-class bias with, for recent history, a focus on leisure of the working classes rather than the social elite (Cannadine 1990) or the middle classes (Lowerson 1993; Thompson 1988). The leisure of women and children has received even less attention (Davies 1992; Horn 1989; Walvin 1983).

The historical debate has also been concerned with the extent to which the leisure habits of one social class were influenced by those of another. Plumb (1973) suggests that a largely middle-class taste was transferred to a generally passive working class but Cunningham (1980) and Hardy (1990) prefer to see popular leisure as a more autonomous creation with people making their own culture. Thompson (1988) has expressed a similar opinion for the middle classes in relation to the social elite. These views certainly question the uncomplicated notion that "mass follows class" in an almost deterministic process (Gormsen 1981; Thurot 1973). Hardy (1990) argues for the interplay of agency and structure; the efforts of human agency to create forms of leisure within the structural context of the time, as a more significant process in leisure formation. Similarly, rather than its being a story of class succession, Bailey (1989:112) suggests that the evolution of leisure has in fact been "erratic, complex and contentious". Nevertheless he does claim that social class has always been a fundamental element in that evolution, with leisure clearly differentiated along class lines.

This chapter has to be highly selective in its choice of themes. It broadly divides recreation and tourism amongst three social groups— working class, middle class and elite—and considers how leisure activities varied in different settings, generally classified as urban and rural. The selection of themes tries to balance the emphasis of earlier chapters, so that the wealthy now receive rather less attention than the poorer in society, and travel abroad, although important, is only generally referred to. On the other hand, a number of themes that are discussed—popular recreations in the countryside, the urban recreations of the working and middle classes, recreation movements from town to countryside and the widening horizons of travel—do reflect topics that have arisen elsewhere in the book. The chapter also considers travel as a leisure experience in its own right, looks at the transformation of landscapes through leisure, and concludes with a discussion of recreation and tourism in the context of lifecycles and lifestyles.

Popular recreations in the countryside

The question of change or continuity in rural recreations in Britain for the late eighteenth and early nineteenth centuries was examined in the concluding parts of chapter 3. There has been a tendency to pass over rural leisure activities, however, once the tensions of this early period have been addressed. Yet despite rapid urbanisation and industrialisation in nineteenth-century Britain, a large sector of its population still lived, worked and played in the countryside and it would be a mistake to see these people merely as a dwindling band of little consequence. Popular rural recreation continued to adapt to new forms of agrarian capitalism. There is no doubting, of course, the major increase in urban population and the 1851 census showed, for the first time, more people in "urban" rather than "rural" situations in England and Wales (Best 1979). But the proportion of rural dwellers was still considerable: 46 per cent of the population of England and Wales in 1851, 41.3 per cent in 1861, 34.8 per cent in 1871 and 29.8 per cent in 1881. Furthermore, as Thompson (1988) points out, rural populations remained numerically much the same size.

There is evidence that some leisure activities in the countryside remained little changed until the 1870s, with old customs such as harvest home, Whitsun walks, agricultural shows, tithe feasts, markets and fairs, surviving the pressures from an urban world. Nevertheless, some rural recreations did largely disappear. Bull- and cock-fighting and other cruel sports were eliminated in most areas of Britain by the 1860s (Malcolmson 1973; Thompson 1988) through the actions of organisations such as the Royal Society for the Prevention of Cruelty to Animals (RSPCA) which was formed in 1824. But these pressures were highly class-specific. Little action was taken against the hunting and shooting pleasures of the landowning classes; what was morally corrupting for one group was apparently beneficial for another. A longer term survivor was the rural fair. Although attacked for their boisterousness by the respectable classes, many fairs survived throughout the nineteenth century. The region that suffered the greatest decline was the zone around London where pressures from magistrates and middle-class opinion were strongest. In the north and west and Scotland, however, fairs continued to be a major feature of rural recreation. This was especially the case if the fair had a strong economic function as well, such as a hiring fair for agricultural labour (Fraser 1990; Thompson 1988). Even so, the nineteenth-century migrating labourer, seeking work in different areas, helped to break down the more localised customs of rural areas (Malcolmson 1973).

From the mid-nineteenth century, recreations in the countryside came under the pressure of paternalism. Respectable local society, typified by the church and squire, felt an obligation to inculcate moral codes of behaviour amongst the population. Friendly Societies, church organisations and other devices were used to close down the rougher popular pastimes; a process noted by Thomas Hardy in rural Dorset (Gittings 1978). Together with the loss of space associated with the enclosure of fields and a general rise in hours of work to fit new methods of agricultural production (Cunningham 1990), rural recreations were continually under pressure from a range of different sources.

Howkins (1981) has provided an interesting case study of one rural holiday custom and how it fared during the nineteenth century. This was the Whitsun holiday in Oxfordshire from about 1800 to about 1900. During this period Whitsun, like other traditional holidays, was under attack. Until the 1830s, the holiday in Oxfordshire consisted of up to 13 days of revels, generally supported by the local gentry. This support was withdrawn, however, as landowners increasingly sought to impose stronger time and work disciplines into agricultural practices. Linked to this was a fundamental change in the nature of the whole agricultural process. As production moved to a scientific basis, so the old quasi-magical celebrations of growth and fertility were removed and therefore the reason for the holiday was undermined. At the same time, traditional Whitsun celebrations came under attack from the established church; the Bishop of Oxford, for instance, was keen to introduce shorter and more rational forms of recreation in the area. As a result church parades led by bands, village clubs, organised sports and sports days gradually became a feature of rural Oxfordshire. These measures had a number of consequences. Instead of the whole village participating in recreations, the old and the females became pushed to the sidelines—observers of male-dominated activities. By 1900, the Oxfordshire Whitsun holiday had been reduced from a 13-day revel to a one-day respectable Bank Holiday. These short holidays did retain one aspect from the past, however. They remained essentially localised affairs and the railways which appeared in the area tempted few villagers to travel to more distant places in search of pleasure (Howkins 1981).

Therefore, despite major changes, it remained the case that rural populations still had the "ability to create a culture for themselves" (Cunningham 1990:304). The family, the pub, football, cricket, were foci for village leisure even if it was less rigorous than a century earlier. Children, especially, were able to continue age-old pastimes tied to the rhythms of rural life (Walvin 1983). As well as football in winter and cricket in summer, there were explorations of the surrounding countryside and Sunday School outings to local beauty spots (Horn 1989). The recollections of Flora Thompson (1939) of rural Oxfordshire in the 1880s give some insight into aspects of rural recreation. She felt that the 1880s saw the last generation of children who kept to the old pastimes, with outside influences becoming dominant after that time. Flora Thompson's record is particularly valuable for highlighting activities, and the significance attached to them, which can be easily lost in the historical record. For instance, she records a month-long holiday visiting relatives in the local town eight miles away when she was eleven and her brother eight. The short journey was a vivid experience in their lives:

> A streak of clear water spouting from a pipe high up in the hedgerow bank was to them what a cataract might have been to more seasoned travellers; and the wagons they met, with names of strange farmers and farms painted across the front, were as exciting as hearing a strange language.
>
> (Thompson 1939:337)

In the local town, these children encountered new worlds where even visiting the shops was a memorable event. The holiday was informally organised, required little expenditure, and had no tourist "industry" involvement, and yet was as much a part of tourism's history as a Grand Tour.

Urban recreations

As chapter 3 has indicated, space for leisure and recreation has long been a feature of urban environments. But the opportunities for leisure and recreation, or the lack of them, for the rapidly expanding urban populations of industrialising regions in the nineteenth century became a matter of public and official concern. In this section, the focus will be on working-class and middle-class urban recreation, the spaces utilised by them, plus some examples of the contest for control of those spaces.

For the urban working classes, the space for recreation was often informal and consisted, pre-eminently, of the areas around their houses, particularly the streets. Other spaces that they might use were often under pressure from other land uses and working populations generally had little control in determining this process. Within working-class districts themselves, there was relatively little conflict with other social classes over the use of the streets. But problems could arise if working people encroached on central areas that were seen as the preserve of the more affluent. The swelling industrial towns saw high-density housing with poor living conditions and very little open space provision. This not only created health problems but also meant that the working classes increasingly impinged on middle-class space. Their use of streets, squares and other areas was highly visible and intrusive and also conflicted with the developing commercial uses of shops, banks, and professional services which were appearing in town centres. These problems could be clearly seen in the new industrial towns of the Rhineland and Westphalia (Abrams 1992). Here, entertainments often had their origins in spontaneous street gatherings with musicians and family theatres spilling over into the surrounding taverns. As industrialisation used up spaces which were previously occupied for recreation, so these street activities encroached on the shared space of the town centre. The urban bourgeois retreated from this area into their private clubs and homes and, from about the 1860s, left the police to regulate street leisure. What had once been a relatively classless general entertainment became class-specific and working-class leisure was pushed from the street into alehouses and taverns.

In Britain, the street was also of paramount importance as an area for working-class leisure (Davies 1992). In Salford and Manchester it was used by different age groups and both sexes, from mundane everyday activities such as women "sitting out" on doorsteps to large-scale annual events such as the Whit Walks. The street formed a strong link in the culture of these neighbourhoods; activities were free or very cheap, used by children playing, youths at street corners or communal street parties and dances. As late as the 1930s itinerant street entertainers were still a feature of Salford life. These working-class street cultures were able to continue partly because they did not impinge on other areas of the city. Something of the atmosphere of the Victorian back streets was captured by Somerset Maugham in *Liza of Lambeth* (1897:5–6):

This Saturday afternoon the street was full of life; no traffic came down Vere Street, and the cemented space between the pavements was given up to children. Several games of cricket were being played by wildly excited boys . . . The girls were more peaceable; they were chiefly employed in skipping . . . The grown-ups were gathered round the open doors; . . . women squatting on the doorstep . . . men leant against the walls.

Away from their own neighbourhoods, public streets could also be important spaces for working-class leisure activity. In Manchester and Salford the annual Whit Walks penetrated into the centre of the urban area but were tolerated because of their infrequency. On the other hand, more regular use of "shared space" could take place. In Glasgow, from the later nineteenth century onwards, the young from the crowded tenement areas would spill out into the city centre on Saturday nights and go "on the pad", strolling up and down Sauchiehall, Buchanan and Argyle Streets. The lighted areas were free and Sauchiehall became "the street of youth and evening promenade" (King 1987:144). There was a critical lack of alternative space in the overcrowded working-class residential districts of Glasgow. The Govanhill area, for instance, was laid out south of the River Clyde and the Gorbals from the 1870s. Between 1869 and 1877 its population grew to over 7000 and by 1891 had risen to 10 000. Yet the only open space for the tenement blocks was the small Govanhill Park which was not created until 1894 (Williamson et al, 1990).

Open space for urban leisure in the form of fashionable parks, squares and promenades had been a feature of urban design since the Renaissance (chapter 2). During the course of the nineteenth century, however, a number of factors created a demand for more formal provision of leisure and recreation space for the urban working classes. Perhaps the most notable result was the creation of public parks which were developed in Britain, Europe and North America from the second half of the century onwards. In most cases the factors underlying urban park creation were very similar: a concern for the physical and mental welfare of the workers, a desire to impose forms of social control and to develop more "rational" forms of recreation within the city and at its edges. The creation of parks could both divert the working class away from bourgeois areas and provide a healthier environment. The idea that open space was intrinsically healthy was based on the nineteenth-century pythogenic theory which mistakenly held that disease was due to bad air (Cartwright 1977). There was also the notion that open space and exercise would improve the moral welfare of people, provide an alternative to taverns and help reduce tension and social unrest. In Britain, the Select Committee on Public Walks was established in 1833 to identify open space sites in urban areas (Conway 1991). Little real progress was made until the 1840s, when the increased importance of municipal authorities and the Victorian concept of social citizenship (the moral obligation to help the poor) acted as a spur to action. Public parks could also serve, of course, as important spatial buffers between working- and middle-class areas of towns (Nuttgens 1973).

Figure 8.1 shows the evolving pattern of urban public parks in Britain. The first park created for an industrial town was Moor Park on the edge of Preston in 1833 when the Borough Council laid out walks, drives and rides on an area of unenclosed land (Conway 1991). Birkenhead, Sheffield and Derby followed in the 1840s, together with parks in London such as the Victoria Park in the East End. Other centres, such as Bath and Edinburgh, developed public parks also, but not necessarily for their working-class populations. Figure 8.1 shows a substantial growth of parks in midland and northern industrial centres from the mid-1840s to 1860; a pattern intensified from the 1860s. In this later period, industrial towns were also joined by some of the larger seaside resort centres such as Brighton, Hastings and Southport which now had sufficient working populations to need as much open space as their visitors. By the 1880s, industrial towns in South Wales, including Swansea and Llanelli, and centres in north-east England had acquired parks, as had cities with more diverse economic bases, such as Bristol (Meller 1976). But although a whole range of urban places developed public parks, the evolving pattern very much reflected the rapidly growing urban industrial centres of the country.

Manchester and Salford were amongst the earliest urban industrial areas to provide public parks for their working populations. In the 1840s Peel Park was established in Salford and Philips and Queen's Parks in Manchester (Davies 1992). Each was located close to large working-class districts and, over time, the various parks became strongly associated with their local communities. Thus Peel Park was linked to the residents of the Aldelphi, Islington and Hope Street areas, Ordsall Park served the dock area and Buile Hill Park catered for Hanky Park, Seedley and Weaste. By 1915, Salford had over 30 parks and recreation grounds. But spatial provision was uneven. The central working-class districts of Manchester had few outlets; Ancoats and Hulme with high population densities had no parks because industrial uses consumed all the available space. As in other cities, the use of the parks was highly focused in time. Weekends and public holidays saw the greatest influxes with Buile Hill sometimes coping with over 10 000 people at a time. Although all age groups used the parks, families and courting couples were major users for promenading, with young males using the space for football,

Figure 8.1   (*opposite*) The growth of public parks in Britain, 1820–1885

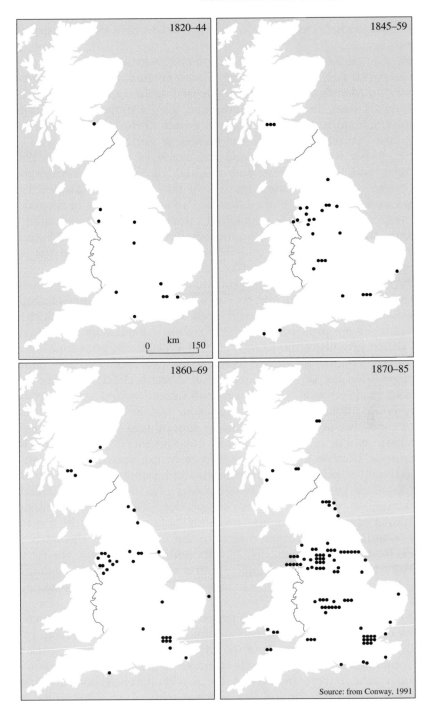

rugby and cricket. During the week, married women were the principal users.

The city authorities hoped to promote rational recreation in their public parks but inevitably these places created their own forms of activity. In Manchester, prostitutes paraded around the edge of the park at Ardwick near the army barracks and they also frequented Trafford Road which led to the docks and ran beside Ordsall Park. Many parks were also gathering grounds for gamblers. Furthermore, despite free access, parks were often beyond the reach of some groups. Young mothers, tied to housework and children, rarely used Salford's parks and were confined to their immediate streets instead (Davies 1992). Social conventions also limited access. Parks were arenas of display for the respectable working population, with best clothes required for Sunday outings. Consequently the very poor were excluded and in many parts of Manchester and Salford the streets remained the most important space for leisure and recreation.

The rapid urban growth in Germany, referred to earlier, also created a demand for public parks and they evolved along similar lines to Britain (Chadwick 1966). The parks and open spaces of the older cities like Düsseldorf were principally for middle-class use but with the industrial and urban growth of the Rhineland and Westphalia, poor housing and unsanitary conditions pushed open space provision into the political limelight from the 1870s onwards. Thus, Abrams (1992) identifies issues such as health, moral welfare, rational recreation and public order as underlying public urban park provision, just as they did in Britain. There was, however, a difference in the process of park creation in Germany where central and local government, together with local businesses, became far more involved from the outset, rather than the varied mix of privatised philanthropy and public initiative found in Britain. Park provision in Germany was also less directly linked to working-class needs in terms of location. For example, although Bochum's authorities saw the need for public open space, the town park was located on common land to the north-east of the town well away from working-class districts. In addition, the park was strictly controlled by wardens and police with a need for users to be "orderly and decently dressed", and unaccompanied children under twelve were prohibited (Abrams 1992:157).

The importance of open space provision for recreation was recognised in the extensive remodelling of Paris following the 1848 uprising. In the 1820s, the main open spaces of the city were the Luxembourg park and the formal Tuileries, together with commercial gardens such as Tivoli and Beaujon which were frequented by a wide cross-section of Parisian society (Green 1990). In addition to these areas, there were on the west side of the city the large wooded Bois de Boulogne and on the east side, the Bois de Vincennes. As the city grew so much open space was lost, and the working population sought refuge at the city edge which attracted unplanned bars and dance halls. By the time of the revolution in 1848, Paris had only 47 acres of municipal park within the city itself, together with an "anarchic turmoil" of unplanned private recreation (Green 1990:74; Herbert 1988). The grandiose urban designs of Louis-Napoleon and Haussmann, which commenced in the 1850s, had a number of aims including the improved circulation of traffic and troop movements within the city, public health and aesthetic appearance, with large avenues and vistas driven through the old chaotic districts of the city. But the leisure dimension was also included. The Bois de Boulogne and Bois de Vincennes were remodelled along the more "natural" lines of the London parks to enhance their attractiveness for the wealthy. In addition, Haussmann provided more local *parcs-intérieurs* at Monceau, Buttes-Chaumont (in the working-class district of Belleville) and Montsouris as well as 20 small neighbourhood parks. By the 1870s, Paris had 4500 acres of park. The Bois de Boulogne, with its racecourse at Longchamp, carriage drives and lakes for boating and winter skating, was an elite and middle-class playground. The upper classes would parade in their carriages and on horseback between 4 p.m. and 7 p.m. in summer and 3 p.m. to 5 p.m. in winter, providing a spectacle for others to watch, including foreign visitors to the city (Chadwick 1966; Herbert 1988).

The urban park movement in North America also had similar roots to those in Europe. Concern over health and mental well-being stemmed from a form of urban growth which left little space for leisure and recreation. Chicago, before 1867, had no plans for open space in the city, with leisure places for the working population confined to small pieces of land left over between intersecting streets, the streets themselves or tenement courtyards (Cranz 1982). When parks were created, they were often on marginal land unsuitable for other uses. Chicago's South Park system was on a former swamp as was Louisiana's central park.

New York's celebrated Central Park (started in 1857) (Figure 8.2) was on poor, rocky ground (Cranz 1982). Often, the sites available were on the city edge and so transport links became vital if the "lungs" of the city were to serve their purpose. Thus for the Golden Gate Park near San Francisco, it was claimed that cheap tram cars had the effect of "equalising the facilities of the entire population for enjoying its facilities" (Cranz 1982:32). The fact that peripheral locations, in reality, frequently precluded the use of parks by the working classes led to the American "reform park" movement later in the century, where space, especially for children, was provided near to poorer areas. Boston's Sand Garden (1885) was simply created by a philanthropist placing a pile of

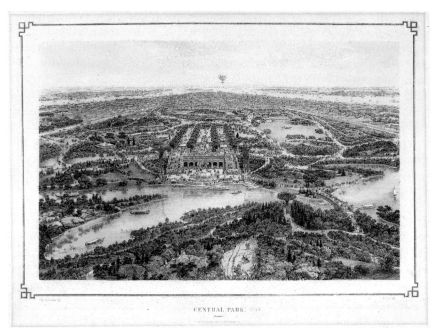

CENTRAL PARK

Figure 8.2 "Central Park, Summer". From its beginnings in the 1850s, the park was intended to provide a leisure space for all social classes in the city. Natural and formal features were provided in this much used "lung" for urban inhabitants (Collection of the New-York Historical Society)

sand in a yard and thus creating a playground. Idealists, however, were soon replaced by public authorities and New York created five parks in its Lower East Side. By 1900, fourteen US cities had supervised space for children in poor working-class areas (Kraus 1971).

A difference between the USA and Europe was the reluctance by the Americans to acknowledge a social-class basis to open space provision; a feature also noticeable in seaside resort development (chapter 7). Thus there was an emphasis on parks for the "weak" in society: the poor, children, the handicapped or the elderly. In addition, urban open space in America had to confront the issue of race, just as it remained a factor in resorts. Parks were often settings for racial conflict and many facilities were segregated (Cranz 1982).

The USA was an innovator in new forms of leisure provision for urban populations. As they led the way in National Park designation (chapter 6) so they were the first to conceive of the idea of integrated metropolitan park systems, linking space in the city with opportunities around its edge (Chadwick 1966). Boston was the originator of this idea with 19 parks and parkways created by 1896 (Newton 1971). The need for an overall coordinated system was made clear by the unequal provision of leisure space by the different municipalities in and around Boston. In 1892, the Metropolitan Parks Bill was passed and its chief proponent, Charles Eliot, outlined the five types of area which would provide the basis for the system (Figure 8.3). They were:

1   Spaces along the ocean front such as Revere Beach north-east of Boston.
2   The shores and islands of the inner Bay.
3   Courses of the larger tidal estuaries with land acquired along the side of the Mystic, Charles and Neponset rivers.
4   Peripheral areas of wild forest such as the Middlesex Fells on the north side and the Blue Hills to the south.
5   Small squares, playgrounds and parks within the built-up area which already existed.

This way of seeing urban open space provision as a continuous system linking central areas to peripheral areas was a major advance and one which was gradually adopted by other North American cities.

The provision of open space in urban areas has, not surprisingly, produced a history of conflict, with competing interests over the use of that space. Both street settings and public parks provide many instances of this basic geographical issue. In Derby, for example, the custom of street football raised the question of "possession of the streets" and the first half of the nineteenth century saw many attempts to suppress this form of recreation. On Shrove Tuesday and Ash Wednesday up to 1000 people could be involved in a robust game that spilled through the centre of the town and across gardens, and the spectacle drew visitors from far afield (Delves 1981). Magistrates tried to stamp out the game and even offered the bribe of a free railway excursion to somewhere else as an alternative. Riots and the use of troops characterised the conflict but the football game was symptomatic of wider leisure issues. In Derby, as elsewhere, loss of space, especially common land at the town edge, meant that the working population were increasingly forced to use the central streets for leisure, thus mixing with the respectable classes. Police and public order controls were used on a daily basis, creating an undercurrent of resentment for which the annual football match symbolised the contest between different social classes as much as the game itself. Nineteenth-century Norwich provides an interesting variation on this theme. Here, the contested space was the urban periphery but it was a conflict between a local working population, for whom the land was economic space, and the middle class of the city who wanted additional recreation space (MacMaster 1990). Mousehold Heath was used by the slum suburb of Pockthorpe for quarrying and brickmaking as well as

1893

0   km   5

Nahant

Central
Boston

Franklin
Park

Quincy
Bay

after Newton, 1971

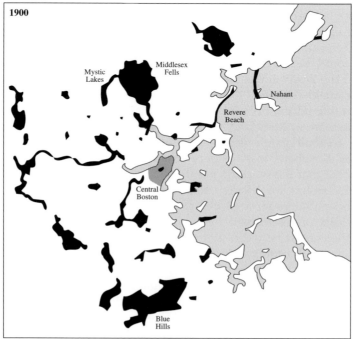

1900

Mystic
Lakes

Middlesex
Fells

Nahant

Revere
Beach

Central
Boston

Blue
Hills

recreational activities such as boxing and gambling. Traditional local employment in handloom weaving had declined and so the Heath provided an alternative source of living. At the same time, the city authorities wished to convert the Heath into an arena of civilised leisure with walks and carriage drives for its middle-class citizens. The result was a dispute which lasted for 25 years from the 1850s, until a public park was created in 1883. Different political interests in Norwich became drawn into the struggle but the surprise is that resistance to park creation was sustained for so long.

Other forms of open space conflict, again essentially between different social classes, could be seen in the industrial city of Worcester, Massachusetts, in the later nineteenth century (Rosenzweig 1979). The town had a diverse economic base with a large immigrant population which propelled its growth from 41 000 in 1870 to 146 000 in 1910. There was a basic class division between the native "yankee" Americans, who owned most of the factories, and the immigrant workers from Ireland, Sweden, Italy, Polish Lithuania and French Canada. The west side of the city was for the affluent, the east side for the immigrants, and the elite controlled Worcester's open space just as they did its politics and industry. Disputes over leisure began in the 1870s with the creation of Elm Park on the west of the city, a landscaped area carefully controlled for the nearby middle classes. In the overcrowded east side, the population demanded a very different kind of leisure space, somewhere for active recreation. Irish immigrant groups petitioned the City Council declaring: "there is no public ground in this vicinity . . . where children or young men can resort, either for health or amusement" (quoted in Rosenzweig 1979:31). During the same period, the west-side residents were pressing for more land near Elm Park to create a reservoir. The issue split the council and the community with the Irish *Worcester Daily Times* declaring: "we, east siders, want more outside room, we want every inch of space the city can afford us" (Rosenzweig 1979:36). The final compromise saw the west side getting its reservoir and the east side a number of playgrounds. But at the same time, it was recognised that Worcester had, in reality, created a system of "class parks", with overcrowded spaces at one end of the town and genteel preserves at the other. Furthermore, the east-side parks did not fulfil the cherished American ambition of acting as "melting pots" for different immigrant groups but rather "provided a leisure space in which workers expressed and preserved their distinct ethnic cultures" (Rosenzweig 1979:42).

Figure 8.3 (*opposite*) The growth of a metropolitan park system around Boston, Massachusetts, 1893–1900 (Newton (1971) *Design on the Land: The Development of Landscape Architecture*, with permission of Harvard University Press)

As well as influencing the location and use of urban parks, the upper and middle classes, through their wealth and power, were able to shape the general leisure environments around their homes. A major feature of many nineteenth-century industrialising towns was increased class segregation, with centrifugal forces drawing the affluent into the "rich and airy suburbs" and centripetal forces confining the poor in "airless slums" (Dicks 1985:91). Furthermore, throughout the century there was a tendency for the middle classes to move from an urban culture of public sociability to the more private domestic pleasures of home and family (Bailey 1978). This movement, and the ability of the middle class to create their own home and leisure environments, can be seen in the westward expansion of middle-class residential areas of Glasgow.

Deteriorating living conditions in the city centre and the encroachment of commercial uses into the Georgian area of the west end, encouraged the Glaswegian middle classes to move further out of town. A number of factors influenced this choice of new residential areas, including environmental quality, the presence of middle-class institutions, and recreation and leisure amenities. Therefore open and airy locations with attractive views across the rivers Kelvin and Clyde were important considerations in the development of Partickhill, Dowanhill and the prestigious Woodlands Hill with its terraces and private gardens. Institutions such as the 21-acre Botanic Gardens in Kelvinside and the University provided further exclusive middle-class amenities in the area. Private leisure space was incorporated into the residential layouts with gardens behind fences and locked gates—suitable for family prome- nades and picnics. The residents were also successful in petitioning the city to provide them with a park at Kelvinside which, although open to all in theory, was controlled by an entrance fee (Dicks 1985). In these various ways, the west-end residential area of nineteenth-century Glasgow became a middle-class residential and leisure enclave separate from a rapidly industrialising city which contained some of the worst living conditions for its working population to be found anywhere in Europe. But it was not just in the areas around their homes and in the city that the urban middle classes' leisure lifestyle operated. Increasingly mobile as the nineteenth century progressed, they moved in growing numbers beyond the city into the surrounding countryside to create an ever-widening recreational hinterland for themselves.

From town to country

The movement of the upper and middle classes into the countryside was not new, of course, and rural retreats were a prominent feature of earlier periods of leisure history (chapter 2). During the nineteenth century, however, the scale of movement in Britain, Europe and North America increased considerably. Although many would see this search for countryside as a rejection of urban environments and values, epitomised in William Cowper's dictum, "God made the country, and man made the town" (Patmore 1970:34), it was never as simple as that. On the continent, urban culture retained a greater potency than it did in Britain and so, for instance, Green (1990) argues for a distinctive Parisian cultural attitude to town and country, with a continuum between the ways the city and the countryside were seen, rather than a sharp break between the two.

Both Green (1990) and Herbert (1988) have traced in detail the expansion of middle-class leisure into the countryside around Paris from the mid-nineteenth century, and Figure 8.4 is an attempt to construct a map of the range of places and activities used by visitors to the areas west of the capital. Wooded landscapes could be reached in areas such as the Bois de Meudon, Forêt de Marly, Forêt de Saint Germain and Forêt de Montmorency. Until the 1830s, many of these visits focused on viewing landed estates and gardens, but after then more "natural" scenes became popular. A further stage was reached when the country homes were not merely viewed but owned by city dwellers and there was a boom from the 1840s in *maisons de campagne*. Easy access to Paris was stressed in the advertising, with the benefits of combining country *and* urban life a major appeal. The River Seine became a focus for leisure with day visits to centres such as Asnières and Argenteuil to the north-west, Sèvres to the south-west, Chatou, Louveciennes and Bougival to the west. This whole river zone was easily reached from the Gare Saint-Lazare which was opened in 1837 and provided special excursion trains for weekends and holidays. Scenes of the nineteenth-century Parisian bourgeoisie at play in these places have become some of the most familiar and popular images in art through Impressionist painters such as Monet, Manet and Renoir (Herbert 1988). The world portrayed in these works evidently has an enduring appeal to twentieth-century audiences with their nostalgic sense of a lost "golden age" of leisure.

Asnières was only ten minutes journey from Saint-Lazare and became hugely popular by the 1860s. The wide range of activities developed there included swimming, rowing, sailing, riding, picnicking, diving, dancing, promenading, regattas, concerts, circuses, fairs and markets. The village grew from 1300 people in 1856 to 15 200 by 1886 and 24 300 by 1896, with a rapidly expanding permanent population swollen by both day and summer visitors. The old houses near the river became swamped by shops, apartment blocks and boating establishments and by the 1870s, villas stretched all along the river banks. Although leisure land uses rarely

234

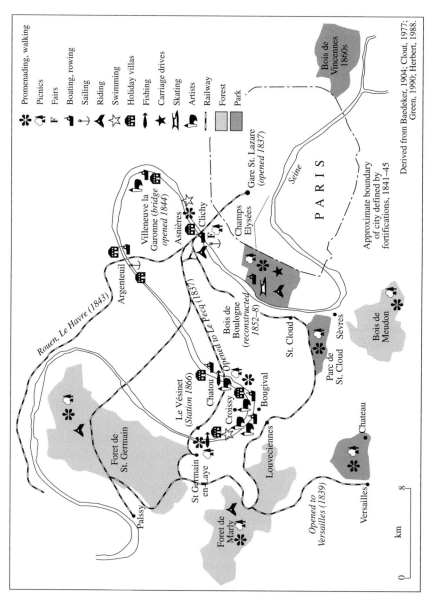

Figure 8.4 Aspects of the pleasure periphery to the west of Paris, c.1830–c.1880

Derived from Baedeker, 1904; Clout, 1977; Green, 1990; Herbert, 1988.

sit happily alongside industrial land uses, at Asnières the landscape of play was immediately opposite the docks, warehouses and factories of Clichy and Saint-Ouen and the sailors from the barges mingled with the weekend sailors, providing interesting local colour. In time, however, artists and other sensitive visitors forsook the industrial backdrop of Asnières and moved further down the Seine to Bougival, Chatou and Port Marly. Here, the willow-filled river banks had restaurants such as the "Grenouillère", painted so often by Monet and Renoir. It was an area that provided boating, regattas and dances as well as the historic interest of seventeenth- and eighteenth-century chateaux (Herbert 1988).

Argenteuil became a famous place for sailing, the River Seine widening here to provide a suitable stretch for yachts. This leisure habit was derived from the British, as a result of a new entrepreneurial Parisian class closely identifying with British progress and adopting a similar recreation culture. Thus, *le sport, le turf, le rowing, les skiffs* and *les yachts*, became familiar vocabulary amongst the Parisian leisure classes.

In addition to creating particular recreation centres, the movement to the countryside from Paris also created more general landscape change. The villas in the "pleasure zone" to the west of the city had their own gardens; their private spaces for leisure. Over time, the traditional plots with their vegetables, fruit trees and animals became converted to flower gardens surrounded by hedges and fences (Figures 8.5 and 8.6). This change, representing a movement from a landscape of work to a land-scape of pleasure, was lamented by some. The geographer Elisée Reclus observed in 1883:

> For strollers walking down the muddy lanes of this make-believe country-side, nature is represented only by well-trimmed bushes and masses of flowers seen through the bars of fences.
>
> (quoted in Herbert 1988:260)

Just as middle-class Parisians were colonising the Seine near Paris during the late nineteenth century, so middle-class Londoners were increasingly using the Thames upriver from London. Although the villas of the upper classes had spread along the river banks from the late seventeenth century onwards (chapter 2), a new middle-class impetus developed especially from the 1870s and 1880s. The Maidenhead area was particularly popular, with Boulter's Lock easily reached by rail. A whole series of regattas (Henley from 1839) and rowing clubs emerged. Regatta days at Marlow could attract nearly 4000 people arriving by train (Burstall 1981). A range of social classes used the Thames for leisure but there was a degree of temporal separation. The social elite tended to use the river in the early summer but later on they moved away to other venues leaving the water and banks to the middle and working classes.

Figure 8.5 "Kitchen Garden at the Hermitage" by Camille Pissarro (1874), who painted traditional village scenes of vegetable plots, fruit trees, chickens and pigs (National Gallery of Scotland, Edinburgh)

The latter increased their presence particularly from the 1880s, as cheap excursion trains to higher reaches of the Thames became common and, inevitably, this led to conflict between them, middle-class recreationists and the local population. Press reports were full of complaints about drunkenness and "inappropriate behaviour". Stereotyped by polite society as "'Arry" and "'Arriet" these visitors earned the reputation now applied to the package tourist in Torremolinos. The social journal *The Dwarf* in 1892 complained of Sundays at Maidenhead where "Houndsditch was let loose" and "Petticoat Lane had come out for an airing", while the *Maidenhead Advertiser* (August 1887) described the 'Arry as follows:

> Having refreshed himself with a gin-and-bitters, he promenades for half an hour or so outside the hostelry of his choice. He is a scrubby and hairy man, with a limp collar, a rumpled shirt front, and a frock coat disclosing no wristband. He smokes a short clay, and wears his hat on the right side of his head.
>
> (quoted in Burstall 1981:30)

His day ends with a rendering of "Auld Lang Syne" and "Rule Britannia".

Figure 8.6 "The Artist's House at Argenteuil" ("La maison de l'artiste à Argenteuil") by Claude Monet (1873) shows how nineteenth-century second homes and rural retreats helped to transform the scenes painted by Pissarro into the flowers, gardens and neat hedges of the urbanite (Art Institute of Chicago, © ADAGP, Paris and DACS, London 1996)

As with seaside resorts, however, it seems that public behaviour and class tolerance had improved by the end of the century and instances of conflict on the Thames began to decline. Furthermore the Thames was not only a recreation space open to all social classes, it played a significant role as a space for women's leisure (Burstall 1981). Women actively participated in river activities such as rowing and punting with a degree of freedom that also became associated with the 1880s and 1890s craze for cycling (see below). But a continuing difficulty for all types of visitors on the river, however, was the question of access to the river banks, where most of the land lay in private ownership. Many Thames backwaters were closed and reserved for private use and a heated debate took place between "the Thames Rights Defence Association" (founded in 1882) which championed the visitors and "The Thames Riparian Owners' Defence Association" (founded in 1884) which upheld the cause of private landowners.

The increase of visitors to the Thames during the second half of the nineteenth century fuelled an increase in tourist services to the area. The demands of tourism meant that the river zone became an area of innovation, providing facilities in advance of places surrounding it. Thus riverside hotels were forerunners in introducing electric lighting by the 1890s (Burstall 1981). Significant employment resulted from the leisure invasion. As well as hotel and restaurant services, boat-building firms increased rapidly in number and size. Large companies were located at Oxford, Streatley, Goring, Pangbourne, Henley, Maidenhead, Windsor and Eton.

Recreation activities centred around rivers were not the only aspect of large-scale movement from the town to the countryside. Bicycling and golf became prominent middle-class pastimes in the later years of the century. The 1890s, in Britain, saw a "cycling boom", which added a new dimension to personal mobility and emancipation (Rubinstein 1977). During the previous decade, improved bicycle designs coincided with the desire to explore the countryside. Women increasingly took to using bicycles and there was much contemporary discussion of the "new woman", her freedom of movement and bicycling dress. As the *Complete Cyclist* of 1897 observed: "now women, even young girls, ride alone or attended only by some casual man friend, for miles together through deserted country roads" (quoted in Alderson 1972:85). Possession of a bicycle opened up a new world: The *Northampton Daily Reporter* enthused in 1891:

> nothing is more delightful than, after a week's hard grind in the office and among the dry ledgers, day books etc. etc., to don your special garments, mount your glittering wheel, and then away to the green lanes, leafy woods, and rippling brooks, to the sweet country, there to mix your blood with sunshine, and to take the wind into your pulses.
>
> (quoted in Lowerson 1993:118)

A flurry of articles and books reinforced the significance of the whole bicycling movement with H.G. Wells, in particular, through his works *The Wheels of Chance* (1896) and *The History of Mr Polly* (1910) emphasising the role of bicycling as an escape from the everyday monotony of the lower middle classes. The Cyclists' Touring Club was founded in 1878 (Lightwood 1928) and published extensive lists of bicycle routes, approved inns and hotels for its members. Membership of the Club rose from 14 000 in 1894 to over 60 000 by 1899 (Rubinstein 1977). There were also numbers of local and regional cycling clubs; London had 300 clubs in 1898 and there were over 2000 in the UK as a whole. Furthermore, all this activity had significant economic impacts for certain areas of Britain, most clearly seen in the growth of the cycle industry in the West Midlands, but also found in Nottingham and London. Most firms were very small but Raleigh in Nottingham employed over 1000 workers. The 1901 census showed that the numbers employed in bicycle making had increased by 86 per cent in the previous ten years, from 11 524 to 21 466 (Rubinstein 1977).

Although bicycling as a leisure activity was widespread through the social classes and was adopted by both males and females, young unmarried men were the main participants. For the lower middle class and working class, groups such as the Clarion Clubs (linked to the socialist *Clarion* newspaper) associated bicycling with wider issues of freedom of movement and the ability of groups to organise their own leisure. But as a purely recreational activity, the bicycling boom of the 1890s faded quite rapidly. The 60 000 membership of the Cyclists' Touring Club collapsed to only 14 000 by 1914 as the bicycle increasingly became a practical means of transport for work rather than a symbol of leisure and freedom. The bicycle continued, however, as important for working-class leisure during the interwar years even though it had lost its fashionable cachet (Howkins and Lowerson 1979; Seebohm Rowntree 1941).

A very similar bicycling trend emerged in the USA (Tobin 1974). The 1880s onwards saw a rapid increase in recreational cycling, the establishment of clubs (such as the League of American Wheelmen) and the involvement of women. As in Britain, the activity was associated strongly with an urban escape to explore the surrounding countryside. In 1896, the American bicycle economy was estimated to be worth $75 million, with over one million bicycles made and employment rising from under 2000 in 1890 to over 20 000 by 1899 (Tobin 1974). Concentrated especially in the major urban centres of the east and mid-west, cyclists' "touring corridors" were developed, radiating from the towns and cities and following the itineraries outlined in maps and guides. Shops, hotels and inns were attracted to these routes, creating an infrastructure that was later to be adopted by early motorists (see below). Ironically, although cycling seemed to symbolise the "freedom to roam", the actual spatial pattern of journeys tended to conform to well-designated routes, with direction signs, service facilities and the companionship of other bicyclists being major considerations. Poor road surfaces in the USA also had the effect of restricting movements (Tobin 1974). As in Britain, the boom of the 1890s was followed by a rapid decline in the early twentieth century for cycling as a fashionable leisure activity.

In the later nineteenth century, another middle-class recreation emerged. In Lowerson's (1993) words, golf was "land hungry" and became an expression of middle-class "spatial hegemony" as areas of land became reserved for their exclusive use. Although golf had a longer history in Scotland, its growth in England was especially important from the 1870s onwards. Until 1900, most courses were found on marginal land, such as coastal links, sandy commons or barely modified farm pasture in zones around the city edge. Increased demand, however, meant that golfcourses encroached on other land uses and took particular advantage of farms which had become redundant. Often, common land could be lost to the game, as happened at Chorley Wood in the 1890s and at Yeovil, so that the recreation space of others succumbed to the pleasures of the rich and powerful. In some areas, a whole network of golfcourses came to form significant elements in the landscape. Stretching east from Edinburgh along the East Lothian coast to North Berwick, the later nineteenth century saw the creation of a string of golfcourses or links. North Berwick had three courses by 1880 and the major course of Muirfield at Gullane was laid out in 1882. The Aberlady, Gullane and North Berwick railway branch which developed in the 1890s was known as "The Golfers' Line" (Hajducki 1992).

As well as using particular sites in the countryside for recreation, the middle classes spread further afield from their urban bases during the nineteenth century. In part, this has been attributed to a growing anti-urban sentiment and a nostalgia for rural scenes that were undergoing major changes as a result of the agricultural depression of the 1870s onwards (Marsh 1982; Walton 1990). The problems of the Victorian city were often attributed to the urban industrial system itself and, for some, the countryside symbolised a rejection of this system and the return to a pre-industrial world. The arts and crafts movement of William Morris is perhaps the best known of these returns to rural ways. For the majority, however, a temporary visit to the countryside did not demand such wholesale rejection of urban life and was simply an escape from routine happily combined with nostalgia. The urban middle classes began to visit certain rural areas in increasing numbers. These were not only the more obvious "scenic" areas, such as the Lake District, Scottish Highlands and North Wales (chapter 6) but included the areas that were simply "rural". One such region was the Cotswolds which saw an influx of visitors from the 1880s onwards (Marsh 1982). Until then, the agricultural landscape and old stone-built villages had been little regarded but places such as Broadway with its picturesque houses were "discovered" by literary and artistic circles. They were quickly followed by sightseers and the village had four guidebooks devoted to its charms by 1904. Books about the countryside, with details of nature lore, local stories and customs became increasingly popular in the later nineteenth century and supplemented guidebooks in reinforcing the attractions of a vanishing world. Richard Jefferies of Wiltshire epitomised this trend and his writings included *The Gamekeeper at Home* (1878), *Wild Life in a Southern County* (1879), *The Amateur Poacher* (1879), *Hodge and his Masters* (1880), and *Round About a Great Estate* (1880).

The influx of middle-class visitors to rural areas had important consequences. Bouquet (1985) for example, has linked the growth of tourism in north Cornwall to the broader context of a changing rural economy and changes in gender roles in a traditional society. Until the first half of the nineteenth century, women had had a diverse role in agricultural practices, being involved in a wide range of tasks around the farms. The penetration of urban markets into the area later on, however, created a new set of circumstances. First, there was a move to dairy farming which created specialised jobs for women away from general food production. Then into this period of change came visitors who stayed on the farms and who, in turn, required services which became almost exclusively provided by women. Thus a major gender division in rural work was created by new forms of farm production and the creation of the farm as a place for leisure and recreation as well as work.

In addition to these social and economic changes, the increased use of the countryside raised the contentious issue of access to the land. To a wish to preserve the "traditional" aesthetics of landscape and its way of life, there was also added pressure to preserve traditional rights of access to the land and to open up more areas for enjoyment. Until the later years of the nineteenth century, large tracts of the countryside remained the exclusive preserve of landowners and their friends but demands were building up from other social groups. The Commons Preservation Society was founded in 1865, followed in 1884 by the National Footpaths Preservation Society, The Lake District Defence Society (1883) and the National Trust in 1895. 1905 saw the establishment of the Federation of Rambling Clubs (Marsh 1982; Shoard 1987). The activities of the Commons Preservation Society were focused especially in the south-east of England where pressures on the land were greatest. In the 1860s, the owners of Berkhamstead Common, 25 miles from London, tried to close off the area but the Society successfully fought them and the area was left for recreation. Another place of conflict was at Epping Forest, again near the capital, where there were disputes between owners—the local population—who used the forest for timber and leisure, and visitors from London. Ultimately, after a Royal Commission report, the City of London took the forest under public ownership and the area was opened to all by Queen Victoria in 1882 (Blunden and Curry 1990).

Pressures over access also built up in other parts of Britain. The Peak District, surrounded by the urban conglomerations of south Yorkshire and south Lancashire, had only one quarter of its open moorland accessible to the public. Most of the land was in private ownership and reserved for grouse shooting. By the 1920s and 1930s, it is estimated that about 15 000 people left Sheffield at the weekend for the Peak District and about the same number were leaving Manchester (Shoard 1987). Radical groups became involved in a struggle for the right to roam and in 1932 there was a celebrated mass invasion of the Duke of Devonshire's grouse moors. In this pressure for countryside access, Blunden and Curry (1990) and Howkins and Lowerson (1979) both draw a distinction between movements based in southern England which were essentially middle-class conservation groups and northern groups who were more radical and working class. Many southern rambling clubs were socially exclusive. The "Sunday Tramps", created in 1879 by Lesley Stephen, attracted members of the London legal, literary and political circles (Walker 1985). Suburbanite country rambles in the Home Counties were very different from the desire to walk the moorland immediately adjacent to the crowded industrial cities of the north. Nevertheless, despite these different emphases, both movements helped to create the momentum of the 1920s and 1930s to establish land which was both conserved for its beauty and had access for recreation. This was eventually enshrined in the National Parks and Access to the Countryside Act of 1949 (Blunden and Curry 1990). But the issue of access has never been resolved in Britain and it remains a matter of dispute between landowners and the public despite over 100 years of debate.

The working classes, especially in the north of England, were part of the movement to gain access to the countryside for recreation, but their wish to escape from the town could be expressed in different ways to those of the middle classes. The exodus of London's East Enders out to the hop fields of Kent in the autumn was a means of combining much needed earnings with pleasure in a setting very different from home. The three- or four-week season in September became increasingly organised, with special railway services provided and the hop pickers provided with purpose-built "hopper huts" on the farms. By the 1890s, about 250 000 hoppers were in Kent during the season, centred on Maidstone, Malling, Tonbridge and Faversham. These numbers were swollen by friends and relatives who would come down at the weekends to visit their acquaintances (Bignell 1977). This whole leisure-work phenomenon was made possible by the increased urban consumption of beer which led to the expansion of the hop fields. But mechanisation, especially after 1945, saw the rapid decline of this institution (Ward and Hardy 1986). While it lasted, it became an established part of East End culture with succeeding generations of families departing for Kent and often staying on the same hop farm. It was a very different way of using the countryside from that of the middle classes and a reminder that social groups may create their own leisure and not simply imitate the habits of others (Hardy 1990). A variation on this theme is well illustrated by Somerset Maugham in *Liza of Lambeth* (1897) where he describes a Bank Holiday coach trip from Lambeth to Chingford on the north side of London. It was an outing for the whole street together, a communal urban expedition, and the countryside was an escape from a restricted urban life. But the rural scene was essentially a backdrop to a social occasion which was more involved with cementing street relationships than exploring a landscape. The episode helps to reinforce the importance of understanding the culture of the generating area (the street life of Lambeth) in order to understand what was happening in the destination area (the countryside near Chingford).

Between the First and Second World Wars there was also a movement by comparatively poor urban people to establish their own second homes in parts of Britain (Hardy and Ward 1984; Hardy 1990). Known as plotlands, old sheds, shacks and railway carriages were placed on cheap marginal areas of land in what was a genuinely self-help movement. Sites likely to flood, steep slopes, shingle ridges, sand dunes, heavy clays and dry chalky uplands began to be colonised as a piece of "Arcadia" for the less affluent in society. In the London area, the banks of the Thames and Lea rivers were popular locations inland, as were parts of the North Downs. Near Manchester, areas of the Pennine edges were occupied and in the west Midlands the River Severn, especially near Bridgnorth, was a favoured spot. Parts of the Tyne Valley, west of Newcastle, also saw a scattering of these rural retreats. The coast, however, witnessed the greatest plotland development, particularly those areas within easy reach of London. Thus, Kent around Dungeness, Camber Sands, and Peacehaven saw concentrations, as did Essex at Canvey Island and Jaywick Sands. The unplanned growth of this do-it-yourself landscape, with its lack of services and untidy appearance, attracted the opposition of some sections of the middle classes and local authorities. Many plotlands were removed under Town and Country Planning Acts in the 1930s and 1940s. Other sites became converted into more substantial dwellings and necessary services were put in. Today, little remains in the landscape as a reminder of this independent movement to carve out a little place of space for pleasure.

Another leisure phenomenon of the early twentieth century which catered for the less affluent was the holiday camp (Pimlott 1947; Ward and Hardy 1986). But whereas the growth of plotlands uncomfortably reflected an anarchic process of creating leisure places, the holiday camp was recreation in a controlled and contained environment. The origins of the camps stemmed from the cycling and pioneer tent camps of the late nineteenth century, generally temporary sites at the coast. In many cases, workers' organisations were involved, such as the Cooperative

Societies. The United Co-op Baking Society of Glasgow, for example, had a summer camp at Rothesay on the Isle of Bute from 1911 until 1974 (Ward and Hardy 1986). This relatively primitive, cheap and popular form of leisure attracted the attention, by the early 1930s, of commercial entrepreneurs such as Butlin, Warner and Pontin who transformed the holiday camp experience by replacing "wholesome" outdoor life with permanent accommodation, commercial entertainment and glamour. Butlin's first camp was at Skegness, closely followed by ones at Clacton and Filey. By 1939, permanent holiday camps were spread around the coast of England and Wales but with concentrations in Kent and Essex (near to London), East Anglia, and North Wales (Ward and Hardy 1986). These holiday camps received a measure of support from local authorities and conservationists if they were well planned and sited. When the geographer J.A. Steers made his coastal survey in the 1940s, he acknowledged that Butlin camps "are not eyesores and they do fill a great need" (quoted in Ward and Hardy 1986:121).

The commercial camps became a kind of fantasy world. They went out of their way to provide a complete contrast with the environments of home and work and often featured the latest architectural designs:

> Images were compressed and interwoven to create a world that was everywhere yet nowhere. Hawaiian bars and Viennese coffee lounges, Hollywood Terraces and South Sea Pools, de luxe Grand Hotel ballrooms and sundecks named after Atlantic liners—all could be part of a day's experience.
>
> (Ward and Hardy 1986:147)

This experience, nonetheless, was one which was mainly for the lower middle classes and skilled working class in British society. Although relatively cheap, the holiday camp was beyond the means of the poorer people in the country.

The wider commercial opportunities offered in recreation and tourism which were being increasingly identified in Britain in the 1920s and 1930s, had been developed at an early stage in the USA. The Americans were particularly innovative in seeing leisure activity in an integrated manner so that just as they evolved metropolitan park systems, so they quickly organised the movement of people from town to countryside on a regional basis. This could be detected on the American west coast by the 1870s and beyond (Fifer 1988). Visitors from the east coast cities and the growing urban centres of San Francisco and Los Angeles formed a buoyant market for entrepreneurs. Much of the initial development came from east coast businesses and even European firms who, through marketing, transport and accommodation investment, both supplied and controlled where visitors went. Thus a form of core–periphery relationship between the

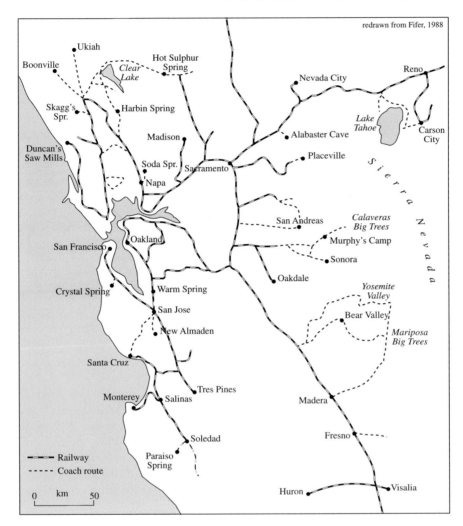

redrawn from Fifer, 1988

Figure 8.7 Tourist attractions, railways and coach routes in central California by the 1870s (The Globe Pequot Press, Connecticut)

American west and American east and Europe was created. For instance, Thomas Cook had a tour of California organised as early as the 1870s, as had the Boston-based firm of Raymond and Whitcomb (Fifer 1988). Figure 8.7 shows the range of places in central California that were being strongly promoted and developed from the 1870s, in a region which stretched from San Francisco along the coast to north and south and inland to Yosemite, Lake Tahoe and Hot Sulphur Springs. Further south, a regionally

Figure 8.8 "Hotel del Coronado, near San Diego, California" (1888). Development came in 1885 as the railway approached San Diego. A fantasy building of white woodwork and red roofs, with electric light installed by Edison, it is now a National Historic landmark (California Historical Society, San Francisco)

integrated recreation system was being encouraged around Los Angeles (Figure 8.9) with the Santa Fe Railroad promoting its "Kite-shaped" day excursions inland to the Bernardino Mountains through Orange, Riverside and San Bernardino Counties (Figure 8.10). As Fifer (1988) points out, Americans on the west coast were, before the turn of the century, aiming to produce well-defined and well-integrated leisure and recreation regions with good internal transport connections, as a way of keeping visitors and their money in particular areas.

Wider horizons

For the wealthy in society during the late nineteenth and early twentieth centuries, the rhythm of their leisure culture appeared to be relatively unchanged. In most western societies, the landed classes and new industrial and commercial rich were able to operate their leisure worlds at provincial, national and international levels. There were variations in habits. The social elite of Italy made their rounds of country estate, provincial town, spa and seaside resort but their travel abroad was limited and rarely extended beyond Switzerland and the South Tyrol

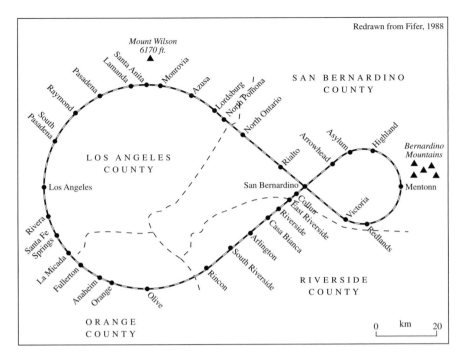

Figure 8.9 Santa Fe Railroad "kite-shaped" day excursion route from Los Angeles (1890s) (The Globe Pequot Press, Connecticut)

(Villari 1905). Similarly, the Spanish elite showed little inclination to journey far beyond their own national frontiers (Barke and Towner 1995). These more bounded visions of travel were presumably more related to cultural attitudes than the constraints of time and money.

In Britain, the London Season continued to operate for the landed classes until the 1880s, as it had done since the late seventeenth century (chapter 2). From London, the retreat to the country estate enabled the pleasures of hunting, shooting and fishing to be undertaken with ease and the house and land remained an important leisure setting for recreation and entertainment. There were some manifestations of change around the house, however. Architectural styles of Gothic fantasy replaced classical dignity, or the Italianate villa was replaced by the Tudor and Elizabethan manor house style (Girouard 1978). The Victorian cult of middle-class respectability and domesticity penetrated the country house and its leisure environment with a new emphasis on family and homely pleasures. Further afield, there also seem to be only slight modifications to leisure behaviour. Europe, especially the Riviera, the continental spas and the exclusive winter resorts of Switzerland, was

Figure 8.10 "Advertisement for the 'Balloon Route' Trolley Trip" by the Los Angeles and Pacific Railroad (late 1890s). Well-coordinated leisure trips were a feature of American recreation and tourism development of the West Coast at this time. Ocean Park in the right-hand corner was laid out as a bathing resort in 1892 (University Research Library, University of California, Los Angeles)

joined by the Middle East, North America, Africa and parts of Asia as tourist zones for the rich. But it would be wrong to fail to distinguish between the old landed classes and the new rich in society. In Britain and Europe the centuries-old lifestyle of the landed elite continued largely unchanged until the 1870s and 1880s. After then, however, the widespread and rapid collapse of agriculture as the basis of Europe's economies, under pressure from imports and industry and commerce, meant that landed wealth became marginalised (Cannadine 1990). In France, the value of land fell by one quarter between 1880 and 1890 and, in Britain, the sales of agricultural land resulted in the greatest turnover since the Norman Conquest and the Dissolution of the Monasteries (see chapter 2). Country houses and estates were sold and so the foundations (both economic and cultural) of landed-class leisure began to crumble. The new rich moved into the rural areas and filled the vacuum so that, as Cannadine (1990:342) puts it, "instead of being a patrician preserve, the countryside was becoming a plutocratic playground".

Where did the old order go in order to escape the pressures of financial worries and the new rich? One answer was to spend more time travelling abroad. In fact, the landed classes of Britain travelled more in the late nineteenth century than ever before but their reasons for doing so were rather different from those of the eighteenth century when travel had been securely based on a dominant position in society. Rather than a clear territorially defined routine of season, health resort and European travel, journeys for the landed classes became a form of aimless wandering (Cannadine 1900). They were escaping from the modern world rather than being at the centre of it. Thus similar patterns of travel can disguise very different reasons for that travel. For the old order it was an expression of retreat, for the new order it was an expression of advance, a demonstration of newly acquired wealth and status.

For the newly affluent upper middle classes, magazines such as the *Queen* give an idea of their travel world. Within Britain, the *Queen Book of Travel* (1914) reveals a wide variety of places for leisure: spas and seaside resorts, walking, cycling and motor tours of regions such as the Lake District, North Wales and the Scottish highlands. To these traditional destinations are now added areas like the New Forest, Welsh Borders and West Midlands. Journeying abroad, summer and winter seasons in Switzerland and the Riviera are outlined and these are supplemented by tours of Italy, France, Belgium and Holland, Germany, Spain, Portugal, Scandinavia, Austria-Hungary and Russia. Beyond Europe, the *Queen* discusses visits to north Africa and Egypt together with world tours which include India, Japan, South America and the USA. Potentially, therefore, much of the world was seen by 1914 as within range of the British upper classes. Amongst this list there were, naturally, particular preferences. Italy was the most popular destination abroad until about the 1860s when the French Riviera became a serious rival especially as a wintering place (Pemble 1988). From the 1880s, Egypt became increasingly popular for the British; an exotic culture mixed with a stable political environment. But outside these zones, the numbers of visitors were actually quite small. Spain and Greece attracted a few, as did Algeria and Palestine (Eisner 1991; Shepherd 1987). Travel firms, notably Thomas Cook (Brendon 1991; Swinglehurst 1974,1982), catered for an affluent clientele and the gradual extension of his "empire" reflected the gradual spread of western tourism. Cook's first tour to Switzerland was in 1863, Italy followed the next year, the USA in 1866, Egypt in 1869, Spain in 1872. But these were an exotic veneer over the general habits of the wealthy. A crude, but possibly realistic measure, of where most of the upper classes went most of the time can be gained from the amount of space devoted by the *Queen* to various countries: France is covered in 64 pages, Switzerland 53, Germany 35, Italy 21, Austria-Hungary 20, Scandinavia 20, Spain and Portugal 13, Belgium and Holland 12. Outside the European zone, only one or two pages are used to describe other destinations.

The widening horizons of upper-class travellers, although evident, can therefore be overexaggerated. Social exclusiveness could also be found within select enclaves in Europe, whether at the spas, the winter season of the Riviera or the health and ski resorts of Switzerland. Cook's *Health Resorts* (1905) reveals a whole network of both summer and winter resorts stretching from San Sebastian on the north coast of Spain, through the summer resorts of the Pyrenees to the winter resorts of the French and Italian Rivieras (Figure 8.11). In Switzerland (Figure 8.12) clusters of ski resorts to the east and west of the country, many with their own rail links, had emerged by the 1920s with Davos (nearly 6000 beds) and St Moritz (6000 beds) in the east and Villars (2000 beds) and Leysin (2800 beds) forming major resort centres (Cook 1929–1930). In his study of tourism in Savoy published in 1934, Miege was able to show the significance of altitude on the pattern of accommodation in the region south of Lake Geneva (Figure 8.13). Skiing had created a new pattern whereby some of the largest accommodation centres were to be found above 1000 metres, especially in the Chamonix region rather than to the west in the lower lying and seemingly more accessible area (Miege 1934).

Travel abroad was also becoming possible for the middle ranks of society, although the actual numbers must have remained small. Organisations such as the Polytechnic Touring Association were offering their own version of the Grand Tour in the 1930s (Figure 8.14), following a spatial pattern very similar to that established in the seventeenth

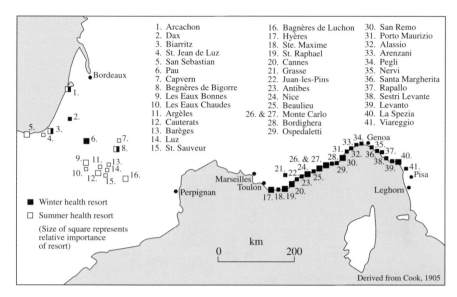

Figure 8.11 Winter and summer health resorts of Italy, the South of France, and Pyrenees in the early twentieth century

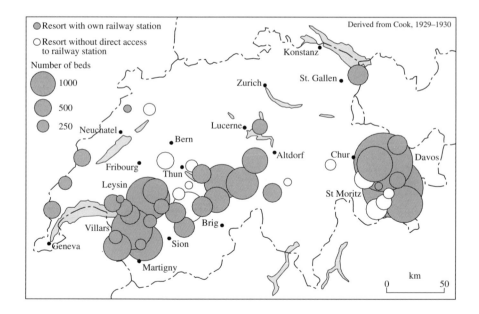

Figure 8.12 The winter sports resorts of Switzerland in the late 1920s

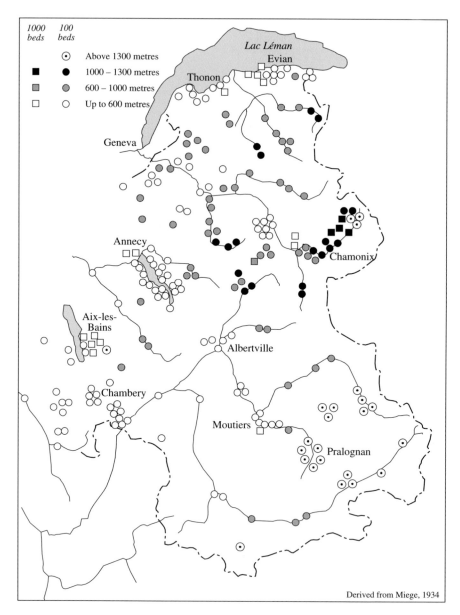

Figure 8.13   The pattern of accommodation by size and altitude in Savoy c.1934

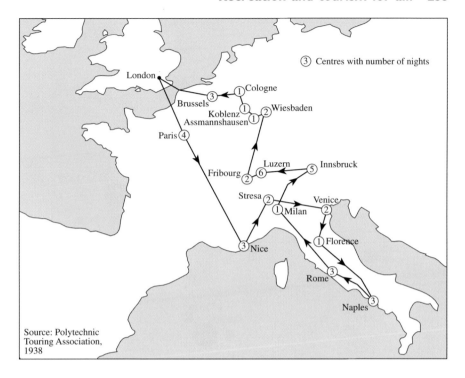

Centres with number of nights

London
Cologne
Brussels
Koblenz
Assmannshausen
Wiesbaden
Paris
Fribourg
Luzern
Innsbruck
Stresa
Venice
Milan
Nice
Florence
Rome
Naples

Source: Polytechnic
Touring Association,
1938

Figure 8.14 A Grand Tour of Europe in 1938

century. The key difference, however, was in time and expenditure. The
Polytechnic tour took 46 days and cost £63. Other groups included the
Workers' Travel Association who offered inexpensive travel abroad to
Belgium and France in the 1920s and 1930s. Most of the clientele,
however, consisted of clerical workers, teachers, civil servants and some
skilled industrial workers (Williams 1960).

The story of the spread of western tourism can, however, be too easily
distorted by the fortunate survival of the archives of a few firms. These
can present an exaggerated picture of the inexorable spread of tourism
out from its European heartland (Towner 1995). The chance survival of
another archive perhaps reveals the more usual pattern of tourism for
many relatively affluent people. This source is the hotel registers of the
Chateau Frontenac in Quebec City in the 1890s (Lundgren 1983). From
the data, it is possible to map the catchment area of this large hotel and
study the changing seasonal pattern of visitor flows (Figure 8.15).

Generally, the hotel relied on the north-east region of North America
throughout the year. Montreal, only half a day's journey away, was
always the dominant generating centre. In the peak summer season, the

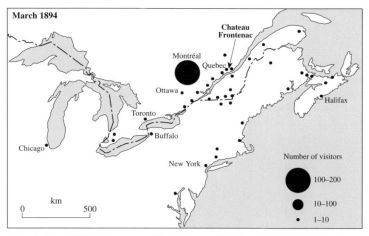

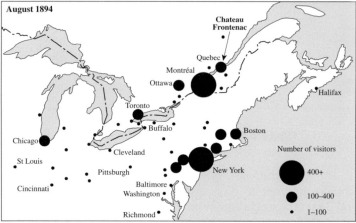

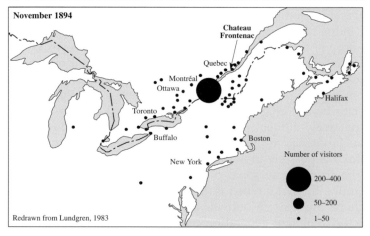

catchment area expanded to include the high-order urban centres of New York, Boston and the manufacturing belt around Pittsburgh and beyond to Cincinnati, St Louis and Chicago. In the low season, the area contracted to depend on Montreal, and to a lesser extent, the cities of Toronto and Ottawa. Annual cycles of visitors as shown by these records must have formed the more typical, if less prestigious and so less frequently mentioned, excursions for tourists in much of the western world.

Travel as a leisure experience

Recreation research writers have long recognised that the journey itself, from home to destination and back, can often be an integral part of the total leisure experience (Clawson 1963; Mercer 1971; Pigram 1983). The letters, diaries and journals of travellers in earlier centuries make clear that, although travel was often slow and uncomfortable, there was pleasure in viewing the slowly unfolding landscape from horseback or from a carriage (chapter 5). This shows that it would be a mistake to simply link delight in a journey with ease of movement. Nevertheless, the improvements in transport which came with the new roads of the eighteenth century, the railways of the nineteenth century and the cycles and motor cars of the turn of the century, had an effect on travellers' perceptions of distance and scenery, and these form part of the historical geography of recreation and tourism.

Thrift (1990) and Schivelbusch (1977) argue that the coming of the railways in the last century introduced a new dimension to travel experience. The sheer increase in speeds from a horse to 50–60 m.p.h. was revolutionary and mid-nineteenth-century writings constantly referred to the effect of the railways on the shrinking of space. They also noted how the railway carriage and the passing landscape became two clearly separated worlds. For instance, the journey from Paris to the Mediterranean almost ceased to be experienced; travellers arrived seemingly untouched by the space traversed, "paying no attention to the invisible landscapes of the journey" (Schivelbusch 1977:38) (Figure 8.16). The increased speed and organisation of travel gave a sense, to some tourists, of being ever more controlled in their movements and experiences. The American William Howells commented in 1883:

> We do not nowadays carry letters recommending us to citizens of the different places . . . No, we buy our through tickets and we put up at the

Figure 8.15 (*opposite*) Chateau Frontenac Hotel, Quebec City: seasonal variations in visitors, 1894

Figure 8.16   "The Travelling Companions" by Augustus Egg (1862) shows two girls in a first-class railway carriage near Menton on the French Riviera. Affluent young women were able to travel in comfort across Europe, although here the view from the window seems to have lost some of its interest (Birmingham Museums and Art Gallery)

hotels praised in the handbook, and we are very glad of a little conversation with any native, however adulterated he may be by contact with the world to which we belong.

(Howells 1883:2:52)

And yet this comment tells us perhaps more about how tourists have a tendency to cast back to "golden ages of travel" than about any fundamental change in a particular era. After all, a version of Howells' sentiments could just as easily be expressed today in a nostalgic regret for the leisurely travel of the 1880s.

Even so, the railway travel encouraged forms of guidebooks which reinforced particular ways of seeing. Railway companies issued guides for passengers presenting the scene as viewed from their railway carriages. (Again, however, the novelty of the railways should not be overemphasised. John Ogilby's (1675) strip-maps of roads presented an image of Britain as seen from horse or carriage by the passing traveller.) George Measom's (1853:33) guide to the South Eastern Railway was typical of the genre where, although he gave information on places away from the line, much of the narrative was concerned with the landscape seen from the carriage window:

Another mile, and we pass the pretty village of Teston, which has a bridge over the Medway—here remarkably picturesque—adding not a little to the charms of the richly cultivated scenery on its banks; adjoining is the demesne of Barham Court . . . The next objects for notice are on the right side both of the river and railway . . .

Cycling and the motor car brought variations in travel experience. Both possessed freedom from the constraints of rail travel with its fixed routes and timetable (Jakle 1985). Cycling was, in some respects, the precursor of the motor car in generating systems of excursion routes out of the city (Tobin 1974) and, particularly in the USA, the car quickly became a fashionable form of leisure transport. Both bicycle and car led to a rebirth of rural roads as significant environments for American travel. Closer contact with landscapes was resumed after it had been lost through rail travel and the early publicity of the two new modes of transport stressed the idea of "freedom". The car built upon the infrastructure created for cyclists with route maps, guides and accommodation. Hotels and inns began to shift their location from city centre to city edge to cater for the more mobile traveller (Jakle 1985) and scenic drives were created around Boston, Kansas City, Philadelphia, New York City and other urban agglomerations in the early years of the century. The car in the USA was seen largely as a leisure form of transport until the 1920s, when like the bicycle before, it then acquired a more utilitarian function.

The initial restriction of car ownership to the wealthy elite gave a new impetus to exclusive travel in America as a substitute for travel abroad (Hugill 1985). This led to a form of "rediscovery" of places which had been made popular in the early nineteenth century by artists and romantic writers (chapter 6). The north-eastern states, in particular, re-emerged as destinations for the leisured classes with the car acting as a form of mobile social enclave. Once again the Catskills, Adirondacks and the Hudson and Connecticut rivers became attractions for the rich. Hugill (1985) traces a nine-day car excursion from Cazenovia, an elite summer resort in New York State, in the early twentieth century (Figure 8.17). The Catskills, Berkshires, Green Mountains, Hudson and Connecticut rivers were seen with new eyes from the comfort of a motor car. With tourists in control of their own itinerary, able to spot and admire the scenery, the new mode of transport created a form of travel experience which encouraged a greater sensibility to the landscape of the journey which had been lost during the railway era (Hugill 1985).

The transformation of landscapes

During the 1930s, a number of geographers, notably in North America, began to write about the increasing significance of recreation and

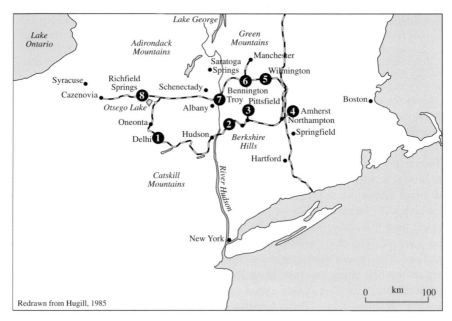

Figure 8.17 A nine-day automobile tour of the Catskills, Berkshires and Green Mountains, 1908 (Elsevier Science Ltd)

tourism as both a land use and a social and economic activity (Brown 1935; Carlson 1938; Chichester 1934; McMurry 1930). This academic interest was a recognition of the fact that leisure was not only capable of creating the townscapes of spa and seaside resort, but had an increasing potential to transform landscapes at a much wider scale.

This process had been evident much earlier, of course, in Europe, where the rich and powerful in society could create large hunting preserves for their pleasure (chapter 2). A more recent example could be found in nineteenth-century Britain with the creation of the deer forests in the Highlands of Scotland (Orr 1982). The ancient deer forests had virtually disappeared by the early nineteenth century with increases in arable and livestock farming but later that century, vast tracts of land were set aside for the sporting interests of a wealthy elite (Figure 8.18). In transforming these landscapes for recreation, the process of development was very much linked to a core–periphery relationship, with a peripheral Highland economy locked to an economic core in southern England. The south provided the investment and the customers for the deer forests. As sheep farming declined, so sport outbid other land uses. Renting or owning a Highland estate brought great prestige and the new commercial and industrial rich joined the old-established land-

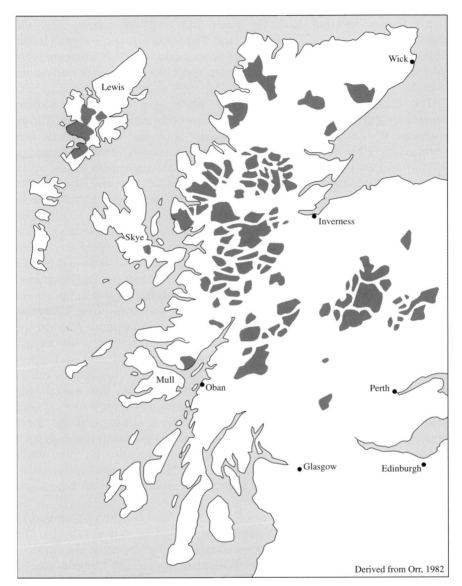

Figure 8.18   Deer forests in the Scottish Highlands by 1884 (John Donald Publishers Ltd, Edinburgh)

owners in the annual migration to the hills of the north. The trans-formation began gradually in the 1820s and 1830s but increased from the 1840s when royal patronage popularised the Highland scene. An equilibrium between farming and pleasure was reached in the 1850s and some forests reverted back to sheep, but southern money and the demand for sport tipped the scales and there was a major increase in the 1880s in forest creation. During this latter period, British interests were joined by affluent visitors and investors from North America and South Africa.

The conversion of so much land from agriculture to moorland reserved for hunting and shooting had clear economic and social consequences. It was argued that the loss of land for local farmers was compensated by new jobs on the estates. However, as the minister of Kintail argued in 1883: "the sums paid as rent are chiefly taken away from the Highlands and expended in London and elsewhere" (Orr 1982:90). Not all income leaked out of the local economy. In addition to a proportion of rates and taxes, some profits were reinvested locally. The Duke of Sutherland, for instance, backed the Helmsdale and Wick Railway and local jobs such as planting, fencing, draining and road building were created. Some food and drink might be supplied locally but luxury items such as wine came from London. The increased accessibility brought by the railways increased the flow of imports. In 1912, the Blackmount Estate brought all its groceries from Glasgow, while others brought everything except bread from London. Around the estates, there were some direct evictions from crofts and a loss of hill pasture. Outsiders tended to become the new local hotel- and innkeepers and these entrepreneurs tended to benefit most from the estates rather than those in the traditional crofting communities. But overall the conversion of Highland landscapes into pleasure areas for a few affluent customers had much longer term consequences. Fundamentally, there was the opportunity cost of lack of investment in alternative sectors such as farming which retarded economic development. By the early twentieth century, 34 per cent of land in crofting communities was in deer forest use, reserved for the seasonal pleasures of those who lived elsewhere.

In North America, the power of recreation and tourism to transform landscapes was perhaps more democratic in that land uses reflected the leisure of a wider cross-section of society than that found in the Scottish Highlands. From the 1890s, the lakes and forests of Ontario saw a significant spread of summer cottages for the nearby urban societies of Canada and the USA, and these cottages became major features of the landscape (Wall 1977; Wolfe 1962, 1967). Also from the 1890s, the landscapes of Maine in north-east USA began to reflect the widespread influence of recreation and tourism. Like the Scottish Highlands, this was a peripheral economy, dependent on agriculture, fishing and mining and resentful of outside influences such as those from urban centres like Boston (Judd 1988). During the 1860s the coast of Maine had been colonised by urban elites in a series of exclusive seaside resorts such as York, Kennebunk, the Casco Islands and Bar Harbor but by the 1890s, Maine's landscape inland was seen as offering commercial leisure potential. Promotion focused on Maine's "pre-industrial" landscape and its healthy environments. These interests, which lived on the region's aesthetic qualities, were in competition with the industrial lobby which lived on the economic resources of timber and water. Over time, it was the tourism perspective that tended to hold sway. Farming and the sporting interests of fish and game had a common desire to conserve Maine's landscapes in order to attract visitors. As a South Portland legislator pointed out in 1921: "For one hundred years we dammed the rivers and praised the builders, and now we are praising the rivers and damning the builders" (quoted in Judd 1988:190). Farmers were urged to improve the beauty of the roadside in recognition of the economic significance of tourism and so contribute to the "rustic beauty of the landscape" (Judd 1988:187).

In 1930 McMurry in the *Annals of the Association of American Geographers* noted that recreation had been neglected as a land use in geographical studies but that now it could be seen as a "major form" in many areas. He was writing in particular of the Great Lakes area but some of the largest changes were occurring in the north-east of the country, especially in New England. A 1938 paper by Carlson produced a detailed study of New Hampshire and, in a series of maps (Figure 8.19), he plotted the distribution of a whole range of accommodation types in the state and identified clearly distinctive tourist regions. At that time, recreation and tourism were already twice the economic value of agriculture and they lay a close second behind the main activity, the textile industry. Furthermore, the forms of tourism had already undergone major changes. The accommodation sector had moved from large hotels based near railway junctions and in the mountain regions, which had been created in the nineteenth century, to a more dispersed pattern of summer cottages, lodgings and cabins based on the motor car. Lodgings (bed and breakfast) although widespread were most important in the mountain and lakes regions, while summer cottages tended to cluster around lake shores. Overnight cabins for motorists were found along the major highways. Much of this new accommodation had followed the agricultural decline of the state. Farms decreased from 29 000 in 1890 to 15 000 by 1930, while summer cottages on these sites rose from 2700 to 10 500 between 1902 and 1932. Carlson also commented on the new landscapes being created along the highways—petrol stations and shops, as well as vegetable stands laid out by farmers to catch the passing trade. Clearly, by the 1930s, this part of the USA was increasingly geared to the need of urban pleasure seekers.

Lifestyles and lifecycles

In the first chapter of this book the need was highlighted for placing particular recreation and tourism episodes within the wider context of people's lifecycles and lifestyles. Too often, research describes a leisure event in isolation from the wider circumstances under which it took place. Furthermore, there is little understanding of how the geography of recreation and tourism changed for people during their lifetime. One major reason for this neglect is the lack of evidence, in the form of long-term records for individuals, although for more recent times the techniques of oral history can offer interesting possibilities (Towner 1994, 1995). Using scattered evidence, a number of examples will illustrate aspects of people's "time-space" diaries as a starting point for this kind of analysis.

The autobiography of Molly Hughes (1934,1946a, b) traces her life from childhood in the London of the 1870s to married life in the 1890s. Within this period we can trace the shifting geography of her leisure: from local routine activities associated first with her childhood but

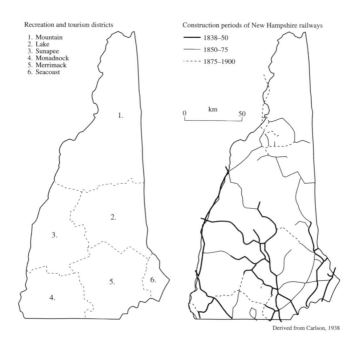

Figure 8.19 The spatial pattern of the recreation and tourism industry in New Hampshire by the 1930s (*Economic Geography*, Clark University, MA)

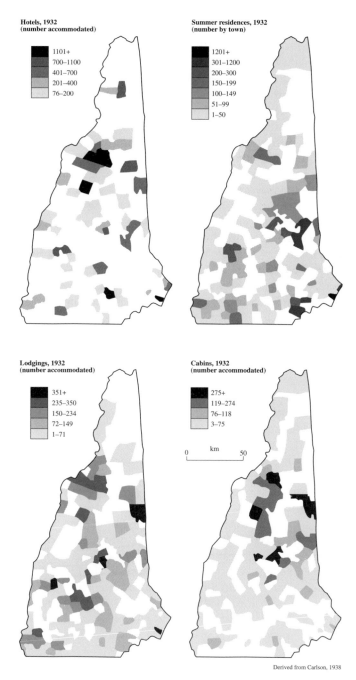

Figure 8.19   (continued)

returned to again as a mother, to longer holidays away which were linked to changes in family connections and wider social networks. As a child of a middle-class family, her early leisure experiences centred on home and weekend excursions to London parks, the river at Richmond, Epping Forest or a boat trip to Greenwich. These were undertaken with her father and brothers. Viewing the shops of the West End was a trip with her mother. Despite these outings it is clear that her brothers had far more opportunities for widening their leisure worlds, while Molly often remained with her mother at home. Family summer holidays were to Cornwall, not because this was a holiday region but to stay with relatives who had always lived there. Her father's death saw a constriction on the family's overall lifestyles, including leisure, during much of her teenage years and a holiday at Clacton in 1884 (when she was 17) was the first lengthy outing for five years. After teacher training at Cambridge, Molly's leisure horizons widened as her social network expanded. Holiday visits to Wales in her twenties were to see her fiancé's family, while visits to Middlesbrough and Guernsey were to see her brothers, who by then were working in these areas. The one visit Molly Hughes made to Europe was in 1895 when she was 28 and was with two fellow lecturers from Bedford College, London. This was to Switzerland. After marrying and having children, her leisure world entered a phase of domestic and local pleasures again. But the value of her record lies not particularly in what she did in her leisure time but in the insight it gives into the changing pattern of recreation and tourism in her life as social and economic circumstances altered. These changes are not, perhaps, surprising, but they are a perspective often missing from the historical and geographical record.

Other insights into leisure worlds come from the chance survival of the ephemera of life left by Miss Agnes Toward (1886–1975) in Glasgow (Ritchie 1984). A shorthand typist living with her mother in a tenement in Garnethill, Agnes Toward kept records of virtually everything she did from childhood to old age. Her two-week annual holiday with pay was spent at Largs or Kirn down the River Clyde, at first with her grandmother or mother, later by herself. She often stayed in the same boarding house or hotel year after year. Her one trip further afield was to Beckenham in Kent, visiting a friend made through the workplace. Otherwise her leisure world was very localised: church outings to the Campsie Fells or occasional visits to Glasgow theatres and dances. Her overall lifestyle (unlike that of Molly Hughes) seems to have barely changed as she progressed through the years and, as a consequence, neither did her world of pleasure.

An example from my own family history can provide another illustration of changing leisure lifestyle. Figure 8.20 shows the summer

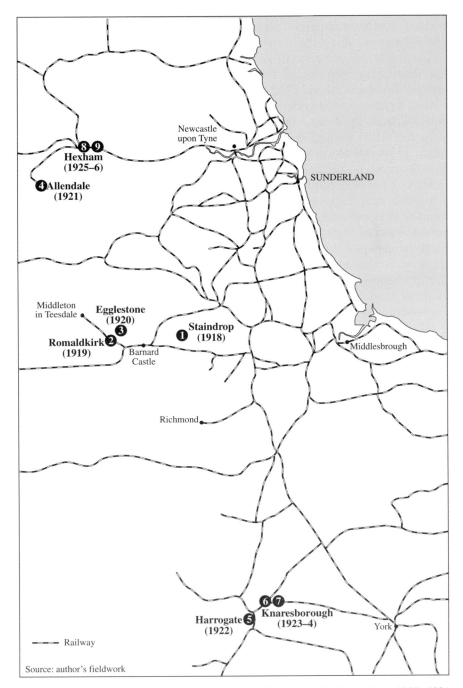

Figure 8.20 Summer holiday destinations of the Robson family, Sunderland, 1918–1926

holiday destinations from 1918 to 1926 of the Robson family, mother and father and three children, who lived in Sunderland.

The father owned a small engineering firm which was dependent on the fluctuating fortunes of the shipbuilding industry, and he had an annual income of about £250–300 a year. In 1918, mother and children rented a cottage at Staindrop in County Durham for a month, and this was followed by similar holidays at nearby Romaldkirk and Eggleston, with the father joining the family only at weekends. A holiday further afield at Harrogate came through a family connection with one of the town's guest house owners and this then led to subsequent visits to nearby Knaresborough. Cheaper farm holidays then resumed in Allendale and near Hexham. All destinations were within a day's journey of home and could be reached by rail and horse-drawn cab. The places selected were found informally by word of mouth or through local newspaper advertisements. Within this annual holiday pattern there was also a routine of visiting friends and relatives, especially grandparents in Clayton West in Yorkshire who were seen in the summer and at Christmas. After 1926, the family group began to disperse as the children grew older and individual holidays with friends marked a new stage in the lifecycle and a new stage in leisure.

This was not the world of the *Queen Book of Travel*, yet although more common for many people, the recreation and tourism of families like the Robsons remains elusive. Ironically we know more about the activities of the few at Nice or Cannes than about the annual patterns of leisure for the majority of the population. Further research into the more recent past will, however, enable us to build up a clearer picture of this changing world of lifestyle and lifecycle and so provide a much richer context for exploring the geographies of recreation and tourism.

This chapter has ranged widely over a number of themes which were a feature of leisure in the nineteenth and early twentieth centuries. It does not pretend to provide a comprehensive overview of all that took place during that era but, in selecting certain episodes, it has tried to capture something of the flavour of recreation and tourism for different social classes in different geographical settings. Rather than retelling the familiar stories of Thomas Cook and the emergence of organised popular travel, I have attempted to show that leisure and pleasure occurred at all levels in society long before the growth of modern tourism.

Postscript

Throughout this book I have attempted to place case studies of recreation and tourism in the past within the overall framework outlined in the first chapter. Where possible, processes have been examined which have taken place in visitor-generating areas, visitor destination areas and the transport and other links which joined them. All three components need to be studied if we wish to understand particular recreation and tourism systems. Within this framework, much of the material has been considered in the context of certain environments: places within and around urban areas, the countryside, both tamed and wild, and the movements which took place between these various settings. This has not been to insist, however, that there was always a fundamental distinction to be made, in terms of activities, between these environments and, in some instances, the creation of a leisure place did not necessarily involve movement. As part of that process of creation, I have included discussions on the values that were accorded to particular environments which made them places for pleasure.

The book has also explored the issues of change and continuity in the geographies of recreation and tourism between different historical eras and as they occurred in Britain, western Europe and North America. Social class and cultural variations in leisure activities have been emphasised as they took place at different times and in different places. And, when information has allowed, I have attempted to balance the geographies of those at play with those who worked to support them.

From amongst this general picture, a number of recurring themes have emerged. I began chapter 2 by raising the idea that the upper classes in western society gradually withdrew from the customs of others and, if this was the case, it would have had geographical consequences for the use of space for recreation and tourism. With a separation of interest there would at times be competition for space when different social groups identified the same areas for leisure and diverging interests would also encourage the search for clearly separate areas in the pursuit of pleasure. Whatever the underlying reasons, there was clearly a social-class component to these processes and the evolution of leisure and issues of power and conflict have been a characteristic of this geography of recreation and tourism. Another theme which can be detected relates to the process of the development of leisure places. This has been linked a number of times in this book, to the relationship between core and periphery areas and the degree of control that core regions had over the growth of resorts and other centres of leisure. Furthermore, viewing these places as centres of consumption and examining the consequent geographies of supply and demand of goods and services, reveals other patterns and moves the study of places beyond simply examining the activities of visitors.

On the other hand, I have tried to show that there should be some reservations over other themes which have sometimes been held to characterise the evolution of recreation and tourism. One of these is the concept of "mass follows class" (or successive class intrusion) which at times has been presented as an inevitable factor in the process of development. But although class differences are vital there is another argument that suggests that different social groups may make their own leisure and not simply imitate the example of others. In the same vein, I have drawn attention to debates over the precise role of transport technology as a fundamental factor for changing recreation and tourism patterns. Different forms of transport were important but the relationship between them and development was more complex than sometimes suggested. At another level, but also relating to change, I have pointed to the doubts that some historians have on the transition from pre-industrial to industrial societies as a basic explanation for alterations in leisure and recreation attitudes and practices. But beyond these ideas, I have made few references to the theories and models which will be familiar to those involved in social science research in the field. I wished to provide a different perspective on this subject and I am also conscious of the problems associated with trying to fit events from the distant past into structures which involve a considerable amount of *post hoc* reasoning. Thus the broad concepts and themes which I have employed reflect a certain caution in seeking analogies between present and past.

These arguments need to be taken a stage further. What is written about in this book can only be a partial view of the history and geography of recreation and tourism. I have not gone back in time to the medieval and classical worlds and I have confined myself to a consideration of parts of the western world. We can hardly make generalised statements about leisure, recreation and tourism development, either today or in the past, when what we have is essentially a western cultural perspective. We seem to know little about the worlds of leisure in other societies but it is hard to believe that this aspect of life has not been expressed in different ways elsewhere. Leisure, recreation and tourism have, so far, been defined and researched in western cultural terms and their history portrayed as a gradual spread from a European heartland to the rest of the world. That history is more likely to be a story of variations in different cultures, at different times and in different places.

A fuller understanding in this field has, therefore, a considerable way to go. Perhaps future developments might include a number of the following ideas. New geographical areas and cultures need to be brought into the picture. We need to know how leisure evolved in other societies and to what extent they can be related to western models of pleasure. Another development which would be helpful would be closer links between historians and recreation and tourism studies researchers so that a process of cross-fertilisation can be encouraged. After all, this book began from a concern that little historical research was penetrating the recreation and tourism area. One advantage for historians is that they have not compartmentalised the field into subdivisions of leisure, recreation and tourism and so have explored the interrelated world of pleasure more realistically. Part of this interrelationship can be usefully developed by employing the context of lifestyles and lifecycles, rather than seeing activities as separate, unconnected events. The changing leisure geographies of people through time is a much needed perspective that needs to be pursued.

Finally, in an area where reliable research evidence is often hard to obtain, there seems to be considerable scope for exploring other forms of material. In this book, I have at times drawn on literature and art to provide an insight into past leisure worlds. But for the more recent past, oral history can be used extensively to study a wide spectrum of people and to enquire into what role leisure, recreation and tourism played in their lives. The possibilities are considerable, challenging and even enjoyable.

Bibliography

Abrams, L. (1992), *Workers' Culture in Imperial Germany*. London: Routledge.

Ackerman, J.S. (1990), *The Villa: Form and Ideology of Country Houses*. London: Thames and Hudson.

Addison, J. (1761), *Remarks on several parts of Italy etc. in the years 1701, 1702, 1703*. (1st publ. 1705). London.

Adhémar, J. (1938), "Les lithographies de paysage en France à l'époque romantique", *Archives de l'art Français*, **19**, 189–364.

Adler, J. (1989), "Origins of sightseeing", *Annals of Tourism Research*, **16**, 7–29.

Alderson, F. (1972), *Bicycling: A History*. Newton Abbot: David and Charles.

Allen, B.S. (1937), *Tides in English Taste (1619–1800)*. Repr. edn 1958, New York: Pageant Books.

Amory, C. (1948), *The Last Resorts*. New York: Harper.

Andrews, M. (1989), *The Search for the Picturesque*. Aldershot: Gower Press.

Ashworth, G.J. and Voogd, H. (1990), *Selling the City: Marketing Approaches in Public Sector Urban Planning*. London: Belhaven.

Austen, J. (1811), *Sense and Sensibility*. London.

Austen, J. (1813), *Pride and Prejudice*. London.

Austen, J. (1815), *Emma*. Republ. 1906, London: Everyman.

Austen, J. (1818), *Persuasion*. London, republ. New York: Modern Library.

Austen, J. (1818), *Northanger Abbey*. London, republ. New York: Modern Library.

Baedeker, K. (1900), *Austria, including Hungary, Transylvania, Dalmatia, and Bosnia*, 9th edn. Leipzig: Baedeker.

Baedeker, K. (1904), *Paris and Environs*, 15th edn. Leipzig: Baedeker.

Baedeker, K. (1910), *Northern Germany as far as the Bavarian and Austrian Frontiers*, 15th edn. Leipzig: Baedeker.

Bailey, P. (1978), *Leisure and Class in Victorian England*. London: Routledge and Kegan Paul.

Bailey, P. (1989), "Leisure, culture and the historian: Reviewing the first generation of leisure historiography in Britain", *Leisure Studies*, **8**, 107–127.

Baillie, G. (1911), *The Household Book of Lady Grisell Baillie, 1692–1733*, ed. R.Scott-Moncrieff, Scottish Historical Society, 2nd series, 1. Edinburgh.

Baker, P.R. (1964), *The Fortunate Pilgrims. Americans in Italy, 1800–1860*. Cambridge, Mass.: Harvard University Press.

Ball, A. (1977), *Yesterday in Bath*. Bath: Kingsmead Press.

Barea, I. (1966), *Vienna, Legend and Reality*. London: Secker and Warburg.

Baridon, M. and Chevignard, B. (eds) (1988), *Voyage et tourisme en Bourgogne à l'époque de Jefferson*. Dijon: Publications de l'université de Bourgogne.

Barke, M. and Towner, J. (1995), "Exploring the history of leisure and tourism in Spain", in M. Barke, J. Towner and M. Newton (eds), *Tourism in Spain: Critical Issues*. Wallingford: CAB International.

Barlow, T. (1836), *A Trip to Rome at Railway Speed*. London.

Barraclough, G. (1979), *Main Trends in History*. New York: Holmes and Meier.

Barrell, J. (1972), *The Idea of Landscape and the Sense of Place 1730–1840. An Approach to the Poetry of John Clare*. Cambridge: Cambridge University Press.

Barrett, J.A. (1958), The seaside resort towns of England and Wales. Doctoral dissertation, London University.

Barwick, G.F. (1904), "Some early guide books", *Transactions of the Bibliographical Society*, **7**, 191–207.

Batten, C.L. (1978), *Pleasurable Instruction. Form and Convention in Eighteenth Century Travel Literature*. Berkeley and London: University of California Press.

Beckford, W. (1928), *The Travel Diaries of William Beckford of Fonthill*, ed. G.Chapman, 2 vols. London: Constable.

Beckinsale, R. and Beckinsale, M. (1980), *The English Heartland*. London: Duckworth.

Bennett, A. (1908), *The Old Wives' Tale*. London: Everyman Library.

Bernard, R. (1815). *A Tour through some Parts of France, Switzerland, Savoy, Germany, and Belgium, during the Summer and Autumn of 1814*. London.

Best, G. (1979), *Mid-Victorian Britain, 1851–1875*. London: Fontana.

Bicknell, P. (1957), *British Hills and Mountains*. London: Collins.

Bicknell, P. and Woof, R. (1982), *The Discovery of the Lake District, 1750–1810: A Context for Wordsworth*. Grasmere: Trustees of Dove Cottage.

Bignell, A. (1977), *Hopping down in Kent*. London: Hale.

Billcliffe, R. (1985), *The Glasgow Boys*. London: Murray.

Black, J. (1992), *The British Abroad: The Grand Tour in the Eighteenth Century*. New York: St Martin's Press.

Blair, A. (1985), *Tea at Miss Cranston's: A Century of Glasgow Memories*. London: Shepheard-Walwyn.

Blunden, J. and Curry, N. (eds) (1990), *A People's Charter?* London: HMSO.

Boorman, D. (1990), "The city and the channel", in R.A. Griffiths (ed.), *The City of Swansea: Challenges and Change*. Stroud: Alan Sutton.

Boorstin, D.J. (1962), *The Image*. Harmondsworth: Penguin.

Borsay, P. (1982), "Culture, status and the English urban landscape", *History*, **67**, 1–12.

Borsay, P. (1986), "The rise of the promenade: The social and cultural use of space in the English provincial town c.1660–1800", *British Journal for Eighteenth Century Studies*, **9**, 2, 125–140.

Borsay, P. (1989), *The English Urban Renaissance: Culture and Society in the Provincial Town, 1660–1770*. Oxford: Clarendon Press.

Borsay, P. (ed.) (1990), *The Eighteenth Century Town: A Reader in English Urban History 1688–1820*. London: Longman.

Boswell, J. (1774), *Journal of a Tour to the Hebrides*. London.

Bouquet, M. (1985), *Family, Servants and Visitors: The Farm Household in Nineteenth and Twentieth Century Devon*. Norwich: Geo. Books.

Boyle, J. (1774), *Letters from Italy, in the years 1754 and 1755, by the late Right Honourable John, Earl of Corke and Orrery*. London.

Boyle, M. and Hughes, G. (1991), "The politics of the representation of 'the real':

Discourses from the left on Glasgow's role as European City of Culture", *Area*, **23**, 3, 217–228.

Brandon, P.F. (1979), "The diffusion of designed landscapes in south-east England", in H.S.A. Fox and R.A. Butlin (eds), *Change in the Countryside: Essays on Rural England 1500–1990*. IBG Special Publication, 10, 165–187.

Braudel, F. (1979), *The Structures of Everyday Life*, vol. 1, *Civilization and Capitalism*, trans. S. Reynolds, 1985. London: Fontana.

Brauer, G.C. (1959), *The Education of a Gentleman. Theories of Gentlemanly Education in England, 1660–1775*. New York: Bookman.

Brendon, P. (1991), *Thomas Cook*. London: Secker and Warburg.

Brewer, J. (1976), *Party Ideology and Popular Politics at the Accession of George III*. Cambridge: Cambridge University Press.

Bridenbaugh, C. (1946), "Baths and watering places of colonial America", *William and Mary Quarterly* (3rd series), **3**, 2, 151–181.

Britton, S.G. (1982), "The political economy of tourism in the Third World", *Annals of Tourism Research*, **9**, 3, 331–358.

Brockedon, W. (1828–29), *Illustrations of the passes of the Alps, by which Italy communicates with France, Switzerland and Germany*. London.

Brockman, C.F. and Merriam, L. (1973), *Recreational Use of Wild Lands*. New York: McGraw-Hill.

Brown, E. (1677), *An account of several travels through a great part of Germany*. London.

Brown, J. (1766), *Description of the Lake and Vale of Keswick*. Newcastle.

Brown, R.M. (1935), "The business of recreation", *Geographical Review*, **25**, 467–475.

Bruford, W.H. (1935), *Germany in the Eighteenth Century. The Social Background of the Literary Revival*. Cambridge: Cambridge University Press.

Budworth, J. (1810), *A Fortnight's Ramble in the Lakes*. London.

Bulley, J.A. (1953), "To Mendip for coal: A study of the Somerset coalfield before 1830", *Proceedings of the Somerset Archaeological and Natural History Society*, **97**, 46–78; **98**, 17–54.

Burdett, R.B. (1970), *Go Great Western: A History of GWR Publicity*. Newton Abbot: David and Charles.

Burkart, A.J. and Medlik, S. (1990), *Historical Development of Tourism*. Université de Droit, d'Economie et des Sciences, Centre des Hautes Etudes Touristiques, Aix-en-Provence.

Burke, J. (1968), "The Grand Tour and the rule of taste", in R.F. Brissenden (ed.), *Studies in the Eighteenth Century*. Canberra: Australian National University Press.

Burke, P. (1978), *Popular Culture in Early Modern Europe*. London: Temple Smith.

Burnet, G. (1686), *Some letters. Containing an account of what seemed most remarkable in Switzerland, Italy, etc.* Rotterdam.

Burnet, T. (1681), *Sacred theory of the Earth*. London.

Burstall, P. (1981), *The Golden Age of the Thames*. Newton Abbot: David and Charles.

Butler, R.W. (1980), "The concept of a tourist area cycle of evolution; implications for management of resources", *Canadian Geographer*, **24**, 1, 5–12.

Butler, R.W. (1985), "Evolution of tourism in the Scottish Highlands", *Annals of Tourism Research*, **12**, 3, 371–391.

Butlin, R.A. (1990), "Regions in England and Wales c.1600–1914", in R.A.

Dodgshon and R.A. Butlin (eds), *An Historical Geography of England and Wales*. 2nd edn. London: Academic Press.

Buzard, J. (1993), *The Beaten Track: European Tourism: Literature, and the Ways to "Culture", 1800–1918*. Oxford: Clarendon Press.

Camden, W. (1586), *Britannia, Or a Choro-Graphicall Description of the Most Flourishing Kingdomes, England, Scotland, and Ireland*, 1610 edn. London.

Cannadine, D. (1978), "The theory and practice of the English leisure classes", *Historical Journal*, **21**, 2, 445–467.

Cannadine, D. (1980), *Lords and Landlords: The Aristocracy and the Towns, 1774–1967*. Leicester: Leicester University Press.

Cannadine, D. (1990), *The Decline and Fall of the British Aristocracy*. New Haven: Yale University Press.

Cariou, A. (1992), *Painting in Brittany: Gaugin and his Friends*. Newcastle: Laing Art Gallery.

Carlson, A.S. (1938), "Recreation industry of New Hampshire", *Economic Geography*, **14**, 255–270.

Cartwright, F.F. (1977), *A Social History of Medicine*. London: Longmans.

Caspari, F. (1954), *Humanism and the Social Order in Tudor England*. Chicago: University of Chicago Press.

Casson, L. (1974), *Travel in the Ancient World*. London: Allen and Unwin.

Castiglione, B. (1528), *The Book of the Courtier*, trans. G.Bull (1967). Harmondsworth: Penguin.

Chadwick, G.F. (1966), *The Park and the Town*. London: Architectural Press.

Charleton, R.J. (1885), *A History of Newcastle-on-Tyne*. Newcastle: Robinson.

Charlton, D.G. (1984), *New Images of the Natural in France: A Study in European Cultural History, 1750–1800*. Cambridge: Cambridge University Press.

Chichester, L.W. (1934), "The importance of recreation as a land use in New England", *Journal of Land and Public Utility Economics*, **10**, 202–209.

Cipolla, C.M. (1981), *Fighting the Plague in Seventeenth Century Italy*. Madison: University of Wisconsin Press.

Clark, J. (1787), *Map of Keswick*, deposited in Keswick Library.

Clark, K. (1949), *Landscape into Art*. London: Murray.

Clarke, E.M.L. (1974), *Canada's landscape through the eyes of nineteenth century American and British travellers*. MA dissertation, Toronto: York University.

Clarke, J. and Critcher, C. (1985), *The Devil Makes Work*. London: Macmillan.

Claval, P. (1984), "Reflections on the cultural geography of the European city", in J. Agnew, J. Mercer and D. Sopher (eds), *The City in Cultural Context*. London: Allen and Unwin.

Clawson, M. (1963), *Land and Water for Recreation—Opportunities, Problems, and Policies*. Chicago: Rand McNally.

Clawson, M. and Knetsch, J. (1966), *Economics of Outdoor Recreation*. Baltimore: Johns Hopkins University Press.

Clenche, J. (1676), *A tour in France and Italy made by an English gentleman*. London.

Clough, S.B. (1964), *The Economic History of Modern Italy*. New York: Columbia University Press.

Clough, S.B. (1968), *European Economic History: The Economic Development of Western Civilization*. New York: McGraw-Hill.

Cloulas, I. (1983), *La vie quotidienne dans les châteaux de la Loire au temps de la Renaissance*. Paris: Hachette.

Clout, E. (ed.) (1977), *Themes in the Historical Geography of France*. London: Academic Press.

Cobbett, J.P. (1830), *Journal of a Tour in Italy, also in part of France and Switzerland*. London.

Coffin, D.R. (1979), *The Villa in the Life of Renaissance Rome*. Princeton, NJ: Princeton University Press.

Cohen, E. (1979), "A phenomenology of tourist experiences", *Sociology*, **13**, 179–201.

Cole, B. and Durack, R. (1990), *Happy as a Sand-boy: Early Railway Posters*. London: HMSO.

Conway, H. (1991), *People's Parks: The Design and Development of Victorian Parks in Britain*. Cambridge: Cambridge University Press.

Cook, T. (1905), *Cook's Handbook to the Health Resorts of the South of France, Riviera and Pyrenees*. London: Thomas Cook.

Cook, T. (1929–1930), *The Traveller's Handbook to Switzerland*. London, Simkin Marshall.

Cooper, J. Fenimore (1823), *The Pioneers*, repr. 1867. London: Routledge.

Cooper, J. Fenimore (1826), *The Last of the Mohicans*, repr. 1867. London: Routledge.

Corbin, A. (1994). *The Lure of the Sea*. Cambridge: Polity Press.

Corfield, P.J. (1982), *The Impact of English Towns, 1700–1800*. Oxford: Oxford University Press.

Cornell, S. (1983), *Art: A History of Changing Style*. Oxford: Phaidon.

Cosgrove, D. (1993), *The Palladian Landscape*. Leicester: Leicester University Press.

Cosgrove, I. and Jackson, R. (1972), *The Geography of Recreation and Leisure*. London: Hutchinson.

Cranz, G. (1982), *The Politics of Park Design: A History of Urban Parks in America*. Cambridge, Mass.: MIT Press.

Cross, G. (1990a), *A Social History of Leisure since 1600*. State College, PA. Venture Publishing.

Cross, G. (1990b), *Worktowners at Blackpool: Mass-observation and Popular Leisure in the 1930s*. London: Routledge.

Crump, J. (1986), "Recreation in Coventry between the wars", in W. Lancaster and A. Mason (eds), *Life and Labour in a Twentieth Century City: The Experience of Coventry*. London: Cryfield Press.

Cunningham, H. (1980), *Leisure in the Industrial Revolution, 1780–1880*. London: Croom Helm.

Cunningham, H. (1990), "Leisure and culture", in F.M.L. Thompson (ed.), *The Cambridge Social History of Britain, 1750–1950*, vol. 2. Cambridge: Cambridge University Press.

Curley, T.M. (1976), *Samuel Johnson and the Age of Travel*. Athens, GA: University of Georgia Press.

Cust, L. (1898), *History of the Society of Dilettanti*. London: Macmillan.

Daiches, D. (1977), *Glasgow*. London: Deutsch.

Dallington, R. (1605?), *A method for travill. Shewed by taking the view of France. As it stoode in the yeare of our Lord 1598*. London.

Daniels, S. and Seymour, S. (1990), "Landscape design and the idea of improvement 1730–1914", in R.A. Dodgshon and R.A. Butlin (eds), *An Historical Geography of England and Wales*, 2nd edn. London: Academic Press.

Davies, A. (1992), *Leisure, Gender and Poverty: Working Class Culture in Salford and Manchester, 1900–1939*. Buckingham: Open University Press.

De Beer, E.S. (1952), "The development of the guidebook until the early nineteenth century", *Journal of the British Archaeological Society* (3rd series), **15**, 35–46.

De Beer, E.S. (1975), "The literature of travel in the seventeenth century", *Annual Report*, Hakluyt Society, 1–6.

De Blainville, P. (1703), *A relation of the journey of the Gentlemen Blathwayt into the north of England in the year seventeen hundred and three*, ed. N. Hardwick, 1977. Gloucester: Gloucester Record Office.

Defoe, D. (1724), *A Tour through the Whole Island of Great Britain*, republ. 1971. Harmondsworth: Penguin.

Delgado, A. (1977), *The Annual Outing and other Excursions*. London: Allen and Unwin.

Delves, A. (1981), "Popular recreation and social conflict in Derby, 1800–1850", in E. Yeo and S. Yeo (eds), *Popular Culture and Class Conflict: Explorations in the History of Labour and Leisure, 1590–1914*. Brighton: Harvester Press.

Demars, S. (1979), "British contributions to American seaside resorts", *Annals of Tourism Research*, **6**, 3, 285–293.

Dent, K.S. (1974), The informal education of the landed classes in the eighteenth century, with particular references to reading. University of Birmingham doctoral dissertation.

Dent, K.S. (1975), "Travel as education. The English landed classes in the eighteenth century", *Educational Studies*, **1**, 3, 171–180.

Derry, T.K. and Williams, T.I. (1960), *A Short History of Technology*. Oxford: Clarendon Press.

De Vries, J. (1978), "Barges and capitalism: Passenger transportation in the Dutch economy, 1632–1839", *Afdeling Agrarische Geschiedenis Bijdragen*, **21**, 33–39.

Dickens, C. (1837), *Pickwick Papers*. London.

Dicks, B. (1985), "Choice and constraint: Further perspectives on socio-residential segregation in nineteenth century Glasgow with particular reference to its West End", in G. Gordon (ed.), *Perspectives of the Scottish City*. Aberdeen: Aberdeen University Press.

Dodgshon, R.A. (1990), "The changing evaluation of space 1500–1914", in R.A. Dodgshon and R.A. Butlin (eds), *An Historical Geography of England and Wales*, 2nd edn. London: Academic Press.

Douglas-Simpson, W. (1930–1931), "Edzell Castle", *Proceedings of the Society of Antiquaries of Scotland*, **65**, 117–173.

Drabble, M. (1979), *A Writer's Britain: Landscape in Literature*. London: Thames and Hudson.

Dugdale, W. (1656), *The antiquities of Warwickshire*, 1765 edn. Coventry.

Dulles, F.R. (1964), *Americans Abroad: Two Centuries of European Travel*. Ann Arbor: University of Michigan Press.

Dulles, F.R. (1965), *A History of Recreation: America Learns to Play*, 2nd edn. New York: Appleton-Century-Crofts.

Dwight, T. (1821–1822), *Travels in New England and New York*. New York.

Ebel, M.J.G. (1820), *The Traveller's Guide through Switzerland*. London.

Edinburgh Review (1806), **8**. Edinburgh.

Eisner, R. (1991), *Travellers to an Antique Land: The History and Literature of Travel to Greece*. Ann Arbor: University of Michigan Press.

Elyot, T. (1531), *The Governor*, repr. edn 1907, Everyman Library. London: Dent.

Eustace, J.C. (1815), *A Classical Tour through Italy*, 4 vols. London.

Evelyn, J. (1955), *The Diary of John Evelyn*, vol. 2, "Kalendarium", 1620–1649, 6 vols, ed. E.S. de Beer. Oxford: Clarendon Press.

Fall, J. (1931), *Memoires of my Lord Drumlangrig's and his brother Lord William's travels abroad for the space of 3 yeares beginning Septr.13 1680*. Edinburgh: Constable.

Farrant, S. (1987), "London by the sea", *Journal of Contemporary History*, **22**, 137–162.

Fawcett, T. (1990), "Eighteenth-century shops and the luxury trade", *Bath History*, **3**, 49–75.

Fedler, A.J. (1987), "Are leisure, recreation and tourism interrelated?" *Annals of Tourism Research*, **14**, 3, 311–313.

Fergusson, A. (1973), *The Sack of Bath*. Salisbury: Compton Russell.

Fielding, H. (1749), *Tom Jones*. London.

Fifer, J.V. (1988), *American Progress: The Growth of the Transport, Tourist, and Information Industries in the Nineteenth Century*. Chester, Conn.: Globe Pequot Press.

Fisher, F.J. (1948), "The development of London as a centre of conspicuous consumption in the seventeenth and eighteenth centuries", *Trans. Royal Historical Society* (4th series), **30**, 37–50.

Flinn, M.W. (1984), *History of the British Coal Industry, 1700–1830*, vol. 2. Oxford: Clarendon Press.

Forbes, R.J. (1957), "Land transport and roadbuilding (1000–1900)", *Janus*, **46**, 2, 104–140; **3**, 201–223.

Ford, B. (1974), "Thomas Jenkins, banker, dealer, and unofficial agent" 416–425; "The Earl-Bishop, an eccentric and capricious patron of the arts" 426–434; "Sir Watkin Williams-Wynn, a Welsh Maecenas" 435–439; "James Byres, principal antiquarian for the English visitors to Rome" 446–461; "Sir John Coxe-Hippisley, an unofficial English envoy to the Vatican" 440–445; "William Constable, an enlightened Yorkshire patron" 408–415. *Apollo*, **99**.

Fordham, H.G. (1925), *Notes on the Itineraries, Road-books and Road-maps of France*. Southampton.

Forsyth, J. (1813), *Remarks on Antiquities, Arts and Letters during an Excursion in Italy, in the years 1802 and 1803*. London.

Fosbroke, T.D. (1818), *The Wye Tour, or Gilpin on the Wye, with Historical and Archaeological Additions*. Ross on Wye.

France, L.A. and Towner, L. (1992), "Open space and public recreation in the nineteenth and early twentieth centuries", in M. Barke and R.J. Buswell (eds), *Newcastle's Changing Map*. Newcastle: City Library.

Franck, C.L. (1966), *The Villas of Frascati, 1550–1750*. London: Tiranti.

Frantz, R.W. (1934), *The English Traveller and the Movement of Ideas, 1660–1732*, repr. 1968. New York: Octagon.

Fraser, W.H. (1990), "Developments in leisure", in W. Hamish Fraser and R.J. Morris (eds), *People and Society in Scotland*, vol. 2, *1830–1914*. Edinburgh: John Donald.

Frye, W.E. (1908), *After Waterloo, Reminiscences of European Travel, 1815–1819*, ed. S. Reinach. London: Heinemann.

Fussell, P. (1965), *The Rhetorical World of Augustan Humanism*. Oxford: Clarendon Press.

Fussell, P. (1980), *Abroad, British Literary Travelling between the Wars*. New York: Oxford University Press.

Gade, D.W. (1982), "The French Riviera as elitist space", *Journal of Cultural Geography*, **3**, 1, 19–28.

Gailhard, J. (1678), *The compleat Gentleman: or directions for the education of youth as to their breeding at home and travelling abroad*. London

Gay, P. (1967), *The Enlightenment*, vol. 1. New York: Knopf.

Gell, W. (1797), *A tour in the Lakes*, ed. W.Rollinson. Newcastle upon Tyne: Frank Graham.

Gentleman's Magazine, **18**, 1748; **53**, 1783. London.

Getz, D. (1992), "Tourism planning and destination life cycle", *Annals of Tourism Research*, **19**, 752–769.

Giddens, A. (1991), "Structuration theory: past, present and future" in C. Bryant and D. Jary (eds), *Giddens' Theory of Structuration*. London: Routledge.

Gifford, J., McWilliam, C. and Walker, D. (1984), *Edinburgh*, The Buildings of Scotland. Harmondsworth: Penguin.

Gilbert, E.W. (1939), "The growth of inland and seaside health resorts in England", *Scottish Geographical Magazine*, **55**, 16–35.

Gilbert, E.W. (1949), "The growth of Brighton", *Geographical Journal*, **114**, 30–52.

Gilbert, E.W. (1954), *Brighton: Old Ocean's Bauble*. London: Methuen.

Gilpin, W. (1782), *Observations on the river Wye, and several parts of South Wales, etc. relative chiefly to picturesque beauty; made in the summer of the year 1770*. London.

Gilpin, W. (1786), *Observations relative chiefly to picturesque beauty, made in the year 1772, on several parts of England; particularly the mountains, and lakes of Cumberland, and Westmoreland*. London.

Gilpin, W. (1789), *Observations relative chiefly to picturesque beauty, made in the year 1776, on several parts of Great Britain; particularly the high-lands of Scotland*. London.

Gilpin, W. (1809), *Observations on several parts of the counties of Cambridge, Norfolk, Suffolk, and Essex. Also on several parts of North Wales, relative chiefly to picturesque beauty in two tours, the former made in . . . 1769, the latter in . . . 1773*. London.

Girouard, M. (1978), *Life in the English Country House*. Harmondsworth: Penguin.

Gittings, R. (1978), *Young Thomas Hardy*. Harmondsworth: Penguin.

Glacken, C. (1960), "Count Buffon on cultural changes of the physical environment", *Annals of the Association of American Geographers*, **50**, 1–21.

Glennie, P.D. (1990), "Industry and towns, 1500–1730" in R.A. Dodgshon and R.A. Butlin (eds), *An Historical Geography of England and Wales*, 2nd edn. London: Academic Press.

Glyptis, S. (1981), "Leisure life-styles", *Leisure Studies*, **15**, 5, 311–326.

Gold, J.R. and Ward, S.V. (eds) (1994), *Place Promotion*. Chichester: Wiley.

Golden, M. (1977), "Travel writing in the 'Monthly Review' and 'Critical Review', 1756–1775", *Papers on Language and Literature*, **13**, 213–223.

Gormsen, E. (1981), "The spatio-temporal development of international tourism: attempts at a centre periphery model", in *La consommation d'espace par le tourisme et sa preservation*. Aix-en-Provence: Centre des Hautes Etudes de Tourisme.

Graburn, N. (1978), "Tourism: the sacred journey", in V.L. Smith (ed.), *Hosts and Guests*. Oxford: Blackwell.

Graham, H.G. (1909), *The Social Life of Scotland in the Eighteenth Century*. London: Black.

Graham, M. (1820), *Three months passed in the mountains east of Rome, during the year 1819*. London.

Granville, A.B. (1841), *The Spas of England, and Principal Sea-bathing Places*, 2 vols, repr. 1971. Bath: Adams and Dart.

Gray, T. (1909), *The Letters of Thomas Gray*, ed. D.C. Tovey, 6 vols. London: Bell.

Green, N. (1990), *The Spectacle of Nature: Landscape and Bourgeois Culture in Nineteenth Century France*. Manchester: Manchester University Press.

Gregory, A. (1991), *The Golden Age of Travel, 1880–1939*. London: Cassell.

Gregory, D. (1990), "'A new and differing face in many places': Three geographies of industrialization", in R.A. Dodgshon and R.A. Butlin (eds), *An Historical Geography of England and Wales*, 2nd edn. London: Academic Press.

Grigson, G. (1975), *Britain Observed*. London: Phaidon.

Grosley, P. (1769), *New Observations on Italy and its Inhabitants*, trans. T. Nugent, 2 vols. London.

Guides Bleus (1930). *Bretagne*. Paris: Hachette.

Gunn, E.A. (1979) *Tourism Planning*. New York: Crane, Russak.

Gutkind, E.A. (1964), *Urban Development in Central Europe*, International History of City Development, vol. 1. London: Collier Macmillan.

Gutkind, E.A. (1967), *Urban Development in Southern Europe: Spain and Portugal*, International History of City Development, vol. 3. London: Collier Macmillan.

Gutkind, E.A. (1969), *Urban Development in Southern Europe: Italy and Greece*, International History of City Development, vol. 4. London: Collier Macmillan.

Gutkind, E.A. (1970), *Urban Development in Western Europe: France and Belgium*, International History of City Development, vol. 5. London: Collier Macmillan.

Gutkind, E.A. (1971), *Urban Development in Western Europe: The Netherlands and Great Britain*, International History of City Development, vol. 6. London: Collier Macmillan.

Habakkuk, H.J. (1965), "Economic functions of English landowners in the seventeenth and eighteenth centuries", in H.G.J. Aitken (ed.), *Explorations in Enterprise*. Cambridge, Mass.: Harvard University Press.

Haddon, J. (1973), *Bath*. London: Batsford.

Hajducki, A.M. (1992), *The North Berwick and Gullane Branch Lines*. Headington: Oakwood Press.

Hamilton, M. (1978), *Bath before Beau Nash: A Guide Based on Gilmore's Map of Bath, 1692–4*. Bath: Kingsmead Press.

Hampson, N. (1968), *The Enlightenment*. Harmondsworth: Penguin.

Hardy, C. (1855), *Sporting Adventures in the New World or Days and Nights Moose-hunting in the Pine Forests of Acadia*. London: Hurst and Blackett.

Hardy, D. (1990), "Sociocultural dimensions of tourism history", *Annals of Tourism Research*, **17**, 541–555.

Hardy, D. and Ward, C. (1984), *Arcadia for All: The Legacy of a Makeshift Landscape*. London: Mansell.

Hart, G. (1981), *A History of Cheltenham*, 2nd edn. Stroud: Alan Sutton.

Hart, T. (1983), "Transport and the economic development: The historical dimension", in K.J. Button and D. Gillingwater (eds), *Transport, Location and Spatial Policy*. Aldershot: Gower.

Harvey, P. D. A. (1980), *The History of Topographical Maps*. London: Thames and Hudson.

Haskell, F. (1959), "The market for Italian art in the seventeenth century", *Past and Present*, **15**, 48–59.

Haug, C. J. (1982), *Leisure and Urbanism in Nineteenth Century Nice*. Lawrence, Kansas: Regents Press.

Hauser, A. (1951), *The Social History of Art*, 2 vols. London: Routledge and Kegan Paul.

Heal, F. (1990), *Hospitality in Early Modern England*. Oxford: Clarendon Press.

Heath, C. (1799), *The excursion down the Wye, from Ross to Monmouth*. Monmouth.

Hembry, P.M. (1990), *The English Spa 1560–1815. A Social History*. London: Athlone.

Herbert, D. (1991), "Place and society in Jane Austen's England", *Geography*, **76**, 3, 193–208.

Herbert, H. (1939), *Henry, Elizabeth and George. Letters and Diaries of Henry, 10th Earl of Pembroke and his Circle*. London: Cape.

Herbert, R. L. (1988), *Impressionism: Art, Leisure and Parisian Society*. New Haven: Yale University Press.

Herbert, R. L. (1994), *Monet on the Normandy Coast: Tourism and Painting, 1867–1886*. New Haven: Yale University Press.

Hibbert, C. (1969), *The Grand Tour*. London: Putnam.

Hill, M. K. (1989), *Bath and the Eighteenth Century Novel*. Bath: Bath University Press.

Hillaby, J. (ed.) (1983), *The Journeys of Celia Fiennes*. London: Macdonald.

Hills, T. L. and Lundgren, J. (1977), "The impact of tourism in the Caribbean: A methodological study", *Annals of Tourism Research*, **4**, 5, 248–267.

Hindle, P. (1989), "Roads, canals and railways", in W. Rollinson (ed.), *The Lake District: Landscape Heritage*.Newton Abbot: David and Charles.

Hipple, W. J. (1957), *The Beautiful, the Sublime, and the Picturesque in Eighteenth Century British Aesthetic Theory*. Illinois: South Illinois University Press.

Holloway, J. and Errington, L. (1978), *The Discovery of Scotland*. Edinburgh: National Gallery of Scotland.

Horn, D. B. (1961), *The British Diplomatic Service, 1689–1789*. Oxford: Clarendon Press.

Horn, P. (1989), *The Victorian and Edwardian Schoolchild*. Gloucester: Alan Sutton.

Horne, J. (1991), "Travelling through the romantic landscapes of the Blue Mountains", *Australian Cultural History* **10**, 84–98.

Houghton, W. E. (1942), "The English virtuoso in the seventeenth century", *Journal of the History of Ideas*, **3**, 51–73, 190–219.

Howell, D.W. and Baber, C. (1990), "Wales" in F.M.L. Thompson (ed.), *The Cambridge Social History of Britain, 1750–1950*, vol. 1. Cambridge: Cambridge University Press.

Howell, J. (1642), *Instructions for Forreine Travel*. London.

Howells, W.D .(1883), *Italian Journeys*, 2 vols. Edinburgh.

Howkins, A. (1981), "The taming of Whitsun: The changing face of a nineteenth century rural holiday", in E. Yeo and S. Yeo (eds), *Popular Culture and Class Conflict: Explorations in the History of Labour and Leisure, 1590–1914*. Brighton: Harvester Press.

Howkins, A. and Lowerson, J. (1979), *Trends in Leisure, 1919–1939*. London: Sports Council/SSRC.

Hudson, K. (1971), *The Fashionable Stone*. Bath: Adams and Dart.

Hughes, E. (1952), *North Country Life in the Eighteenth Century*. London: Oxford University Press.

Hughes, G. (1991), "Conceiving of tourism", *Area*, **23**, 3, 263–267.

Hughes, G. (1992), "Tourism and the geographical imagination", *Leisure Studies*, **11**, 31–42.

Hughes, M. (1934), *A London Child of the 1870s*. Oxford: Oxford University Press.

Hughes, M. (1946a), *A London Family 1870-1900*. Oxford: Oxford University Press.

Hughes, M. (1946b), *A London Home in the Nineties*. Oxford: Oxford University Press.

Hugill, P.J. (1985), "The rediscovery of America: Elite automobile touring", *Annals of Tourism Research*, **12**, 3, 435–447.

Hume Brown, P. (1891), *Early Travellers in Scotland*, republ. 1978. Edinburgh: James Thin.

Hurtley, T. (1786), *Natural Curiosities of Malham*. London.

Hussey, C. (1927), *The Picturesque*, repr. edn. London: Cass.

Huth, H. (1957), *Nature and the American: Three Centuries of Changing Attitudes*. Berkeley: University of California Press.

Irving, W. (1819–1820), "Rip van Winkle", "The legend of Sleepy Hollow", in *The Sketch Book of Geoffrey Crayon Gent.*, republ. 1909. London: Cassell.

Jackson, A.A. (1991), *The Middle Classes, 1900–1950*. Nairn: David St John Thomas.

Jacques, D. (1983), *Georgian Gardens: The Reign of Nature*. London: Batsford.

Jafari, J. (1981), *The Unbounded Reaches of Leisure, Recreation and Tourism in the Paradigm of Play*. Vienna: AIEST.

Jakle, J.A. (1977), *Images of the Ohio Valley: A Historical Geography of Travel, 1740 to 1860*. New York: Oxford University Press.

Jakle, J.A. (1985), *The Tourist: Travel in Twentieth Century North America*. Lincoln: University of Nebraska Press.

Jarvis, J.F. (1993), *The Rise of the Devon Seaside Resorts, 1750–1900*. Exeter: University of Exeter Press.

Jefferies, R. (1878), *The Gamekeeper at Home*. London: Smith, Elder.

Jefferies, R. (1879), *The Amateur Poacher*, repr. 1911. London: Nelson.

Jefferies, R. (1879), *Wild Life in a Southern County*, repr. 1934. London: Cape.

Jefferies, R. (1880), *Hodge and his Masters*. London: Smith Elder.

Jefferies, R. (1880), *Round about a Great Estate*. London: Smith Elder.

Jeffreys, D. (1742), *A Journal from London to Rome, by way of Paris, Lyons, Turin, Florence, etc*. London.

Jenkyns, R. (1980), *The Victorians and Ancient Greece*. Oxford: Blackwell.

Joanne (1912), *The Seaside Resorts of Brittany*. Paris: Hachette.

Johnson, S. (1775), *A Journey to the Western Islands of Scotland*. London.

Johnston, R. (1991), *A Question of Place*. Oxford: Blackwell.

Jones, S.G. (1986), *Workers at Play: A Social and Economic History of Leisure, 1918–1939*. London: Routledge and Kegan Paul.

Jones, S.G. (1987), "State intervention in sport and leisure in Britain between the wars", *Journal of Contemporary History*, **22**, 163–182.

Judd, R.W. (1988), "Reshaping Maine's landscape: Rural culture, tourism and conservation, 1890–1929", *Journal of Forest History*, **32**, 4, 180–190.

Kaufman, P. (1960), *Borrowings from the Bristol Library, 1773–1784*. Charlottesville: University of Virginia Press.

Kearns, G. and Philo, C. (1993), *Selling Places: The City as Cultural Capital, Past and Present*. Oxford: Pergamon.

Keir, D. (ed.) (1966), *The City of Edinburgh*, Third statistical account of Scotland. Glasgow: Collins.

Kilvert, F. (1977), *Kilvert's Diary, 1870–1879*, ed. W. Plomer. Harmondsworth: Penguin.

King, E. (1987), "Popular culture in Glasgow", in R.A. Cage (ed.), *The Working Class in Glasgow 1750–1914*. Beckenham: Croom Helm.

Knecht, R.J. (1982), *Francis I*. Cambridge: Cambridge University Press.

Kostof, S. (1992), *The City Assembled: The Elements of Urban Form through History*. London: Thames and Hudson.

Kraus, R. (1971), *Recreation and Leisure in Modern Society*. New York: Appleton-Century-Crofts.

Lachs, P.S. (1965), *The Diplomatic Corps under Charles II and James II*. New Brunswick: Rutgers University Press.

Lamb, C. (1802), "Letter to Thomas Manning", repr. in E.V. Lucas (ed.), *The Letters of Charles Lamb* (1935). London.

Lambert, R.S. (ed.) (1935), *The Grand Tour*. London: Faber and Faber.

Lambert, R.S. (1950), *The Fortunate Traveller*. London: Melrose.

Lane, M. (1988), *A Charming Place: Bath in the Life and Times of Jane Austen*. Bath: Millstream Books.

Lassels, R. (1686), *The voyage of Italy: or a compleat journey through Italy*. London.

Lawrence, H.W. (1983), "Southern spas: source of the American resort tradition", *Landscape*, **27**, 2, 1–12.

Lawrence, H.W. (1988), "Origins of the tree-lined Boulevard", *Geographical Review*, **78**, 4, 355–374.

Lee, L. (1959), *Cider with Rosie*. Harmondsworth: Penguin.

Lee, S. (1910), *The French Renaissance in England*. Oxford: Clarendon Press.

Lehne, I. and Johnson, L. (1985), *Vienna—The Past in the Present*. Vienna: Österreichischer Bundesverlag.

Leiper, N. (1979) "The framework of tourism: Towards a definition of tourism, tourist and the tourist industry", *Annals of Tourism Research*, **6**, 4, 390–407.

Lemaistre, J.G. (1806), *Travels after the Peace of Amiens, through parts of France, Switzerland, Italy and Germany*, 3 vols. London.

Lennox, C. (1752), *Female Quixote*. London.

Lewis, R. (1980), "Seaside holiday resorts in the United States and Britain: A review", *Urban History Yearbook*, 44–52.

Lickorish, L.J. and Kershaw, A.G. (1958). *The Travel Trade*. London: Practical Press.

Liddle, J. (1982), "Estate management and land reform politics: The Hesketh and Scarisbrick families and the making of Southport, 1842–1914", in D. Cannadine (ed.), *Patricians, Power and Politics in Nineteenth Century Towns*. Leicester: Leicester University Press.

Lightwood, J.T. (1928), *The Cyclists' Touring Club: Being the Romance of Fifty Years' Cycling*. London: CTC.

Lindsay, M. (1979), *The Discovery of Scotland*. London: Hale.

Lister, M. (1698), *A journey to Paris in the year 1698*. London.

Lough, J. (1984), *France Observed in the Seventeenth Century by British Travellers*. Stocksfield: Oriel Press.

Lowenthal, D. (1985), *The Past is a Foreign Country*. Cambridge: Cambridge University Press.

Lowenthal, D. and Prince, H.C. (1965), "English landscape tastes", *Geographical Review*, **55**, 186–222.

Lowerson, J. (1993), *Sport and the English Middle Classes, 1870–1914*. Manchester: Manchester University Press.

Lowerson, J., and Myerscough, J. (1977), *Time to Spare in Victorian England.* Hassocks: Harvester Press.

Lundgren, J. (1983), "The market area of the turn of the century hotel: The Chateau Frontenac in Quebec City", *Recreation Research Review*, **10**, 3, 11–21, University of Waterloo.

MacMaster, N. (1990), "The battle for Mousehold Heath 1857–1884: 'Popular politics' and the Victorian public park", *Past and Present*, **127**, 117–154.

Mains, J.A. (1966), British travellers in Switzerland, with special reference to some women travellers between 1750 and 1850. University of Edinburgh doctoral dissertation.

Malcolmson, R.W. (1973), *Popular Recreations in English Society, 1700–1850.* Cambridge: Cambridge University Press.

Malins, E. (1966), *English Landscaping and Literature, 1660–1840.* Oxford: Oxford University Press.

Mann, T. (1902), *Buddenbrooks*, republ. 1957. Harmondsworth: Penguin.

Manwaring, E. (1925), *Italian Landscape in Eighteenth Century England.* Oxford: Oxford University Press.

Marsh, J. (1982), *Back to the Land: The Pastoral Impulse in Victorian England, from 1880 to 1914.* London: Quartet.

Marshall, J.D. (1971), *Old Lakeland: Some Cumbrian Social History.* Newton Abbot: David and Charles.

Marshall, J.D. and Walton, J.K. (1981), *The Lake Counties: From 1830 to the Mid-twentieth Century.* Manchester: Manchester University Press.

Martyn, T. (1768) *The English Connoisseur.* London.

Martyn, T. (1791), *A tour through Italy. Containing full directions for travelling in that country.* London.

Mathias, P. (1957–1958), "The social structure in the eighteenth century: A calculation by Joseph Massie", *Economic History Review* (2nd series), **10**, 30–45.

Matthews, H. (1822), *The Diary of an Invalid*, 2 vols. London.

Maugham, S. (1897), *Liza of Lambeth*, repr. 1978. London: Pan.

Mayne, J. (1909), *The Journal of John Mayne. During a Tour on the Continent upon its Reopening after the Fall of Napoleon, 1814*, ed. J.M. Colles. London: Bodley Head.

McCrorie, I. (1986), *Clyde Pleasure Steamers: An Illustrated History.* Greenock: Orr, Pollock.

McInnes, A. (1988), "The emergence of a leisure town: Shrewsbury 1660–1760", *Past and Present*, **120**, 53–87.

McIntyre, S. (1981), "Bath: the rise of a resort town, 1660–1800", in P. Clark (ed.), *Country Towns in Pre-industrial England.* Leicester: Leicester University Press.

McKendrick, N., Brewer, J. and Plumb, J. (1982), *The Birth of a Consumer Society: the Commercialisation of Eighteenth Century England.* Bloomington: Indiana University Press.

McMurry, K.C. (1930), "The use of land for recreation", *Annals of the Association of American Geographers*, **20**, 7–20.

Mead, W.E. (1914), *The Grand Tour in the Eighteenth Century.* New York: Houghton Mifflin.

Measom, G. (1853), *The Official Illustrated Guide to the South-Eastern Railway.* London.

Meller, H.E. (1976), *Leisure and the Changing City, 1870–1914.* London: Routledge and Kegan Paul.

Mercer, D. (1971), "The role of perception in the recreation experience: A review and discussion", *Journal of Leisure Research*, **3**, 4, 261–276.

Meyer, P.J.B. (1978), No land too remote: Women travellers in the Georgian age. University of Massachusetts doctoral dissertation.

Michaelis-Jena, R. and Merson, W. (eds) (1988), *A Lady Travels: Journeys in England and Scotland from the Diaries of Johanna Schopenhauer*. London: Routledge.

Middlebrook, S. (1950), *Newcastle upon Tyne, its Growth and Achievement*. Newcastle: Kemsley House.

Miege, J. (1934), "La vie touristique en Savoie", *Revue de Géographie Alpine*, **23**, 749–817; **24**, 5–213.

Mingay, G.E. (1963), *Landed Society in the Eighteenth Century*. London: Routledge and Kegan Paul.

Mingay, G.E. (1976), *The Gentry: The Rise and Fall of a Ruling Class*. London: Longman.

Misson, M. (1714), *A New Voyage to Italy*, 4 vols. London.

Mitchell, L.S. and Murphy, P.E. (1991), "Geography and tourism", *Annals of Tourism Research*, **18**, 1, 57–70.

Moffat, C.A. (1982), "The development of tourism in Nova Scotia", in G. Wall and J. Marsh (eds), *Recreational Land Use: Perspectives on its Evolution in Canada*. Ottawa: Carleton University.

Moir, E. (1964), *The Discovery of Britain. The English Tourists 1540–1840*. London: Routledge and Kegan Paul.

Moloney, B. (1968), *Florence and England*. Florence: Biblioteca Dell Archivum Romanicom 104.

Monthly Review, **94** (series 2), London.

Moore, J. (1781), *A View of Society and Manners in France, Switzerland and Germany*. 2 vols. London.

Morgan, N. and Trainor, R.H. (1990), "The dominant classes", in W. Hamish Fraser and R.J. Morris (eds), *People and Society in Scotland*, vol. 2, *1830–1914*. Edinburgh: John Donald.

Morgan, P. (1983), "From a death to a view: The hunt for the Welsh past in the romantic period", in E. Hobsbawm and T. Ranger (eds), *The Invention of Tradition*. Cambridge: Cambridge University Press.

Morgan, S. (1821), *Italy*, 3 vols. London.

Mortoft, F. (1925), *Francis Mortoft: His Book. Being his travels through France and Italy, 1658–1659*. M. Letts, Hakluyt Society, 2nd series **57**.

Moryson, F. (1617), *An Itinerary. Containing his ten yeares travell through the twelve dominions of Germany, Bohmerland, Sweitzerland, Netherland, Denmarke, Poland, Italy, Turkey, France, England, Scotland, and Ireland*. London. Repr. 1907. Glasgow: MacLehose.

Mougel, F. C. (1978), "Une société de culture en Grande-Bretagne au XVIIIe. La Société des Dilettanti, 1734–1800", *Revue Historique*, **526**, 389–414.

Mowl, G. and Towner, J. (1995), "Women, gender, leisure and place: Towards a more 'humanistic' geography of women's leisure", *Leisure Studies*, **14**, 102–116.

Mowl, T. (1990), "A trial run for Regent's Park: Repton and Nash at Bath, 1796", *Bath History*, **3**, 76–89.

Mulvey, C. (1983), *Anglo-American Landscapes: A Study of Nineteenth-century Anglo-American Travel Literature*. Cambridge: Cambridge University Press.

Muraro, M. (1986), *Venetian Villas: The History and Culture*. New York: Rizzoli.

Murray, J. (1838), *A Handbook for Travellers in Switzerland, and the Alps of Savoy and Piedmont*, London, ed. J. Simmons, Victorian Library edn, 1970. Leicester: Leicester University Press.

Murray, S. (1799), *A Companion and Useful Guide to the Beauties of Scotland*, republ. 1982. Hawick: Byway Books.

Namier, L. (1961), *England in the Age of the American Revolution*, 2nd edn. London: Macmillan.

Nash, D. (1977), "Tourism as a form of imperialism", in V.L. Smith (ed.), *Hosts and Guests: The Anthropology of Tourism*. Philadelphia: University of Pennsylvania Press.

Nash, D. (1979), "The rise and fall of an aristocratic tourist culture: Nice 1763–1936", *Annals of Tourism Research*, **6**, 1, 61–75.

Nash, R. (1963), "The American wilderness in historical perspective", *Forest History*, **6**, 4.

Nash, R. (1967), *Wilderness and the American Mind*. New Haven: Yale University Press.

Neale, R.S. (1976), "Bath: Ideology and utopia, 1700–1760", in R.F. Brissenden and J.C. Eade (eds), *Studies in the Eighteenth Century*, 3. Canberra: Australian National University.

Neale, R.S. (1981), *Bath: A Social History 1680–1850*. London: Routledge and Kegan Paul.

Neave, D. (1991), "Violent idleness: The eighteenth century East Riding gentleman at leisure", *Journal of Regional and Local Studies*, **11**, 1, 3–15.

Nelson, J. G. (1982), "Canada's national parks: past, present and future", in G. Wall and J. Marsh (eds), *Recreational Land Use: Perspectives on its Evolution in Canada*. Ottawa: Carleton University.

Newby, P.T. (1981), "Literature and the fashioning of tourist taste", in D.C.D. Pocock (ed.), *Humanistic Geography and Literature*. London: Croom Helm.

Newton, M.T. (1995), "Tourism and public administration in Spain", in M. Barke, J. Towner and M. Newton (eds), *Tourism in Spain: Critical Issues*. Wallingford: CAB International.

Newton, N.T. (1971), *Design on the Land: The Development of Landscape Architecture*. Cambridge, Mass.: Harvard University Press.

Nichols, J. (1812–1815), *Literary Anecdotes of the Eighteenth Century*, 9 vols. London.

Nichols, J. and Nichols, J.B. (1817–1858), *Illustrations of the Literary History of the Eighteenth Century*, 8 vols. London.

Nicolson, M.H. (1959), *Mountain Gloom and Mountain Glory: The Development of the Aesthetics of the Infinite*. Ithaca, NY: Cornell University Press.

Nicolson, N. (1955), *The Lakers*. London: Robert Hale.

Norgate, E. (1649), *Miniatura or the Art of Limning*. London.

Norton, W. (1984), *Historical Analysis in Geography*. London: Longman.

Norval, A.J. (1934), *The Tourist Industry*. London: Pitman.

Nugent, T. (1756), *The Grand Tour, or, a journey through the Netherlands, Germany, Italy and France*, 2nd edn. London.

Nuttgens, P. (1973), "The people and the park", *Parks and Sports Grounds*, **38**, 2, 512–518.

Ogden, H.V.S. and M.S. Ogden (1955), *English Taste in Landscape in the Seventeenth Century*. Ann Arbor: University of Michigan Press.

Ogilby, J. (1675), *Britannia: or an illustration of the Kingdom of England and the Dominion of Wales: by a geographical and historical description of the principal roads thereof*. London.

Ogilvie, F. W. (1933), *The Tourist Movement: An Economic Survey*. London: P.S. King.

Olmsted, F. L. and Kimball, T. (1971), *Forty Years of Landscape Architecture: Central Park*. Cambridge, Mass.: MIT Press.

Orr, W. (1982), *Deer Forests, Landlords and Crofters: The Western Highlands in Victorian and Edwardian Times*. Edinburgh: John Donald.

Ousby, I. (1990), *The Englishman's England*. Cambridge: Cambridge University Press.

Owen, J. (1796), *Travels into different parts of Europe, in the years 1791 and 1792, with familiar remarks on places, men and manners*, 2 vols. London.

Palin, M. (1987), *Happy Holidays: The Golden Age of Railway Posters*. London: Pavilion.

Parks, G.B. (1951), "Travel as education", in *The Seventeenth Century: Studies in the History of English Thought and Literature from Bacon to Pope*, ed. R.E. Jones. London: Oxford University Press.

Parks, G.B. (1954), *The English Traveller to Italy. The Middle Ages (to 1525)*. Rome: Edizioni di Storia e Letteratura.

Parks, G.B. (1964), "The turn to the romantic in the travel literature of the eighteenth century", *Modern Language Quarterly*, **25**, 22–33.

Paterson, A.J.S. (1969), *The Golden Years of the Clyde Steamers*. Newton Abbot: David and Charles.

Paterson, A.J.S. (1972), *The Victorian Summer of the Clyde Steamers*. Newton Abbot: David and Charles.

Patmore, J.A. (1963), *Atlas of Harrogate*. Harrogate: Harrogate Corporation.

Patmore, J.A. (1968), "The spa towns of Britain", in R.P. Beckinsale and J.M. Houston (eds), *Urbanisation and its Problems*. Oxford: Blackwell.

Patmore, J.A. (1970), *Land and Leisure*. Harmondsworth: Penguin.

Patmore, J.A. (1983), *Recreation and Resources*. Oxford: Blackwell.

Peacham, H. (1612), *The Art of Drawing with the Pen and Limning in Water Colours*, London.

Pearce, D. (1978), "Form and function in French resorts", *Annals of Tourism Research*, **5**, 1, 142–156.

Pearce, D. (1987), *Tourism Today*. London: Longmans.

Pearce, D. (1989), *Tourist Development*, 2nd edn. London: Longman.

Pearce, P.L. (1982), *The Social Psychology of Tourist Behaviour*. Oxford: Pergamon.

Pearson, L.F. (1990), "The seaside resort as an international phenomenon", *Planning History*, **12**, 2, 34–35.

Pearson, R.E. (1968) "Railways in relation to resort development in east Lincolnshire", *East Midland Geographer*, **40**, 281–295.

Pemble, J. (1988) *The Mediterranean Passion, Victorians and Edwardians in the South*. Oxford: Oxford University Press.

Pennant, T. (1774), *A Tour of Scotland, 1769*. Warrington.

Pennington, T. (1825), *A Journey into Various Parts of Europe; and a Residence in them, during the years 1818, 1819, 1820 and 1821*, 2 vols. London.

Perkin, H. (1976), "The 'social tone' of Victorian seaside resorts in the north-west", *Northern History*, **11**, 180–194.

Perth, James Earl of (1968) *Letters from James Earl of Perth, Lord Chancellor of Scotland etc. to his sister; the Countess of Erroll etc.* ed. W. Jerdan, Camden Society, old series 33. London: Ams. Press.

Piggott, S. (1950), *William Stukeley: An Eighteenth Century Antiquary*. London: Thames and Hudson.

Pigram, J. (1983) *Outdoor Recreation and Resource Management*. London: Croom Helm.

Pimlott, J.A.R. (1947), *The Englishman's Holiday: A Social History*. London: Faber and Faber.

Piozzi, H.L. (1789), *Observations and Reflections made in the Course of a Journey through France, Italy and Germany*. Dublin.

Plumb, J.H. (1973) *The Commercialisation of Leisure in Eighteenth Century England*. Stenton Lecture, Reading: University of Reading.

Plumb, J.H. (1975) "The new world of children in the eighteenth century", *Past and Present*, **65**, 64–95.

Polytechnic Touring Association (1938), *Polytechnic Holidays Abroad, 1938*. London: Polytechnic Touring Assoc.

Poole, S. (1990), "Radicalism, Loyalism and the 'Reign of Terror' in Bath, 1792–1804", *Bath History*, **3**, 114–137.

Pottle, F.A. (ed.) (1952–1955), *Boswell in Holland, 1763–1764; Boswell on the Grand Tour, Germany and Switzerland 1764; Boswell on the Grand Tour, Italy, Corsica and France*, Yale edn of the private papers of James Boswell. London: Heinemann.

Prince, H. (1967), *Parks in England*. Isle of Wight, Shalfleet Manor: Pinhorns.

Queen (1914), *The "Queen" Newspaper Book of Travel*. London: Field and Queen.

Radcliffe, A. (1795), *A Journey made in the Summer of 1794, through Holland and the Western Frontiers of Germany with a Return down the Rhine*, 2 vols. London.

Rasmussen, S.E. (1934), *London: The Unique City*. Cambridge, Mass.: MIT Press.

Rawlinson (1852), *Rawlinson's Report*, deposited in Keswick Library.

Ray, J. (1691), *The wisdom of God manifested in the works of Creation*. London.

Raymond, J. (1648), *An itinerary contayning a voyage made through Italy, in the yeare 1646 and 1647*. London.

Redfern, A. (1983), "Crewe: Leisure in a railway town", in J.K. Walton and J. Walvin (eds), *Leisure in Britain 1780–1939*. Manchester: Manchester University Press.

Rees, R. (1973), "Geography and landscape painting: An introduction to a neglected field", *Scottish Geographical Magazine*, **89**, 3, 147–157.

Reichard, M. (1829), *A Descriptive Road-book of France*. London.

Reresby, J. (1904), *Memoirs and Travels of Sir John Reresby*, London, 1813, repr. ed. A. Ivatt, Dryden House Memoirs. London: Kegan Paul.

Richards, J. and MacKenzie, J. (1986), *The Railway Station*. Oxford: Oxford University Press.

Ritchie, L. (1832), *Travelling Sketches in the North of Italy, the Tyrol, and on the Rhine*. London.

Ritchie, W.K. (1984), *Miss Toward of the Tenement House*. Edinburgh: National Trust for Scotland.

Roberts, R. (1982), "Leasehold estates and municipal enterprise: Landowners, local government and the development of Bournemouth, c.1850 to 1914", in D. Cannadine (ed.), *Patricians, Power and Politics in Nineteenth Century Towns*. Leicester: Leicester University Press.

Rogers, S. (1956), *The Italian Journal of Samuel Rogers*, ed. J.R. Hale. London: Faber and Faber.

Rollinson, W. (1967), *A History of Man in the Lake District*. London: Dent.

Rosenzweig, R. (1979) "Middle class parks and working class play: The struggle over recreational space in Worcester, Massachusetts, 1870-1910", *Radical History Review*, **21**, 31-46.

Rousseau, J.J. (1759), *La Nouvelle Héloïse,* trans. M. Cranston, 1968. Harmondsworth: Penguin.

Rousseau, J.J. (1762), *Emile,* trans. and ed. W. Boyd, Classics in Education, 10. New York: Columbia University Press.

Rousseau, J.J. (1778) *The Reveries of a Solitary,* trans. P. France 1980. Harmondsworth: Penguin.

Rowlands, R. (1576), *The Post. For divers partes of the world; travaile from one notable citie unto an other, with a description of the antiquitie of divers famous cities in Europe.* London.

Rubinstein, D. (1977), "Cycling in the 1890s", *Victorian Studies,* **21**, 47–71.

Rudney, R. (1980), "The development of tourism on the Côte d'Azure: An historical perspective", in D.E. Hawkins, E.L. Shafer and J.M. Rovelstad (eds), *Tourism Planning and Development Issues.* Washington, DC: George Washington University Press.

Rule, J. (1986), *The Labouring Classes in Early Industrial England, 1750–1850.* London: Longman.

Russell, R. (1752), *Dissertation on the Use of Sea-water.* London.

Russell, R. (1979), *A Guide to British Topographical Prints.* Newton Abbot: David and Charles.

Salter, R. (1972), "Bath and its entertainments", in J. Wroughton (ed.), *Bath in the Age of Reform.* Bath: Morgan Books.

Schama, S. (1987) *The Embarrassment of Riches: An Interpretation of Dutch Culture in the Golden Age.* London: Collins.

Schivelbusch, W. (1977), *The Railway Journey: The Industrialisation of Time and Space in the Nineteenth Century.* Leamington Spa: Berg.

Schudt, L. (1959), *Italianreisen im 17, und 18, jahrhundert.* Vienna: Schroll Verlag.

Scott, J. (1982), *The Upper Classes. Property and Privilege in Britain.* London: Macmillan.

Scott, W. (1802–1803), *The Minstrelsy of the Scottish Border,* repr. in: *The Poetical Works of Sir Walter Scott,* 1908. Oxford.

Scott, W. (1805), *The Lay of the Last Minstrel,* repr. in: *The Poetical Works of Sir Walter Scott,* 1908. Oxford.

Scott, W. (1808), *Marmion,* repr. in: *The Poetical Works of Sir Walter Scott,* 1908. Oxford.

Scott, W. (1810), *The Lady of the Lake.* repr. in: *The Poetical Works of Sir Walter Scott,* 1908. Oxford.

Sears, J.F. (1989), *Sacred Places: American Tourist Attractions in the Nineteenth Century.* New York: Oxford University Press.

Seebohm Rowntree, B. (1941), *Poverty and Progress, a Second Social Survey of York.* London: Longmans Green.

Sells, A.L. (1964), *The Paradise of Travellers: The Italian Influence on Englishmen in the Seventeenth Century.* London: Allen and Unwin.

Shackleton, J.T. (1976), *The Golden Age of the Railway Poster.* London: New English Library.

Sharp, S. (1767), *Letters from Italy. Describing the Customs and Manners of that country, in the years 1765 and 1766.* London.

Shepherd, N. (1987), *The Zealous Intruders: The Western Rediscovery of Palestine.* London: Collins.

Shoard, M. (1987), *This Land Is Our Land.* London: Paladin.

Shubert, A. (1990), *A Social History of Modern Spain.* London: Unwin Hyman.

Sigsworth, E.M. (ed.) (1980), *Ports and Resorts in the Regions.* Hull: Hull College of Higher Education.

Simmons, J. (ed.) (1969), *Journeys in England.* Newton Abbot: David and Charles.

Simmons, J. (1986), *The Railway in Town and Country, 1830–1914.* Newton Abbot: David and Charles.

Singer, C., Holmyard, E.J., Hall, A.R. and Williams, T. (1957), *A History of Technology,* vol. 3, *From the Renaissance to the Industrial Revolution, c.1500– c.1750.* Oxford: Clarendon Press.

Skinner, B. (1966), *Scots in Italy in the Eighteenth Century.* Edinburgh: National Gallery of Scotland.

Sleigh, A.B.W. (1853), *Pine Forests and Hackmatack Clearings or Travel, Life and Adventure in the British North American Provinces.* London: Bentley.

Smith, C.T. (1967), *An Historical Geography of Western Europe before 1800.* London: Longmans.

Smollett, T. (1771), *Humphry Clinker.* London.

Smollett, T. (1979), *Travels through France and Italy,* ed. F. Felsenstein. Oxford: Oxford University Press.

Snow, R. and Wright, D. (1976), "Coney Island: A case study in popular culture and technological change", *Journal of Popular Culture,* **9**, 4, 960–975.

Soane, J.V.N. (1993), *Fashionable Resort Regions: Their Evolution and Transformation.* Wallingford: CAB International.

Spence, J. (1975), *Letters from the Grand Tour,* ed. S. Klima. Montreal and London: McGill–Queen's University Press.

Spencer, T. (1954) *Fair Greece Sad Relic: Literary Philhellenism from Shakespeare to Byron.* London: Weidenfeld and Nicolson.

Spring, D. (ed.) (1978) *European Landed Elites in the Nineteenth Century.* Baltimore: Johns Hopkins University Press.

Squire, S.J. (1988), "Wordsworth and Lake District tourism: Romantic reshaping of place", *Canadian Geographer,* **32**, 3, 237–247.

Stansfield, C.A. (1972), "The development of modern seaside resorts", *Parks and Recreation,* **5**, 10, 14–17, 43–46.

Stansfield, C. A. (1978), "Atlantic city and the resort cycle", *Annals of Tourism Research,* **5**, 2, 238–251.

Starke, M. (1800), *Letters from Italy, between the Years 1792 and 1798,* 2 vols. London.

Starke, M.(1820), *Travels on the Continent: Written for the Use and Particular Information of Travellers.* London.

Stevens, T.(1990), "Tourism and leisure", in R.A. Griffiths (ed.), *The City of Swansea: Challenges and Change.* Stroud: Alan Sutton.

Stone, L. (1965), *The Crisis of the Aristocracy, 1558–1641.* Oxford: Clarendon Press.

Stone, L. (1966), "Social mobility in England, 1500–1700", *Past and Present,* **33**, 16–55.

Stone, L. (ed.) (1975), *The University in Society,* vol. 1. Oxford: Oxford University Press.

Stoye, J.W. (1952), *English Travellers Abroad, 1604–1667.* London: Cape.

Strong, R. (1973), *Splendour at Court: Renaissance Spectacle and Illusion.* London: Weidenfeld and Nicolson.

Strout, C. (1963), *The American Image of the Old World.* New York: Harper and Row.

Sutton, D. (1982), *Souvenirs of the Grand Tour.* London: Wildenstein.

Swinglehurst, E. (1974). *The Romantic Journey: The Story of Thomas Cook and Victorian Travel*. London: Pica.

Swinglehurst, E. (1982), *Cook's Tours: The Story of Popular Travel*. Poole: Blandford Press.

Taylor, C.D. (1983), *Portrait of Windermere*. London: Hale.

Thomas, K. (1964), "Work and leisure in pre-industrial society", *Past and Present*, **29**, 50–62.

Thomas, K. (1983), *Man and the Natural World: Changing Attitudes in England 1500–1800*. London: Allen Lane.

Thomas, W. (1549), *The history of Italy. A book exceeding profitable to be read because it entreateth of the state of Mary and divers commonwealths how they have been and now be governed*. Repr. ed. G.B. Parks, Folger documents of Tudor and Stuart Civilization. New York: Cornell University.

Thompson, E.P. (1963), *The Making of the English Working Class*. Harmondsworth: Penguin.

Thompson, E.P. (1975), *Whigs and Hunters: The Origins of the Black Acts*. London: Allen Lane.

Thompson, F. (1939), *Lark Rise to Candleford*, repr. 1973. Harmondsworth: Penguin.

Thompson, F.M.L. (1988), *The Rise of Respectable Society: A Social History of Victorian Britain, 1830–1900*. London: Fontana.

Thompson, F.M.L. (1990), "Town and city" in F.M.L. Thompson (ed.), *The Cambridge Social History of Britain, 1750–1950*, vol. 1. Cambridge: Cambridge University Press.

Thompson, T. (1981), *Edwardian Childhoods*. London: Routledge and Kegan Paul.

Thrift, N. (1990), "Transport and communication" in R.A. Dodgshon and R.A. Butlin (eds), *An Historical Geography of England and Wales*, 2nd edn. London: Academic Press.

Thrupp, G.A. (1877), *The History of Coaches*. London: Kerby and Endean.

Thurot, J.M. (1973), "Le tourisme tropical balnéaire: le modèle Caraïbe et ses extensions". Aix-en-Provence: Centre d'Etudes du Tourisme.

Timbs, J. (1898), *Clubs and Club Life in London*. London: Chatto and Windus.

Tinniswood, A. (1989), *A History of Country House Visiting*. Oxford and London: Blackwell and National Trust.

Tobin, G.A. (1974). "The bicycle boom of the 1890s", *Journal of Popular Culture*, **8**, 838–849.

Topham, E. (1775), *Edinburgh Life in the Eighteenth Century*, repr. 1989. Glasgow: Lang Syne.

Towner, J. (1984a), "The Grand Tour: Sources and a methodology for an historical study of tourism", *Tourism Management*, **5**, 3, 215–222.

Towner, J. (1984b), The European Grand Tour, c.1550–1840: A study of its role in the history of tourism. University of Birmingham doctoral dissertation.

Towner, J. (1985), "The Grand Tour: A key phase in the history of tourism", *Annals of Tourism Research*, **12**, 3, 297–333.

Towner, J. (1988), "Approaches to tourism history", *Annals of Tourism Research*, **15**, 1, 47–62.

Towner, J. (1994), "Tourism history: Past, present and future" in A.V. Seaton et al (eds), *Tourism: The State of the Art*. Chichester: Wiley.

Towner, J. (1995), "What is tourism's history?" *Tourism Management*, **16**, 5, 339–343.

Towner, J. and Wall, G. (1991), "History and tourism", *Annals of Tourism Research*, **18**, 1, 71–84.

Trease, G. (1967), *The Grand Tour*. London: Heinemann.

Trevor Roper, H. (1983), "The invention of tradition: The Highland tradition of Scotland", in E. Hobsbawm and T. Ranger (eds), *The Invention of Tradition*. Cambridge: Cambridge University Press.

Tuan, Y.F. (1971), *Man and Nature*, Commission on College geography, resource paper 10. Association of American Geographers.

Turgenev, I. (1871), *Spring Torrents*, repr. 1972. Harmondsworth: Penguin.

Tylden-Wright, D. (1991), *John Aubrey: A Life*. London: Harper Collins.

Urry, J. (1990), *The Tourist Gaze*. London: Sage.

Vaughan, J. (1974), *The English Guide Book, c.1780–1870*. Newton Abbot: David and Charles.

Vida, M. (1992), *Spas in Hungary in Ancient Times and Today*. Budapest: Semmelweis Kiado.

Villari, L. (1905), *Italian Life in Town and Country*. London: Newner.

Wadsworth, J. (1641), *The European mercury. Describing the highways and stages from place to place, through the most remarkable parts of Christendome. With a catalogue of the principal fairs, marts, and markets, thorowout the same*. London.

Walker, A. (1790), *Ideas, suggested on the spot in a late excursion through Flanders, Germany, France and Italy*. London.

Walker, H. (1985), "The popularisation of the outdoor movement, 1900–1940", *British Journal of Sports History*, **2**, 140–153.

Wall, G. (1977), "Recreational land use in Muskoka", *Ontario Geography*, **11**, 11–28.

Wall, G. (1982a), "Changing views of the land as a recreational resource", in G. Wall and J. Marsh (eds), *Recreational Land Use: Perspectives on its Evolution in Canada*. Ottawa: Carleton University.

Wall, G. (1982b), "The fluctuating fortunes of water-based recreational places", in G. Wall and J. Marsh (eds), *Recreational Land Use: Perspectives on its Evolution in Canada*. Ottawa: Carleton University.

Wall, G. (1989), "Temporal change and the history of recreation" in C. Cooper (ed.), *Progress in Tourism, Recreation and Hospitality Management*, 1. London: Belhaven Press.

Walton, J.K. (1978), *The Blackpool Landlady*. Manchester: Manchester University Press.

Walton, J.K. (1979), "Railways and resort development in Victorian England: The case of Silloth", *Northern History*, **15**, 191–208.

Walton, J.K. (1980), "Railways and resort development in north-west England", in E.M. Sigsworth (ed.), *Ports and Resorts in the Regions*. Hull: Hull College of Higher Education.

Walton, J.K. (1981), "The demand for working-class seaside holidays in Victorian England", *Economic History Review*, **34**, 2, 249–265.

Walton, J.K. (1983), *The English Seaside Resort: A Social History, 1750–1914*. Leicester: Leicester University Press.

Walton, J.K. and McGloin, P.R. (1981), "The tourist trade in Victorian Lakeland", *Northern History*, **17**, 153–182.

Walton, J.K. and Smith, J. (1995), "The first century of beach tourism in Spain: San Sebastian and the 'playas del norte' from the 1830s to the 1930s", in M. Barke, J. Towner and M. Newton (eds), *Tourism in Spain: Critical Issues*. Wallingford: CAB International.

Walton, J.K. and Walvin, J. (eds) (1983), *Leisure in Britain, 1780–1939*. Manchester: Manchester University Press.

Walton, J.R. (1990) "Agriculture and rural society 1730–1914", in R.A. Dodgshon and R.A. Butlin (eds), *An Historical Geography of England and Wales*, 2nd edn. London: Academic Press.

Walvin, J. (1978), *Beside the Seaside: a Social History of the Popular Seaside Holiday*. London: Allen Lane.

Walvin, J. (1983) "Children's pleasures", in J.K. Walton and J. Walvin (eds), *Leisure in Britain, 1780–1939*. Manchester: Manchester University Press.

Ward, C. and Hardy, D. (1986) *Goodnight Campers! The History of the British Holiday Camp*. London: Mansell.

Ward Lock (1905), *A Pictorial and Descriptive Guide to Glasgow and the Clyde*, 3rd edn. London: Ward Lock.

Ward, S.V. (1988) "Promoting holiday resorts: A review of early history to 1921", *Planning History*, **10**, 2, 7–11.

Ward, S.V. (1994), "Place marketing: Some historical thoughts", *Planning History*, **16**, 1, 16–28.

Wechsberg, J. (1979), *The Lost World of the Great Spas*. London: Weidenfeld and Nicolson.

Weight, B. (1972), "Public health and housing in Bath", in J. Wroughton (ed.), *Bath in the Age of Reform*. Bath: Morgan Books.

Wells, H.G. (1896) *The Wheels of Chance*. London: Dent.

Wells, H.G. (1910), *The History of Mr Polly*. London: Dent.

West, T. (1780), *Guide to the Lakes*, 2nd edn. London.

Whyman, J. (1973), "A Hanoverian watering-place: Margate before the railway", in A. Everitt (ed.), *Perspectives in English Urban History*. London: Macmillan.

Whyman, J. (1980), "Water communications and their effect on the growth and character of Margate, c.1750 to c.1840", in E.M. Sigsworth (ed.), *Ports and Resorts in the Regions*. Hull: Hull College of Higher Education.

Wightman, D. and Wall, G. (1985), "The spa experience at Radium Hot Springs", *Annals of Tourism Research*, **12**, 3, 393–416.

Wilberforce, W. (1779), *Journey to the Lake District from Cambridge*, ed. C.C. Wrangham. Stocksfield: Oriel Press.

Wilkinson, P. F. (1988), "The historical roots of urban open space planning", *Leisure Studies*, **7**, 125–143.

Williams, A. (1915), *Life in a Railway Factory*, republ. 1984. Stroud: Alan Sutton.

Williams, F. (1960), *Journey into Adventure: The Story of the Workers' Travel Association*. London: Odhams Press.

Williams, R. (1973), *The Country and the City*. London: Chatto and Windus.

Williamson, E., Riches, A. and Higgs, M. (1990), *Glasgow*, The Buildings of Scotland. Harmondsworth: Penguin.

Williamson, T. and Bellamy, L. (1987), *Property and Landscape*. London: George Philip.

Wilson, D. (1825), *Letters from an absent brother: Containing some account of a tour through parts of the Netherlands, Switzerland, North Italy, and France; in the summer of 1823*, 2 vols. London.

Wilton, A. (1980), *Turner and the Sublime*. London: British Museum.

Winchester, A. (1989), "The farming landscape", in W. Rollinson (ed.), *The Lake District: Landscape Heritage*. Newton Abbot: David and Charles.

Wittkower, R. (1974), *Palladio and English Palladianism*. London: Thames and Hudson.

Wolfe, R.I. (1952), "Wasaga Beach—the divorce from the geographic environment", *Canadian Geographer*, **2**, 57–66.

Wolfe, R.I. (1962), "The summer resorts of Ontario in the nineteenth century", *Ontario History*, **54**, 3, 149–160.

Wolfe, R. I. (1967), "The changing patterns of tourism in Ontario", in E.G. Firth (ed.), *Profiles of a Province: Studies in the History of Ontario*. Toronto: Ontario Historical Society.

Wood, M. (1951), "The growth of Edinburgh, 1800–1950", in *Scientific Survey of south-east Scotland*. Edinburgh: British Association.

Woodforde, J. (1978), *The Diary of a Country Parson 1758–1802*, ed. J. Beresford. Oxford: Oxford University Press

Woodward, C. (1992), *The Building of Bath*. Bath: Advantage Press.

Woof, R. (1986), "The matter of fact paradise", in *The Lake District: A Sort of National Property*. Cheltenham and London: Countryside Commission and Victoria and Albert Museum.

Woolf, S.J. (1968), "Venice and the Terrafirma: Problems of the change from commercial to landed activities", in B. Pullan (ed.), *Crisis and Change in the Venetian Economy in the Sixteenth and Seventeenth Centuries*. London: Methuen.

Wordsworth, D. (1941), "A tour on the continent", in *The Journals of Dorothy Wordsworth*, ed. E. de Selincourt, 2 vols. London: Macmillan.

Wordsworth, W. (1822), *Guide to the Lakes*, repr. 1970. ed. E. de Selincourt. Oxford: Oxford University Press.

Wordsworth, W. (1940–1949), *The Poetical Works of William Wordsworth*, ed. E. de Selincourt and H. Darbishire, 5 vols. Oxford: Clarendon Press.

Wright, J.K. (1947), "Terrae incognitae: the place of imagination in geography", *Geographical Review*, **37**, 1–15.

Wright, L.B. (1935), *Middle-class Culture in Elizabethan England*. Chapel Hill: University of North Carolina Press.

Wroughton, J. (1972), "Bath and its workers", in J. Wroughton (ed.), *Bath in the Age of Reform*. Bath: Morgan Books.

Yelling, J. (1990), "Agriculture 1500–1730", in R.A. Dodgshon and R.A. Butlin (eds), *An Historical Geography of England and Wales*, 2nd edn. London: Academic Press.

Youngson, A.J. (1966), *The Making of Classical Edinburgh*. Edinburgh: Edinburgh University Press.

Youngson, A.J. (1974), *Beyond the Highland Line*. London: Collins.

Index